REGIONAL POLICY
Past Experience and
New Directions

GLASGOW SOCIAL AND ECONOMIC RESEARCH STUDIES

AN INTRODUCTION TO THE ITALIAN ECONOMY
Kevin Allen and Andrew Stevenson

THE INDUSTRIAL RELATIONS ACT
A. W. J. Thomson and S. R. Engleman

THE ECONOMICS OF INFLATION
Charles Mulvey and James Trevithick

AGRARIAN CHANGE IN THE SCOTTISH HIGHLANDS
John Bryden and George Houston

THE ECONOMIC ANALYSIS OF TRADE UNIONS
Charles Mulvey

REGIONAL POLICY
Past Experience and New Directions

EDITED BY

Duncan Maclennan
John B. Parr

DEPARTMENT OF SOCIAL AND ECONOMIC RESEARCH,
& CENTRE FOR URBAN AND REGIONAL RESEARCH
UNIVERSITY OF GLASGOW

GLASGOW SOCIAL & ECONOMIC
RESEARCH STUDIES 6

1979

Martin Robertson

First published in 1979 by Martin Robertson & Company Ltd., 108 Cowley Road, Oxford OX4 1JF.

ISBN 0 85520 216 5 (paperback)
ISBN 0 85520 217 3 (case)

Typeset by Santype International Ltd., Salisbury, Wilts.
Printed and bound by Richard Clay Ltd., Bungay, Suffolk

Contents

Lists of tables and figures   vii

Foreword by Sir Alec Cairncross   xi

Introduction by Duncan Maclennan and John B. Parr   xix

PART I: Regional Policy: Past and Present   I

CHAPTER 1 The Development of British Regional Policy *by J.
           D. McCallum*   3

CHAPTER 2 The Effect of Regional Policy on the Movement of
           Industry in Great Britain *by Brian Ashcroft and Jim
           Taylor*   43

CHAPTER 3 An Examination of Assisted Labour Mobility Policy
           by P. B. Beaumont   65

CHAPTER 4 Regional Policy and the National Interest *by Thomas
           Wilson*   81

PART II: The Changing Economic Environment   109

CHAPTER 5 The Changing Nature of the Regional Economic Prob-
           lem since 1965 *by J. N. Randall*   111

CHAPTER 6 Changing Metropolitan Structure *by P. A. Stone*   133

CHAPTER 7 Regional Development and North Sea Oil and Gas
           by G. A. Mackay   159

PART III: Neglected Aspects in Regional Policy   171

CHAPTER 8 An Urban Approach to Regional Problems *by J.
           T. Hughes*   173

CHAPTER 9 Spatial Structure as a Factor in Economic Adjust-
           ment and Regional Policy *by John B. Parr*   191

CHAPTER 10 The Limits and Means of 'Self-Reliant' Regional
            Economic Growth *by N. S. Segal*   212

v

CHAPTER 11   Entrepreneurship and Regional Development: Impli-
              cations for Regional Policy *by J. K. Swales*   225

PART IV: **Regional Policy in an Emerging Political Frame-
             work**   243

CHAPTER 12   Regional Policy in a European Framework *by M.
              C. MacLennan*   245

CHAPTER 13   Devolution: The Changing Political Economy of
              Regional Policy *by John R. Firn and Duncan Maclennan*   273

CHAPTER 14   The National Industrial Strategy and Regional
              Policy *by Gordon C. Cameron*   297

Postscript by Duncan Maclennan and John B. Parr   323

Index of Names   330

Index of Subjects

List of Tables

1.1   New industrial building approved, 1945–55   8
1.2   Employees in selected industrial sectors in the United Kingdom   10
1.3   Changes in employees in the United Kingdom in selected
       industrial sectors, 1951–68   11
1.4   Regional differentials in incentives, 1970 and 1972   22
1.5   Regional-policy funds by major heading, 1962–63 to 1977–78   32
1.6   Regional distribution of regionally relevant expenditures on
       trade, industry and employment   33
1.7   Changes in regional unemployment rates, 1974–78   34
2.1   Industrial movement in the United Kingdom in four sub-per-
       iods   45
2.2   Origin of interregional moves   46
2.3   Destination of interregional moves   46

2.4 Regression analysis of the movement of industry, 1952–71: the generation of industrial movement and its distribution to the Development Areas of Great Britain with a one-year lag on the policy variables   55

2.5 Regression analysis of the movement of industry, 1952–71: the generation of industrial movement and its distribution to the Development Areas of Great Britain with a two-year lag on the policy variables   56

2.6 The effect of individual regional-policy instruments on the movement of industry to the Development Areas, 1961–71   60

3.1 The willingness and ability of the assisted migrant sample to move in the absence of transfer scheme assistance   73

3.2 Regression results for the willingness and ability to move in the absence of assistance under the ETS   75

3.3 Size of the return migration flows from ten of the survey exchanges   76

4.1 Public expenditure per capita   89

4.2 Gross domestic product (GDP) and regionally relevant public expenditure (RRPE)   90

5.1 Per capita gross domestic product by region at factor cost, 1966–74   117

5.2 Regional unemployment rates relative to Great Britain   118

5.3 Rates of change of population and employees by region, 1965–75   121

6.1 Population changes in the South East   137

6.2 Employment by major sector, 1961 and 1974   137

6.3 Average annual percentage change in employment by major sector   138

6.4 Analysis of employment changes for London and Rest of the South East, 1961–71   140

6.5 Components of industrial decline in Greater London, 1966–74   141

6.6 Male resident unemployment rates in April and October, 1971–76   145

6.7 Unfilled vacancies and unemployment among males in London and Rest of the South East, March 1974   146

6.8 Average employment earnings by area of residence, 1974–75   148

6.9 Population changes, 1961–76   150

6.10 Employment changes by major sector, 1966–71   151

6.11 Composition of employment in the conurbations, 1971   153

6.12 Actual and expected employment in 1971 by major sector
      in the English conurbations   154

8.1   Population change in British Metropolitan Areas, 1951–66   176

8.2   Population and employment change by urban zone in Great
      Britain, 1951–71   176

8.3   Population and employment change by urban zone in selected
      Economic Planning Regions, 1951–71   178

8.4   Analysis of Metropolitan Area employment, 1959–68   180–81

8.5   Components of manufacturing employment decentralisation,
      1958–68   185

14.1 Regional distribution of accelerated projects, April 1975–Sep-
      tember 1976   305

14.2 Net output per employee as a percentage of the United King-
      dom average (manufacturing industry, Orders 3–19), 1971   310

14.3 Net output per employee in manufacturing industry, 1971   311

14.4 Percentages of United Kingdom net output, employment and
      capital for manufacturing industry (assisted areas and non-
      assisted areas), selected years   312

14.5 Net output per employee in the super sectors in relation
      to the national average, 1970–73   315

14.6 Engineering industries selected for Sector Working Parties
      and for productivity analyses   316

14.7 Net output per employee in the Industrial Strategy engineering
      sectors in relation to the national average, 1970–72   318

List of Figures

1.1   Economic Planning Regions   26

1.2   Assisted areas as of November 1977   27

4.1   Gross domestic product (GDP) and regionally relevant public
      expenditure (RRPE) by region   91

Foreword

Interest in regional economic problems quickened in the 1930s, as it became apparent that recovery from the slump was highly lopsided. In Britain some parts of the country, notably those in or near London, were conspicuously prosperous and had relatively low unemployment rates. They attracted a continuing inflow of migrants, while other parts of the country remained obstinately depressed, with heavy, long-term unemployment in their major industries and an outflow of workers in search of employment elsewhere. A similar situation existed in other countries. A Canadian friend, for example, wrote to me in 1937 asking what prescription Keynes would offer to a country that was enjoying a boom in some provinces but faced an unyielding depression in the others.

It was natural to feel at that time that the most important problem was mass unemployment and to regard a deficiency of demand as its obvious cause. This meant laying emphasis on the general level of demand, with only casual reference to the bottlenecks that expansion might encounter in some parts of the country or to structural factors that might complicate and limit the process of recovery in others. Indeed, in reaction to the pre-Keynesian analysis of unemployment there was a tendency for economists to play down structural factors and to argue that any general deficiency of demand almost inevitably hit some industries and some regions harder than others, so intensifying any *appearance* of structural weakness. A sustained and world-wide recovery in demand might be expected to overcome these weaknesses in the course of time.

If one looks back at the popular view of regional problems in this period, as expressed for example in the Barlow report of 1940, what is striking is the absence of any attempt to link it with Keynesian thinking. The emphasis was entirely on micro-economic, to the neglect of macro-economic, explanations. Thus the Barlow Report made no attempt to review the influence on regional development of an approach to full employment. It attacked the congestion resulting from the greater prosperity of the south and east, without much effort to define congestion and without much evidence that it was of real importance in any sense in the particular places where new industry was growing up. When people talked about congestion, they were partly reacting in the traditional way against London, the Great Wen, and partly expressing disquiet that so much new construction should go on in an already rich area when there was redundant social capital in the 'depressed areas'.

Similarly, analysis of the problems of those areas dwelt on the decline of their staple industries and on the lack of new industry to take its place. That is, it was nearly always specific local circumstances that were emphasised, not the side effects of a general world depression. The remedies proposed accorded with this emphasis. They took the form of schemes of labour transference involving retraining for work available in other regions, schemes of work creation to provide temporary employment (pending what?) and to improve social amenities, schemes for providing finance for promising small businesses, and schemes for creating trading estates to bring in new branches of manufacturing industry. All of these had fairly modest results. Most workers who moved did so without benefit of government help; the schemes of work creation did little to change the balance between regions; the small businesses remained small; the trading estates were usually dominated by firms dependent on government orders. So long as the world depression continued, the regional contrasts did not fade away. Devaluation, tariff protection and a building boom allowed domestic demand to recover, but the recovery was concentrated in the southern half of the country.

When the war came, the question was no longer how to bring work to the 'depressed areas' but how to find labour for the war effort. In some areas the shortage was acute from an early stage; in others a surplus persisted. The differences were symbolised in the coloured pins used in government departments on maps of labour supply to mark the contrasts. Red pins indicated dangerous shortages and hence areas to be avoided in the building of new factories or the placing of government contracts. Green pins indicated a clear field for additional employment. Yellow pins were neutral. What became increasingly apparent as the war went on was that it was not possible to treat labour supply as the only significant localising factor. In fact, it was often extremely difficult to persuade companies to locate new factories in the regions remote from London. Rolls Royce, for example, pointed to the burden on top management of putting in a weekly (or more frequent) journey to a site well away from Derby (the site of the parent factory). The convenience of management and the availability of labour pointed in two different directions.

The moral for the post-war period was plain. The regional problem would return in response to the greater gravitational pull of locations in the south. To offset this would call for policies more stringent than those favoured in the 1930s. The Board of Trade took this view very strongly, mainly under the influence of Douglas Jay. It came to be accepted that compulsion should be used—not positive compulsion to go to particular areas but denial of the right to locate in areas judged to be already at full employment. The post-war period started off under the influence of two dominant ideas: first, that action should be concentrated on the provision of factory space and the location of branch factories; and second that this action should be governed by the level of unemployment in each region. The idea of growth or of a change in the long-term balance between regions did not enter because in 1945 attention was fastened on short-term issues of employment, not long-term issues of growth.

As time went on, it became clear that growth could not be left out. It just had to be asked *why* new industry elected to go to certain regions rather than others and whether the growth of industrial employment was the key factor in regional differences. It was increasingly evident that in spite of the compulsions applied under the Industrial Development Certificate (IDC) legislation, the pattern of regional unemployment remained remarkably stable. The level of unemployment, although high in certain localities, was no higher on the average in the peripheral regions than it had been in the most prosperous regions of Great Britain before the war. At the same time there was a growing reluctance to rely on compulsion as a localising factor, when no one knew the social cost of compulsion: promising new developments in 'red' areas were simply abandoned altogether when, in the absence of compulsion, they might have displaced other work. On top of this, a little arithmetic showed the comparative triviality *in the short term* of employment in new branch factories and this in turn made one reflect that the longer-term consequences might, in contrast, be large but adverse.

Full employment in half the country and nearly full employment in the other half made regional policy seem less urgent. Nevertheless, in the late 1950s the government, having relaxed the IDC procedure, began to take direct action affecting a limited number of major investment decisions. This action was a response to political pressure (especially from Scotland) and not an expression of well-considered economic planning. The example of the steel industry, where government intervention resulted in the construction of two strip mills that were both too small to be internationally competitive, was far from reassuring. There was no virtue in pushing well-conducted businesses into putting their limited capital into unprofitable plants, even with government help. Much the same applied to the motor car industry where again government pressure was applied without any thorough examination of the impact on the industry's power to compete internationally.

This experience and the increasingly Laodicean enforcement of the IDC legislation in the 1950s, led to a switch to financial inducements to locate in regions of high unemployment. First, there was the offer of 'free depreciation' in the 1963 Budget (at that time confined to the 'Development Districts'). Then there was the introduction of the Regional Employment Premium (REP) in 1966. Both these measures were deliberately on a *regional* basis. Earlier, the incentives to locate in areas of high unemployment were on a more local basis and made sense only on the assumption that the right response to high local unemployment, in however small a district, was to provide incentives to locate in that district. Debate on

REP brought to a head the controversies over regional policy that had raged for the past twenty years. Some important considerations, however, were given insufficient weight.

First of all, regional problems were treated as purely domestic, although they often originated in the failure of local industries to meet foreign competition. It was rare to find any attempt to link the theory of regional development with the theory of international economic development—and this is still the case. Ohlin had drawn the parallel, but in terms of equilibrium, not growth. A little reflection made some of the propositions on regional policy look less convincing in the context of what was known about international economics.

Second, some of the proposals for action were suspect because they rested on the current state of the balance of payments, which is a very dubious basis for settling the location of economic activity, unless it is contemplated that there should be frequent changes in location. Regional policy was treated as a kind of substitute for devaluation.

Third, and most significant, it was thought sufficient to base action on regional unemployment percentages without regard to other indicators of pressure in the labour market. Migration was treated as a separate phenomenon that might conceivably justify action along the same lines, not as a reflection of the same deficiency of demand that generated relatively high unemployment. In the same way, the fact that earnings were lower in the peripheral regions was regarded as a separate issue, not a reflection of a differential pressure of demand.

Neglect of these considerations, particularly the last, tended to give rise to an underestimate of the scale of action required. Calculations were made implying that x more jobs would bring down unemployment by x. It was assumed that the provision of additional jobs would offer no check to outward migration and produce little or no overflow of demand to goods and services furnished by workers in other regions. The post-war tendency to treat regional growth exclusively in terms of unemployment percentages persisted. Yet it should have required little demonstration that the hierarchy of unemployment percentages reflected a corresponding hierarchy in locational preferences. If the aim was to overturn the one hierarchy, it presupposed a capacity to overturn the other. To achieve a higher pressure of demand in the assisted areas required an actual *preference* for these locations over locations elsewhere. If such a preference manifested itself, it would not only bring down the level of unemployment in the assisted areas but would stem the outflow of labour from them and raise the level of earnings in comparison with other regions.

It is doubtful whether any government in post-war Britain would ever have been prepared to go quite so far as to aim at reversing the existing hierarchy. Aid is one thing; but turning preferences upside-down is another matter altogether. The market is less inhibited and can offer incentives more powerful than governments are usually willing to contemplate. North

Sea oil might yet do what no regional policy has ever done and make Scotland more attractive to producers than locations in the south and east. All one can say is that it has not happened yet.

As time has gone on, we have come closer to a marriage of macro-economic and micro-economic considerations in regional analysis. The overconcentration on unemployment has been replaced by a broader view of labour-market pressures. The need to achieve full employment is now set alongside the need to secure steady growth. The problem of maintaining equilibrium is seen in the context of cumulative factors in development that tug against any existing equilibrium. Growth cannot avoid being at different rates in different parts of a large, developed economy.

At the end of the day, we come back to that antithesis between cyclical and structural factors from which the whole analysis started. We know that, given time, in the long run, structures can be changed. Labour moves to new locations or new employment comes to replace the old. The issue is always: how long will either process take? Mobility is a concept that makes no sense except against a background of the lapse of time. But the one thing that is startlingly absent from most economic analysis is the length of time that things take. The importance of the regional problem is measured by the relative magnitudes of industrial and occupational mobility, as compared with geographical mobility. If it were as easy to move between regions as between occupations there would be no specifically regional problems. Before the war, David Champernowne showed, in a neglected two-part article in the *Review of Economic Studies* (Vol. 5, pp. 93–106 and Vol. 6, pp. 111–126), that in a region of high unemployment there was a process of diffusion that raised unemployment in all industries above the level in more fortunate regions. If the process of diffusion worked as effectively between regions as between industries, would that not remove differences in the pressure of demand and so in unemployment percentages? In the long run, the answer is 'yes', but in the short run, 'no'. The same rate of transfer between regions has less effect because, if those who move quit a job (and it is usually the *employed* who move), their move reduces demand as well as supply and recreates some of the disequilibrium that the move destroys. Thus, if migration were the complete answer, it would be necessary for geographical mobility to be *higher* than industrial or occupational mobility.

So where do we stand now? It seems to me that we still have to start from the importance of macro-economic forces. If the pressure of demand is sufficiently high to secure full employment in the leading regions, this should help to keep unemployment within limits in the regions that lag behind. Not every region can be in the lead, and so long as the spread is not very wide, regional policy as such is of subordinate importance. Sustained pressure of demand in the leading regions is perhaps the most powerful aid that can be offered to the lagging regions—a proposition that has so far been more easily accepted when expressed in terms of the relations between industrial countries and developing countries (under conditions of free trade).

That said, we are in the area of structural policy and this is necessarily somewhat vague since one cannot legislate simultaneously for every economy or count on every government to translate policy recommendations into action with equal effectiveness. Most policy prescriptions imply that sheer labour availability must be transformed by government action into some definite locational advantage. But it is perhaps more important to *create* these advantages by training labour or making the environment more attractive, or by counteracting the disadvantages of distance from the major centres of economic activity. Those disadvantages are by no means limited to high transport costs, which are often of quite subordinate importance.

The fact is that accelerating development in regions that are lagging behind has to face much the same difficulties when the regions are within one country as when they constitute separate countries. In some ways the difficulties are greater because the spread in labour costs and labour availability within one country is usually much narrower; in other ways the difficulties are less because a lagging region escapes most of the financial handicaps of a poor country, or can turn to a single government to redress the balance of advantage with taxpayers' money, while there is no single government to exercise its jurisdiction over the economies of competing countries so as to influence or dictate the choice of location. But the similarities are more striking than the differences. Each region, like each country, offers itself as a location in competing with others and has to find ways of enhancing its attractions and bringing them into play at times when there is an overflow from established locations. Both regions and countries find that the path of economic development is hard in any circumstances—either because the prosperity of other regions reinforces their attractions or because bad times elsewhere dampen external demand and lessen the disposition to move to a new location. It might seem that the lagging regions are doomed to fall progressively further behind, just as the gap between developed and developing countries is often alleged to be predestined to increase. But, in fact, regions like countries rise and fall in the batting order, and regional policy has so far been a relatively minor influence on such changes as have occurred.

So far as the future of regional economics is concerned, it seems inevitable that the trend will be towards closer incorporation in the general body of theory. The spatial aspects of equilibrium and growth cannot be disregarded and are a necessary part of that theory. At the same time the issues they raise have much in common with other factors labelled structural, so that it is not so much a separate branch of theory that is required as an adaptation of a general theory of the interaction of structural and conjunctural factors.

Alec Cairncross
St. Peter's College, Oxford

Introduction

Duncan Maclennan and John B. Parr

The origins of this volume go back to two meetings that took place at the University of Glasgow in 1976. These meetings were held under the auspices of the Urban and Regional Economics Seminar Group, which is organised by the University of Glasgow under the sponsorship of the Social Science Research Council. A number of papers on regional policy in Great Britain were presented at these meetings, and it was felt that these formed the core of a volume on regional policy, a subject that continues to occupy the energies and interests of researchers in a number of fields. Accordingly, additional chapters were invited, in order to provide an element of balance and to cover a range of important issues not dealt with at the earlier meetings. The chapters were selected primarily to reflect the current state of regional policy in Great Britain and to provide an assessment of its changing character. Naturally, the responsibility for the selection of chapters lies with the editors.

Regional policy has existed in Great Britain in one form or another for over fifty years. Throughout its existence, regional policy has been accorded varying degrees of importance by successive governments, but it is only in the last decade or so that regional policy has attained its present status. While there has always been academic interest in the question of regional problems and regional policy, it was not until the 1960s that a significant research effort in this area emerged. This has contributed much to our understanding of regional economic problems and the nature of particular regional-policy responses, although there are still disturbingly large gaps in our knowledge. One reason for this has been the lack of an adequate system for monitoring the effects of regional policy and, more particularly, changes in regional policy. A second reason concerns the fact that the development of theoretical approaches may have outstripped our capacity for empirical investigation. This has been due, in part, to the quality of regional and interregional statistics which, though considerably improved in recent years, are still inadequate for the kinds of analyses that need to be undertaken, and continue to be inferior to those available in other countries of the developed world.

At the present time, concern with regional policy is widespread. To some extent, this may be because the traditional approaches to regional

policy appear to be increasingly inappropriate or ill-conceived. Also, the
dramatic changes in the economic climate during the present decade have
meant that the nature of the regional problem, to which regional policy
is supposed to be responding, has changed considerably. Furthermore, the
implications of North Sea oil discoveries, entry into the European Community and the proposed arrangements for devolution have added further
dimensions of interest to regional policy. Thus, whether because of the
apparent ineffectiveness of policies under present conditions or as a result
of changing institutional circumstances, awareness of the regional problem
and concern with regional policy are both at a high level.

Considerations such as these have provided the basic impetus for this
volume, the intention of which is to examine British regional policy up
to the present, to assess its current relevance and to speculate on its role
and significance in the foreseeable future. This final objective is particularly
elusive, by virtue of the numerous uncertainties in the economic and
political structure of the nation. It is a worthy objective, nonetheless,
in view of the fact that a number of researchers have expressed the opinion
that regional policy is rapidly approaching its demise. While this is a
rather extreme prognosis, it is one that merits attention in the light of
recent trends and current developments, and it is hoped that the following
chapters will be able to cast light on this controversial issue.

It is important to stress that the term 'regional policy' is being used
here in a particular sense. Throughout the volume the term is used to
indicate policies with specific regional objectives or particular regional
applications. There are, of course, many other elements of public policy
that have differential regional impacts and thus significant regional implications, and in a very real sense these should be regarded as important
components of regional policy. For example, the national structure of public
finance and the interregional transfers of income underlying this, together
with the policies of the nationalised industries, have a very strong effect
on levels of regional welfare. Such 'indirect' regional policy represents
a neglected area of research, and given the relative sparseness and inaccessibi-
lity of official statistics, this is likely to remain the case for some time to
come. While certain chapters do draw attention to this indirect form of
regional policy, there is no explicit treatment of the topic within the volume.

This volume is concerned primarily with Great Britain, rather than
the United Kingdom. The reason for this is that regional policy in Northern
Ireland has been legislatively and administratively distinct from that pursued
in Great Britain, with the result that it would have been difficult to
generalise at the level of the United Kingdom. In the few cases where
the relevant statistics were published on a United Kingdom basis in such
a manner that it was not possible to extract the pertinent information
for Great Britain, the United Kingdom figures have been presented. Also,
in certain chapters involving topics relating to the United Kingdom as

a whole (those on North Sea oil, membership of the European Community, devolution and the national Industrial Strategy), it was logical to focus on the United Kingdom, although any explicit consideration of regional policy in these chapters has been limited to Great Britain.

If only because of limitations of space, a work of this nature can never be comprehensive, and there are a number of important topics that are not dealt with. For example, chapters on transport, environmental quality, resource management and rural development might well have been usefully included, but this has not been possible. Broadly speaking, the chapters of this volume are concerned with the recent development of regional policy in Great Britain, its major shortcomings at the conceptual as well as the operational level and the changing conditions under which it must operate. The various contributions do not appear *en bloc*, but have been divided into four parts, each part representing a major theme of the volume. It will be observed on several occasions that certain chapters are not in total agreement on particular points. Usually, this is more apparent than real, and results from a difference in emphasis or perspective. More importantly, perhaps, it may also be a reflection of the basic complexity of the problems being treated. No attempt has been made editorially to modify those points of difference, in the expectation that they will be of interest to the reader.

The structure of the volume may be briefly outlined. Part I (Regional Policy: Past and Present) traces the development of regional policy, particularly in the post-war period, and examines its major elements. Consideration is also given to how regional policy relates to, and interacts with, other aspects of national economic policy. In Part II (The Changing Economic Environment) an attempt is made to emphasise the fact that the nature of the regional problem has undergone substantial modification in the last ten to fifteen years. Particular attention is focused on the increasingly important metropolitan dimension of regional policy and on the impact of North Sea oil. The chapters that form Part III of the volume (Neglected Aspects in Regional Policy) discuss a number of considerations that have received inadequate attention in the formulation and implementation of regional policy. The principal concerns here are with the spatial framework within which regional policy is implemented and with the kinds of economic development that should be fostered within the problem regions. Part IV of the volume (Regional Policy in an Emerging Political Framework) looks toward the future and considers the operation of regional policy under changing institutional conditions, particularly with respect to Community membership, devolved government and the operation of the national Industrial Strategy.

The analysis of regional problems and the examination of regional policy cannot be the exclusive province of a single discipline, although there is probably not universal agreement on this point. In any comprehensive analysis of regional problems designed to improve the formulation and implementation of regional policy, it becomes apparent sooner or later that the contributions of a number of fields are necessary. The general tenor of the approach taken in the following pages is a regional economic one. It will be apparent, however, that the volume also reflects the influence of other disciplines, such as economic geography, planning and political science, and it seems only reasonable to acknowledge the debt to these other fields.

This multi-disciplinary nature of the subject makes the difficulties encountered by those who administer regional policy even more formidable, and thus renders policy administrators all the more susceptible to criticism from those outside government. It is virtually inevitable in a work that deals with public policy that criticisms, implied or direct, of those who are responsible for the implementation of policy must occur, either on specific details of operation or in a more general sense with regard to perceptions, misconceptions or biases. This volume is no exception, and while the various authors would no doubt wish to stand by their criticism, it is conceded that such criticism is made from an academic vantage point, from which the subtleties of policy implementation and pressures to which administrators are subject are often not apparent.

We would like to express our gratitude to those who have contributed chapters to this volume. Our special thanks are due to Sir Alec Cairncross for taking time from his duties as Master of St Peter's College, Oxford, to write the Foreword to this volume. We are also grateful to the publishers' referees for their valuable suggestions on preliminary drafts of the volume, as well as to the publishers, Martin Robertson, for their cooperation and assistance at all stages of preparation. Professor Max Gaskin of Aberdeen and Professor Laurence Hunter of Glasgow have provided us with much useful advice and encouragement and we wish to thank the Social Science Research Council for its cooperation in the preparation of the volume. Finally, we gratefully acknowledge the generous financial support of the Publications Board of the University of Glasgow and the Carnegie Trust, without which publication of this volume would not have been possible.

PART I

Regional Policy: Past and Present

Policies aimed deliberately at the reduction of regional differences in welfare levels and unemployment rates have been undertaken in Great Britain for more than half a century. During this period there has been a remarkable degree of uniformity in the instruments used to pursue regional policy. However, in the post-war era, there have not only been marked real increases in expenditure, but the scope of regional policy has expanded and its overall complexity has increased. Since many of the major characteristics of present-day regional policies have evolved over a lengthy time span, it is important that any analysis of the current situation and speculation about future trends take adequate account of the historical evolution of regional policy. Throughout the major phases of regional policy, interregional welfare redistribution has continued to be the central goal, although there have also been secondary goals, and these have tended to change over the years. In the immediate post-war period, regional policy was deemed desirable as a means of aiding the return of the national economy to a peacetime basis. By the 1960s it was felt that regional policy could assist economic expansion by stimulating the use of idle resources in lagging economies of the problem regions. This argument, largely concerned with the allocative-efficiency gains from regional policy rather than its redistributive benefits, was revised and extended during the early part of the 1970s, and for a short period was viewed by many regional economists as being the principal objective of policy. It was argued that regional policy would enable the national economy to attain a faster growth rate without generating substantial balance of payments difficulties or domestic inflationary pressure.

The retrospective analysis of policy deals first with a general history of British regional policy, and then with two sets of policy measures, which are usually viewed as alternatives rather than as complementary approaches—the movement of capital to workers and the migration of labour to work opportunities. Attempts at reducing regional disparities in unemployment and welfare levels have generally been pursued by increasing regional demand for labour and, in the longer term, expanding regional supply capacities. Increased income and employment in the problem regions have generally been attained by the strategy of reconstituting the export bases of the regions concerned. This renovation of the regional export bases was, in turn, achieved by diverting manufacturing investment away from congested regions by a series of controls and incentives that favoured the problem regions. Such diversion of manufacturing investment has formed the core of British regional policy, and it is only during the last five years that the diversion of service industries or the development of the indigenous sector within the economies of problem regions have been given serious consideration. The policy of moving work to workers, rather than the encouragement of labour migration, as the means to reduce regional-unemployment and activity rate differentials, has held sway in the major 'policy-on' periods. By contrast, the possibility of influencing labour market adjustment by encouraging interregional migration has received scant attention throughout most of the history of British regional policy. This limited role of assisted-mobility policies is somewhat difficult to comprehend, and to redress this imbalance in policy thinking and research, an evaluation of assisted labour mobility policy is included as an important element of this part of the volume.

In the current climate of economic uncertainty, calls are frequently made for a general reassessment of economic policies and there is no reason to suppose that regional policy will be immune from such examination. Some commentators have argued that regional policies have ceased to operate in the best interests of national economic performance. Policies that have been instituted in the past could well have escaped general scrutiny in periods of relative economic prosperity. In any event, the opportunity costs of regional policy require more detailed economic evaluation. Furthermore, with increasing concern over the level of public expenditure, doubts are bound to arise about the cost effectiveness of regional policy and more generally about the suitability of existing measures for coping with present problems. Finally, the mutual interrelationship between regional policy and national economic performance must continue to be recognised. A sound regional policy can contribute much to well-being throughout the nation, but at the same time the pursuit of an effective regional policy is largely conditional upon the existence of a thriving national economy.

CHAPTER 1

The Development of British Regional Policy

J. D. McCallum*

Foundations: from the Great Depression to 1947

The beginnings of regional policy in Great Britain can be dated to the late 1920s, when the unemployment problems of the post-war decade began to look more permanent and serious than originally thought.[1] Significantly, there was a growing awareness that the country's economic problems were different from those of the more familiar pre-war business cycles. A crucial difference was the failure of many of Britain's major export industries to recover from the slump. With their world markets collapsed, coalmining, iron and steel manufacture, shipbuilding and marine engineering and much of heavy engineering staggered along at reduced levels of output and employment. Correspondingly, because of the spatial concentration of these basic industries in certain parts of the country, persistent regional concentrations of unemployment became clear. Government awareness of the problems arising from this concentration was heightened by the rise of the Labour Party, which brought into Parliament a large and vocal group representing the industrial working class—those most directly affected by these new economic problems. In any event, the unemployment statistics themselves were powerfully clear. In May 1928 unemployment rates were between 2 and 5 per cent in London and the Home Counties, but in South Wales and North East England the rates were 20 to 25 per cent.

The first significant government response came in January 1928, when the Minister of Labour appointed the Industrial Transference Board (ITB) '. . . for the purpose of facilitating the transfer of workers, and in particular of miners, for whom opportunities of employment in their own district or occupation are no longer available' (Great Britain, 1928, p. 1). The Board thus embodied that basic diagnosis of the problem which was to underlie regional policy for nearly fifty years: secularly declining industries concentrated in particular regions. Coalmining, which under the ITB and

*Department of Town and Regional Planning and Centre for Urban and Regional Research, University of Glasgow.

many subsequent initiatives received special treatment, illustrated this analysis of the problem in extreme form. Mining villages were typically in isolated locations, with no alternative employment nearby. The surplus of employees in that industry automatically became a spatially concentrated surplus of labour, unable to respond to the situation by shifting to other jobs. The approach of the ITB was orthodox in the sense that it relied on the accepted 'market' mechanism of labour movement between regions and industries; but given the low rates of unemployment then (1928) prevailing in the South and Midlands of England, it was by no means an inappropriate solution. Unfortunately, as the Depression deepened, the unemployment rates in the more prosperous regions rose, with a corresponding reduction in the success of interregional labour mobility. In the end, despite assisting a large number of moves (approximately 200,000 in ten years), the programme was considered to have had little lasting impact. This judgement was probably unfair, as A. J. Brown (1972, pp. 281–4) argues, but it unquestionably coloured subsequent attitudes toward what constituted 'appropriate' policy solutions (Beaumont, chapter 3 of this volume; Pitfield, 1978).

Meanwhile, the unemployment situation continued to get worse, and the pressures on the Government for further action became increasingly intense. A variety of industrial and area surveys were carried out, the most important being published in 1934 as *Reports of Investigations into the Industrial Conditions in Certain Depressed Areas* (Great Britain, 1934). These four reports covered what had come to be widely accepted as the 'depressed areas': Central Scotland, South Wales, North East England and North West England (West Cumberland). They described the extreme distress of these areas and argued not only that traditional employments were simply not recovering, but also that new or alternative jobs were not forthcoming. Unemployment (over 50 per cent in many local employment exchanges) had not been alleviated either by 'natural' economic forces or by previous government initiatives, and all four reports called for new programmes and policies. One report concluded that the depressed areas '. . . can only escape from the vicious cycle, where depression created unemployment and unemployment intensified depression, by means of some positive external assistance' (Great Britain, 1934, p. 106).

The Government duly brought forward a measure of 'positive external assistance' with the Special Areas (Development and Improvement) Act 1934. Four Special Areas were designated covering the areas investigated in the *Reports*, and two Commissioners (one for Scotland, one for England and Wales) were appointed to administer the legislation. Initially the Commissioners had few resources, and in the first year '. . . expenditure was almost entirely limited to sewerage schemes and settlement of labour on the land' (McCrone, 1969, p. 95). In 1936 loan capital was made available for small business in the Special Areas through the Special Areas Reconstruction Association set up by the Bank of England. The Special Areas (Amendments) Act 1937 then empowered the Treasury to give loans to larger businesses in the assisted areas; it also allowed the Commissioners to make contributions toward firms' taxes, rent and rates for a limited period (Pitfield, 1978). Additionally, Special Area firms could be exempted from the National Defence Tax (started in 1937).[2] The proportion of total funds expended going to private industry remained very small, at only about 10 per cent. By the outbreak of war only around £2m had been disbursed as government loans to industry, and a mere £50,000 in contributions towards taxes and rents; programmes at this scale of expenditure 'were little more than a token effort' (Sundquist, 1975, p. 40). More visible success came with public sponsorship of industrial estates. The first of these was established in 1936, and their development was encouraged by the 1937 Amendments, which broadened the Commissioners' powers to build and let factories and otherwise promote employment growth on the new estates. By 1938 government-built factories were employing around 12,000 people in the Special Areas, and the apparent success of the industrial estate approach firmly established it as a favoured regional-policy tool.

By 1939 the Special Areas Commissioners had built up a fairly broad range of powers and gained considerable experience in dealing with problems of depressed areas (see Great Britain, 1935a–1938b). Although their activities had not produced any dramatic effect (unemployment rates only began to drop significantly in 1939 with the impact of the war economy), it must be remembered that most of their more important powers were grossly underfinanced and had only a very short period in which to prove themselves. But at least the potential efficacy of their developmental powers, according to Brown (1972, p. 285), '. . . may be regarded . . . as having been demonstrated'. Moreover, for whatever reasons, the proportion of new factories in the United Kingdom going to the Special Areas rose from 2 to 3 per cent in the period 1932–36 to 17 per cent in 1938.

Because of the persistence of severe regional economic problems, and because of continuing concern about the conditions of life in the large industrial centres of the nation, a Royal Commission (Great Britain, 1940, p. 1) had been established in July 1937:

> . . . to inquire into the causes which have influenced the present geographical distribution of the industrial population of Great Britain and the probable direction of any change in that distribution in the future; to consider what social, economic or strategical disadvantages arise from the concentration of industries or of the industrial population in large towns or in particular areas of the country; and to report what remedial measures if any should be taken in the national interest.

The Commission's Report, subsequently well known as the Barlow Report, was completed in August 1939 and published the following January. Many of its key issues had been previously explored in policy discussions. The

1934 investigators, for example, had already sounded two themes that were to reappear in Barlow: first, a firm conviction that large conurbations were undesirable; and, second, explicit acceptance of government control and direction of private industry as a necessary means of securing a satisfactory regional pattern of economic activity. Thus the authors of the *Reports* (Great Britain, 1934, p. 107) argued:

> The evils, actual and potential, of this increasing agglomeration of human beings are so generally recognised as to need no comment. It is suggested, therefore, that the time has come when the Government can no longer regard with indifference a line of development which, while it may possess the initial advantage of providing more employment, appears upon a long view to be detrimental to the best interests of the country; and the first practical step which could be taken towards exercising a measure of control in this direction would seem to be some form of national planning of industry.

Sir Malcolm Stewart (Special Areas Commissioner for England and Wales) later put forward similar views (Great Britain, 1936a), including a strong argument that depressed-area problems could not be solved without coordinated control over development in the more prosperous regions. Though overlapping with these concerns, the Barlow Commission had a scope greater than just the problems of the depressed areas, as is clear from the three principal 'objectives of national action' identified in its Report (Great Britain, 1940, pp. 201–2):

> a) Continued and further redevelopment of congested urban areas, where necessary.
> b) Decentralisation or dispersal, both of industries and industrial population, from such areas.
> c) Encouragement of a reasonable balance of industrial development, so far as possible, throughout the various divisions or regions of Great Britain, coupled with appropriate diversification of industry in each division or region throughout the country.

The effect of Barlow's analysis and prescriptions upon planning and urban policy was fundamental; as Cullingworth (1970, p. 27) argued:

> The Barlow Report is of significance not merely because it is an important historical landmark, but also because some of its major policy recommendations have been accepted by all post-war governments as a basis for planning policy. Only recently have these policies been questioned.

The Report had a lesser, but still significant, influence upon regional-development policy. According to McCrone (1969, p. 104), it

> . . . was a landmark in the development of thought on the regional problem in Britain. . . . In several respects it was ahead of its time and many of the innovations which have been introduced into British regional policy in the 1960s were given clear expression in the Report some twenty years earlier.

Translation of Barlow's general ideals into official policy soon followed.

In 1943 the Ministry of Town and Country Planning was set up, and in 1944 the White Paper on Employment Policy (Great Britain, 1944) devoted one of its six chapters to 'The Balanced Distribution of Industry and Labour' and explicitly committed the Government to the objective of reducing regional economic inequalities. Then, following the election in 1945 of a Labour Government strongly committed to an activist regional economic policy, came the Distribution of Industry Act 1945. Broadly similar in its powers to those accumulated by the Special Areas Commissioners before the war, the Act remained the basis of regional policy until 1960. The Board of Trade could build factories, make provision for basic services, help reclaim derelict land and make loans to industrial-estate undertakings. The Treasury, with the advice of a Development Areas Treasury Advisory Committee (DATAC) provided grants or loans to specific firms, although there was no longer any direct tax incentive. The areas designated were Central Scotland, South Wales, North East England and West Cumberland. These were broadly as under the 1934 Act, but with the addition of major cities (Glasgow, Dundee, Cardiff, Swansea, Newcastle, Teeside) which had not been included in the former Special Areas. Wrexham (1946), Wigan–St. Helens (1946), Scottish Highlands (1947), Merseyside (1949) and North East Lancashire (1953) were subsequently added to the original 1945 Development Areas, which were themselves extended on occasion. Finally, the name was changed to Development Areas, presumably to give a more positive and dynamic connotation.

Conspicuously absent from the 1945 Act (despite the recommendations of Barlow and the 1944 White Paper) was any formal power of control over industrial development in the non-assisted areas. However, the government was able to use its discretionary control over scarce (usually rationed) building materials and its temporarily continued war-time building licence system to influence location of new industrial development. Control was regularised, two years later, through the 1947 Town and Country Planning Act, which introduced the Industrial Development Certificate (IDC) as a prerequisite for granting of planning permission, thus formalising '... the relationship between distribution policy and town and country planning' (Great Britain, 1948, p. 12). Industrial developments over a fixed size (originally 5,000 sq.ft.) were thereby required to secure an IDC from the Board of Trade certifying that the development was consistent with the 'proper' distribution of industry *before* planning permission could be given.[3]

Further expression of the Barlow-stimulated concern for the interrelationship of regional economic with urban planning themes can be seen in the post-war consensus supporting the control of growth in the big cities of the South (especially London). On the one hand, control was needed to 'push' industry to the high-unemployment regions; on the other hand, control was needed to ease congestion and assist urban redevelopment.

Such consistency among objectives and approaches, however, was often more apparent than real. In practice, New Town and overspill policies often operated against the interregional redistribution of industry. Following the plans of Abercrombie (1945 and 1949), urban problems and solutions were seen almost exclusively in an intraregional context; and since the planning orthodoxy (following the Garden City idea) called for 'balance' of jobs and homes, a great deal of industry moved from London, not to the development areas, but simply to the New Towns in the outer metropolitan area. In effect, the New Towns competed directly with the assisted areas.[4]

The general conditions in the early post-war period were quite favourable to a redistribution of industry. The existence of some 13m sq.ft. of surplus ordnance factories in the assisted areas (where they had been located in a war-time policy of strategic dispersal) was of great benefit, since these were immediately available at a time of severe national shortage of premises. Equally, the generally tight national labour market meant that the relative availability of labour in the assisted areas was itself an important attraction. Finally, there was so much pent-up demand for capital investment (and such a scarcity of immediately available resources) that industry was more concerned to get a plant going than to worry about where it was located. The assistance available under the 1945 Distribution of Industry Act was of some significance; but the financial incentives were relatively small, and the biggest impact initially was through industrial estates and provision of factories. More important was the extent to which government was willing to enforce its controls (through IDCs or through rationing of building materials); in the early period these were fairly rigorously enforced. As a result of all this, the Development Areas gained their greatest ever share of total new industrial investment: over 50 per cent of total national development (by area) in the period 1945–47 (see Table 1.1). This success was visible, and it implanted in many minds the idea that regional problems could effectively be tackled by government policy. Unfortunately, it also suggested to some people that the problem

TABLE 1.1
New industrial building approved, 1945–55 (annual average during period)

Period	Development Areas		Rest of Great Britain	
	Square feet	Percentage of total	Square feet	Percentage of total
1945–47	15,734,000	51.3	14,949,000	48.7
1948–51	8,602,000	19.4	35,819,000	80.6
1952–55	9,906,000	17.4	47,180,000	82.6

Source: Odber, Allen and Bowden (1957, Table V).

was practically solved and it eroded previous feelings of urgency (based on the Depression experience) and paved the way psychologically for later reductions in development area priorities.

Consolidation and Gradual Change: 1947 to 1964

1947–1958: the 'Lull' in Regional Policy
The situation changed dramatically following the October 1947 balance of payments crisis, which forced the Government into public expenditure cuts, shifted emphasis to export production, and focussed attention on national (rather than regional) problems. The Government decided, however reluctantly, that it could no longer give regional development its former high priority. Control measures (IDCs and materials rationing) were loosened, the building of advance factories in Development Areas was stopped, and regional-policy expenditure was cut (from about £12.1m per annum 1947–48 to 1948–49 down to about £6.5m per annum 1949–50 to 1950–51). At the same time, the stock of war-time factories in Development Areas had largely been taken up, and interregional labour supply differentials were no longer so important. Industrialists were no longer so willing to ignore location in their rush to begin production. In consequence, the Development Areas' share of approved industrial expansion fell sharply in the 1948–51 period, down to about 19.4 per cent of the national total— roughly their share of the national industrial labour force. In absolute terms, the average annual square footage in Development Areas dropped over 45 per cent, whereas in the rest of the country it more than doubled, as is indicated in Table 1.1.

This 'de-emphasis' of regional assistance, acceded to unwillingly by the Labour Government, was embraced openly by the Conservative Government elected in 1951. Controls over development were deliberately weakened: the building licence system was abolished by 1954 and IDCs became relatively easy to obtain. Industrial-estate activities were cut back. Total expenditures under the 1945 Act dropped from £8.13m per annum in the last three Labour years down to £4.76m per annum in the first eight Conservative years. Odber (1965, p. 339) is certainly correct in his judgement that '. . . from 1951 to 1958 development area policy was in abeyance': The major reason for this long hiatus in regional policy was the Conservative Government's opposition to such forms of national planning or control over industry (Harris, 1966; Cullingworth, 1970). This ideological predisposition was reinforced by a number of other factors, particularly the continued low levels of unemployment nationally and regionally: from 1951 to 1957 unemployment in Scotland averaged 2.7 per cent, in the North 2.1 per cent and in Wales 2.5 per cent, with a national average of 1.4 per cent (Odber, 1965, Table 4). In contrast to pre-war experience and post-war fears, many of those industrial sectors that had caused such problems in the assisted regions during the Depression seemed to be doing well in the 1951–58 period. Coalmining, shipbuilding and marine engineering, and railway vehicles and equipment (all heavily concentrated in the problem regions) maintained their national total of a million and a quarter employees throughout this period; see Tables 1.2 and 1.3. Interestingly, the new Government did not need to made any change in the instruments of policy. The basic legislation (the 1945 Act, with the minor changes of the Distribution of Industry Act 1950) remained in force. The Government simply lowered the authorisation for Board of Trade to spend on industrial estates, factories, loans, etc. Equally, the IDC system remained nominally in force, but the rigour of its application was reduced.

The Reactivation of Regional Policy: 1958–1964

In 1958, however, economic conditions began to change. Unemployment rose nationally and the 1958–1959 recession left the problem regions at a level of unemployment well above the long-term post-war average. Part of the problem during this time is indicated in Tables 1.2 and 1.3. After remaining stable for the seven years 1951–58, the three 'weak' industry sectors (coalmining, shipbuilding, railway equipment) shed over a quarter of a million employees (one-fifth of the total) in the five years 1958–63, and most of these were in the traditionally distressed regions. The immediate government response was the Distribution of Industry (Industrial Finance)

TABLE 1.2

Employees in selected industrial sectors in the United Kingdom (thousands of employees in employment)

Sector (1958 SIC)	1948	1951	1958	1963	1968	1973
All employment	20,732	21,171	22,290	23,393	23,667	22,662
Manufacturing and mining, total	9,130	9,773	10,207	9,609	9,456	—[a]
Coalmining	803	780	786	625	446	315
Shipbuilding and marine engineering	343	306	315	242	207	187
Railway equipment and vehicles	179	172	160	120	60	41
Subtotal, 3 groupings	1,325	1,258	1,261	987	713	543
All other manufacturing	7,805	8,515	8,946	8,622	8,743	—[a]
Employment excluding mining and manufacturing	11,602	11,398	12,083	13,784	14,211	—[a]

[a] Data not available.

Note: data for 1973 are based on the 1968 Standard Industrial Classification and are not strictly comparable with earlier years, although in these particular sectors the differences are small.

Source: figures have been taken from various volumes of the *Annual Abstract of Statistics*.

TABLE 1.3

Changes in employees in the United Kingdom in selected industrial sectors, 1951–68

Sectors:	1951–58		1958–63		1963–68	
	Number	Percentage	Number	Percentage	Number	Percentage
All employment	+1,119	+5.3	+1,103	+ 4.9	+274	+ 1.2
Manufacturing and mining	+ 434	+4.4	− 598	− 5.9	−153	− 1.6
Coalmining	+ 6	+0.8	− 161	−20.5	−179	−28.6
Shipbuilding and marine engineering	+ 9	+2.9	− 73	−23.2	− 35	−14.5
Railway equipment and vehicles	− 12	−7.0	− 40	−25.0	− 60	−50.0
Sub-total, 3 groupings	+ 3	+0.2	− 274	−21.9	−274	−27.8
All other mining and manufacturing	+ 431	+5.1	− 324	− 3.6	+121	+ 1.4
Employment excluding mining and manufacturing	+ 640	+5.6	+1,701	+14.1	+427	+ 3.1

Source: Table 1.2.

Act of 1958. This supplemented but did not replace the 1945 Act. It rather confused matters by making a number of places outside the Development Areas eligible for loan and grant assistance on the basis of local registered unemployment. Assistance was also made available to non-industrial undertakings, and expenditures under the legislation were increased from £3.6m in 1958–59 to £8.6m in 1959–60 and £11.8m in 1960–61 (this last amount still being less than was spent in 1947–48).

The continued deterioration of conditions in the problem areas (especially Scotland) was not visibly arrested by extant measures. Equally, the 1959 General Election gave certain political warnings. Despite a national swing to the incumbent Government (up from 54.6 per cent of seats to 58.0 per cent), the Conservatives lost substantially in Scotland, dropping from 50.7 per cent to 43.7 per cent of seats. Finally, politicians and officials alike were unhappy with the administrative confusion introduced by the 1958 Act. Accordingly, the Local Employment Act 1960 was brought forward, repealing the 1945, 1950 and 1958 Distribution of Industry Acts and recasting regional policy. The Local Employment Act 1960 retained all the important incentive features of the 1945 Act, and added the ability to give grants to businessmen building their own factories in Development Areas. The administration of loans and grants to enterprises, formerly undertaken by the Treasury, was transferred to the Board of Trade, thus putting all the main powers in one department. The Board, however, was required to secure general Treasury approval for its loan and grant activities and had to consult a special Board of Trade Advisory Committee (BOTAC).[5] An interesting step was that loans and grants were made available for non-manufacturing firms. This step was first taken in the 1958 Act and ran counter to the manufacturing orientation of policy since 1934. Also, the basis for loan eligibility was loosened; formerly required to show that alternative finance was not available, the firm was now only required to show reasonable prospects of success. This was a change from supplementing the private capital market to competing directly with it. Reflecting these changes, expenditure on policy more than doubled from £11.8m in 1960–61 to £24.0m in 1961–62.

A most significant change in the 1960 Act was the abolition of the old Development Areas (which had remained largely unchanged in definition since 1945 except for the additions during the period 1946–53) and their replacement by Development Districts. These were based on local employment exchanges and could be quite small. Their designation as Development Districts was by the Board of Trade, within the general guideline that a high rate of unemployment already exists or is likely to exist. This approach was felt to be flexible and to allow direct discrimination in favour of areas experiencing high unemployment. But since Development Districts could be scheduled and descheduled according to movements in unemployment rates, the extent of coverage could vary rapidly. Development Districts covered 12.5 per cent of the population of Great Britain in 1961, but only 7.2 per cent the following year, later reaching a maximum of 16.8 per cent in 1966. The disadvantages of this for financial planning are obvious, and it is impossible to gauge the extent to which firms were discouraged from investing in certain Development Districts because of the uncertainty of knowing when or where incentives would be available. Another result was that instead of large economic regions (which was at least partly the objective of the Development Area approach to designation), assisted areas became a patchwork of non-contiguous labour exchanges scattered across the country, including some in otherwise very prosperous regions. It also meant the inclusion of rural areas, which had largely been excluded from earlier designation on the grounds of being unsuitable for industrial growth, though this change was consistent with the earlier (1958) widening of eligibility to non-industrial firms.

Regional problems, of course, were not solved by the passage of this new legislation. On the contrary, the problems worsened in the 1962–63 recession, causing such concern that a Minister (Lord Hailsham) was given special responsibility for the North East, which along with Scotland (already possessing its own Minister) was most hard hit. In late 1963 White Papers for Central Scotland (Great Britain, 1963a) and for North East England (Great Britain, 1963b) were issued, to indicate the developmental lines along which the Government intended to proceed. In the Central Scotland White Paper emphasis was placed on '. . . growth areas chosen as potentially the best locations for industrial expansion' and the building up of these areas '. . . by providing for them, in accordance with a coherent plan, all the "infrastructure" services . . .' (Great Britain, 1963a, p. 5). These proposed growth areas were to be allowed to maintain Development District status even if local unemployment rates dropped below the set limit for descheduling. Concern was also expressed for the problems of housing supply and of transport and communication as constraints on growth. This meant a heavy emphasis on roadbuilding, bridges and port development. It was noted that some of the New Towns (especially East Kilbride) had become centres of industrial growth and employment expansion, and four of the eight proposed growth areas were based on the New Towns. In all these ways, the White Paper reflected a welcome emphasis on the spatial dimensions of regional-development strategies (Parr, chapter 9 of this volume). On the other hand, there was no discussion about changes in the nature and scale of financial incentives to industry, presumably on the assumption that the 1960 Local Employment Act would remain the basic instrument.

In many ways, the White Paper for the North East (Great Britain, 1963b) was similar to the Scottish White Paper, although its spatial focus was on a 'growth zone' as opposed to the several separate 'growth areas' of Central Scotland. This was a rather vague concept in practice, since the zone included practically all the industrial areas of the North East. The White Paper put enormous emphasis on construction of a huge network of roads. As a result, expenditure on road construction in the North rose from 4.8 per cent of total road expenditures in Great Britain in 1963 to 12.8 per cent in 1969; in the period 1969–71 road construction expenditures exceeded those for house building (Northern Region Strategy Team, 1975b). The White Paper suggested more support for non-industrial developments like offices, however.

Also in 1963 there appeared two major reports from the National Economic Development Council (NEDC): *Growth of the United Kingdom Economy to 1966* (Great Britain, 1963c) and *Conditions Favourable to Faster Growth* (Great Britain, 1963d). The former was a study of the '. . . implications of an annual rate of growth of 4 per cent for the period 1961–1966' (Great Britain, 1963c, p. viii), while the latter was a policy-oriented paper suggesting some of the specific ways in which public and private sectors would need to perform to achieve this growth. It contained not only a lengthy discussion of 'Regional Questions', but also an explicit statement (Great Britain, 1963d, p. 14) that regional policy should be considered something more than spatially concentrated welfare measures:

> The level of unemployment in different regions of the country varies widely,
> and high unemployment associated with the lack of employment opportunities

in the less prosperous regions is usually thought of as a social problem. Policies aim, therefore, to prevent unemployment rising to politically intolerable levels and expenditure to this end is often considered as a necessary burden to the nation, urelated to any economic gain that might accrue from it. But the relatively high unemployment rates and, more important still, the relatively low activity rates in these regions also indicate considerable labour reserves. To draw these reserves into employment would make a substantial contribution to national employment and national growth.

Given this view of unemployed labour as a 'resource', an important interdependence between the national and the regional economies was then posited: 'A national policy of expansion would improve the regional picture; and, in turn, a successful regional development programme would make it easier to achieve a national growth programme' (Great Britain, 1963d, p. 29).

Another of the regional-policy issues discussed was the increasing congestion of development in the South East and the Midlands and the need for effective countermeasures. It was argued that there were important social costs (such as high costs of public-service provision, inflationary pressures on land prices and on wages, and increased transport congestion) resulting from the apparent rapid rate of urban and industrial development in these growing regions. In this respect a suggestion was made for extending development controls to offices, a step taken shortly afterwards. There was also argument for an explicit growth area approach (as in the two White Papers), as well as a suggestion that larger policy regions would be more appropriate than the Development Districts of the 1960 Act. Additionally, it was recommended that government expenditure on physical infrastructure in the problem regions be continued at a high level.

In terms of official policy measures, the Government introduced the Finance and Local Employment Acts of 1963, to strengthen and extend the incentives available. Standard grants for plant and machinery (not previously available under the 1960 Act) were made available at 10 per cent and the building grant (introduced in 1960) was set at a standard 25 per cent; both were limited to manufacturing (subject to an employment creation criterion).[6] More important was the entitlement of firms in Development Districts to depreciate investment in plant and machinery at any rate; this was in effect an interest-free loan from the Inland Revenue to any profit-making firm that wished to postpone its tax liabilities. The net result of the 1963 Acts was a further expansion of financial assistance to industry in Development Districts. Finally, in 1963, the Government set up the Location of Offices Bureau (LOB) to work toward reducing the concentration of office building and employment in London, although in this initial form LOB's role was advisory and promotional only. Unlike the case for manufacturing industry, there was no power to refuse permission for development. Equally, the emphasis quickly came down to a concern for suburbanisation of offices rather than a dispersal to far-distant regions.

The Boom in Regional Policy: 1964–1970

After a campaign in which economic planning and regional development had been made key issues, Labour came to power in October 1964 largely on the strength of voting shifts in the poorer regions and could reasonably consider themselves to have received a mandate for a major expansion of regional development activities.[7] One campaign pledge was quickly redeemed with the establishment of the Department of Economic Affairs (DEA), a new ministry headed by the Deputy Prime Minister and intended to assume a leading role in economic planning and management. Indicating the importance attached to regional problems, the DEA included a regional planning group as one of its four main divisions, thus establishing regional planning at the heart of the Government's new economic policy-making machinery. Steps were also taken to establish a uniform set of official regions, both to coordinate the work of existing ministries and to provide the basis for two new sets of regional planning organisations. In each of these new Economic Planning Regions (eight in England, one each for Scotland, Wales and Northern Ireland) there was established a Regional Economic Planning Council and a Regional Economic Planning Board. The Councils, appointed by the Government, drew upon 'leaders' in the region (businessmen, trade unionists, academics etc.) and provided (it was hoped) a body both knowledgeable about the region and roughly representative of it. The functions of the Councils were advisory only; they were concerned with broad strategy on regional development and with the formulation of regional plans. The Boards, comprising civil servants from various government departments already working in the region, were expected to coordinate (under a DEA-appointed chairman) their departmental activities and to form the nuclei of integrated regional administrative centres.

Initially, the Government worked within the framework of existing legislation (the 1960 and 1963 Acts), but with increased vigour. Expenditure on industrial estates and advance factories was boosted from the 1961–62 to 1963–64 average of £5.5m per annum to an average of £13.2m per annum for 1964–65 to 1966–67. In October 1965 sixteen more areas were added to the list of Development Districts, considerably expanding the geographic coverage of policy assistance and making the Districts into somewhat more coherent spatial units. There was also an immediate tightening of IDC control to make certificates mandatory for all industrial development in excess of 1,000 sq.ft., down from the earlier cut-off limit of 5,000. In early 1965 the Control of Office and Industrial Development Act established the requirement of obtaining an Office Development Permit (ODP) before office development in the controlled areas could proceed—a procedure analogous to the IDC (Rhodes and Kan, 1971). A further demonstration of the Government's commitment to regional policy came in September 1965 with the publication of *The National Plan*. The plan viewed regional

planning, not simply as large-scale land use planning, but as being '.
. . concerned with decisions to develop the infrastructure of the economy,
and with the location of employment and population' (Great Britain,
1965, p. 84). Echoing earlier views of the NEDC (Great Britain, 1963d),
the Plan dealt at length with the contribution of regional policy to national
economic growth, especially in terms of utilisation of idle resources and
expansion of the labour force. It constituted an explicit argument that
regional policy could serve *both* national economic growth and regional
redistribution objectives.

In November 1965 another new step in regional economic development
was taken with the setting up of the Highlands and Islands Development
Board. Responsible for the seven sparsely populated counties of northern
and western Scotland, the Board was given an unprecedentedly wide range
of powers, combining planning and advisory with developmental and financial activities. The Board established itself quickly as a crucial force in
Highland development—so well that it survived changes of government
in 1970 and 1974 and local government reorganisation in 1975.

In January 1966 a plan for Scotland was published (Great Britain,
1966). While primarily of interest as a regional economic programme,
it devoted considerable attention to location of infrastructure, transport
and communication, and housing. In particular, it urged the idea of concentration into growth centres as the way to maximise the growth impact
of new development, carrying on the ideas raised in the 1963 White Paper.
It was a further step in official efforts to integrate local planning and
regional economic development.

In late March 1966 another General Election was held, and the
Labour Government converted its thin 1964 majority into a commanding
lead: 97 seats over all other parties combined. Reinforced by this electoral
endorsement, the Government proceeded to develop and carry through
its legislative programmes, and especially those concerning regional
policy. In August the Government passed the Industrial Development
Act 1966, which was to be the legislative cornerstone of its industrial
and regional policies. In line with the aim of promoting investment
nationally, a 20 per cent grant was to be given for manufacturing investment, nation-wide. But in the Development Areas the rate was 40 per
cent (later the rates were raised to 25 per cent and 45 per cent), thus
providing a significant financial incentive on the basis of an automatic
grant.[8] The free depreciation of the 1963 legislation was dropped, though
initial allowances of 30 per cent for plant and 15 per cent for buildings
were still allowed nationally. The basic building grant remained unchanged
at 25 per cent in Development Areas and was unavailable elsewhere.
Negotiated grants and loans under the Local Employment Acts continued
to be available, but were soon overshadowed by the sheer scale of funds
disbursed under the Industrial Development Act. Once again, the basis

of geographic designation was changed. The old Development Districts were replaced by new Development Areas—large regions selected on the basis of unemployment, population change, migration and 'the objectives of regional policy'. The five initial Development Areas covered Scotland (except Edinburgh), the North (entire), Wales (except the coastal strips in the south, Cardiff–Swansea, and north), Cornwall and West Devon (in the South West), and Merseyside (in the North West). About 20 per cent of the population of Great Britain lived in these areas.

In September 1967 a Regional Employment Premium (REP) was introduced, involving payment of £1.50 per week per adult male employee (lower rates for women and juveniles) to manufacturing industries in the Development Areas. These industries were also allowed to retain a premium that had earlier been added to the regular rebate of Selective Employment Tax (SET) but that had been abolished in 1967 for employers outside Development Areas. These two measures together provided a subsidy of £1.87½ per week per man, and was not dependent upon profit, performance, creation of new jobs or any other criterion. It was a massive subsidy, both absolutely (nearly £130m in the first full year) and in terms of value to firms. McCrone (1969) estimated it to represent something like an 8 per cent reduction in an average firm's wages bill, while Kaldor (1970) considered it equivalent to a 5 or 6 per cent reduction in 'efficiency wages'; see also Great Britain (1967) and Brown, Lind and Bowers (1967). A by-product of the REP legislation was the setting up in September 1967 of the Hunt Committee. A number of regions that did not qualify as Development Areas but that nonetheless could not be considered prosperous had for some time felt themselves 'left-out' by regional policy. Alarmed by the £100m per annum that the REP would be injecting into the Development Areas, these regions (then called 'grey areas' and later termed 'intermediate areas') agitated for consideration of their special needs and problems. Accordingly, the Government set up a Committee of Inquiry into the Intermediate Areas (Great Britain, 1969b, p. 1)

> . . . to examine in relation to the economic welfare of the country as a whole and the needs of the development areas, the situation in other areas where the rate of economic growth gives cause (or may give cause) for concern, and to suggest whether revised policies to influence economic growth in such areas are desirable and, if so, what measures should be adopted.

In November 1967 the Government announced the designation of Special Development Areas: locales within existing Development Areas that, because of some special economic distress, were made eligible for extra assistance, in addition to regular Development Area aid. Initially (and until 1971) these Special Development Areas were almost exclusively small coalmining districts, particularly those hard hit by accelerating pit closures; the national coalmining labour force shrank by nearly 30 per cent during the period 1963–68 (Tables 1.2 and 1.3), and these losses were heavily concentrated

in the older coalfields of the Development Areas. Special assistance, extended
to new or incoming manufacturing projects, included rent-free periods
of up to five years in industrial-estate premises (two years in Development
Areas), building grants of 35 per cent (25 per cent in Development Areas),
loans toward the balance of building costs and one measure without direct
parallel in the Development Area assistance: an 'Operational Grant' intended to help in the early, high-cost years of establishment in the new
location (these were negotiable and related to employment creation). For
the remainder of the Labour term of office the tools and approaches worked
out in the 1964–67 period were brought into full operation and applied
vigorously. The most visible result was a massive increase in the amounts
of regional aid expended: in real terms the amount in the Labour Government's last two years (1968–69 and 1969–70) was over four times what
it had been in its first two (1964–65 and 1965–66), and nearly twelve
times what it had been in the last two years of the Conservative Government
(1962–63 and 1963–64).

In early 1969 *The Task Ahead: Economic Assessment to 1972* (Great Britain,
1969a, p. 6) was published as an updated statement of the Government's
economic aims, and for the nation as a whole certain 'broad objectives'
were laid down as the basis for obtaining a 'satisfactory rate of growth
of output':

> First, the achievement of a substantial surplus in the balance of payments
> . . . . Secondly (and partly to maintain the better trade balance), a steady
> improvement of the competitive efficiency of the economy . . . . Third, a
> fuller utilisation of resources, including an improvement in the regional balance
> of the economy; this involves a further and more marked reduction in the
> disparity between rates of unemployment in the Development Areas and the
> rest of the country.

Regional balance was once more confirmed in its place of importance
among the nation's economic objectives—the place it had held officially
since the White Paper on Employment Policy (Great Britain, 1944) twenty-
five years earlier. The chapter on 'Regional Strategy and Prospect'
offered little in the way of new suggestions or programmes, the Government
apparently feeling satisfied with the regional policy tools already in existence.

In April 1969 the Hunt Committee Report (Great Britain, 1969b)
on Intermediate Area problems was published. Concerned primarily with
the older industrial areas of the North West and Yorkshire and Humberside,
the Committee (Great Britain, 1969b, p. 7) emphasised the 'total environment' as a factor in these areas' problems:

> We mean by this the full range of the social, educational, cultural, industrial,
> and commercial facilities, as well as the physical infrastructure of buildings,
> roads, docks and the like which houses and sustains them. Our conclusion
> is that poverty in the total environment is often associated with slow economic
> growth and net outward migration, and is an important component of the
> complex of inter-related factors which make it difficult for areas to recapture
> their former dynamism.

The majority report specified a number of policy recommendations, including: (a) a 25 per cent grant for industrial building; (b) extension of Development Area training benefits to Intermediate Areas; (c) extension of the activities of the Industrial Estate Corporations; (d) new programmes of derelict land clearance with the Development Area level of 85 per cent assistance; (e) establishment of 'growth zones'; (f) raising the IDC limit to 10,000 sq.ft. and making them more freely available in the Intermediate Areas; and (g) downgrading Merseyside from a Development Area to an Intermediate Area. These recommendations were intended to cover most of the North West and Yorkshire and Humberside Regions. A strong note of dissent was registered by Professor A. J. Brown, who thought the recommendations put too much emphasis on infrastructure at the expense of financial measures; he also questioned the wisdom of relaxing controls (because of the danger to the Development Areas) and of the descheduling of Merseyside, which he felt needed full Development Area assistance—a pessimism fully confirmed by Merseyside's disastrous economic decline in the 1970s.

In the event, the Government implemented few of the majority or minority recommendations. It did pass the Local Employment Act 1970, which designated a number of small Intermediate Areas encompassing only part of the two Economic Planning Regions (excluding the major cities). It also added a few other small areas in the South West, South Wales, Scotland and the East Midlands—the first three being 'border' areas adjacent to Development Areas and the last being a problem coalfield area. The Act did introduce a 25 per cent building grant for the Intermediate Areas, and it did extend the Development Area training and industrial-estate activities into them. Finally, a 75 per cent grant for derelict land clearance was instituted, and the eligible areas were not only the Intermediate Areas but the whole of the North West and Yorkshire and Humberside. The Hunt Committee's emphasis on environmental improvement, at least, received a reasonably full endorsement. In its last year the Labour Government formally wound up the diminished DEA (G. Brown, 1972, pp. 109–16) and brought together (under a new Secretary of State for Local Government and Regional Planning) the Ministry of Housing and Local Government, the Ministry of Transport and most of the regional planning elements of the expired DEA.

The Unsuccessful Counter-Revolution: 1970–1974

In the June 1970 General Election the Labour Party lost only 7 per cent of their seats (compared to 1966) in the assisted areas, but in the rest of the country they lost 29 per cent and so lost office. The new Conservative Government was opposed on ideological grounds to much of the Labour Government's work, and changes soon began to be made. Both industrial and office development controls were relaxed; in its first year the new Government approved over twice the square footage of office development in Central London as had the Labour Government in the preceding year. The Government also announced that the Regional Employment Premium (opposed strongly by them when in Opposition) would be discontinued in September 1974 when its original seven-year commitment ran out. It was still to be paid up to that time, but of course potential investors would discount payments that they knew to be ending in 1974.

The main lines of the new Government's regional policy were specified in an October 1970 White Paper (Great Britain, 1970). Following their frequently expressed preference for tax allowances and dislike of grants, the Government ended the Investment Grants introduced in 1966. A new system of depreciation allowances was introduced in its place. Free (100 per cent) depreciation was allowed for plant and machinery in the Development Areas, as opposed to a 60 per cent initial allowance elsewhere. In addition, the temporarily increased initial allowance for industrial buildings of 40 per cent was to be retained in Development Areas and Intermediate Areas, while the 30 per cent rate applicable elsewhere was to be reduced to 15 per cent in 1972. The rates of building grants were raised from 25 per cent (Development Areas) and 35 per cent (Special Development Areas) to 35 per cent and 45 per cent, respectively; the Intermediate Area rate was not changed. Finally, the 'Operational Grants' available in Special Development Areas were changed, from the old 10 per cent of cumulative building, plant and machinery costs in the first three years, to a rate of 20 per cent of wage and salary costs during the first three years (subject as before to an upper limit relating to jobs provided).

The Government also announced an intention to increase discretionary aid under the Local Employment Acts in order to put more emphasis on the 'selective' instruments of policy. But as the Labour Government had already significantly expanded these expenditures (reaching £83.9m in 1969–70) the extra £25m promised in the White Paper looked small. In the event, moreover, the Conservatives actually spent *less* than their predecessors. The Government also announced its intention to rely on increased infrastructure spending in regional development. But again, there had been a massive build-up during Labour's term of office: per capita infrastructure spending in the four poorer regions was 25 per cent above the national average in 1968–69, up from 18 per cent above in 1965–66. Finally, there was another government reorganisation, in October 1970. A new Department of Trade and Industry (DTI) was created by amalgamation of the old Board of Trade and the previously enlarged Ministry of Technology. A second 'super-ministry' was established with the Department of the Environment (DOE), which brought together land use planning, housing, transport, local government, water and sewerage, and countryside and amenity functions. DOE was given a 'leading responsibility' for regional strategies, with important executive powers for the development of regional infrastructure and regional services. But DTI retained control over regional financial incentives and location of industry policy.

Economic events, however, overtook the Government's efforts to disengage from national and regional economic policy. The winter of 1970–71 brought a deepening recession, with the highest unemployment rates since the war. The Government felt it had to act to soften the growing impact of high unemployment in the problem regions. Its first response came in February 1971 when several of the worst-hit industrial areas were designated Special Development Areas: West Central Scotland (Glasgow and Clydeside), North East England (Tyneside and Wearside) and more of South Wales.[9] This meant that about 8.5 per cent of the nation's insured population was in Special Development Areas, as opposed to roughly 1.8 per cent before. In addition, the incentives were increased: the Operational Grant was raised from 20 per cent to 30 per cent. In the following month a number of additional districts were given Intermediate Area status: Edinburgh and vicinity; and small 'border' areas in the West Midlands and Yorkshire and Humberside. As 1971 progressed, the economy continued to decline, and in July the Government brought out a mildly reflationary Budget. To stimulate investment further, the initial tax allowance for plant and machinery was raised from 60 per cent to 80 per cent nation-wide, thus reducing the differential in favour of assisted areas (where the rate was still 100 per cent). The only compensating step (a small one) was to extend free depreciation to service industries in the Development and Special Development Areas. The assisted areas, not surprisingly, reacted strongly against their advantage being eroded in this way. The associated announcement of an extra £100m of capital expenditure on roads, schools and health facilities in the assisted areas did little to allay their fears; they recognised the measure as a short-run public works programme mainly designed to help the construction industry.

The Budget failed to have the desired effect on the national economy, and conditions continued to worsen into the winter of 1971–72. The difficulties in the regions were illustrated by the January 1972 announcement that estimated new jobs from industrial projects begun during 1971 in Development Areas and Special Development Areas totalled only 66,000—40 per cent below the 1970 figure. By this time it was being widely argued that the Government's October 1970 measures had not only been ineffective nationally, but even damaging regionally. For example, it was pointed out that a time of low profits, low corporate liquidity and substantial idle capacity was a particularly bad time to switch from capital grants to tax allowances. One review concluded: 'The recent changes have virtually eradicated the advantage of investing in development areas, as compared with similar investment in non-development areas. . . .' (Scholefield and Franks, 1972). The Government, itself, produced figures that showed that the differential in favour of development areas for a 'typical' industrial

TABLE 1.4

Regional differentials in incentives, 1970 and 1972

	Pre-October 1970 system	Post-October 1970 system	Industry Act 1972 system
Industrial buildings	19.2	25.8	19.0
Plant and machinery	13.25	2.0	19.0
Typical project	14.45	6.7	19.0

Note: Figures are for the differential between net present values of grants and tax savings from capital allowances, (expressed as a percentage of cost of investment) on investment in Development Areas and investment outside assisted areas.

Source: Great Britain (1972b, p. 147).

project had dropped from about 14.5 per cent under the pre-October 1970 system down to about 6.7 per cent under the October 1970 system; see Table 1.4.

In March 1972 there was a major reflationary Budget, which among other things further raised initial allowances nation-wide (this time to 100 per cent for plant and machinery and 40 per cent for buildings), thus eliminating the assisted areas' advantage. But in its White Paper, *Industrial and Regional Development* (Great Britain, 1972a), the Government reversed its approach to regional policy. Enacted in August as the Industry Act 1972, this new approach went back to the type of standard grant system established by Labour in 1966, and eschewed any reliance on tax incentives. It also systematised and retained the types of assistance developed under the various Local Employment Acts (which had themselves earlier been 'tidied up' by a consolidating Act, the Local Employment Act 1972). Part I of the Industry Act provided for the Regional Development Grant (RDG). This was paid at the rate of 20 per cent in Development Areas (22 per cent in Special Development Areas) in respect of investment in plant and machinery and for industrial buildings; Intermediate Areas qualified only for the 20 per cent Industrial Buildings grant. Two important differences over the 1966 Act system were that the grant portion was allowable against tax and that firms already in the assisted areas ('indigenous' firms) qualified equally with new or incoming firms. No job creation requirement was attached to receipt of RDGs. Only manufacturing and construction industries qualified (initially) for assistance.

Section 7 of the Industry Act dealt with selective financial assistance in assisted areas. It took over most of the powers of the Local Employment Acts, leaving little other than government factory building and industrial-estate activities under the rump Local Employment Act 1972. The criteria for assistance were broader than before; not only did projects that create additional employment qualify (as they generally had since the 1930s), but projects 'for modernisation or rationalisation, which do not provide extra jobs but maintain or safeguard existing employment', also qualified;

and in case that was not broad enough, 'There may be exceptional cases which fall into neither of these categories and these are decided in the light of circumstances' (Great Britain, 1973e, p. 38). Initially, the main forms of aid under Section 7 were loans at concessionary rates (sometimes completely interest free), interest relief grants and removal grants (up to 80 per cent of costs). Regional offices were set up within DTI, along with regional advisory boards, to promote decision-making in the regions rather than in Whitehall. According to the Government's own calculations (Table 1.4) the Industry Act package of aids greatly improved the attractiveness of investment in the assisted areas. The regional differential nearly trebled over the Government's own earlier measures, and was an increase of nearly a third over the 1966 Labour package. The other main feature was that the 1972 package was designed to give more of this increased aid to 'indigenous' industry than had been the case under the 1966 Act. As to the remaining major element of regional aid, the Government announced in the White Paper (Great Britain, 1972a, p. 7) that REP was to be 'phased out over a period from September 1974' and not suddenly and totally cut off at that date. Finally, it was decided to extend Intermediate Area status to the entire remainder of the North West, Yorkshire and Humberside, and Wales, as recommended by the Hunt Committee two years earlier. This extension, combined with earlier extensions in 1970 and 1971 meant that almost half of the nation's population lived in assisted areas.

Working in a somewhat contrary direction, though, the Government in July 1972 raised the exemption limits for IDCs to 15,000 sq.ft. nationally and to 10,000 sq.ft. in the South East; these were the highest (i.e., least strict) limits yet used. The Government also eliminated altogether the necessity for obtaining an IDC in Development and Special Development Areas. This was merely an administrative tidying-up, since IDCs were automatically given in such areas anyway; but it did mean the end of a most useful statistical check on the progress of industrial development in the assisted areas. As to office controls, the Government said that it would retain the ODP system, but '. . . special account will be taken of the importance of enhancing the prospects of London as an international financial and commercial centre' (Great Britain, 1972a, p. 7). This carried an implication that efforts to steer office development into the regions would be even further loosened. The loss of the negative control was particularly important because the Government did not then propose any positive incentives for office decentralisation. Fortunately, the 1971–72 recession was beginning to moderate, and in late 1972 unemployment rates began to come down. This relieved much of the pressure on the regions, and on the Government. For the remaining 15 months of its term of office the Government simply put into operation the policies it had latterly established (with regional funds in 1973–74 being one-fifth up on 1972–73).

At the same time, however, a lengthy and detailed review of regional policy was being undertaken by the Trade and Industry Sub-Committee of the House of Commons Expenditure Committee, beginning in October 1972 (just at the time, of course, that the Government was sweeping away previous legislation with the Industry Act 1972). The Report was published in December 1973, along with extensive supporting materials (Great Britain, 1973b, 1973c, 1973d). Its conclusions were largely critical: 'Much has been spent and much may well have been wasted. Regional policy has been empiricism run mad, a game of hit-and-miss, played with more enthusiasm than success' (Great Britain, 1973c, p. 72). The Report added: 'Everything in this inquiry pointed to the need for Government to create a more rational and systematic basis for the formulation and execution of regional policy' (Great Britain, 1973c, p. 73). The Committee was particularly concerned about the failure of policy makers (and especially their officials) to assess effectiveness of different policies. It was also critical of the rapid changes in policies, which had made private-sector planning nearly impossible—a potent charge at a time when policies had been radically changed twice in under three years. The Committee's work, with its lengthy Minutes of Evidence from interested parties and important contributions from academic analysts, should provide valuable guidance for future regional-policy formulation. Whether it proves to have any effect may well depend upon whether the Whitehall civil servants (who were criticised) pay much attention to what is after all merely a House Committee report, and upon whether Cabinet-level politicians (also criticised) are willing or able to heed the Report's calls for a more considered and rational progression of policy.

An Age of Uncertainty: the Rise and Fall of Regional Policy 1974–1978

In March 1974 Labour took office once again.) The voting patterns of the February General Election had been inconclusive in overall effect, but they had confirmed the immensely strong hold of Labour on the allegiance of the assisted areas.) True to its political roots as well as to its own past policy, the Labour Government announced its firm commitment to regional development activism. But it also made it clear that the 1972 Industry Act, although passed by a Conservative government, was an excellent instrument for industrial and regional intervention and so would be retained as the basis for its own policy. The new Government also announced that REP would not be ended as the previous government had threatened. Indeed, the rates paid (which, being flat rates, had been badly eroded by inflation) were later doubled. There were immediate changes in organisation.) DTI, which had already lost its energy functions to the new Department of Energy in January 1974, was split in March. The now separate Department of Industry kept the Industry Act powers and administration, including the Industrial Development Executive. In July, regional Department of Industry offices were empowered to deal with Section 7 applications of up to £1m, as a further step towards decentralising the decision making and making it more responsive to local needs. Earlier, in April, the new local-government system for England and Wales came into force, changing the historic county boundaries and, consequently, changing the boundaries of some of the Economic Planning Regions (Figure 1.1). The definition of assisted areas (Figure 1.2) was not affected, since this was based on employment office areas.

Also in July 1974 the Government announced a major programme to disperse government offices from London: 31,000 jobs were to be dispersed, mostly to the assisted areas (7,000 to Clydeside, 7,000 to South Wales, 5,400 to the North East and 3,400 to Merseyside). A year before, the Hardman Report (Great Britain, 1973a) had given the results of the Civil Service's view on dispersal, which scheduled relatively few jobs for the assisted areas and generally endorsed departmental preferences for 'desirable' locations in the South East and South West. The new Labour Government found the Hardman proposals 'unacceptable' and made clear its determination to use government office dispersal as a major tool of regional policy.[10] Indeed, in April 1974 they had already announced the transfer of the Offshore Supplies Office (set up in early 1973) to Glasgow. In August 1974 there was another expansion of assisted-area designation, with Merseyside being raised to Special Development Area status, Edinburgh and Cardiff to Development Area status, and Chesterfield to Intermediate Area status. In September 1974 IDC limits were tightened, being lowered to 5,000 sq. ft. for the South East, 10,000 sq. ft. for other non-assisted areas, and 15,000 sq.ft. for Intermediate Areas. The Government had already proclaimed its intention to clamp down on office building in Central London, partly to take advantage of growing public reaction against the highly publicised bonanza for property speculators unleashed by the Conservatives in the early 1970s. In the last year of the Conservative Government, 1973–74, some 21.9m sq.ft. of office space were sanctioned in Central London; in its first year, 1974–75, the Labour Government cut this down to 11.4m sq.ft.

In October came the second General Election of 1974, which produced only minor changes in results as compared to February. Labour still held power, though the challenge of the Nationalists in the traditionally Labour areas of Scotland and Wales continued to strengthen. In a sense, the election was just in time for the Government. Unemployment began to rise in the autumn of 1974—a rise that has continued for four years. In early 1975, in response to growing clamour about industrial decline in London, a whole class of small developments was given special treatment; in effect, the IDC limit was raised again to 10,000 sq.ft, despite the lack

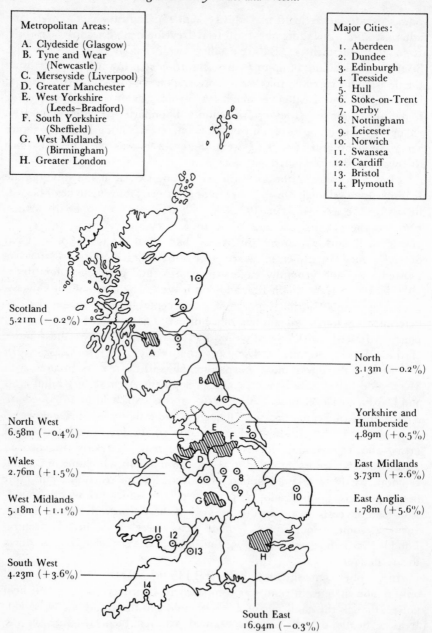

Metropolitan Areas:

A. Clydeside (Glasgow)
B. Tyne and Wear
   (Newcastle)
C. Merseyside (Liverpool)
D. Greater Manchester
E. West Yorkshire
   (Leeds–Bradford)
F. South Yorkshire
   (Sheffield)
G. West Midlands
   (Birmingham)
H. Greater London

Major Cities:

1. Aberdeen
2. Dundee
3. Edinburgh
4. Teesside
5. Hull
6. Stoke-on-Trent
7. Derby
8. Nottingham
9. Leicester
10. Norwich
11. Swansea
12. Cardiff
13. Bristol
14. Plymouth

Scotland
5.21m (−0.2%)

North
3.13m (−0.2%)

North West
6.58m (−0.4%)

Yorkshire and
Humberside
4.89m (+0.5%)

Wales
2.76m (+1.5%)

East Midlands
3.73m (+2.6%)

West Midlands
5.18m (+1.1%)

East Anglia
1.78m (+5.6%)

South West
4.23m (+3.6%)

South East
16.94m (−0.3%)

Under the name of each region is its estimated 1975 population, followed in parentheses by the 1971–75 population change.

Solid lines show the present (post-April 1974) boundaries of the Economic Planning Regions. Dotted lines show boundaries of the 1965–74 period.

FIGURE 1.1
Economic Planning Regions

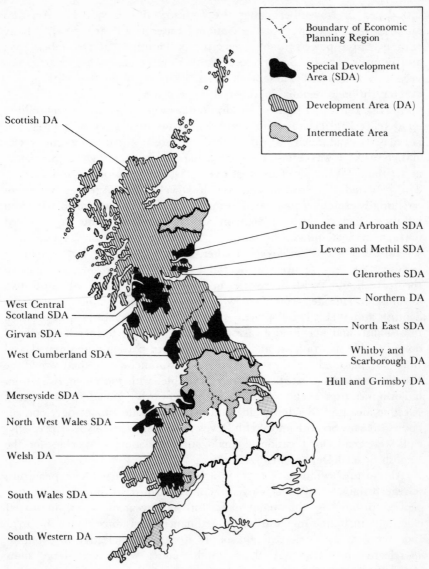

FIGURE 1.2
Assisted areas as of November, 1977

of evidence that IDC controls have any significant effect on local industrial decline (Stone, chapter 6 of this volume).

More importantly, in 1975 the Government began to develop its new industrial strategy, which would rely on greatly increased public intervention with the prime aims of stimulating investment and promoting competitive efficiency. The Industry Act 1972 became the basis of this strategy, with certain modifications (which removed constraints on equity participation)

introduced in November under the Industry Act 1975. That Act also
authorised the setting up of the National Enterprise Board (NEB), a body
with extensive powers to intervene in UK industry. In December 1975
and January 1976 the Scottish and Welsh Development Agencies, respectively, were established. These were regional versions of the NEB, with powers
of intervention in regional industry; they were also given the former Scottish
and Welsh Industrial Estates Corporations, as well as certain responsibilities
for derelict land clearance programmes. While their scale of funding was
not massive (and much was ear-marked for industrial-estate and land recla-
mation work), it was certainly enough to make an impact: £200m (Scotland)
and £100m (Wales) over the first five years, with possibilities of increases.
The NEB and the Scottish and Welsh Development Agencies were not
territorially exclusive, however. The NEB could intervene in United Kingdom
industry which might have plant in Scotland or Wales; this has involved
the NEB in Scotland, for instance, in Rolls Royce, British Leyland and
several other major employers. Earlier, in July 1975, the Department of
Industry Section 7 powers in Scotland and Wales were handed over to
the Scottish and Welsh Secretaries in a further extension of administrative
devolution. This step, combined with the subsequent establishment of the
Scottish and Welsh Development Agencies, created a serious split between
the English and non-English assisted areas, with the former feeling hard
done by. The North East and Merseyside were particularly agitated and
were not placated by the Government's assurances that they would be
equally and fairly treated. This was inevitable, with the move away from
uniform measures (such as standard grants) towards regionally administered
selective measures (Section 7 aid) and regionally autonomous development
bodies (like the Scottish and Welsh Development Agencies). Not surprisingly,
calls were made for creation of analogous Development Agencies for the
English Special Development Areas.

Also at the beginning of 1976, in a White Paper on public expenditure
(Great Britain, 1976), the Government reaffirmed its intention to give
general priority to the maintenance or improvement of UK industrial
efficiency, including increased selective financial assistance under the 1972
Industry Act. This referred not simply to regional selective aid, but to
all selective industrial aid, the umbrella under which very large sums
of money were being used to assist, for example, British Leyland (most
of whose labour force is in non-assisted areas). In practice, moreover,
regional expenditures seem to have become less selective: regional development grants increased by over 50 per cent from 1974–5 to 1975–6, whereas
selective regional assistance increased by only 3 per cent. During the year,
however, the economic situation remained difficult, with unemployment
continuing to rise. The July 1976 Budget reflected the grim situation,
with severe public expenditure cuts. Regional funds were cut back in
two ways. First, mining and construction were excluded from RDGs and

all grants were to be paid three months in arrears, starting in April 1977. Second, REP was both reduced and delayed. The old system (£3 per adult male and £1.50 per adult female) was replaced with a flat rate of £2 per employee. This eliminated the discriminatory feature of the old rate (in line with the spirit of the equal-pay legislation), but since the labour force in manufacturing is biased towards males the new £2 rate was *lower* than the average of the old rates. Reaction in the regions was, predictably, hostile. One region, the North, estimated that the July measures amounted to a loss of £17m a year in funds to the region, with a loss of 6,000 jobs.

The severity of the economic situation and consequent pressures on the Government were also illustrated in the extension of the Job Creation programme. Established in late 1975, by July 1976 it had created nearly 30,000 jobs, in a variety of projects intended to have both training and social-benefit purposes. Although a nation-wide programme, its 'take-up' was greatest in the assisted areas. Scotland alone accounted for one-third of the total number of jobs under the programme, and in one local authority (Western Isles) Job Creation accounted for around 5 per cent of total employment. In a situation of this kind it was inevitable that the programme would be continued in some form or another (as happened with its replacement in 1978 by the Special Temporary Employment Programme and related measures).

In October 1976 it was announced that Section 7 aid would be made available to service industries and offices; but since only large concerns that were not local-serving and that had a genuine choice of locations were eligible, the impact has been quite small. The final development in 1976 was the December mini-Budget, which brought in the most massive expenditure squeeze yet. Regional aid was affected even more adversely than it had been in July: REP was ended immediately. This constituted the most drastic single cut in regional expenditures ever. Some assisted areas were stunned by the announcement (which had not been publicly rumoured in advance). The Secretary of the CBI (Scotland) was particularly concerned about the effects of this withdrawal on the liquidity of Scottish companies, and he estimated that it would cost Scotland £80m in aid and mean the loss of 10,000 jobs. A later assessment (Moore, Rhodes and Tyler, 1977) estimated a total loss (to 1980) of as much as 50,000 jobs in the assisted areas. This is particularly relevant remembering the Expenditure Committee's earlier warning: 'Our evidence however left us in little doubt that the withdrawal of REP without any comparable replacement could create operating difficulties for many firms' (Great Britain, 1973c, p. 75). Finally, it is ironic that the Labour Government that originated REP, and that in 1974 dramatically rescued it, should be the Government to eliminate it summarily.[11]

In April 1977 the Government announced that they did not intend to designate any assisted areas additional to those presently existing; accordingly, the only changes announced were movements from one category of assistance to another. Hull, Grimsby and vicinity, on Humberside, and also North Wales were upgraded from Intermediate Area to Development Area status; and Lanark, Dundee, Cumnock, Kilbirnie and Arbroath, in Scotland, were upgraded from Development Area status to Special Development Area status. In a new departure, however, certain areas were actually downgraded. Aberdeen and vicinity, in Scotland, and Malton, Northallerton, Richmond, Pickering, Thirsk in Yorkshire and Humberside were dropped from Development Area status to Intermediate Area status, although most projects in these areas remained eligible for Development Area assistance for a transitional year. This was the first time (since the 1966 Act began this approach to designation) that assisted areas had actually been downgraded in terms of eligibility. It brought loud complaints from the areas affected, but on the whole it was considered an overdue reaction to the very low unemployment rates prevailing in those areas. In May it was the turn of office controls to face the axe. It was announced that ODPs would be greatly relaxed, with higher limits (30,000 sq.ft.—the highest yet) and with outright exemption for small employment (200–300 workers). This meant the exempting of about 55 per cent of all applications. In addition, the Location of Offices Bureau was to be 'turned on its head' by giving it a new objective: to bring office jobs back into London! These measures spelled the end of office development control as an effective instrument of regional policy, although the powers were nominally continued in being. Significantly, in the first month after the relaxation 1m sq.ft. of office space were approved in London.

By the summer of 1977 it was also clear that the 1974 plan to disperse government office employment was at a virtual standstill. The plans had come under immediate fire from the civil-service unions and the Greater London Council, and the Government was either unable or unwilling to force the issue. Officially, it was announced that the programme had 'slipped' back in time; unofficially, few people expected the more unpopular intended destinations (such as Glasgow) ever to see more than a much reduced fraction of the original promise. Also by the summer of 1977 a study prepared by the NEB was given to the Government, and in June its recommendation for wider differentials in assistance between Development Areas and Special Development Areas was accepted. The Government stated it would increase from two to three years the period for interest-free loans or interest relief grants for viable job-creating projects in SDAS, and also SDA advance factories could have their rent-free periods extended in certain cases. These measures did not, however, meet the more fundamental (and often-urged) need to increase the percentage differential in the rate of grant—arguments frequently made by both West Central Scotland and North East England.

By 1978 the context of regional policy had changed significantly, and as in 1971–72 the change was not the result of a new government. There are four main strands to this changed situation (these are discussed more fully in other chapters of this volume). First, the recession that began in 1974 has become the severest since before the Second World War. Impelled by the exigencies of domestic and external economic factors, the Government (reminiscent of 1947) has been forced into a series of public expenditure cuts that are themselves the most severe for over a generation (Wilson, chapter 4 of this volume). Regional policy has finally become a victim of this general squeeze, and the drop in regional funds from 1975–76 to 1977–78 will probably turn out to be around 25 per cent in real terms; see Table 1.5.

Second, the Government has been promoting a new industrial strategy that is based on nation-wide intervention in (and assistance to) industry (Cameron, chapter 14 of this volume). This strategy, which is based both on Labour Party ideology and on an assessment of what is required to revitalise the obviously ailing British economy, has very important implications for regional policy (Holland, 1976). The most obvious of these is the fact that extremely large amounts of money are being channelled into industry in the 'prosperous' regions. The West Midlands is being assisted enormously by the aid to British Leyland—aid that dwarfs that previously given to shipbuilders in the 'less prosperous' regions. Equally, the huge sums spent on subsidising a British civilian aerospace industry are largely devoted to the prosperous regions of the South. The Government has occasionally made polite noises about not allowing this to hurt the less prosperous regions, frequently citing the Scottish and Welsh Development Agencies as evidence. But so far the facts belie such assertions, and there is reason to believe that if all industrial aids were examined together (regional and other), the regional incidence of that aid could be different from traditional expectations. The figures in Table 1.6, which are for a period well before the introduction of the NEB and the new Labour industrial strategy, show the importance of non-regional programmes. Scotland, Wales and the North received 79 per cent of funds for 'Regional Support and Regeneration'—nearly four times their population share of 20.8 per cent. But these regional funds were only 16.5 per cent of total trade, industry and employment expenditures; so when both regional and non-regional funds are taken together, the three regions obtained 35.8 per cent of the grand total—only about three-quarters above their population share.

A third strand in the changing context of regional policy has been the unusual pattern of changes in unemployment (Randall, chapter 5 of this volume). Initially, from the second quarter of 1974 to the first quarter of 1976, unemployment rose much more dramatically in the prosperous regions than in the assisted areas; see Table 1.7. In the West

TABLE 1.5

Regional-policy funds by major heading, 1962–63 to 1977–78 (thousands of pounds at constant 1970–71 prices)

	Local Employment Acts	REP and SET	1966 Industry Act investment grants	1972 Industry Act Regional Development Grants	1972 Industry Act Section 7 Aid	All funds	Net tax items	Grand total net funds
1962–63	22,500	0	0	0	0	22,500	−300	22,200
1963–64	41,500	0	0	0	0	41,500	−1,000	40,500
1964–65	53,600	0	0	0	0	53,600	−100	53,400
1965–66	53,200	0	0	0	0	53,200	+63,900	117,100
1966–67	67,200	0	0	0	0	67,200	+40,600	107,800
1967–68	55,400	42,300	88,300	0	0	186,000	−13,500	172,500
1968–69	61,900	145,500	100,400	0	0	307,800	−19,500	288,300
1969–70	89,900	147,800	107,200	0	0	344,900	−20,700	324,200
1970–71	70,200	118,700	123,500	0	0	312,400	−21,500	290,900
1971–72	59,300	101,000	82,500	0	0	242,800	+2,900	245,700
1972–73	58,800	86,600	56,800	6,800	2,900	211,900	+20,400	232,300
1973–74	29,300	82,600	22,900	83,100	14,100	232,000	−5,400	226,600
1974–75	29,100	101,900	10,200	140,700	48,400	330,300	−3,300	327,000
1975–76	10,300	111,900	2,900	170,100	39,600	334,800	−3,100	331,700
1976–77	8,500	72,200	2,200	186,800	41,300	311,000	−ᵃ	311,000
1977–78ᵇ	6,000	0	1,000	200,000	40,000	247,000	−ᵃ	247,000

ᵃ Data not available.
ᵇ Estimated.

Note: All figures have been rounded to nearest £100,000. These data also include funds which have a large recoverable element (such as loans and factory building) and so do not represent true ultimate net cost.

Source: Annual reports of the 1972 Industry Act; Northern Region Strategy Team (1975a, Appendix B); unpublished data from Department of Employment.

TABLE 1.6

Regional distribution of regionally relevant expenditures on trade, industry and employment (average for the period 1969-70 to 1973-74)

Type of expenditure	North	Yorks, & Humberside	East Midlands	East Anglia	South East	South West	West Midlands	North West	Wales	Scotland	Share of each programme in GB total
Regional support and regeneration	29.0	2.2	0.2	0	0	2.1	0	16.5	16.0	34.0	16.5
Industrial innovation	2.0	0.5	20.9	1.0	22.3	28.5	4.3	7.4	0.1	13.0	16.1
General support for industry	15.0	6.1	4.2	2.7	23.3	5.1	6.7	14.2	8.1	14.6	37.9
Support for nationalised industries	10.1	11.1	9.2	3.6	27.8	3.9	7.9	14.7	7.2	10.2	12.9
Regulation of domestic trade and consumer protection	4.7	14.2	0	9.6	14.4	9.5	14.2	23.7	9.6	0	0.1
Functioning of the labour market	8.4	7.8	5.5	2.3	31.3	5.4	8.1	14.6	6.3	10.4	9.6
Central and miscellaneous services	6.3	3.2	1.0	0.4	58.8	2.2	2.3	6.6	11.0	8.4	6.1
Total	11.5	5.3	6.8	1.9	21.9	8.0	5.2	13.1	8.1	16.2	100.0
Region's share in GB population, 1971 Census	6.1	8.9	6.3	3.1	31.9	7.0	9.5	12.5	5.0	9.7	–
Ratio of share of expenditures to share of population	1.885	0.596	1.079	0.613	0.687	1.143	0.547	1.048	1.620	1.670	–

Source: Northern Region Strategy Team (1976, Table 6.2).

TABLE 1.7
Changes in regional unemployment rates, 1974–1978

Region	Quarterly unemployment rate			Percentage change	
	Second quarter 1974	First quarter 1976	Second quarter 1978	II/1974 to I/1976	I/1976 to II/1978
South East	1.5	3.8	4.1	+153.3	+7.9
East Anglia	1.9	4.6	4.8	+142.1	+4.3
South West	2.6	6.1	6.3	+134.6	+3.3
West Midlands	2.0	5.4	5.2	+170.0	−3.7
East Midlands	2.1	4.5	4.8	+114.3	+6.7
Yorshire & Humberside	2.5	5.1	5.6	+104.0	+9.8
North West	3.2	6.4	6.9	+100.0	+7.8
North	4.3	6.7	8.1	+55.8	+20.9
Wales	3.6	6.9	7.9	+91.7	+14.5
Scotland	3.9	6.3	7.7	+61.5	+22.2
Great Britain	2.4	5.2	5.6	+116.7	+7.7

Note: figures refer to wholly unemployed (seasonally adjusted).

Midlands it rose by 170 per cent, and in the South East by over 150 per cent; at the same time it rose by only 56 per cent in the North and 61.5 per cent in Scotland. From a regional point of view this convergence of unemployment rates was to be welcomed (the well-off areas ceased to be so much above average and the poorer areas were no longer so far below average). But this convergence caused near panic in regions unaccustomed to high unemployment. Quite remarkable scare stories were circulating, and even the more careful and sober analysis of the West Midlands County Council (1974; 1975) spent a great deal of time lamenting the harmful effects of regional policy despite the lack of evidence to support such contentions. With high unemployment becoming more of a nation-wide phenomenon, there was a more competitive spirit among regions—more resentment at any other region getting any special favours or assistance. Certainly, the alarming rise in West Midlands unemployment was a vital factor in the Government decision to commit major resources to British Leyland. Critics also began pointing accusing fingers at aid in places like East Scotland, where the underlying health of the economy was boosted by North Sea oil to the point that many local exchanges had unemployment rates well below the national average and yet were still assisted areas; this was the basis for the April 1977 downgrading of Aberdeen. However, during the second phase of the recession, say from the first quarter of 1976 to the second quarter of 1978, the position changed again. Unemployment rates in Scotland, Wales and the North rose faster than the national average, while in the non-assisted areas they rose rather less. In the West Midlands the rate even declined. When one considers that the employment from North Sea oil exploitation in Scotland and the North probably peaked during 1976 or 1977 (the very years of these sharp rises in unemployment) the future seems very worrying. In particular, if the underlying trends now are against the assisted areas, and yet regional-policy funds are being cut and funds are being diverted to the non-assisted areas, the regional situation could well deteriorate further over the next year or so, even if the national economy begins to recover slowly in 1979.

The fourth strand in the changing context of regional policy is partly related to the third but is also a continuation of past confusions and conflicts in regional policy and urban planning. The recession has highlighted what is now called the 'problem of the inner cities'. Despite decades of planned renewal, the central areas of most big cities are physically deteriorated and economically weak, typically with a population distribution skewed towards the less skilled, the elderly, and the low income generally. What has come to be of concern has been the loss of jobs in the city centres, especially the loss of manufacturing jobs (Stone, chapter 6 of this volume). Within individual regions there are marked variations in unemployment rates; for example, some Greater London Council boroughs have rates equal to those in some assisted areas. Major new government initiatives for inner-city regeneration have been discussed (and in the case of Glasgow's East End, begun). The result is a feeling that the spatial pattern of national assistance should be much finer than in the past, with a new emphasis on inner-city problem areas in all regions of the nation (Hughes, chapter 8 of this volume). Aid should certainly continue to go to Clydeside and Merseyside, but it should be redirected to inner London, inner Birmingham and inner Manchester instead of North East Scotland or Yorkshire, so the argument runs (Townsend, 1977).

Conclusions: Continuity and Change in Regional Policy

From the early 1930s to the mid-1970s the development of regional policy was steady, and despite the occasional 'hiccough' (as in 1970–71), there was a great deal of continuity of attitude and approach. For instance, unemployment discrepancies have always been the basic, almost exclusive, dynamic of regional policy, despite references to migration, growth, income, or other welfare indicators.[12] This focus has been associated with a firm belief in the overriding importance of interregional equalisation. The problem of the trade-off between regional welfare distribution and national economic efficiency has generally been ignored, or at least heavily down-played.[13]

There was also a high degree of agreement upon a 'structural' explanation of regional economic problems, originating from the experience of the Great Depression, reinforced by the radical labour force shifts of the 1960s. A third theme was the emphasis on 'place prosperity'—the focus on geographical areas (regions) rather than on people. This grew partly out of the welfare state assumption that uniform national programmes (unemployment compensation, national health service, pensions, etc.) would adequately handle individual problems and needs. Regional-scale problems, it was apparently assumed, required different, aggregative solutions. It also arose partly from the (probably mistaken) impression that labour migration was an unsuccessful as well as intrinsically undesirable policy (Beaumont, chapter 3 of this volume; Pitfield, 1978). The primacy of 'work to the workers' was never seriously challenged. A fourth theme was the assumption of a relatively passive public posture, in which government's role was to induce private industry to take an initiative. This reflected a belief in the proper roles of public and private sectors that some consider oversimplified (Holland, 1976).

Because of these basic views, regional policy came to have a number of particular emphases. The most prominent was the almost exclusive emphasis on capital mobility and on investment in manufacturing. Another important emphasis was on non-selectivity. Regional policy encompassed ever larger assisted areas and never seriously attempted any 'growth centre strategy' (Parr, chapter 9 of this volume); it did not attempt to differentiate among industries and remained sectorally non-selective, despite the logical inference that restructuring means favouring particular sectors; it did not differentiate among firms, regardless of their different capabilities and intentions. Finally, behind many of the policies (especially controls such as IDC and ODP) lay an assumption that there was a secular growth trend in the national economy that would generate (especially in the more prosperous regions) a continuous flow of new industrial investment, some of which could be diverted to the poorer regions.

In the mid-1970s, however, this well-established 'consensus' view of regional policy began to be shaken. The apparent convergence of unemployment discrepancies between 1974 and 1976, combined with rapid rises in the absolute rate in formerly more prosperous regions (Table 1.7), undermined the general acceptance of the unemployment justification for regional policy. Additionally, the simple 'structural' explanation of regional economic performance was widely challenged. No one attempted to deny that there were structural factors, but it was shown that structural explanations accounted for only a part of the problem (Randall, 1973; West Central Scotland Plan, 1974a, 1974b; Northern Region Strategy Team, 1975b). It was also argued that the indigenous sector, largely ignored by regional policy before the 1972 Act, was crucial for any regional economic regeneration (Segal, chapter 10 of this volume).[14] The gradual drying-up of the supply of so-called mobile firms, owing to decreased mobility amongst firms generally and to lower levels of industrial investment overall from 1974 on, forced attention to be directed more toward the economic needs and problems of established enterprises. This, of course, called for subsidies and incentives aimed at competitive efficiency rather than at locational choice.[15]

Perhaps most damaging for the traditional view of regional policy has been the shift of national concern towards a non-spatial industry policy based on individual firms and sectors. This is not a wholly new development, since both major acts upon which regional financial aid has been based (the 1966 and 1972 Acts) represented legislation for general industrial stimulation into which a regional element was built. This shift interacts with two other factors in an important way. First, there is the contemporary loss of confidence in the underlying health of the economy, which means that the idea of shifting around industrial investment loses significance while the idea of promoting industrial growth *anywhere* gains. Second, the move away from structural explanations of economic problems (whether regional or national) into realms dealing with capital investment, finance, entrepreneurship, labour relations, productivity, etc., makes it all the easier to lose the spatial (regional) element of national economic or industrial policy.

The emergence of the Scottish and Welsh Development Agencies has heralded yet another shift: the move toward agency-based instead of general department-administered assistance. It also represents a move from the passive to the active mode for government involvement. Equally, there has come to be a more active interest by local authorities in the problems of economic development. Urban areas have traditionally concerned themselves with housing and education and related services, paying scant attention to industrial or economic affairs. Under the stimulus of the new Inner City policies, however, local authority activity has been redirected much more toward employment issues, in non-assisted regions as well as in assisted areas.

It is important to emphasise, finally, that the present uncertain state of regional policy, which may prove to be the beginning of the end of nearly fifty years of policy evolution, does not result from a change of Government. Some of the variations in application of regional policy over the years have undeniably been due to a change of Government and consequent change of prevailing ideology. The new Labour administrations of 1945 and 1964 brought bursts of regional policy activity, while the Conservatives in 1951 and 1970 tried hard to rein back on regional policy. However, it is equally true that Governments have sometimes been forced, usually by economic crises, into changes against their predispositions: the Labour Government's cut-back in 1947 and the Conservative Government's expansion in 1972 are examples. The Labour Government's current (1976–78) de-emphasis of regional policy is partly in this latter category, insofar as the lengthy recession is one major cause of financial cut-backs. Nonetheless, the Government's own ideas and views are changing, as are those of the Opposition; even with economic recovery, regional policy may well not be revitalised, but instead may continue to be subordinated to various national industrial and inner-city policies.)Enough of the traditional interpretations and prescriptions have been 'shaken to make the future of British regional policy fundamentally uncertain. A consensus, nearly fifty years in the making, is probably collapsing; it is unclear what will take its place. The following chapters in this volume will explore these issues and suggest some answers.

Notes

1. Regional development policies for Northern Ireland are legislatively and administratively different from those for the rest of the United Kingdom. Accordingly this chapter deals with regional policies in Great Britain only (i.e., England, Scotland, and Wales).

2. As McCrone (1969, p. 97) points out, 'This was the first time tax incentives had been given on a regional basis in the United Kingdom and they were not to be used again until Mr Maudling's 1963 Budget'.

3. Securing an IDC was a necessary but not a sufficient condition for approval of the development proposal: the local planning authority still had to be satisfied on planning grounds. It was a double hurdle, each barrier being judged on different criteria by different officials.

4. By the end of 1954 the floorspace of new factories completed or under construction in the eight London New Towns was nearly five times as great as that in the five New Towns in the peripheral regions.

5. This shift did not significantly alter the conservative view taken by the Treasury, as illustrated by Odber (1965, pp. 344–7). BOTAC wanted to keep interest rates low, for example, on the loans granted to firms being helped. However, they were always aware that if they went outside 'pretty narrow limits' they would be overruled by the Treasury. 'Thus the Treasury mind translates a requirement to charge no more than a commercial rate into a doctrine of charging no less than a commercial rate' (Odber, p. 346).

6. General cost-per-job yardsticks were used by BOTAC in its evaluation of applications. These were flexible to a degree, and higher costs per job were certainly tolerated for projects in particular problem areas, as well as for politically important projects like the establishment of the automobile industry on Merseyside and Clydeside. But there was also conflict between the Treasury (wanting rigid, lower guidelines) and the Board of Trade (wanting more flexible, higher guidelines). As a result, '. . . there was little economic justification for the criteria applied' (Northern Region Strategy Team, 1975a, p. A.9).

7. Compared to the 1959 General Election results, the Conservatives in 1964 lost 27.8 per cent of their seats in Scotland, Wales, and northern regions of England, whereas they only lost 11.6 per cent in the rest of the country. Since an across-the-board loss of 11.6 per cent would have retained the Conservatives in power, it was the heavy voting shift in the poorer regions that turned them out of office.

8. While the regional differential was apparently 20 per cent, it was lower in practice owing to two factors: first, the delay in payment (usually 12 to 18 months); and second, the ruling by the Treasury that permitted tax allowances only against the non-grant portion of capital expenditure.

9. The announcement of the Special Development Area extensions appeared just before the news of the dramatic collapse of Rolls-Royce. The company then employed 12,000 in Scotland (mostly in the Glasgow area), and the potential consequences of a heavy loss of jobs in one of the region's (and nation's) most prestigious firms helped to convince the Government to accept the idea of extending SDA status to the Clydeside and Tyneside areas.

10. There were precedents in the 1960s when large departments were moved: the Post Office Savings Bank went to Glasgow, the Post Office GIRO to Merseyside, and much of the Department of Health and Social Security to Newcastle. The only moves actually accomplished by Labour since returning to power in 1974 are of new agencies not previously established elsewhere: Offshore Supplies Office and British National Oil Corporation (BNOC), both to Glasgow. Significantly, in mid-1977 BNOC still had a larger staff in London than in its Glasgow headquarters.

11. It is likely that the Government was also influenced by the desire of the European Community to secure conformity with its general rules about forms of development assistance (MacLennan, chapter 12 of this volume).

12. Some regional analysts and regional planners have used other welfare indicators with a considerable degree of sophistication, e.g., the work of the West Central Scotland Plan (published 1974–75) and of the Northern Region Strategy Team (published 1975–77). However, the overriding political and popular criterion remained unemployment—nothing else receives headline treatment every month upon release of the official statistics.

13. The work of Moore and Rhodes (1973a, 1973b, 1974a, 1974b, 1976, 1977) has stimulated a great deal of discussion about the real long-term economic and financial costs of regional policy. Their general proposition that true costs have been much lower than apparent costs has led many people to argue that regional policy is in a sense costless, or at least capable of generating sufficient offsetting benefits, though their methodology is not without criticism (Chisholm, 1976).

14. For example, Moore and Rhodes (1974b) showed that for Scotland the loss of jobs in establishments already in the indigenous sector more than offset the gain of jobs from incoming industry.

15. It is curious, therefore, that the existing regional aid of greatest immediate benefit to the indigenous sector, REP, should be the one category of aid to be eliminated in late 1976.

References

Abercrombie, P. (1945) *Greater London Plan 1944*. Report prepared for the Standing Conference on London Regional Planning. London: HMSO.

Abercrombie, P. (1949) *The Clyde Valley Regional Plan 1946*. Report prepared for the Clyde Valley Regional Planning Committee. Edinburgh: HMSO.

Brown, A. J. (1972) *The Framework of Regional Economics in the United Kingdom*. Cambridge: Cambridge University Press.

Brown, A. J., Lind, H. and Bowers, J. (1967) 'The "Green Paper" on the Development Areas', *National Institute Economic Review*, No. 40, pp. 26–33.

Brown, G. (1972) *Going My Way*. Harmondsworth: Penguin Books.

Chisholm, M. (1976) 'Regional Policies in an Era of Slow Population Growth and High Unemployment', *Regional Studies*, Vol. 10, pp. 201–13.

Cullingworth, J. B. (1970) *Town and Country Planning in England and Wales*. Third edition. London: George Allen and Unwin.

Great Britain (1928) Ministry of Labour. *Report of the Industrial Transference Board* Cmd. 3156. London: HMSO.

Great Britain (1934) Ministry of Labour. *Reports of Investigations into the Industrial Conditions in Certain Depressed Areas*. Cmd. 4728. London: HMSO.

Great Britain (1935a) Ministry of Labour. *First Report of the Commissioner for the Special Areas (England and Wales)*. Cmd. 4927. London: HMSO.

Great Britain (1935b) Scottish Office. *Commissioner for the Special Areas in Scotland: Report for the Period 21st December 1934–30th June 1935*. Cmd. 4958. London: HMSO.

Great Britain (1936a) Ministry of Labour. *Second Report of the Commissioner for the Special Areas (England and Wales)*. Cmd. 5090. London: HMSO.

Great Britain (1936b) Scottish Office. *Commissioner for the Special Areas in Scotland: Report for the period 1 July 1935–31 December, 1935.* Cmd. 5089. London: HMSO.

Great Britain (1936c) Ministry of Labour. *Third Report of the Commissioner for the Special Areas (England and Wales).* Cmd. 5303. London: HMSO.

Great Britain (1936d) Scottish Office. *Commissioner for the Special Areas in Scotland: Final Report of Sir Arthur Rose.* Cmd. 5245, London: HMSO.

Great Britain (1937a) Ministry of Labour. *Report of the Commissioner for the Special Areas (England and Wales).* Cmd. 5595. London: HMSO.

Great Britain (1937b) Scottish Office. *Report of the Commissioner for the Special Areas in Scotland.* Cmd. 5604. London: HMSO.

Great Britain (1938a) Ministry of Labour. *Report of the Commissioner for the Special Areas (England and Wales).* Cmd. 5896. London: HMSO.

Great Britain (1938b) Scottish Office. *Report of the Commissioner for the Special Areas in Scotland.* Cmd. 5905. London: HMSO.

Great Britain (1940) Royal Commission on the Distribution of the Industrial Population. *Report.* Cmd. 6153. London: HMSO.

Great Britain (1944) Ministry of Labour. *Employment Policy.* Cmd. 6527. London: HMSO.

Great Britain (1948) Board of Trade and Scottish Office. *Distribution of Industry.* Cmd. 7540. London: HMSO.

Great Britain (1963a) Scottish Development Department. *Central Scotland: A Programme for Development and Growth.* Cmnd. 2188. Edinburgh: HMSO.

Great Britain (1963b) Board of Trade. *The North East: A Programme for Regional Development and Growth.* Cmnd. 2206. London: HMSO.

Great Britain (1963c) National Economic Development Council. *Growth of the United Kingdom Economy to 1966.* London: HMSO.

Great Britain (1963d) National Economic Development Council. *Conditions Favourable to Faster Growth.* London: HMSO.

Great Britain (1965) Department of Economic Affairs. *The National Plan.* Cmnd. 2764. London: HMSO.

Great Britain (1966) Scottish Office. *The Scottish Economy 1965 to 1970: A Plan for Expansion.* Cmnd. 2864. Edinburgh: HMSO.

Great Britain (1967) Department of Economic Affairs. *The Development Areas: A Proposal for a Regional Employment Premium.* London: HMSO.

Great Britain (1969a) Department of Economic Affairs. *The Task Ahead: Economic Assessment to 1972.* London, HMSO.

Great Britain (1969b) Department of Economic Affairs. *The Intermediate Areas: Report of a Committee of Inquiry under the Chairmanship of Sir Joseph Hunt.* Cmnd. 3998. London: HMSO.

Great Britain (1970) Department of Trade and Industry. *Investment Incentives.* Cmnd. 4516. London: HMSO.

Great Britain (1972a) Department of Trade and Industry. *Industrial and Regional Development.* Cmnd. 4942. London: HMSO.

Great Britain (1972b) Department of Trade and Industry. *Trade and Industry,* Vol. 7, p. 147.

Great Britain (1973a) Civil Service Department. *The Dispersal of Government Work from London.* Cmnd. 5322.

Great Britain (1973b) House of Commons. Expenditure Committee (Trade and Industry Sub-Committee) Session 1972–73. *Regional Development Incentives: Minutes of Evidence (from October 1972 to June 1973) and Appendices.* House of Commons Paper 327. London: HMSO.

Great Britain (1973c) House of Commons. Expenditure Committee (Trade and Industry Sub-Committee) Session 1973–74. *Regional Development Incentives: Report.* House of Commons Paper 85. London: HMSO.

Great Britain (1973d) House of Commons. Expenditure Committee (Trade and Industry Sub-Committee) Session 1973–74. *Regional Development Incentives: Minutes of Evidence (from July 1973), Appendices and Index.* House of Commons Paper 85–I. London: HMSO.

Great Britain (1973e) Department of Trade and Industry. *Industry Act 1972: Annual Report 1972–73.* London: HMSO.

Great Britain (1976) The Treasury. *Public Expenditure 1979–80.* Cmnd. 6393. London. HMSO.

Harris, D. (1966) 'Regional Planning in its Context', 'Regional Planning Out of the Doldrums', 'The Regional Problem: Why Interfere?', 'Regional Planning: The Idea of the

Growth Area', and 'The Task of Regional Planning', *Official Architecture and Planning*, Vol. 29.

Holland, S. (1976) *Capital versus the Regions*. London: Macmillan.

Kaldor, N. (1970) 'The Case for Regional Policies', *Scottish Journal of Political Economy*, Vol. 17, pp. 337–48.

McCrone, G. (1969) *Regional Policy in Britain*. London: Allen and Unwin.

Moore, B. and Rhodes, J. (1973a) 'The Economic and Exchequer Implications of Regional Policy', Memorandum 24, *Minutes of Evidence (from October 1972 to June 1973) and Appendices, Regional Development Incentives*. Expenditure Committee (Trade and Industry Sub-Committee), Session 1972–73. London: HMSO.

Moore, B. and Rhodes, J. (1973b) 'Evaluating the Effects of British Regional Economic Policy', *Economic Journal*, Vol. 83, pp. 87–110.

Moore, B. and Rhodes, J. (1974a) 'The effect of Regional Economic Policy in the United Kingdom' in M. Sant (ed.), *Regional Policy and Planning for Europe*, Farnborough: Saxon House.

Moore, B. and Rhodes, J. (1974a) 'The Effect of Regional Economic Policy in the United Kingdom' in M. Sant (ed.), *Regional Policy and Planning for Europe*. Farnborough: Saxon House.

Moore, B. and Rhodes, J. (1976) 'A Quantitative Analysis of the Effects of the Regional Employment Premium and Other Regional Policy Instruments' in A. Whiting (ed.), *The Economics of Industrial Subsidies*, London: HMSO.

Moore, B., Rhodes, J. and Tyler, P. (1977) 'The Impact of Regional Policy in the 1970s', *CES Review*, No. 1, pp. 67–77.

Northern Region Strategy Team (1975a) 'Evaluating the Impact of Regional Policy on Manufacturing Industry in the Northern Region', Technical Report No. 2, Northern Region Strategy Team, Newcastle.

Northern Region Strategy Team (1975b) 'First Interim Report', Northern Region Strategy Team, Newcastle.

Northern Region Strategy Team (1976) 'Public Expenditure in the Northern Region and other British Regions 1969/70–1973/74', Technical Report, No. 12, Northern Region Strategy Team, Newcastle.

Odber, A. J. (1965) 'Regional Policy in Great Britain' in *Area Redevelopment Policies in Britain and the Countries of the Common Market*. Washington, D.C.: US Government Printing Office.

Odber, A. J., Allen, E. and Bowden, P. J. (1957) *Development Area Policy in the North East of England*. Newcastle: North East Industrial and Development Association.

Pitfield, D. E. (1978) 'The Quest for an Effective Regional Policy 1934–1937', *Regional Studies*, Vol. 12, pp. 429–43.

Randall, J. (1973) 'Shift-Share Analysis as a Guide to the Employment Performance of West Central Scotland', *Scottish Journal of Political Economy*, Vol. 20, pp. 1–26.

Rhodes, J. and Kan, A. (1971) *Office Dispersal and Regional Policy*. Department of Applied Economics, University of Cambridge, Occasional Papers No. 30. Cambridge: Cambridge University Press.

Scholefield, H. H. and Franks, J. R. (1972) 'Investment Incentives and Regional Policy', *National Westminster Bank Quarterly Review*, February, pp. 34–40.

Sundquist, J. L. (1975) *Dispersing Population: What America can Learn from Europe*. Washington, D.C.: The Brookings Institution.

Townsend, A. R. (1977) 'The Relationship of Inner City Problems to Regional Policy', *Regional Studies*, Vol. 11, pp. 225–51.

West Central Scotland Plan (1974a) *West Central Scotland—A Programme of Action*. Glasgow: West Central Scotland Plan.

West Central Scotland Plan (1974b) *The Regional Economy*. Supplementary Report, No. 1. Glasgow: West Central Scotland Plan.

West Midlands County Council (1974) *A Time for Action: Economic and Social Trends in the West Midlands*. Birmingham: West Midlands County Council.

West Midlands County Council (1975) *A Time for Action: Policy Proposals*. Birmingham: West Midlands County Council.

CHAPTER 2

The Effect of Regional Policy on the Movement of Industry in Great Britain

*Brian Ashcroft and Jim Taylor**

Introduction

The previous chapter drew attention to the heavy emphasis placed on 'taking work to the workers' in the historical development of British regional policy. The predominating theme of British regional policy has been to encourage manufacturing industry to move to designated assisted areas, in order to create jobs in those parts of the country suffering from persistently high rates of unemployment. These assisted areas will be referred to as Development Areas (DAS) and are defined in the Appendix. In this chapter, we seek to estimate the effect that regional policy has had on the movement of industry to the Development Areas of Great Britain during the period 1961–71. After describing the broad trends in industrial movement during the period 1945–71, we discuss a model of industrial movement, the purpose of which is to estimate the effect of regional policy on the movement of industry to the DAS. The key feature of this model is that it separates the explanation of industrial movement into two components: first, the generation of industrial movement, and second, its regional distribution. We discuss some empirical tests of the generation–distribution model. Finally, the model is used to estimate the effect of regional policy on the movement of industry, including an estimate of the individual effect of the two major policy instruments used to encourage more industry to move to the DAS, namely location controls and investment incentives. The main conclusion to be drawn from our analysis is that although regional policy had a substantial effect on the movement of manufacturing industry to the Development Areas of Great Britain during the period 1961–71, the success of the redistribution of industry component of regional policy has been very heavily dependent upon the rate of industrial expansion in the economy as a whole. Given that the objective of the redistribution of industry policy

* Department of Economics, University of Strathclyde, and Department of Economics, University of Lancaster. The authors are indebted to the Nuffield Foundation for supporting the research reported in this chapter, and to R. R. MacKay, B. Moore, J. Rhodes and the Department of Industry for the use of unpublished data. The comments of these individuals (together with those of H. Armstrong and J. Wright) on the authors' earlier work are also gratefully acknowledged.

43

is to induce new industrial capacity to locate in DAS rather than in non-DAS, a high level of national investment activity is necessary if the policy is to be successful.

The Movement of Manufacturing Industry in Great Britain, 1945-71

The Meaning of Industrial Movement
Industrial movement is defined in this chapter as the setting-up of an establishment in an area by a firm that did not previously have any producing capacity in that area. The setting-up of an establishment can take the form of either a transfer of existing plant or the creation of entirely new plant—or a combination of both. Ideally, we should prefer to measure industrial movement either in terms of the real value of the capital actually involved, or in terms of the number of jobs created as a direct consequence of the industrial movement. Data limitations force us to use a proxy variable, namely, the number of establishments actually moving. We are interested in the movement of industry to the DAS, primarily because of the extra jobs that such an inflow of capital might bring to the relatively less prosperous regions. An examination of the relationship between the number of moves and the employment directly associated with these moves does, fortunately, support the use of movement data as a proxy for job creation (Sant, 1975, Appendix C). However, the relationship is not as simple and straightforward as might be expected. In order to obtain a close positive correlation between the number of moves and the employment associated with these moves, it is necessary to allow for the build-up of employment over time. Yet, even allowing for this build-up of employment over the longer run, the relationship has not been stable in Britain during the study period. Industrial movement generated fewer jobs per move at the end of the study period than during earlier years.

Broad Trends in Industrial Movement, 1945-71
The movement of industry in Great Britain has exhibited considerable variation over the course of the study period. The number of establishments 'on the move' varied from a low of 94 in 1958 to a peak of 335 in 1968. Similarly, only 15 establishments moved into the DAS in 1958 compared to 134 in 1969. Clearly, the period was one of considerable volatility as far as the movement of industry is concerned. To obtain an overview of the possible effect of regional policy on the movement of industry, the study period can be divided into four sub-periods: 1946-51, 1952-59, 1960-65 and 1966-71. These broadly agree with the phases identified by McCallum (chapter 1 of this volume). Table 2.1 shows the main pattern of industrial movement in Great Britain during each period. Two facts stand out. First, both total movement (M) and the movement of industry

TABLE 2.1

Industrial movement in the United Kingdom in four sub-periods (annual averages)

Period	Total movement (M)	Movement to the DAS (MDA)	Movement to the non-DAS $(MNDA)$	MDA/M
1946–51	224	99	125	0.44
1952–59	146	28	118	0.19
1960–65	223	65	158	0.29
1966–71	264	102	162	0.39

Note: see Appendix for a description of the data.

to the DAS (MDA) fell dramatically during the 1950s and did not recover to the high levels reached during the early post-war years until the end of the 1960s. Second, dividing total movement into the movement of industry to the DAS and the movement to the non-DAS indicates that it is the former that was responsible for the low level of total movement during the 1950s. The fact that the movement of industry to the non-DAS fluctuated around a rising trend during the study period is consistent with the view that industrial movement is a function of the growth of productive capacity.

The Origin and Destination of Industrial Movement

Every move has both an origin and a destination. This origin–destination feature of industrial movement suggests that an understanding of movement requires an analysis of: (a) the forces responsible for generating movement; and (b) the forces determining the geographical distribution of movement. A model of industrial movement based upon the distinction between the generation and the distribution of movement is discussed in a later section. Some of the broad features of interregional movement are provided in Tables 2.2 and 2.3, which show the origin and destination of interregional moves during the four policy sub-periods. By far the most important 'generator' of interregional movement in Great Britain is the South East, which accounted for 44 per cent of total interregional moves between 1945 and 1971. No other region approached this figure, though the two Midlands regions certainly contributed substantially (and more than their 'fair share') to the flow of interregional moves. The importance of moves from abroad, which accounted for about 14 per cent of interregional movement, should also be noted. The picture is, of course, reversed when we consider the geographical distribution of interregional moves. Wales, East Anglia, the North, Scotland and the South West (in that order) did particularly well relative to their size. The high rank of East Anglia is a consequence of its proximity to the South East. It has benefited both from the overspill from Greater London and from the imposition of industrial location controls, which have caused firms to search for nearby alternative locations to their preferred locations in the South East.

TABLE 2.2
Origin of interregional moves

Region of origin	Number of moves[a]				Percentage of total moves, 1945–71	Percentage of establishments in Great Britain, 1963[b]
	1945–51	1952–59	1960–65	1966–71		
Scotland	9	7	12	13	1.5	7.4
Wales	4	7	5	14	1.1	2.7
North	4	5	8	19	1.3	3.3
North West	64	43	44	59	7.6	14.0
South West	7	14	17	23	2.2	4.6
Yorks. & Humberside	66	36	36	55	7.0	11.0
East Midlands	48	30	50	74	7.3	6.6
West Midlands	76	41	98	121	12.1	12.0
East Anglia	7	4	10	17	1.4	2.0
South East	251	129	352	495	44.4	36.3
Abroad	55	77	126	133	14.1	–
Total	591	393	758	1023	100.0	100.0

[a] 1945–65 moves surviving to 1965; 1966–71 moves surviving to 1971. The data are described in the Appendix.
[b] Figures based on Great Britain (1970, parts 131 and 133).

TABLE 2.3
Destination of interregional moves

Region of destination	Number of moves[a]				Percentage of total moves, 1945–71	Percentage of establishments in Great Britain, 1963[b]
	1945–51	1952–59	1960–65	1966–71		
Scotland	77	50	132	140	15.3	7.4
Wales	154	45	86	196	18.4	2.7
North	107	34	79	157	14.5	3.3
North West	63	52	100	78	11.3	14.0
South West	33	36	95	89	9.7	4.6
Yorks. & Humberside	49	31	32	36	5.7	11.0
East Midlands	25	34	47	86	7.4	6.6
West Midlands	18	19	21	17	2.9	12.0
East Anglia	20	23	84	118	9.4	2.0
South East	21	48	35	40	5.5	36.3
Total[c]	567	372	711	957	100.0	100.0

[a] 1945–65 moves surviving to 1965; 1966–71 moves surviving to 1971. The data are described in the Appendix.
[b] Figures based on Great Britain, 1970, parts 131 and 133.
[c] The difference between the totals in Table 2.2 and Table 2.3 is due to the omission of unknown origins (i.e., origins unallocated) in Table 2.3.

The Distribution of Industry and Regional Policy

Since there can be little doubt that regional policy was largely non-existent in Great Britain during the period 1952–59, and since regional policy was almost certainly 'stronger' during the 1960s, this suggests a possible way of making an initial 'first guess' at estimating the effect of regional policy on industrial movement. We begin by assuming that regional policy had no effect on the movement of industry to the DAs during 1952–60. Since the movement of industry to the DAs increased from 29 per annum in the period 1952–60 to 88 per annum in the period 1961–71, this suggests that regional policy had the effect of raising the movement of industry to the DAs by around 59 moves per annum, or by about 650 moves in total during the period 1961–71. However, this rough estimate of the effect of regional policy on the movement of industry to the DAs cannot be taken seriously as it stands. It would be quite hazardous automatically to assume that the number of moves to DAs during the assumed 'policy-off' period (1952–60) is necessarily a good approximation of the moves that *would* have taken place during 1961–71 if regional policy had not been strengthened during the 1960s. It is therefore necessary to construct a model of industrial movement that is specifically designed to produce 'policy-off' estimates of the movement of industry during the period 1961–71 if we are to obtain reasonably reliable estimates of the effect of regional policy on the movement of industry to the DAs.

A Model of Industrial Movement

The previous section discussed the broad trends in the geographical pattern of industrial movement during the period 1945–71. In this section, we discuss a model of industrial movement that is subsequently used to estimate the effect of regional policy on the movement of industry.

The Movement Decision, the Location Decision and the Effect of Regional Policy on Industrial Movement

We have argued elsewhere (Ashcroft and Taylor, 1977) that it is analytically useful to regard the decision to move and the decision to locate as two quite separate decisions. The factors that determine the decision to move are not necessarily the same as those that determine the decision to locate, though the two decisions will often overlap in practice. A firm may wish to expand its capacity but because of a supply constraint at its existing location (e.g., a shortage of labour), it may decide to transfer its plant to a new location or create additional capacity at a new location. If there exists more than one satisfactory alternative location, the final choice may well be made on the basis of other criteria such as the availability of regional-policy incentives, or the quality of local amenities.

Distinguishing between the movement decision and the location decision is of importance in the present context because regional policy may have a different effect on each of these two decisions. Regional policy may affect the movement decision in so far as location controls prevent expansion in non-DA locations and therefore force firms to search for a location where permission to expand will be granted. In addition, the availability of regional-policy incentives (in the form of capital or labour subsidies) may encourage firms to shift their productive activities to regions where these subsidies are available. But even if regional policy has no effect on the decision to move, it may still have an effect on industrial movement through its effect on the location decision. Regional-policy incentives, for example, may induce firms that are already 'on the move' to locate their plant and equipment in the DAS, while location controls will tend to divert mobile capital away from the non-DAS. To the extent that the volume of industrial movement varies over time owing to factors other than variations in the strength of regional policy, it follows that the movement of industry to the DAS is also likely to be affected by factors other than regional policy.

Since it is analytically convenient to break down the process of industrial movement into a decision to move and a decision to locate, this suggests that regional policy may have a dual effect on industrial movement. It may affect either the generation of industrial movement or the regional distribution of industrial movement, or both. Hence, to examine the effect of regional policy on industrial movement we require a two-component model—a generation component and a distribution component. It will be useful to discuss each of these two components separately.

The Generation of Industrial Movement

Empirical surveys of firm movement suggest that a major proportion of moves are a direct consequence of constraints on productive capacity at existing locations (Townroe, 1973, 1976; Keeble, 1971). As demand expands, firms reach their capacity ceilings and have to look for suitable sites for their new capacity. Previous studies have, indeed, discovered a positive relationship between industrial movement and the pressure of demand (Beacham and Osborn, 1970; Moore and Rhodes, 1976). Extending this argument, we suggest that the influence of the pressure of demand on industrial movement is more likely to come through its effect on investment spending, which in turn is likely to be an important determinant of industrial movement (Danielsson, 1964). If industrial movement is a consequence, in the main, of firms reaching their capacity ceilings at their existing locations, this implies that industrial movement will respond positively to industrial investment. However, we should also recognise that not all industrial movement is a consequence of capacity constraints at the firm's existing location. Some movement will occur simply because alternative regions become more attractive locations for production than the region in which the firm has been operating. Movement in this case will consist of transfers of existing capacity rather than net additions to capacity. Since an increase in the pressure of demand causes labour shortages in some regions much more quickly than in others, firms may actually decide to transfer existing plant to regions where labour is more abundant, in order to avoid the problems that may result from labour shortages at their existing locations.

Dividing the total movement of industry into net additions to capacity and the transfer of existing plant, we therefore suggest that the former is likely to be positively related to current investment activity whereas the latter is likely to respond to fluctuations in the pressure of demand. Using a spare-capacity index as a measure of the pressure of demand, allowing for a one-year lag in the effect of the pressure of demand on the transfer of existing plant, and assuming a linear relationship, we can write

$$M_t = a + bI_t + cS_{t-1} \qquad (b > 0; \ c < 0) \tag{1}$$

where:

M_t = total movement of industry in period t;

I_t = aggregate industrial investment expenditure in period t;

S_{t-1} = index of spare capacity in period $t-1$.

Note that the effect of spare capacity is postulated to be negative because a rise in spare capacity will occur as the pressure of demand falls.

Using a modified capital stock adjustment model to explain aggregate investment, we can write[1]

$$I_t = \alpha\beta\gamma \, \Delta Y_t - \alpha\beta\gamma\delta S_{t-1} + (1 - \alpha)I_{t-1}$$

where ΔY_t = annual change in index of manufacturing output, (between periods $t - 1$ and t). Substituting the investment function into the movement equation, we obtain

$$M_t = d_0 + d_1 \, \Delta Y_t + d_2 S_{t-1} + d_3 I_{t-1} \qquad (d_1 > 0; \ d_2 < 0; \ d_3 > 0) \tag{2}$$

where:

$d_0 = a$;

$d_1 = \alpha\beta\gamma b$;

$d_2 = -(\alpha\beta\gamma\delta b - c)$;

$d_3 = (1 - \alpha)b$.

An *ad hoc* extension to equation (2) is made in the next section to allow for the possible effect of regional policy on total industrial movement.

(iii) *The Distribution of Industrial Movement*

The use of regionally differentiated investment incentives and labour subsidies is designed, in part, to enhance the relative economic attractiveness of the DAS to mobile industry. An increase in investment incentives and labour subsidies can be expected to induce more industry to move to the DAS relative to other regions. In addition, the relative economic attractiveness of the DAS may vary independently of the strength of regional-policy measures. Since fluctuations in aggregate demand fall unevenly on different regions, we might expect regional differences to emerge in *either* factor prices (e.g., regional differences in wage rates for similar occupational groups) *or* the utilisation rate of factor inputs. The existence of wide and persistent disparities in unemployment between regions, together with the rapid transmission of wage inflation between regions (MacKay and Hart, 1975), implies that it is likely to be unused factor inputs (particularly labour) that enhance the relative economic attractiveness of the DAS rather than lower factor prices. We can therefore write:

$$\frac{M_t^r}{M_t} = h(A_{t-\theta}^r). \tag{3}$$

where:

M_t^r = movement of industry to region r in period t;

M_t = total movement of industry in period t;

$A_{t-\theta}^r$ = index of the relative economic attractiveness of region r in period $t - \theta$, where θ is a time lag.

Once again, an *ad hoc* extension of equation (3) is made in the next section to accommodate the possible effect of regional-policy measures on the distribution of industrial movement.

Empirical Analysis of the Movement of Industry, 1951–71

Data and Variables

To test the hypotheses outlined in the previous section, data are required to construct empirical proxies for the dependent and explanatory variables of the model. The various industrial movement variables were constructed from unpublished Department of Industry data. Two sets of data were used, covering survivors and closures of manufacturing units that had moved between geographical sub-divisions of the United Kingdom during the periods 1945–65 and 1966–71; see Appendix. Certain adjustments had to be made to the data. First, account had to be taken of the increased number of sub-divisions used to collect the movement data in the 1966-71 period. Second, when the number of moves to each region was calculated, the data on closures had to be adjusted to remove those closures that had moved solely within each region. Third, moves between Great Britain and Northern Ireland had to be removed because of differences in policy measures adopted in the latter. The methods used are explained in the Appendix.

The annual time series for the total movement of industry (M) represents the total moves of manufacturing units that crossed at least one of the boundaries of the 49 sub-divisions of Great Britain during each year of the period 1945–71. The series for the movement of industry to the DAS (which is designated MDA) was obtained by summing the moves into each DA originating from sub-divisions outside the DAS as a whole.

To measure the relative economic attractiveness of the DAS, we have used a simple ratio based on unemployment rates. Since the majority of firms, according to surveys of industrial movement (Keeble, 1971), cite labour availability as an important factor determining their choice of location, we use the unemployment rate in the DAS relative to the unemployment rate in the South East as a measure of the relative economic attractiveness of the DAS. The non-policy variables in the generation component of the model have already been discussed in the previous section. They are defined in detail in the following sub-section.

The main regional-policy measures adopted by governments during the study period can be divided into three categories: capital subsidies, labour subsidies and controls on the location of new industrial building. Three measures of the value of regional capital subsidies are used. The first, designated II, is a measure of the value of investment incentives available in DAS from 1963 following the Local Employment Act (1963). It is the difference between the present value of investment incentives available in DAS and investment incentives available in non-DAS. The second measure, designated SDA, is a measure of the extra value of the investment incentives available in the Special Development Areas, which were set up at the end of 1967. SDA is simply the 'difference between the present value of investment incentives available in SDAS and investment incentives available in DAS. We have also allowed for the possibility that the grants and loans made to manufacturing firms under the 1960 Local Employment Act may have had an effect on the movement of industry. In the absence of more direct information on the intensity of regional policy between the 1960 and 1963 Local Employment Acts, we have included a dummy variable (D) to allow for an upward shift in industrial movement following the 1960 Act. Although this Act continued in force after 1963, we have assumed that the capital subsidies index (II) fully reflected the effect of capital subsidies available under numerous Acts from 1963 onwards. It should finally be noted that we have not attempted to estimate the extra movement that may have occurred as a consequence of the government's own factory building programme, but it is likely that the effect of this programme will be proxied, at least in part, by the three variables included to measure the effect of financial incentives.

We would expect investment incentives to have a positive effect on the distribution of movement to each DA. The position is not so clear, however, with regard to the impact of the *SDA* differential. Of the 47 employment exchange areas given SDA status in 1967, 42 were in Wales and the North and 5 were in Scotland. The SDAs in Scotland covered relatively remote areas of Central Scotland whereas those in Wales and the North were much larger and more central. Scotland may therefore have suffered a deterioration in attractiveness as a result of the introduction of SDAs (West Central Scotland Plan, 1974). The same argument applies, with perhaps greater force, to the Development Areas of the North West and South West (MacKay, 1976).

Unlike earlier studies (Moore and Rhodes, 1976; Ashcroft and Taylor, 1977), a labour subsidy index has not been included in the empirical analysis. We are persuaded by the view (MacKay, 1976) that the designation of the SDAs in 1967 is likely to have had a greater impact on industrial movement than the Regional Employment Premium which was introduced in the same year.[2] Although there was little difference between expenditure on capital and labour subsidies during the last three years of the study period (Begg *et al.*, 1975), the bulk of the expenditure on the Regional Employment Premium went to firms already operating in the DAs. For the vast majority of firms moving plant to the DAs, the labour subsidies were considerably less attractive than the capital subsidies.

To measure the strength of location controls, the number of applications for an Industrial Development Certificate (IDC) that were refused in the South East and West Midlands was expressed as a percentage of the total number of applications (refusals plus approvals) in these two regions. This measure, designated *IDC*, is used as an indicator of the intensity with which the government operated its control over the construction of new industrial building in the two regions that were responsible for generating a large proportion of the industrial movement. It is assumed that the numerical value of this measure will increase when the government's commitment to regional policy becomes stronger. A more detailed explanation of the weaknesses of the proxy is discussed by Ashcroft and Taylor (1977).

(ii) *The Lagged Effect of Regional Policy*
The complexity of the investment and movement decision makes the exact nature of time lags difficult to specify *a priori*. There is little empirical evidence, for example, to indicate the length of the lag between a given change in regional policy and its subsequent impact on the movement of industry (Moore and Rhodes, 1973). Although it is not possible to specify the lags on the regional-policy variables with confidence, some clues were nevertheless provided in our discussion of the determinants of industrial movement in the previous section. Industrial movement consists

of a large number of heterogeneous establishments and there are likely to be substantial differences not only in the locational requirements of different types of move, but also in the manner in which location decisions are reached by different firms. Some firms, for example, move because they are 'pushed' out of their existing locations. Extending capacity at existing locations may be either too costly or simply not possible because firms cannot obtain government permission to expand. Other firms may move because of the attractiveness of locations that offer lower production costs, either because of a lower demand for factors of production at other locations or because of the availability of government subsidies.

Suppose a firm requires more capacity and plans to expand at its existing location. If the subsequent application for an IDC is refused, the firm will amend its expansion plans by seeking an alternative location for its planned increase in capacity. This is the stage at which the Department of Industry clarifies the incentives available to the firm if it locates its new plant in a DA. The search for a suitable location in a DA, however, is likely to take time and only when one is found will the firm decide whether or not to go ahead with its planned expansion. But since time has elapsed between the initial decision to expand and the subsequent search for a suitable location, the firm is likely to confirm its original investment decision in the light of the appearance of more recent information on the expected growth in demand. If previous demand expectations are not confirmed, the firm will accordingly amend its plans to expand capacity. The comparatively large number of proposed expansions that are abandoned before the move to a new location is implemented[3] suggests that this is how firms behave. Furthermore, surveys of industrial movement indicate that firms take the decision to invest more seriously than the location decision (Loasby, 1967). The lag in the response of industrial movement to changes in regional policy may therefore be longer than the lag in the response to changes in the expected growth of demand. Evidence is cited by Moore and Rhodes (1973, p. 89, footnote 2) that a lag of one to two years occurs between an IDC approval and the subsequent occupation of the building. The lag may, in fact, vary from one policy instrument to another, but we have not investigated this possibility here.

The lagged effect of policy changes may be different for those firms attracted to alternative locations by lower production costs. Firms facing a labour shortage at their existing location, for example, may be induced to transfer their operations to a DA location because of the availability of regional incentives. The lagged response to policy changes is likely to be short in the case of firms voluntarily moving to more attractive locations since they are likely to move more quickly than firms that are 'forced' into moving to a DA location because they fail to obtain an IDC for expanding at their existing location. The evidence, however, is not conclusive (Townroe, 1972). Since we have not been able to specify the lags on the regional-policy variables *a priori*, we have experimented with two sets of lags in the following empirical analysis. First, all the regional-policy variables are lagged by one year, which implies that changes in regional policy and changes in the expected growth of demand affect industrial movement simultaneously. Secondly, all the regional-policy variables are lagged by two years, which implies that firms respond more slowly to changes in regional policy than they do to changes in the expected growth of demand when deciding whether or not to move. Finally, the relative-attractiveness variable in the distribution component of the model is given the same lag as the regional-policy variables.

Before we discuss the results, it may be convenient to summarise the notation employed in the analysis; in the case of the independent variables, the nature of the data is also indicated:

M = recorded moves in Great Britain;

MDA = recorded moves to the DAS of Great Britain;

$SCOT$ = recorded moves to Scotland;

$WALES$ = recorded moves to Welsh DAS;

$NORTH$ = recorded moves to the North;

SW = recorded moves to DAS in the South West;

$MERSEY$ = recorded moves to Merseyside;

I = index of gross fixed capital formation in the UK manufacturing sector, 1948=100 (at constant wholesale prices);

S = index of spare capacity measured in units of output in the UK production sector (Taylor, Winter and Pearce, 1970);

ΔY = annual change in index of UK manufacturing production, 1970=100;

IDC = percentage of refusals to total applications for an IDC (measured in terms of employees expected to be employed in the new establishment) in the South East and West Midlands (Moore and Rhodes, 1976);

D = shift dummy to reflect impact of 1960 Local Employment Act: 1952–59, 1963–71 = 0; 1960–62 = 1;

II = differential investment incentive available to firms expanding in DAS (Mellis and Richardson, 1976);

SDA = differential investment incentive available to firms expanding in SDAS (West Central Scotland Plan, 1974);

A = U_r/U_{SE} where U_r is the unemployment rate in region r.

(iii) *Results*

Multiple regression was employed to test the generation–distribution model of industrial movement outlined in the previous section. Two sets of estimated regression equations, using the ordinary least-squares procedure, are given in Tables 2.4 and 2.5. The first set of estimated regression equations (Table

TABLE 2.4

Regression analysis of the movement of industry, 1952–71: the generation of industrial movement and its distribution to the Development Areas of Great Britain with a one-year lag on the policy variables.

Equation number	Dependent variable	Constant term	S_{-1}	ΔY	I_{-1}	IDC_{-1}	D_{-1}	II_{-1}	SDA_{-1}	A_{-1}	$\bar{R}^2$	DW
(i)	M	105.45 (3.91)	−24.47 (5.25)	17.66 (5.88)	0.66 (3.77)	2.80 (2.65)					0.84	1.38
(ii)	MDA/M	0.158 (1.53)				−0.0004 (0.16)	0.0715 (1.92)	0.0121 (3.40)	0.0055 (1.07)	0.0118 (0.36)	0.86	1.44
1952–70												
(iii)	$SCOT/M$	0.050 (1.86)				0.0001 (0.07)	0.0086 (0.86)	0.0041 (4.31)	−0.0048 (3.06)	0.0063 (0.69)	0.80	2.45
(iv)	$WALES/M$	0.008 (0.27)				0.0001 (0.16)	−0.0043 (0.44)	0.0005 (0.56)	0.0060 (4.94)	0.0109 (0.97)	0.73	1.70
(v)	$NORTH/M$	0.020 (0.92)				−0.0006 (0.76)	0.0040 (0.38)	0.0033 (3.12)	0.0024 (1.84)	0.0116 (1.17)	0.82	2.46
(vi)	SW/M	0.004 (0.31)				−0.0000 (0.11)	0.012 (2.31)	0.0014 (2.52)	0.0004 (0.55)	0.0001 (1.09)	0.70	1.49

Note: the t-ratios are shown in parentheses. The estimated regression equation for $MERSEY/M$ is not reported, since the value for $\bar{R}^2$ was not significantly different from zero at the 0.05 level.

TABLE 2.5

Regression analysis of the movement of industry, 1952–71: the generation of industrial movement and its distribution to the Development Areas of Great Britain with a two-year lag on the policy variables

Equation number	Dependent variable	Constant term	S_{-1}	ΔY	I_{-1}	IDC_{-2}	D_{-2}	II_{-2}	SDA_{-2}	A_{-2}	$\bar{R}^2$	DW
(i)	M	88.42 (3.27)	−22.05 (4.49)	17.68 (5.92)	0.72 (4.43)	2.59 (2.67)					0.84	1.88
(ii)	MDA/M	0.135 (1.35)				0.0034 (1.96)	0.0750 (2.38)	0.0083 (2.88)	0.0077 (1.53)	0.0079 (0.24)	0.86	1.80
1952–70												
(iii)	$SCOT/M$	0.056 (1.28)				0.0002 (0.18)	0.0362 (2.18)	0.0037 (2.51)	−0.0053 (1.84)	0.0041 (0.28)	0.58	1.79
(iv)	$WALES/M$	−0.028 (1.27)				0.0002 (0.27)	0.0050 (0.52)	0.0013 (1.66)	0.0054 (4.29)	0.0236 (2.57)	0.79	1.93
(v)	$NORTH/M$	0.017 (0.81)				0.0006 (1.02)	0.0248 (2.41)	0.0025 (2.66)	0.0041 (2.89)	0.0075 (0.77)	0.86	2.13
(vi)	SW/M	0.040 (2.51)				−0.0007 (1.90)	0.0253 (4.18)	0.0024 (4.13)	−0.0001 (0.014)	−0.0001 (1.05)	0.70	1.18
(vii)	$MERSEY/M$	0.029 (1.23)				0.0026 (3.61)	−0.0217 (1.83)	−0.0027 (2.67)	0.0008 (0.45)	−0.0000 (0.36)	0.31	1.95

Note: the *t*-ratios are shown in parentheses.

2.4) assumes that regional policy affected industrial movement with a one-year lag. The second set (Table 2.5) assumes a two-year lag between a change in regional policy and its effect on industrial movement. The following discussion is confined to the second set of results, since the estimated equations which use a two-year lag on the regional-policy variables are on the whole statistically more satisfactory. The statistical analysis lends tentative support to the argument that the generation of industrial movement is partly dependent upon investment activity. Equation (i) in Table 2.5 suggests that the individual determinants of investment help to explain temporal fluctuations in total industrial movement. In addition, industrial location controls appear to have had the expected effect on industrial movement, stimulating movement when the location controls were more vigorously applied. The three financial incentive variables, D_{-2}, II_{-2} and SDA_{-2}, were omitted from the equation, since the three estimated coefficients had t-ratios very close to zero.

In the distribution component of the model, only the regional-policy variables are seen to be important in explaining the distribution of total movement to the DAS as a whole (MDA/M). The relative attractiveness of the DAS (as measured by relative unemployment rates) had apparently no effect on the movement of industry to the DAS. The one possible exception to this is that the relative abundance of labour in Wales appears to have had a positive effect on the inflow of industry. There is no evidence that the relative abundance of labour had similar effects in any of the other DAS.

As far as the regional-policy instruments are concerned, the clearest result is that both investment incentives and the grants and loans available under the 1960 Local Employment Act have had the expected positive effect on the movement of industry into the DAS. The main exception to this result is that Merseyside appears to have suffered from the availability of capital subsidies in the DAS. One reason for this may be that Merseyside has had to compete with nearby New Towns for industry that has moved from other sub-regions within the North West. The strong positive effect of the additional incentives available in the SDAS of Wales and the North adds further support to the view that capital subsidies have had the postulated effect on movement. The negative coefficient on the SDA variable for Scotland is not unexpected, in view of the fact that the Scottish SDAS were relatively more remote from the major industrial centres than those in Wales and the North. The results suggest that the success of the SDAS in Wales and the North had the effect of attracting moves away from Scotland at the end of the study period.

The influence of location controls on the distribution of industrial movement is less certain. Equation (ii) in Table 2.5 suggests that location controls had the expected positive effect on the movement of industry to the DAS as a whole, whereas the estimated equations for individual DAS indicate that location controls did not have a significant effect on the movement of industry to individual DAS apart from Merseyside. Indeed, the negative coefficient on the location controls proxy for the South West suggests that controls on the location of industry had a disadvantageous effect on the movement of industry to this region, perhaps reflecting the government's desire to steer industry away from the south of England as a whole.

The main conclusions to be drawn from the regression analysis are: first, the investment–demand explanation of the generation of industrial movement is tentatively supported by the empirical investigation of total industrial movement between the sub-regions of Great Britain over the period 1952–71 ; second, controls on the location of industry had the expected positive effect on total movement; third, both controls on the location of industry and the provision of capital subsidies had a positive effect on the movement of industry to the DAS as a whole. The following section attempts to estimate the actual effect of individual regional-policy instruments on the movement of industry to the DAS as a whole.

The Effect of Regional Policy on the Movement of Industry, 1961–71

With the help of the estimated regression equations given in Table 2.5 we can construct some tentative estimates of the effect of regional policy on the movement of industry. Since regional policy affects both the generation and the distribution of industrial movement, the analysis divides into two parts. First, location controls were seen to have a positive effect on the total movement of industry (M). The effect of location controls during the period 1961–71 is easily estimated. Since the coefficient on the location controls proxy (IDC_{-2}) indicates the effect of those controls on industrial movement, the difference between the 'policy-on' and the 'policy-off' value of IDC_{-2} reflects the intensity of the location controls. It was suggested earlier that the period 1952–59 was one of passive regional policy. We now go further and assume that regional policy was entirely non-existent during the period 1953–57. The 1953–57 average of the location controls proxy (i.e., $IDC = 4.9$ per cent during 1953–57) is consequently assumed to reflect a policy-off situation. In other words, we are assuming that location controls have been used not only to divert industry to the DAS, but also to prevent further industrial growth within the major conurbations; hence the assumption that an IDC refusal rate of 4.9 per cent represents a policy-off situation. Even if the policy of diverting industry to the DAS had been abandoned, controls would still have been used to divert industry to less-densely populated locations within the more rapidly growing regions. In view of the doubt, however, about the regional-policy content of location controls, we have provided two estimates of the effect of location controls on the movement of industry: the first assumes that the 1953–57 average for *IDC* represents a policy-off situation, and the second assumes that the policy-off position is represented by a value of zero for *IDC*.

Assuming that a refusal rate for an IDC of 4.9 per cent represents a policy-off situation, the (average annual) effect of location controls on total movement (1961–71) is calculated in two steps:

(a) 4.9 per cent is subtracted from the average value of IDC_{-2} for the period 1959–69 (i.e., allowing for the two-year lag of the effect of location controls on industrial movement);

(b) the result of step (a) is then multiplied by the estimated regression coefficient on IDC_{-2} in equation (i), Table 2.5.

The same procedure applies when a refusal rate (for an IDC) of zero per cent is used to represent a policy-off situation. Using this method, we estimate that location controls raised total moves during 1961–71 by between 470 (assuming a policy-off refusal rate of 4.9 per cent) and 610 (assuming a policy-off refusal rate of zero per cent). In other words, total moves were between 21 per cent and 29 per cent higher than they would have been if location controls had not been used to steer industry towards the DAS.

A similar procedure is used to estimate the effect of individual regional-policy instruments on the movement of industry to the DAS. A policy-off value is selected for each policy instrument. The assumed policy-off value of the policy instrument is subtracted from the actual value and the result is multiplied by the estimated regression coefficient on this variable (in the distribution component of the model). This provides us with an estimate of the effect of each policy instrument on the proportion of industry moving to the DAS, i.e. *MDA/M*. Multiplying the estimated effect on *MDA/M* by *M*, we obtain the effect of each policy instrument on *MDA*. Thus, to estimate the effect of investment incentives (*II*) on the movement of industry to the DAS, the procedure is as follows:

(a) multiply the estimated coefficient on II_{-2} (viz. 0.0083) by the average value of II_{-2} for the period during which the investment incentives were available (i.e., 1963–69), allowing for the two-year lag in the effect of these incentives on industrial movement: $0.0083 \times 14.40 = 0.1195$;

(b) multiply the result of step (a) by the total number of moves during the years when the policy was in operation: $1,861 \times 0.1195 = 222$.

The results of this exercise are given in Table 2.6, from which it can be seen that both location controls and capital subsidies contributed fairly substantially to the total movement of industry to the DAS during 1961–71. The estimates suggest that over 50 per cent of the moves to the DAS during 1961–71 were the direct consequence of regional policy.

These estimates of the effect of regional policy on the movement of industry to the DAS are lower than those of Moore and Rhodes (1976),

TABLE 2.6

The effect of individual regional-policy instruments on the movement of industry to the Development Areas, 1961–71

Regional-policy instrument	Period during which the policy was in operation (1960–71)[a]	Estimated effect on MDA
Location controls (*IDC*)	1960–71	153(198)[d]
Grants and loans, Local Employment Act 1960 (*D*)	1960–62[b]	50
Capital subsidies (*II*)	1963–71	222
Additional capital subsidies available in SDAS (*SDA*)	1967–71[c]	45
Total effect	1961–71	470(515)

[a] Each of the policy instruments was assumed to have an effect on the movement of industry with a two-year lag.

[b] The 1960 Act continued in force throughout the remainder of the study period, but we have assumed that the capital subsidies index (*II*) fully reflected the effect of capital subsidies from 1963 onwards.

[c] Additional capital subsidies were available in designated Special Development Areas from the fourth quarter of 1967.

[d] The figure in parentheses assumes a policy-off IDC of zero; see text.

but higher in total than our own previous estimates (Ashcroft and Taylor, 1977). Our estimates differ from those of Moore and Rhodes (1976), because we use a model which is distinguishable from theirs in several fundamental respects (Ashcroft and Taylor, 1977). The estimates in this chapter differ from our own previous estimates because we have altered the specification of our earlier model by lagging the regional-policy variables by two periods instead of one period, and because we have also allowed for the possible effect of the 1960 Local Employment Act on industrial movement.

Conclusions and Policy Implications

This chapter reaches three main conclusions. First, using a generation–distribution model of industrial movement, we conclude that regional policy had a substantial effect on the movement of industry into the DAS. Our estimates indicate that regional policy increased the number of establishments moving into the DAS by about 500 during 1961–71. In other words, over 50 per cent of the movement of industry into the Development Areas of Great Britain during 1961–71 was the direct result of regional policy. Expressed in terms of the number of direct jobs created by these moves, we estimate that the additional moves into the DAS raised the level of employment in these areas by around 100,000. Second, as far as individual policy instruments are concerned, both location controls and capital subsidies had a substantial effect on the movement of industry to the DAS. A major difference between these two policy instruments, however, is that location controls appear to have affected both the generation and the distribution of industrial movement (stimulating more movement in aggregate as well as inducing more movement into the DAS), whereas capital subsidies had only a distribution effect. Third, perhaps the most significant conclusion is that the movement of industry to the DAS depends extremely heavily upon the movement of industry in aggregate, which itself appears to be dependent upon the level of aggregate investment spending. Location controls and capital subsidies may be a necessary condition for steering more industry into the DAS, but these instruments are not adequate *per se*.

Appendix: Notes on Data and Definitions

The Industrial Movement Data

The data on industrial movement in the United Kingdom were collected by the Department of Industry (formerly the Board of Trade) over two periods. In the first period, 1945–65, the United Kingdom was divided into 50 sub-divisions: 38 in England; 8 in Scotland; 3 in Wales; and 1 in Northern Ireland; see Howard (1968). Industrial movement was defined as the opening of a new manufacturing unit in a sub-division in which a firm did not have any producing units. A move could result either from the complete transfer of a producing unit or from the creation of a branch unit, including moves from abroad. The definition did *not* include: the movement of units employing less than ten people; the opening of a unit by an entirely new firm with no previous origin; the takeover of a firm by another firm that had not manufactured in that area previously; the opening of new premises by a firm in the same sub-division; and the transfer of productive capacity from an existing unit in one sub-division to an existing unit in another sub-division.

For the period 1966–71, the moves were collated for the 62 planning sub-regions of the United Kingdom: 45 in England, 8 in Scotland, 8 in Wales and 1 in Northern Ireland. The moves in this period were recorded as follows:

(a) first occupiers of new premises of 5,000 sq.ft. or more of a new site for which an IDC was issued;

(b) occupiers of premises of 5,000 sq.ft. or more for which an IDC was issued for a change of use;

(c) occupiers of other sorts of premises provided that: (i) employment had at some time reached a minimum level, which varied from region to region but which lay between 11 and 100 employees; and (ii) the establishment had not transferred from other premises in the same 'travel-to-work' group of employment exchange areas. This definition indicates a much more comprehensive coverage of movement in the 1966–71 period than in the preceding period. In particular, the coverage is extended to cover *intra*-sub-divisional movement and the opening of new manufacturing units by firms that had not previously manufactured. Fortunately, the data were made available to us in such a way that these extra moves could be removed to make the two sets of data as compatible as possible.

Adjustments to the Movement and Closure Data
Two important adjustments were made to the data:

(a) An adjustment had to be made to make the 62 × 62 matrix used to collate the data in the 1966–71 period conform as closely as possible with the 50 × 50 matrix used for the 1945–65 period. Where one area in the old matrix had been sub-divided in the new matrix, the moves between those areas were removed by treating them as a single area. Alternatively, an allowance was made for additional moves where an area in the new matrix represented an approximate aggregation of two or more areas in the old matrix. These adjustments produced a net number of moves to be deducted from the total interarea movement in the 1966–71 period. To obtain the total movement for 1966–71, the net deduction for the *whole* period was multiplied by the ratio of (i) actual total movement in each year (from the 62 × 62 matrix) to (ii) the total movement in the whole period. The result was then subtracted from actual total movement in each year to give a corrected figure for total movement. This estimate should be similar to the one that would have been recorded if the same 50 × 50 matrix used for the 1945–65 period had been used in subsequent years.

(b) To calculate movement in any one year between 1945 and 1965, the moves that had survived to 1966 had to be added to the data on the closures of firms that had moved but had not survived by the end of the study period. For moves *to each region* the data on the closure of mobile firms in the region had to be adjusted to remove the closure of firms that had moved solely *within* the region in question. This was accomplished by assuming that the proportion of intraregional moves closing to the total closure of mobile firms in the region would be equal to the proportion of intraregional surviving moves to total surviving moves to the region in the year under consideration.

Regional-Investment Incentives
The proxy for the differential investment incentives available in the DAS (i.e., *II*) was obtained from estimates of the real value of United Kingdom and DA incentives provided by Mellis and Richardson (1976). The value of the differential incentive was found by subtracting the Discounted Cash Flow (DCF) value of the subsidies (as a percentage of capital cost) for

the United Kingdom from the corresponding figure for the DAS. The value of the differential in favour of the Special Development Areas was similarly obtained (from data contained in the West Central Scotland Plan, 1974) by subtracting the DCF value of the subsidies for the DAS from the corresponding figures for the SDAS. It should be noted that the DCF values were calculated on the assumption of a 'mixed project', i.e., the DCF values of schemes for plant, machinery and industrial buildings were weighted on the basis of a ratio of 4 : 1. Finally, adjustments were made to the estimated differential values to put the data on a calendar year basis.

The Definition of the Development Areas

The areas defined in the text as the DAS correspond broadly to those areas designated for regional assistance under the Industrial Development Act, 1966 (McCallum, chapter 1 of this volume). Since the eligible areas were smaller prior to 1966, it is possible that the estimates of the effect of regional policy given in Table 2.5 overstate the impact of regional policy on the movement of industry to the DAS during 1961–71 (Chisholm, 1976). The overestimate will probably be small, however, because the pre-1966 Development Districts covered the major industrial centres to which firms were most likely to be attracted, with the result that the extension of spatial coverage in 1966 should have had a minimal effect on the estimates (Moore and Rhodes, 1976).

Notes

1. A desired investment function $I_t^* = \beta(K_t^* - K_{t-1})$, where $0 \leq \beta \leq 1$, is combined with a desired capital stock (K_t^*) function after allowing for the possibility that the capital stock (K) was not optimally adjusted in the previous period, i.e., $K_t^* = \gamma Y_t$ where $\gamma > 0$, and $K_{t-1} = \gamma(Y_{t-1} + \gamma S_{t-1})$ where Y is output and S is spare capacity. This combination of equations provides a function explaining desired investment spending. By substituting this into the partial adjustment equation

$$I_t - I_{t-1} = \alpha(I_t^* - I_{t-1}), \qquad (0 \leq \alpha \leq 1)$$

we obtain the empirically testable investment function given in the main text; see Junankar (1970) for statistical tests of this function in the United Kingdom.

2. For an alternative view, see Moore and Rhodes (1976). The high correlation ($R^2 = 0.85$) between (a) an index designed to measure the magnitude of the Regional Employment Premium and (b) the SDA incentives, precludes the inclusion of both variables in the same regression equation. Hence, to the extent that the REP had an effect on the movement of industry, it is inseparable (in our analysis) from the effect of the SDA incentives.

3. According to Department of Industry figures, of the firms that failed to obtain an IDC for a proposed extension at their existing location, 13 per cent abandoned their plans to expand their capacity between 1958 and 1971; for an interesting discussion of this point, see Smith (1971).

References

Ashcroft, B. and Taylor, J. (1977) 'The Movement of Manufacturing Industry and the Effect of Regional Policy', *Oxford Economic Papers*, Vol. 29, pp. 84–101.

Beacham, A. and Osborn, W. T. (1970) 'The Movement of Manufacturing Industry', *Regional Studies*, Vol. 4, pp. 41–7.

Begg, H. M., Lythe, C. M., Sorley, R. and Macdonald, D. R. (1975) 'Expenditure on Regional Assistance to Industry', *Economic Journal*, Vol. 85, pp. 884–7.

Brown, A. J. (1972) *The Framework of Regional Economics in the United Kingdom*. Cambridge: Cambridge University Press.

Chisholm, M. (1976) 'Regional Policies in an Era of Slow Population Growth and Higher Unemployment', *Regional Studies*, Vol. 10, pp. 201–13.

Danielsson, A. (1964) 'The Location Decision from the Point of View of the Individual Company', *Ekonomisk Tidskift*, Vol. 66, pp. 47–87.

Great Britain (1970) Board of Trade. *Report on the Census of Production 1963*. London: HMSO.

Howard, R. S. (1968) *The Movement of Manufacturing Industry in the U.K., 1945–65*. London: HMSO.

Junankar, P. N. (1970) 'The Relationship between Investment and Spare Capacity in the United Kingdom, 1957–66', *Economica*, Vol. 37, pp. 277–92.

Keeble, D. E. (1971) 'Employment Mobility in Britain' in M. Chisholm and G. Manners (eds.), *Spatial Problems of the British Economy*. Cambridge: Cambridge University Press.

Loasby, B. (1967) 'Making Location Policy Work', *Lloyds Bank Review*, No. 83, pp. 34–47.

McCrone, G. (1969) *Regional Policy in Britain*. London: Allen and Unwin.

MacKay, D. and Hart, R. (1975) 'Wage Inflation and the Regional Wage Structure' in M. Parkin and A. R. Nobay (eds.), *Contemporary Issues in Economics*. Manchester: Manchester University Press.

MacKay, R. R. (1976) 'The Impact of the Regional Employment Premium' in A. Whiting (ed.), *The Economics of Industrial Subsidies*. London: HMSO.

Mellis, C. L. and Richardson, P. W. (1976) 'Value of Investment Incentives for Manufacturing Industry, 1946 to 1974' in A. Whiting (ed.), *The Economics of Industrial Subsidies*. London: HMSO.

Moore, B. and Rhodes, J. (1973) 'Evaluating the Effects of British Regional Economic Policy', *Economic Journal*, Vol. 83, pp. 87–110.

Moore, B. and Rhodes, J. (1976) 'Regional Economic Policy and the Movement of Manufacturing Firms to Development Areas', *Economica*, Vol. 43, pp. 17–31.

Sant, M. (1975) *Industrial Movement and Regional Development*. Oxford: Pergamon.

Smith, B. M. D. (1971) 'Industrial Development Certificate Control: an Institutional Influence on Industrial Mobility', *Journal of the Royal Town Planning Institute*, Vol. 57, pp. 65–70.

Taylor, J., Winter, D. and Pearce, D. W. (1970) 'A 19 Industry Quarterly Series of Capacity Utilisation in the United Kingdom, 1948–1968', *Oxford Bulletin*, Vol. 32, pp. 113–32.

Townroe, P. M. (1972) 'Some Behavioural Considerations in the Industrial Location Decision', *Regional Studies*, Vol. 6, pp. 261–72.

Townroe, P. M. (1973) 'The Supply of Mobile Industry: A Cross-Sectional Analysis', *Regional and Urban Economics*, Vol. 2, pp. 371–86.

Townroe, P. M. (1976) 'Settling-in Costs in Mobile Plants', *Urban Studies*, Vol. 13, pp. 67–70.

West Central Scotland Plan (1974) *The Regional Economy*. Supplementary Report, No. 1. Glasgow: West Central Scotland Plan.

CHAPTER 3

An Examination of
Assisted Labour Mobility Policy

*P. B. Beaumont**

Introduction

In general both academics and policy makers in Great Britain have been
highly sceptical of the potential value of assisted labour mobility policy
as a major instrument for remedying spatial inequalities in economic welfare
(Organisation for Economic Co-operation and Development, 1970, p. 18).
This scepticism has been based on two basic lines of argument: one stressing
the high incidence of social costs likely to accompany the operation of
such a policy, and the other emphasising the likelihood of only minimal
social benefits being generated by a scheme of this type. The proponents
of the high-cost view have argued that, contrary to the predictions of
the static neoclassical labour market model, assisted labour mobility policies
will generate disequilibrating labour flows that lead to a widening, rather
than a narrowing, of interregional unemployment and income differentials
(Thirlwall, 1966). This non-convergent solution is held to be the result
of various negative externalities stemming from the assisted migration process, which adversely affect the welfare of non-migrants in both the regions
of origin and the regions of destination (Riew, 1973).

The existence of external costs from the assisted migration process is
alleged to result from the removal of the following assumptions of the
neoclassical labour market model: independent labour supply and demand
functions, constant returns to scale production functions and a homogeneous
supply of labour (Greenwood, 1975, pp. 414–418). In fact, the removal
of these three assumptions does not necessarily produce a non-convergent
or disequilibrium solution between regional income and employment levels,
although it does have the effect of removing the automatic tendency to
equilibrium that is built into the neoclassical labour market model (Easterlin,
1958, pp. 324–5). But it is the disequilibrium potential of externalities
from the assisted-migration process that has been so much emphasised
by economists and policy makers in Britain. According to this school of

* *Department of Social and Economic Research, University of Glasgow.*

thought, the operation of assisted labour mobility policy would have the following undesirable effects on non-migrants in the regions of origin and the regions of destination:

(a) The policy would siphon off the younger and more skilled members of the outmigration area's unemployed workforce thereby leading to a decline in the quality of the residual workforce. This selective outmigration process would, in turn, act as a constraint on any policy attempt to attract new industry to the high unemployment areas.

(b) If one was to encourage and assist the outmigration of labour from the high-unemployment regions, this would result in a drainage of purchasing power, which would, in turn, produce downward income–expenditure multiplier effects in the local demand-oriented business sector sufficient to cause considerable secondary (demand-deficient) unemployment.

(c) Assisted labour migrants have invariably been characterised as persons moving from the uncongested parts of the high unemployment regions of the North to the large, physically congested conurbation areas of the Midlands and South East England. Such a direction of movement, it has been claimed, would inevitably lead to below-optimal use of the social capital stock in the areas of outmigration, while at the same time placing extra demand pressure on the already heavily utilised social capital stock of the destination areas. The latter effect would necessitate additional investment expenditure in housing, schools and other welfare facilities in order to accommodate the migrants, and this, in turn, would be likely to have an inflationary effect in the tight labour market conditions of these areas.

The basic conclusion to be drawn from these arguments is that the assisted labour mobility process would lead to such a substantial divergence between social and private costs of movement that the operation of the policy would seriously add to the longer-term recovery difficulties of the high unemployment, outmigration regions (Thirlwall, 1974, pp. 2–5).

The second strand of criticism of assisted labour mobility policy is a less well-developed line of argument, which has received rather less prominence in the regional policy literature than the 'high-cost' view outlined above. The essence of the argument, however, appears to be that the operation of assisted labour mobility policy will not result in a fundamentally 'new' or 'different' type of labour migration flow from the one already in existence on an unassisted basis. A policy of this type will not produce movements of labour that differ in more than a matter of degree from the direction, composition and effects of existing, unassisted migration flows and hence its major effect is simply to 'lubricate' these ongoing flows of labour. The result is that knowledge and use of the mobility assistance has insufficient independent influence on the migrants' decision-making process to be capable of generating substantial social benefits from assisting the geographical movement of unemployed labour.

There are two specific, testable hypotheses that derive from this view of the operation of assisted labour mobility policy (Nelson and Tweeten, 1973, pp. 64–6). First, there is the contention that a disproportionate number of the assisted movers will not be marginal migrants, but rather will be persons assisted to undertake a move that they would have made even in the absence of the policy assistance. If this is the case, then there will clearly be few social benefits resulting from the operation of the policy, since it will have done little more than subsidise a movement of labour that would have come about anyway in the normal course of time. The second contention is that the operation of such schemes will not result in a significant reduction in unemployment numbers, owing to the fact that a large percentage of the persons assisted to move will not make permanent shifts in location. This is because many of the assisted migrants will not adjust to (and remain in) the destination areas for any length of time, but will quickly return to their areas of origin, quite often coming back to a situation of unemployment. The operation of the policy will therefore only temporarily alleviate the unemployment problem in the regions of origin.

It is essential to emphasise that the various arguments outlined in this section are no more than contentions. There has certainly been no lack of armchair speculation about the likely effects of such policies, but 'hard' facts generated by detailed empirical investigation are few in number. Certain of the contentions outlined above contain implicit assumptions of a questionable nature that can be challenged on analytical grounds (Richardson, 1969, pp. 392–7). But the only way to resolve satisfactorily any doubts about the validity and/or magnitude of the allegedly unfavourable effects of assisted labour mobility is to undertake an empirical examination of the workings and impact of such a scheme. Accordingly this chapter will present some of the major findings obtained from the first detailed empirical study made of the operation of assisted labour mobility policy in Britain. However, before turning to this analysis, some reference must be made to the position and role of assisted labour mobility policy in the overall programme of regional policy in Britain. This review provides the necessary background for the later empirical sections of the chapter.

A Brief History of Assisted Labour Mobility Policy

The major emphasis of regional policy in Great Britain, both currently and in the past, has been on taking work to the high-unemployment regions by means of a system of investment incentives and controls. As a result, assisted labour mobility policy has played very much a minor role in overall regional policy. There has only been one policy period in which it was considered both necessary and desirable to encourage a large-scale movement of labour out of the high-unemployment regions. This was during the years 1928–38 when the Industrial Transference Board was set up with the aim of encouraging the movement of labour out of the depressed northern regions of the country.

The importance of this policy episode, at least for our purposes, is that much of the existing scepticism about the potential value of assisted labour mobility derives from the experience of these years. Certainly most of the standard criticisms of this form of policy had their origins in this particular policy period (Singer, 1940). Some recent work, however, suggests that the Board, in spite of the severe constraints under which it operated, achieved somewhat more than its critics have been prepared to concede (Pitfield, 1973). But even if this were not the case, the exceptionally unfavourable operating circumstances of the 1930s would seem to limit the generality of any lessons drawn from this policy experience.

The next stage in the history of assisted labour mobility policy in Great Britain came with the introduction of the Resettlement Transfer Scheme as part of the Employment and Training Act of 1948. This scheme sought to aid the movement of unemployed workers from areas of substantial labour surplus, and to assist the adjustment of ex-regular military personnel to civilian life. At the same time, a temporary transfer scheme operated to assist the movement of married workers forced to take up temporary work outside their local areas until work became available nearer to home. In September 1962 the various features of these two schemes were combined in order to extend the coverage of the Resettlement Transfer Scheme to unemployed workers throughout the country. The level of financial assistance under the policy was increased in 1965, 1969 and 1971 but the basic structure of the scheme remained unaltered until 1972 (Schnitzer, 1970, pp. 65–6).

The number of movers under the Resettlement Transfer Scheme, was extremely small. The largest number of assisted migrants in any one year was 8,368 in 1971–72. The small-scale operation of the scheme was seen to be the result of two major factors. First, the level and range of financial benefits under the Resettlement Transfer Scheme appeared to compare unfavourably with the scale of assistance available under similar schemes elsewhere (International Labour Office, 1962, p. 168). That is, the levels of financial assistance were generally considered barely adequate to make the idea of relocation acceptable (much less attractive), '. . . as the grants and allowances are no more than a contribution to the minimum expenses of removal' (Great Britain, 1963, p. 11).

A second constraint on the effectiveness of the scheme, in terms of its ability to assist the movement of a greater number of unemployed workers, was the limited knowledge of its availability. A number of unemployment surveys revealed that only a small percentage of unemployed workers even knew of the scheme's existence, let alone had any detailed knowledge of the individual benefits and provisions available (Daniel, 1972, p. 116).

Introduction of the Employment Transfer Scheme

A serious attempt was made to overcome these operational problems with the introduction of the Employment Transfer Scheme (ETS). This scheme was begun by the Conservative Government in April 1972 with the express intention of seeking to double the number of persons assisted to move under the Resettlement Transfer Scheme in the previous year (8,368). In the context of rising unemployment it was hoped that some 20,000 unemployed workers would be assisted to move under the ETS in 1972–73. In order to qualify for assistance under the ETS a worker had to be unemployed or liable to redundancy within six months and had to transfer beyond daily travelling distance of his present home so as to take up full-time employment in a new area. There were additional qualifying conditions for workers who did not live in assisted areas. A full statement of the terms and conditions of the scheme has been published (Great Britain, 1972b).

The new scheme contained additional forms of assistance (most notably a rehousing grant) and much higher levels of financial benefit than had generally been available under the Resettlement Transfer Scheme. In addition, the Secretary of State for Employment indicated that it was intended to relax certain of the previous scheme's rather strict eligibility conditions for obtaining mobility assistance (Great Britain, 1972a). The introduction of the ETS was accompanied by an extensive publicity campaign in the news media and managers of local employment exchanges were instructed to draw the attention of major local employers to the existence of the new scheme. The substantial increase in benefit levels, the relaxation of certain eligibility conditions, the publicity campaign and the setting of a numerical target to be achieved by the scheme were all innovations that suggested that for the first time a reasonably serious attempt was to be made to increase the role and status of assisted labour mobility policy in the overall regional-policy programme.

In 1972–73 the ETS just failed to meet its designated target (20,000 migrants) with 18,557 assisted migrants for a total expenditure outlay of £4,463,000. This may be compared with the maximum figures under the Resettlement Transfer Scheme in 1971–72 of 8,368 migrants for an expenditure outlay of £1,645,129. In 1973–74, however, migrant numbers fell to 15,237 for an expenditure outlay of £4,518,000. This downturn in migrant numbers was of concern to the Employment Service Agency and led to a number of changes in the scheme. These changes will be discussed in a later section of the chapter.

Operation of the ETS: Some Preliminary Findings

A breakdown of assisted migrant movement by regions of origin and destination for the years 1966–67 to 1973–74 revealed that out of the total number of 68,166 migrants the largest single group (29 per cent) originated in Scotland. The total number of persons assisted to move under the transference programme was (and still is) extremely small in relation to regional population, workforce and unemployment levels. Assisted migration is also a very small percentage of the overall migration flows from the high-unemployment regions. The number of assisted migrants from Scotland, for example, pales into insignificance alongside the net loss through migration of some 628,000 persons from the region during the years 1951–71. The small-scale nature of the ETS had a number of implications for the proposed study. First, it meant that not all of the contentions outlined in the first section of this chapter could be examined in the study. Those contentions that necessarily assumed a situation in which assisted migrant numbers were of such magnitude as to constitute a major determinant of any absolute change in the size of the base population of the regions of origin or destination fell into this category. This effectively ruled out any attempt to test the hypotheses that assisted-migration policy would result in below-optimal use of the social capital stock in the region of origin, and an above-optimal use of the social capital stock in the destination areas, necessitating additional investment expenditure that would be likely to have an inflationary impact there. In addition to restricting our ability to test the full range of allegedly harmful effects of assisted labour mobility policy, the small-scale operation of the ETS suggests that a number of our findings may not be capable of generalisation to the operation of schemes of assisted labour mobility that involve a much more substantial scale of movement relative to regional population and unemployment numbers. This note of caution must continually be borne in mind when considering the implications of the various findings presented in this chapter.

The basic data–set utilised in the analysis of this chapter was derived from a postal questionnaire sent to a sample group of Scottish assisted migrants to one of twelve employment exchange areas in England and Scotland during the twelve-month period July 1974 to June 1975. The twelve exchanges were the oil employment centres of Aberdeen, Invergordon and Inverness in Scotland, the new towns of Glenrothes and Livingston in Scotland, the one-plant-dominated labour market centres of Corby, Dagenham, Luton and Rugby in England and finally three employment exchanges situated in London. These particular exchange areas were among the leading destination centres for Scottish assisted migrants under the scheme. The final sample consisted of 222 assisted migrants, a figure that represented a 73 per cent response rate to the questionnaire. Various follow-up procedures, including a cross-check with the application form information lodged with the relevant employment exchanges, revealed no obvious selectivity or non-response bias among the respondents, at least as regards their major personal and labour market characteristics. The official application forms of the migrants also proved a useful source of data in their own right for examining a number of the hypotheses set out at the beginning of this chapter.

The Secondary Costs of Labour Mobility Policy

This section presents an outline of some findings for the major external costs alleged to be associated with the operation of assisted labour mobility policy. First, in order to examine the contention that assisted migrants would exhibit a strong locational preference for inner-city destinations, especially those of London and Birmingham, the overall regional flows under the scheme were broken down by local employment exchange areas. This exercise revealed that the pattern of movement was essentially spatially diffuse in destination area terms, with a large number and variety of cities and towns in England and Scotland each absorbing small groups of assisted migrants. The largest individual group of migrants in all regions of the country made intraregional moves; the number of migrants to outer-metropolitan centres far exceeded those to inner-metropolitan destinations and movement to Birmingham and London appeared to constitute less than 10 per cent of all movement under the ETS.

It is important to recognise the fact that these findings are likely to be specific to this particular policy period. If this is indeed the case then they cannot be used to dispute the argument advanced in the early sixties that the majority of assisted migrants under a large-scale labour transference policy would move to London and Birmingham and thereby add to the existing physical congestion and public-service provision difficulties within these centres. The use of our findings for such a purpose would necessitate making the assumption that the locational preferences identified here were essentially independent of differential employment opportunity, which in turn was largely independent of the influence of the dominant regional (industrial relocation) policy of this period. The validity of both of these assumptions would seem highly questionable.

The likelihood of a disproportionate number of younger assisted migrants was strongly confirmed by the fact that 92 per cent of the sample were aged below 45 years. This finding may be compared with the 1971 Census figures, which indicated that only some 61 per cent of the economically active population in Scotland were aged below 45. There was, however, little obvious support for the alleged skill drain effect of such policies. Some 68 per cent of the sample were unskilled, semi-skilled or sales workers, with the largest single group in the sample being the unskilled manual group. The findings for skill composition constitute a definite break with the results of previous studies of *unassisted* migration in Britain, which

have all found a positive relationship between higher occupation/skill status
and the extent of geographical mobility (Mann, 1973). The skill composition
of our sample, when taken in conjunction with the findings for certain
other personal and labour market characteristics, suggests that the assisted
labour mobility process may, at least in certain important respects, differ
from that of unassisted labour mobility in more than just a matter of
degree. The implication of this is that one cannot satisfactorily discuss
the impact of assisted labour mobility policy by simply generalising from
the results of studies of the unassisted migration process. Unfortunately,
this highly questionable practice has been all too common in the regional-
policy literature in Britain.

The questionnaire returns indicated the amount of unemployment benefit
received by the unemployed migrants prior to movement from their home
area which, together with information for average weekly earnings in Scotland during the survey period, was used, in conjunction with estimates
by Archibald (1967, pp. 35–6) for the size of the regional multiplier effect
and the proportion of expenditure from unemployment benefit that goes
directly to factor incomes in the local area of origin, to calculate the
magnitude of the secondary unemployment effect due to the migrants'
draining off purchasing power from their local areas of origin. The mean
unemployment benefit figure suggested a 1 : 11 job displacement ratio,
that is, the outmigration of eleven unemployed workers would on average
cause the loss of one extra job in the local area of origin. This was a
much less damaging result than Archibald's 'minimum' level estimate
of a 1 : 7 displacement ratio. The extent of variation around the mean
figure was such that some 33 per cent of the unemployed migrant group
received benefit payments sufficiently large to yield a ratio of 1 : 6.

The results from the testing of this particular hypothesis are at most
suggestive, as they lack an adequate empirical foundation from which
one could feel reasonably confident in generalising about the magnitude
of the induced-demand effects of assisting the outmigration of unemployed
labour. There is clearly a need for a great deal more empirical work
on this subject before one can produce more than illustrative figures of
the kind outlined above. In summary, the results of the survey provided
little apparent support for the claim that substantial secondary costs in
both regions of origin and destination will necessarily be an inevitable
accompaniment to the operation of policies of assisted labour mobility.
These largely 'favourable' findings (in the sense of being less damaging
than appears to have been widely believed) were very much offset, however,
by the poor performance of the ETS in relation to the two measures of
social benefit from assisting the geographical movement of unemployed
labour adopted in this study. It is to these two indicators of performance
that we now turn.

The Benefits of Labour Mobility Policy

The most basic requirement in any assessment of the performance of assisted labour mobility policy is to identify whether or not the policy users would have been able to move in the absence of the mobility assistance (Beaumont, 1977a). If the scheme merely acts to subsidise the migration costs of persons who would have moved anyway, the social benefits from a policy of this type are clearly minimal, unless it can be shown that the policy did independently influence these migrants' decision-making process in some socially desirable manner. The method employed in obtaining information on this matter was to ask the sample group directly whether they would, in the absence of access to financial aid under the ETS, have both wanted to and been able to migrate during this particular period of time. The major reservation about using this straightforward technique was the possibility of picking up 'halo' effects—some movers might feel compelled to answer that they could not have moved without the scheme in order to avoid the stigma of being seen as 'free riders' (persons who had taken something for nothing). In practice this fear proved groundless, as is only too well evidenced by the distribution of answers presented in Table 3.1.

TABLE 3.1

The willingness and ability of the assisted migrant sample to move in the absence of transfer scheme assistance

	Would you have wanted to move in the absence of assistance?	Would you have been able to move in the absence of assistance?
Yes (per cent)	88.2	69.4
No (per cent)	11.8	30.6
Column total	220	216

In the questionnaire the issue of movement in the absence of mobility assistance was split into the sub-categories of the incentive to move and the ability to move. The results from the examination of this issue are set out in Table 3.1. Over 88 per cent of the sample indicated a willingness to move anyway; hence, knowledge of the availability of financial assistance rarely provided the incentive for the sample to consider migration as a possible solution to their unemployment problem. The scheme was somewhat more successful in translating desired mobility into actual movement with some 31 per cent of the sample claiming that the ETS provided the financial resources necessary for undertaking their desired move. Nevertheless, with some 69 per cent of the migrants being subsidised to undertake a move that they would have made anyway, it is clear that marginal migrants constituted very much a minority of the sample. However, some social benefits may still result from the operation of the policy, if it has independently influenced or modified the movement decisions of this 69 per cent of the sample in any perceptible way.

Our results do provide some indication of a distinct policy influence among the migrants who admitted to being able to move in the absence of ETS assistance. The most important area of influence was in the timing of the move, with approximately 25 per cent of the group claiming that the financial assistance had permitted an earlier move than would otherwise have been possible; a further 8 per cent claimed that the assistance had permitted a longer-distance move. Nevertheless, the fact remains that some 64 per cent of the group were wholly uninfluenced by the scheme in terms of the timing or destination area of their move. It appears that their subsidised move differed in no perceptible way from the move they fully intended to make on an unassisted basis.

In attempting to improve the performance of the ETS in this regard, it is important to know whether the particular answers recorded in Table 3.1 were randomly distributed throughout the sample, as opposed to being disproportionately concentrated among specific sub-groups of the migrants. An answer to this question was sought through the estimation of regression equations for both the willingness to move (*WILL*) and the ability to move (*ABIL*) in the absence of mobility assistance. The equations, which took exactly the same form, were as follows:

$$WILL \ (ABIL) = a_1 + a_2A + a_3M + a_4S + a_5H + a_6D + e.$$

The dependent variables *WILL* and *ABIL* (the answers in columns 1 and 2 respectively of Table 3.1) were coded 1 for 'Yes' and 0 for 'No'.[1] The independent variables were as follows:

A = the age dummy, coded 1 for below 30 and 0 otherwise;

M = the marital status dummy, coded 1 for unmarried and 0 otherwise;

S = the skill status dummy, coded 1 for persons moving to higher skilled employment and 0 for those moving to lesser skilled positions;[2]

H = the pre-move housing tenure dummy, coded 1 for those tenure types considered least likely to restrict mobility and 0 for the other tenure groups;[3]

D = the distance of movement dummy, coded 1 for intraregional (short distance) moves and 0 for interregional (long distance) moves;

e = the random error term.

The regression estimates for the two equations are set out in Table 3.2. The age and marital status variables[4] were significant in both equations, while skill was highly significant in the *ABIL* equation. If we concentrate solely on the *ABIL* equation, which has a much higher level of overall explanatory power than the *WILL* equation, then we find that persons aged above 30, married and in lesser skilled employment had the lowest

TABLE 3.2

Regression results for the willingness and ability to move in the absence of assistance under the ETS

	WILL	ABIL
Constant	0.78803	0.30258
Age	0.18156[a]	0.12698[a]
	(0.05945)	(0.07666)
Marital status	−0.12541[a]	0.23846[a]
	(0.06118)	(0.07826)
Skill	0.00456	0.22321[a]
	(0.04490)	(0.05740)
Pre-move housing	0.07044	0.05301
	(0.05788)	(0.07466)
Distance of move	−0.01803	0.03412
	(0.04324)	(0.05557)
F	2.59588	15.22061
R^2	0.05744	0.26693
N	219	215

[a] Significant at the 0.05 level or better.

Note: standard errors shown in parentheses.

probability of being able to move without assistance. The implication of these results is that, to increase the proportion of users of the ETS who could not otherwise have moved, particular attention should be paid to encouraging and facilitating the relocation of members of the older, married and lesser skilled sub-groups of the unemployed workforce.[5]

When considering the implications of these findings, it should be borne in mind that they may be specific to the present level and structure of financial payments provided under the ETS. Under the present arrangements, single (presumably young) movers receive the minimum level and range of financial assistance as marital status is one of the few criteria upon which payments under the scheme are currently differentiated. Thus one might well obtain a quite different set of results if the present subsidy structure was for some reason altered in favour of younger, single movers.

The second hypothesis to be examined under the low benefit heading involves the question of whether or not the ETS is helping to bring about permanent shifts in the location of unemployed labour. The importance of this issue may be gauged from the results of a number of American studies which have suggested that the full realisation of wage/employment gains under a policy of assisted labour mobility requires the migrants to remain employed in the destination areas for at least a twelve-month period (Reesman and Zimmerman, 1975, pp. 171–8). If a similar requirement is necessary for 'success' under the ETS, then it is important to establish what proportion of assisted migrants remain employed in their respective destination areas for at least a certain specified period of time. The data used to examine this particular hypothesis identify the post-migration employment position of just under 890 assisted migrants to ten of our twelve exchanges (the Aberdeen and Invergordon exchanges had to be excluded from this exercise on administrative grounds) during the survey period July 1974 to June 1975. This data set was not derived from the questionnaire returns, but was provided by the migrants' application form records, which were lodged with the relevant employment exchanges. This source was used in order to avoid problems of non-contact that would undoubtedly have plagued the study if we had attempted to obtain the necessary information through questionnaire returns.

The results of this exercise are set out in Table 3.3. The figures indicate that fully 51 per cent (452) of the 886 assisted migrants had left employment in the destination areas at some stage during this twelve-month period.

TABLE 3.3
Size of the return migration flows from ten of the survey exchanges

Exchange	Total number of incomers during the relevant study period	Percentage of incomers recorded as no longer being employed in the area
Corby[b]	121	25.6
Croydon	17	47.1
Dagenham[b]	90	70.1
Glenrothes[a]	35	77.1
Inverness[a]	39	5.1
Kings Cross	14	–
Livingston[a]	50	52.0
Luton[b]	312	83.2
Rugby	10	90.0
Westminster	198	12.6
Total	886	51.0

[a] Figures for the quarter ending June 1975 only.
[b] All incomers regardless of region of origin.

In the vast majority of cases this meant, according to the local employment exchange officers, that the migrants had returned to their area of origin. Although sizeable inter-exchange variations in the rate of return migration exist, it does appear that high return rates are the rule rather than the exception under the current operation of ETS. The nature of employment in the different destination areas, and differences in certain personal and labour market characteristics of the migrants, appeared to be the factors associated with the sizeable inter-area variations in return migration rates (Beaumont, 1977d).

In order to evaluate correctly the success of assisted movement under the ETS there must be a specified length of stay in the destination areas which is necessary before a move can be deemed successful. Accordingly, an examination of the timing of these return moves was made, specifically with a view to identifying any critical period of adjustment beyond which the probability of return migration declined sharply. The results indicated that some 75 per cent of the migrants who left employment in the destination areas to return home did so within the first ten weeks after their original move. If a newcomer stayed more than ten weeks in the destination area, the probability of experiencing further adjustment problems sufficient to precipitate a return move was relatively slight (Beaumont, 1977b). In terms of policy reform, this finding suggests that, if adjustment difficulties are essentially financial ones, the assistance payments should be disproportionately concentrated in the first ten weeks after the move, rather than dispersed evenly through time—the present practice.

In summary, the results of this study have tended to support the low-benefit rather than the high-cost school of thought concerning the operation of assisted labour mobility policy. The findings presented in this section suggest that if the ETS is ever to generate substantial social benefits from assisting the geographical movement of unemployed labour, then there must be a sizeable reduction in the proportion of scheme users who would have moved in the absence of assistance. Similarly, there must be a reduction in the proportion of assisted migrants who fail to remain in employment in the destination areas for at least some minimum specified period of time. A number of the major influences on the assisted migrants' decision-making process are exogeneous to the control of the Employment Service Agency (Beaumont, 1977c), and hence it is not possible to set out a simple blueprint for policy reform that will guarantee the achievement of these two aims. There does, however, appear to be a case for making a special attempt to encourage the movement of older, married unemployed workers, as they have a low probability of being able to move of their own accord, but when assisted to move seem to have an above-average probability of remaining successfully in employment in the destination areas. The means for achieving this end could be to differentiate the subsidy payments strongly in their favour, or, alternatively, to have local employment exchange officers make a concerted attempt actively to 'sell' the idea of relocation to these particular workers. More generally, the indications are that a significant increase in the level of benefits from the operation of the ETS will only materialise if a serious attempt is made to influence positively the composition and direction of flows under the scheme, rather than continuing with the present approach, which simply seeks to increase the volume of assisted labour mobility (Beaumont, 1977d).

Recent Changes in the ETS

A number of essentially minor changes have been made to the terms and conditions of the ETS since the completion of this study. These changes were anticipated in a policy document (Great Britain, 1974, pp. 22–3) which set out a number of proposed changes to the scheme. These proposals included the establishment of specific objectives to be achieved by the scheme, the formal linking of employment exchanges in certain related areas of origin and destination, and the introduction of a new scheme of job search payments. A modest increase in local exchange staff numbers working on the scheme was also envisaged. In the following July the Employment Service Agency expressed concern over the fact that not enough use was being made of the ETS. This concern reflected the fact that, in spite of rising unemployment levels, assisted migrant numbers had fallen from the high point achieved in the year immediately following the introduction of the scheme. The subsequent changes, which were announced in November 1975, made no fundamental difference to the way in which the scheme was administered. The level of financial payments was raised, a grant for migrants purchasing their first home was introduced, and a related set of job search payments was also established. In keeping with past practice these changes reflected the scheme's continued preoccupation with trying to increase the volume of assisted migration. This aim was to be achieved by making relocation an increasingly attractive option to potential movers through raising the level and range of financial benefits available. The latest figures indicate that 14,333 persons were assisted to move in 1974–75 and 15,701 in 1975–76. The relevant expenditure levels for these two years were £4,372,000 and £5,965,000, respectively.

The Future Shape of Assisted Labour Mobility Policy

The results of the study presented in this chapter suggest that changes far more 'radical' than those set out above will be necessary before the ETS can be expected to produce substantial social benefits from assisting the geographical mobility of unemployed labour. These findings point to the need for a more fundamental re-evaluation of the role and shape of assisted labour mobility policy in the overall regional-policy programme. This re-evaluation should ideally consider the role of the ETS in relation to industrial relocation policy, i.e., whether assisted labour mobility policy should receive more emphasis in the overall regional-policy package. Unfortunately, the data necessary for undertaking this exercise are not currently available. A more workable approach is therefore to concentrate on devising the appropriate means for improving the internal operating efficiency of the scheme. This task will involve devising solutions to eliminate the major weaknesses of this scheme revealed in our study, namely the high proportion of persons assisted to move who would have moved anyway and the large number of migrants who do not remain in employment in the destination areas for any significant length of time. The first steps in this reconsideration of the policy's future were taken with the announcement by the Manpower Services Commission that 'The Commission recognises that the ETS was originally introduced at a time of high pressure of demand in the country as a whole, and that its present form may not be entirely appropriate for a period of generally high unemployment' (Great Britain, 1976a, p. 26). More recently the Commission has acknowledged that the present deficiencies of the ETS are the result of its unselective orientation, and that therefore consideration should be given to operating a scheme designed to facilitate 'desirable' mobility as defined by either the characteristics of the migrants or the length and direction of their proposed moves (Great Britain, 1976b, p. 27). Following a review of the operation of the ETS three basic changes were announced: applicants for ETS assistance must apply before they take up their job in the new area; students leaving a course of higher education would not be eligible for ETS assistance until they had been in the labour market for six months; rehousing grants are to be phased so that applicants are not entitled to the full payment until a year after taking up their job (Great Britain, 1978, p. 441). Although these changes certainly constitute a step in the right direction, they appear insufficient to make a serious inroad into the problems of operation of the ETS that have been detailed in this chapter.

Notes

1. It is acknowledged that the use of ordinary least squares to estimate an equation containing a dichotomous dependent variable may give rise to certain statistical biases. Theoretically more sound techniques do exist, but various studies employing both ordinary least squares and logit analysis have found little difference between the two sets of estimates (Gunderson, 1974).

2. This was not a simple white-collar/blue-collar division, as the former category contained skilled manual workers as well as clerical, administrative and professional workers, while the latter contained sales workers as well as unskilled and semi-skilled manual workers.

3. The former category included private renters, those in temporary accommodation and persons living with their parents or family, while the latter group contained public renters and owner occupiers. This particular division was based on the results of earlier housing–labour mobility studies in Britain (Johnson *et al.*, 1974, pp. 109–11).

4. Given the quite different circumstances and motives involved in answering these questions there does not seem to be anything inconsistent about the different signs on the marital status variable in the two equations.

5. The separate influence of single variables only was examined in these two equations. Interaction terms were subsequently created for the significant variables, but none proved statistically significant and there was no resulting improvement in the level of overall explanatory power.

References

Archibald, G. C. (1967) 'Regional Multiplier Effects in the U.K.', *Oxford Economic Papers*, Vol. 19, pp. 22–45.
Beaumont, P. B. (1977a) 'Assessing the Performance of Assisted Labour Mobility Policy in Britain', *Scottish Journal of Political Economy*, Vol. 24, pp. 55–65.

Beaumont, P. B. (1977b) 'A Further Look at Return Migration Rates under the Employment Transfer Scheme', *British Journal of Industrial Relations*, Vol. 15, pp. 108–12.

Beaumont, P. B. (1977c) 'The Means of Finding Jobs Outside the Local Labour Market', *Industrial Relations Journal*, Vol. 8, pp. 62–9.

Beaumont, P. B. (1977d) *The Operation of Assisted Labour Mobility Policy in a High Unemployment Region.* London: HMSO.

Daniel, W. W. (1972) *Whatever Happened to the Workers in Woolwich?* London: Political and Economic Planning.

Easterlin, R. A. (1958) 'Longer Term Regional Income Changes: Some Suggested Factors', *Papers and Proceedings of the Regional Science Association*, Vol. 4, pp. 313–28.

Great Britain (1963) National Economic Development Council. *Conditions Favourable to Faster Growth.* London: HMSO.

Great Britain (1972a) House of Commons. *Official Report*, Fifth Series. Parliamentary Debates, Vol. 832, cols. 350–1. London: HMSO.

Great Britain (1972b) Department of Employment. *Department of Employment Gazette*, Vol. 80, pp. 354–5.

Great Britain (1974) The Employment Service Agency. *The Employment Service: Plans and Programmes.* London: HMSO.

Great Britain (1976a) Manpower Services Commission. *Annual Report*, 1975–76. London: HMSO.

Great Britain (1976b) Manpower Services Commission. *Towards a Comprehensive Manpower Policy.* London: HMSO.

Great Britain (1978) Department of Employment. *Department of Employment Gazette*, Vol. 86, p. 441.

Greenwood, M. J. (1975) 'Research on Internal Migration in the United States: A Survey', *Journal of Economic Literature*, Vol. 13, pp. 397–433.

Gunderson, M. (1974) 'Retention of Trainees: A Study with Dichotomous Dependent Variables', *Journal of Econometrics*, Vol. 2, pp. 79–93.

International Labour Office (1962) *Unemployment and Structural Change.* Geneva: International Labour Office.

Johnson, J. H. *et al.* (1974) *Housing and the Migration of Labour in England and Wales.* Farnborough: Saxon House.

Mann, M. (1973) *Workers on the Move.* London: Cambridge University Press.

Nelson, J. and Tweeten L. (1973) 'Subsidized Labor Mobility—An Alternative Use of Development Funds', *The Annals of Regional Science*, Vol. 7, pp. 57–66.

Organisation for Economic Co-operation and Development (1970) *Manpower Policy in the United Kingdom.* Paris: Organisation for Economic Co-operation and Development.

Pitfield D. (1973) 'Labour Migration and the Regional Problem in Britain, 1920–39', unpublished PhD thesis, University of Stirling.

Reesman, C. J. and Zimmerman, D. R. (1975) 'Worker Relocation, 1965–1972', report to the US Department of Labor, Manpower Administration, Washington D.C.

Richardson, H. W. (1969) *Regional Economics.* London: Weidenfeld and Nicolson.

Riew, J. (1973) 'Migration and Public Policy', *Journal of Regional Science*, Vol. 13, pp. 65–76.

Schnitzer, M. (1970) *Regional Unemployment and the Relocation of Workers.* New York: Praeger.

Singer, H. W. (1940) *Unemployment and the Unemployed.* London: King and Son.

Thirlwall, A. P. (1966) 'Migration and Regional Unemployment: Some Lessons for Regional Planning', *Westminster Bank Review*, November, pp. 31–44.

Thirlwall, A. P. (1974) 'Regional Economic Disparities and Regional Policy in the Common Market', *Urban Studies*, Vol. 11, pp. 1–12.

CHAPTER 4

Regional Policy and the National Interest

Thomas Wilson*

Introduction

When a country is faced with grave economic difficulties, should it persist with policies selectively designed to foster industrial development in the less prosperous regions? On two important occasions in Great Britain, 1947 and 1977, the response of the government of the day was in the negative. After 1947, regional policies were curtailed and remained largely abandoned for more than a decade. In 1977, the dismantling of the measures in force was more limited; but the Regional Employment Premium (REP), which had accounted for about a third of total expenditure in regional inducements, was finally scrapped after a period of curtailment. Thus, on these two occasions, it was apparently decided that the special needs of the less prosperous areas would have to give way to the more general needs of the economy as a whole. This attitude implies, as does the phrasing of our opening question, that regional policies can impose a burden on the rest of the community. It is a burden that may be accepted at times of national prosperity, but is liable to be laid down when times are bad.

A very different official attitude was adopted in the 1960s. When the National Economic Development Council was presenting its programme for growth (Great Britain, 1963), measures to assist the less prosperous regions were included and such measures formed part of the National Plan (Great Britain, 1965). During this period, regional policies were commended not only for the help they were expected to bring to the regions concerned but also for the benefits to be conferred on the nation as a whole. From a Paretian standpoint, welfare would be increased; from a political standpoint, conflict would not arise. In particular it was held that the national labour force might thus be raised by something like one per cent and this would add to the level of national output. Admittedly it would not have added much (the equivalent of only three or four months growth). When REP was introduced it was claimed that the net

* Department of Political Economy and Centre for Urban and Regional Research, University of Glasgow.

cost would be zero: national output would rise and with it taxable capacity, so that in due course there would be no burden on the Exchequer. The bread cast upon the water would come back again (Great Britain, 1967a; 1967b). A similar optimistic claim for regional policy in general was later made by Moore and Rhodes (1973; 1975); see also MacKay (1974) and, for a discussion of the earlier evolution of policy, McCrone (1969).

Subsequently, there has been a marked change in the official attitude, but this shift is not one that can be explained by reference to party politics, although it is true that party politics have indeed introduced a special element of instability into regional policy.[1] The change could, however, reflect a new assessment, in the light of further experience, of the effectiveness of regional inducements. But the most obvious explanation is that the assessment has changed, rightly or wrongly, because general economic conditions have changed. It is not merely that the nation is better able to help the assisted areas when times are good. It is also that a growing economy may find itself short of manpower and regional policy may ease the strain slightly by reducing structural unemployment and raising the activity rate. This argument loses much of its force when unemployment is at an uncomfortably high level throughout the whole economy and the Keynesian approach, so long officially accepted, would require not cuts in public expenditure but rather substantial increases. It is true that in the assisted areas less might be spent on investment subsidies than would be the case in boom periods, simply because investment there, as elsewhere, was stagnant. But the Keynesian inference might then be that more should be spent not only on infrastructure but also on subsidies such as REP that would help to maintain employment until a cyclical recovery could be initiated. This would, at one time, have been the orthodox answer, but it is not one that has the same support in the mid-1970s; heavy unemployment has been accompanied by severe inflation and, for a time, by an appallingly weak balance of payments. Thus restrictions have been placed on the growth of public expenditure. The special nature of the recession of the 1970s has affected regional policy as well as other policies, but it is always possible that more expansive measures will be thought appropriate once more when recovery finally takes place. Unfortunately, regional development is one of the many fields of public policy where some steadiness of purpose and some stability in the methods used are desirable.

It is not, in any case, to be taken for granted that even when recovery takes place this will be thought to justify a return to the easy-going attitude to public expenditure that had prevailed for so long before the downturn of 1974. First of all, public expenditure had been allowed to rise over a period of years to such a high proportion of the Gross National Product (GNP) as to make it extremely difficult, perhaps impossible, to control inflation. The main effect of the economy campaign has been to prevent further increases in public expenditure as a proportion of GNP. In order to reduce expenditure to a significantly lower proportion of GNP, it would have to be held down for an extended period of years, with GNP, exports, industrial investment, and also private consumption from income derived from production, all growing at faster rates. If this attitude were maintained, public expenditure on regional policies might continue to be watched with a more critical eye. This, in turn, underlines the need for a much more selective approach in order to ensure that what is being spent will bring with it as much benefit as possible. Of course, cost-effectiveness always deserved close attention but it did not receive the consideration that it deserved in the formulation of regional policy as well as in other aspects of public policy.

North Sea oil strengthens the balance of payments and contributes to public revenue (Mackay, chapter 7 of this volume). It should not be inferred, however, that what has been said about the need for cost-effectiveness in regional policy will then lose its force. First, it is important not to exaggerate the effect of North Sea oil. To assess this effect at all is obviously a hazardous undertaking and an understanding of the official estimates (Great Britain, 1976; 1977) is all the more difficult because the assumptions have not been fully explained. If, however, we take the official view, then the gain to the balance of payments may be equivalent to about $3\frac{1}{2}$ per cent of GNP in 1980, and this means that the reduction in real income caused by the decision of the Organisation of Petroleum Exporting Countries to increase the price of oil will be fully offset. By 1985, the percentage may be, say, 5 per cent, which will leave the nation with a slightly increased margin in her favour amounting to, say, $1-1\frac{1}{2}$ per cent of GNP. Second, North Sea oil will not last indefinitely. It will provide a valuable opportunity to alter the structure and to improve the efficiency of the British economy and to do so with less hardship and inconvenience. Third, the strengthening of the balance of payments means a stronger pound than we should otherwise have. It will, to this extent, be all the more important to keep down money costs and to raise efficiency if industry in Great Britain is to compete satisfactorily in domestic and foreign markets. In any case, efficiency remains of crucial importance, for competitiveness cannot be painlessly preserved or achieved merely by progressive devaluation of the currency. Unfortunately even by 1978 it had already become apparent that the benefit from North Sea oil was preventing balance-of-payments problems rather than providing a large surplus that could be expected to continue. The prospects for the balance of payments seemed disappointingly precarious and it was no longer reasonable to suppose that the oil would provide a respite of one or two decades over which inflation could be brought under control and the desirable industrial readjustments could be carried out at an easy and comfortable pace.

The measures designed to assist the less developed regions constitute a very mixed bag. Some may be costly in public money and harmful to efficiency. Fortunately, in other cases this may not be so. Clearly, an important step is to distinguish between two approaches to the industrial problems of the regions, which should be regarded as complementary rather than as alternatives. First, there is the use of measures designed to help industry in these regions by the use of subsidies and controls. The need to ensure the highest possible degree of cost-effectiveness is obvious. Second, there is the possibility of placing a greater reliance upon market forces. What may then be required in particular may be the correction of distortions introduced in part by government itself. No net increase in budgetary expenditure need be expected under this second heading and there may even be savings if there is then less need for some other measures.

The expression 'regional policy' is conventionally used to mean assistance to the less prosperous regions in the form mainly of industrial subventions of one kind or another. When we bring in the second line of policy mentioned above, the removal or at least the easing of obstacles to market forces, the scope of the enquiry naturally widens. But it has to be widened still more than this. For the assistance provided under the first heading is only one of the ways in which certain regions are provided with interregional transfers of public money. It has, indeed, always been recognised that they can also be helped by special assistance with infrastructure, although such assistance has not usually been sharply identified and entered in the statistics as one of the costs of regional policy, not at least in Great Britain. Nor is this all: it is necessary to look at the whole field of public expenditure in the different regions relative to their contributions to national revenue. This is a new approach to regional policy and it is a natural consequence of proposals for devolution. It is comprehensive with regard to the items included and extensive in scope in that it reaches beyond the assisted areas. Two practical results may be anticipated. The first is that there is likely to be a closer and more jealous watch on interregional transfers, and this, in turn, underlines the need for economies and cost-effectiveness. The second result is that whatever economies are required can be spread over a broad field and need not be confined to regional policy in the narrow conventional sense which we shall now designate 'regional development policy'. On the contrary, if it is indeed the case that the latter policies are well designed and are such as to benefit both the nation as a whole and the regions assisted directly, there would be a case for protecting them against cuts. By doing so, such policies would also be made more effective. For their capacity to achieve satisfactory results is reduced when, as in the past, these measures are subject to such frequent alterations as to make it hard for the firms concerned to plan their affairs in a sensible manner—a point much stressed by the industrialists who gave evidence to the Expenditure Committee (Great

Britain, 1973b); see also Finer (1975). In order to pursue these matters further we now need to look more closely at the objectives of regional policy and at the means by which it may be pursued.

Regional Disparities and the Objectives of Policy

Regional policy is designed to reduce disparities between the more prosperous and the less prosperous regions. In Great Britain, the main emphasis has been placed on the reduction of the relatively high levels of unemployment in the latter regions, and to this has been added as a minor theme the scope for raising participation rates. Disparities in levels of output and in rates of growth have also received some attention. In this context, as in others, the term 'disparity' may suggest departure from a norm that is in some sense taken to be 'natural' and certainly desirable. It is then tempting to infer that disparities represent a distortion that can be attributed to some general features of the economic system—even, for example, to the power exercised by the wildly abused multi-nationals! With such notions apparently current, it is necessary to recognise that regional differences in labour markets, in output per capita and in other economic indicators are quite common throughout the world and are to be found in Communist countries as well as in the West. Indeed, these regional differences are small within Great Britain as compared with those in some other countries. This has been shown very clearly with regard to income per capita in the MacDougall Report (European Communities, 1977). Thus the ratio of the richest region to the poorest region came to 2.9 in the USA, 2.2 in Canada, 2.5 in Italy, 1.8 in Germany, 1.7 in France, and 1.6 in the United Kingdom. (For Great Britain, i.e., with Northern Ireland excluded, the ratio would be about 1.8.) The Gini coefficient for the United Kingdom gives a similar impression when compared with those for other countries (European Communities, 1977, p. 27.) The unemployment differential has also been substantially less in Great Britain (and even in the United Kingdom) than in Canada, for example.

Regional disparities can, in fact, be expected to persist as the natural outcome of change and will thus be a permanent feature of any dynamic economy. The disparities may, indeed, be reduced both by market forces that are allowed to operate effectively and by appropriately devised regional policies, but the differences are unlikely to be completely eliminated. This is the first point to be made and it follows that the need for both regional development policies and for some movement of population is also likely to be permanent. Admittedly, the course of events may be such as to remove this need substantially in some countries but, in general, the need is likely to remain, as long as change is taking place. It would be wrong, therefore, to suppose that we are concerned here with a once-and-for-all operation which will dispose of the problem. The words 'temporary' and 'permanent' may, however, be applied in different ways with quite basic implications for policy. To say that there is a lasting need for regional policy is not to imply that the same areas will always require assistance. With the passage of time, one would expect natural locational advantages to alter and the incidence of policy would then have to be adjusted accordingly. The second point is that insofar as assistance takes the form of subsidies to industry, the help given to *particular firms* within any assisted regions need not be permanent. The purpose of the assistance may rather be to help some firms to become established or to carry through certain changes designed to raise their efficiency by changing their products and their processes. If this is the intention, then the firms are being helped to achieve a breakthrough and regional policy can be regarded as an application of the infant-industry argument, so long familiar in the literature on international trade. Permanent subsidisation of individual concerns designed to offset permanent locational disadvantages is a different matter. For this will impose a lasting burden on the rest of the country. It is a burden that may indeed be accepted on political or on broad social grounds. Economists, for their part, have no right to say that such assistance is wrong, for this would commit them to the value judgement that a higher level of real income or a faster growth of national real income, as conventionally measured, is the only legitimate objective or is one that must, in any event, take precedence over others. What is, however, quite proper is to point out that if assistance is permanent in this last sense of the term, it must impose a burden on the rest of the community. This burden may well be resented as has been seen most strikingly, perhaps, in a Communist country, Yugoslavia, where there has been a conflict of interest between the richer north and the poorer south.

These points are clearly relevant to what was said in the preceding paragraphs. If the assistance given to firms in the less prosperous areas is designed with the purpose of enabling them to stand eventually on their own feet, then the conflict between regional interests and national interests will naturally be smaller and perhaps only temporary. But if industry is to be supported indefinitely on the basis of subventions from the rest of the country, then the conflict of interests must be viewed in a different light. There are obvious implications when choosing between different forms of industrial assistance. As far as is practicable, these should be so chosen as to have as large an impact as possible at the margin when decisions are being made, and should consist to the least possible extent of subventions that will be received anyway, even if firms are doing nothing that they would not otherwise have done to raise their efficiency. Assistance of the former kind, designed to facilitate a breakthrough, should form the core of regional industrial policy. More than this may be thought desirable on general political and 'social' grounds, but the conflict between national and regional interests may then become sufficiently marked at times of crisis that some measure of retrenchment may be thought to be unavoidable. The word 'social', so often used in this context, can, of course, be misleading. It is not being suggested that market forces are non-social! On the contrary, the market is a remarkably effective social device for the transmission of preferences, for relating preferences to costs, for stimulating efficiency and so on. The special use of the term 'social' is meant to convey the fact that non-market considerations also need to be taken into account.

The implications of this approach to policy affect not only the selection of the package of industrial inducements but also affect the choice of the areas within which these inducements will be available. In the nature of the case, these areas should be chosen with regard to need, but need should not be the only criterion. Proper regard must also be paid to potentialities.[2] The areas selected much be chosen so as to include within them some promising locations. This was, of course, part of the growth centre concept on which there is an extensive literature (Parr, chapter 9 of this volume). On occasions this concept may have been pursued too strongly and it has certainly come under criticism. But it contains an important element of truth that remains valid even in the face of changing economic circumstances. It would, of course, be wrong to suggest that the inducements should be confined to firms locating themselves in selected growth centres. If some firms feel that other locations are more promising they should be free to choose them. One of the advantages of industrial inducements related to the establishment of new factories or the extension or improvement of existing ones is that these are provided in such a form that no expense need be incurred unless industrial management believes the prospect to be sufficiently attractive to warrant the investment of private capital as well as public money. Infrastructure is a different matter.[3] The need to improve the infrastructure of less prosperous regions is generally recognised, but in this case government must commit itself more definitely to views about the future location of industry. The planning of the transport system is an obvious example.

There is another respect in which expenditure on infrastructure is different from expenditure on industrial inducements: its effect on general industrial expansion is harder to predict in advance. It is true that there have been important cases where improvements in transport or in the provision of housing can be linked to particular projects for industrial expansion that can be envisaged with reasonable confidence. When this is so a joint planning exercise is obviously appropriate. But in large measure the effect on industrial development of expenditure on infrastructure is bound to be uncertain. It is therefore somewhat odd that there has been, from time to time, a strong tendency in some circles to maintain that regional policy should be confined to assistance with infrastructure. Apparently, it was felt that such assistance would involve less interference with the working of market forces. But subsidies for infrastructure also involve heavier taxation on the rest of the economy, and it is by no means obvious that this will be less burdensome and less wasteful than assistance provided to firms in order to help them to achieve self-sustaining growth.

The cost of regional policy is often assessed as expenditure on various forms of assistance to industry and labour; but this is too narrow a view and is, indeed, inconsistent with the usual assumption that improvement of the infrastructure is part of regional policy. This unduly narrow way of looking at the accounts can only be regarded as the accidental outcome of the way in which statistics are presented when, as in Great Britain, there is centralised government. Expenditure on infrastructure should be taken into account but, even if this has been done, we are still confining attention to only part of the interregional transfers that actually take place. In the MacDougall Report it is rightly pointed out that regional policy in the narrow sense of aid to industry, accounts for only a fairly small part of the transfers that take place among the different regions of the nations whose accounts were examined (European Communities, 1977, p. 37). Naturally, this fact has not been concealed in federal countries and we can anticipate that it will receive increasing attention even in Britain as a by-product of the current interest in devolution (Firn and Maclennan, chapter 13 of this volume). We have here a new and broader approach to regional policy to which we must now direct our attention.

Even in the absence of any special measures designed to strengthen industrial development in the less prosperous regions, the normal fiscal arrangements cause funds to be transferred from the richer to the poorer regions. The former have a stronger tax base and contribute more per capita; but the entitlement to central-government expenditure is not related to contributions to tax revenue as levied at uniform national *rates* of taxation, since all regions have the same claims according to what, in the context of Northern Ireland's public finance, used to be termed 'the principle of parity'. Expenditure should reflect not only differences in the cost of providing a given service but also differences in needs, as distinct from differences in taxable capacity. Thus the regions with relatively more unemployment or a relatively high sickness rate or a relatively large proportion of retired people should receive relatively more from the public purse irrespective of their contribution to that purse. This is what follows from the principle of parity. Admittedly, the practical application of the principle is not easy. Although parity can be determined more or less exactly in the case of cash benefits such as old age pensions, unemployment benefit and the like, this is not so with regard to other forms of public expenditure. An element of judgement is entailed and there may also be an element of bargaining, for example, between the Scottish Office and the Treasury. It would therefore be going too far to claim that parity is precisely achieved.

It remains true, however, that in the poorer regions, expenditure per capita can be expected to be larger relative to taxation per capita than in the more prosperous regions. The Royal Commission on the Constitution (Great Britain, 1973a, p. 180) expressed the view not only that this has occurred but that it has done so to a startling extent. Any calculation of this kind is open to damaging criticism on the ground that it is exceedingly difficult, if not impossible, to establish with confidence the ultimate incidence of all taxes. Even with this qualification, it is possible to conclude that substantial transfers in favour of the poorer regions do in fact take place. On the basis of the assumptions about incidence made in the MacDougall Report, these transfers amount to rather less than 4 per cent of GNP in the United Kingdom (European Communities, 1977). This implies that the transfers are equivalent to just under 8 per cent of public expenditure.

It would be premature to suppose that such transfers from the richer to the poorer regions are simply to be regarded as subsidies; the higher level of public expenditure thus made possible in the poorer regions may confer advantages on the richer regions themselves. This justification of fiscal transfers on the ground of externalities has been developed most fully in the USA, notably by Oates (1972). That is perhaps what one might expect in view of the federal structure of that country and the traditional restrictions thus imposed, admittedly with diminishing severity, on the role of the federal government. It may be of interest to supplement what has been said by referring to some estimates of public expenditure per capita, even if these are given without corresponding figures on the revenue side; see Table 4.1. Data on Gross Domestic Product (GDP) and

TABLE 4.1
Public expenditure per capita

Year	England	Wales	Scotland	Northern Ireland
1963–64[a]	100	116	118	103
1965–66[a]	100	114	114	108
1969–70[a]	100	116	131	118
1969–70[b]	100	120	136	115
1973–74[b]	100	105	120	117
1974–75[b]	100	103	119	118

[a] The figures for 1963–64 to 1969–70 are from Great Britain (1973a, p. 178): These figures include expenditure by local authorities but exclude general services such as defence, overseas aid and representation, and debt interest, and also for statistical reasons, certain other services such as agricultural support, subsidies to nationalised transport and some capital expenditure of nationalised industries'.

[b] The figures for 1969–70 to 1974–75 are from Great Britain (1975, col. 478). For the years 1973–74 and 1974–75 the figures for Northern Ireland have been scaled down in order to allow for abnormal expenditure on law and order.

Note: since the figures from the two sources are not strictly comparable, those from both sources are given for 1969–70.

TABLE 4.2

Gross domestic product (GDP) and regionally relevant public expenditure (RRPE)

Region	Billions of pounds		Index of		Index of RRPE per capita as a percentage of index of GDP per capita
	GDP in 1973	RRPE in 1973–74	GDP per capita	RRPE per capita	
North	3.3	1.7	88.2	112.0	127.0
Yorks. & Humberside	5.0	1.9	90.9	85.9	94.5
East Midlands	3.8	1.5	96.2	93.5	97.2
East Anglia	1.8	0.7	92.5	94.4	102.1
South East	22.8	8.2	115.0	104.9	91.2
South West	4.0	1.7	91.0	94.5	103.8
West Midlands	5.9	1.9	99.5	81.1	81.5
North West	7.4	3.0	95.3	98.9	103.8
England	54.2	20.6	101.7	97.7	96.1
Wales	2.7	1.4	86.3	110.9	128.5
Scotland	5.5	2.7	92.2	113.9	123.5
Great Britain	62.5	24.6	100.0	100.0	100.0

Note: what is deemed to be 'regionally relevant' is partly a matter of judgement.

Source: the estimates for GDP (at factor cost) by region are derived from Kemp-Smith and Hartley (1976; Table 1A); the estimates of regionally-relevant public expenditure are taken from the Northern Region Strategy Team (1976).

regionally relevant public expenditure are given in Table 4.2 and are presented in graphic form in Figure 4.1.

One implication of the application of parity is that public expenditure per capita is likely to be higher, relative to regional GDP, in the poorer regions than it is in the richer ones. Table 4.2 and Figure 4.1 indicate that some such relationship exists, if only roughly. (The positions in Figure 4.1 of the West Midlands and, to a lesser extent, of Yorkshire and Humberside, clearly deserve attention.) It may be suggested that the higher relative level of public expenditure in the poorer regions implies some distortion of preferences. Perhaps people in the poorer regions would prefer to receive a larger proportion of their income in the form of higher take-home pay. This would only be possible, however, if taxation could also be varied regionally. Whether, in fact, preferences are being distorted can only be a matter for speculation while government remains centralised; but there are three other conclusions that can be drawn.

First, these poorer regions are more vulnerable to *general* cuts in public expenditure (not just cuts aimed at curtailing regional-development policies) than are the richer ones. This is so because they depend rather more on such general public expenditure for personal incomes and for the local employment generated by expenditure from such incomes. How much

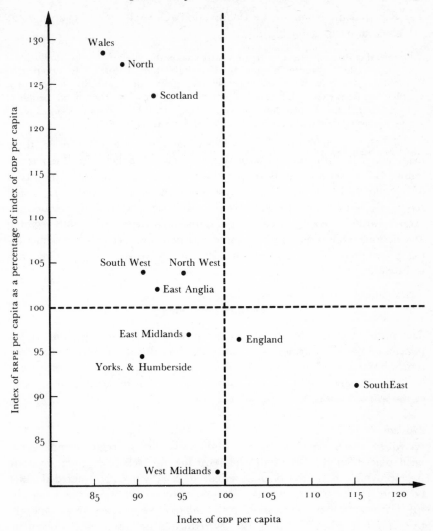

FIGURE 4.1

Gross domestic product (GDP) and regionally relevant public expenditure (RRPE) by region (based on Table 4.2)

more would involve a difficult calculation, even if the figures for public expenditure in each region were available in detail. There are large leakages in the form of imports from the rest of the country (Brown, 1972; Brown, Lind and Bowers, 1967) and regional multipliers should not be applied to gross expenditure but to net value added in the region (Wilson, 1968).

Second, as a consequence of this broader assessment, we must anticipate that a sharper and more jealous watch will be kept on regional transfers.

The Royal Commission on the Constitution (Great Britain, 1973a, p. 172) has given a warning to this effect:

> Financial autonomy in the regions will make the debate public, and the attitudes of the negotiating parties would inevitably harden. Such a development would introduce a spirit of contention and divisiveness into British politics which would weaken the unity of the country. On the other hand people may feel that more open controversy is needed in the interests of democracy and to ensure that financial justice is being done to all regions.

The third conclusion is that, when economies have to be made, these need not fall with special severity on 'regional policy' in the narrow sense of that term, that is to say, policies designed to foster industrial development. It is primarily because these industrial policies are costed separately and because the costs are published separately, that they become targets during an economy campaign. On a longer view, with both regional and national conditions in mind, there may be a stronger case for economising elsewhere, if the constitutional machinery is such as to allow this to be done.

Regional Policies

The purpose of this section is not to provide a detailed account of the policies adopted in Great Britain, since this has already been done (McCallum, chapter 1 of this volume). The aim here is rather to provide a commentary and to do so with *national* interests in mind as well as those of the assisted areas.

Migration

As we have observed, the main emphasis in British regional policy has been placed on the desirability of reducing the relatively high levels of unemployment that have been experienced, usually over protracted periods, in some regions of the country. This objective could be pursued: (a) by stimulating industrial expansion in the relatively depressed areas; and (b) by facilitating migration or at least by reducing the obstacles to movement. The movement of workers in pursuit of work has, in fact, taken place on a substantial scale in the past. Migration has, however, been too politically sensitive an issue to receive much explicit support from successive governments in Britain.

There is now some sign of a change in official attitude, as shown, for example, by the provision of subsidies to migrants (Beaumont, chapter 3 of this volume). What is needed, however, is not only (or even mainly) the provision of subsidies but also a reduction in the barriers to movement, often erected by government itself. Housing policies constitute the outstanding example. Rent controls and security of tenure in the private rental sector have contributed to the long-term decline in the supply of accommodation to let. This decline was extended to furnished accommodation by the 1974 Rent Act, and the problems of movement have thus been further aggravated instead of being eased for would-be migrants. Public-sector housing has generally replaced private renting and is particularly important in the assisted areas, and in this case housing allocation criteria and pricing policies impede mobility. Despite central-government advice, local housing authorities still tend to ascribe lower housing priority to migrants than to local residents and inter area exchange schemes are usually unimportant. The variations in local pricing policies for public renting may also imply that potential movers are faced with markedly different rents for similar houses in different parts of the country. Moreover, it is often held that the local-authority planners and architects have paid too little attention to the desirability of providing people with the kind of accommodation that they prefer. In the owner-occupied sector rising property values (especially where there are marked regional variations in inflation rates) may also hamper mobility, and conveyancing costs, Stamp Duty, etc. can act as an effective deterrent to mobility. Thus housing affords a clear case of the way in which impediments to the working of the market have contributed to regional difficulties. This is a complicated subject but it would be hard to avoid the conclusion that a freer housing market is urgently required, combined with, of course, assistance for poor families that are in genuine need.

A further area for concern relates to unemployment pay. A Soviet policy of having no unemployment pay provided as of right might have a dramatic effect on mobility and might greatly reduce unemployment that is structural in nature. In the years of labour shortage in the West Midlands and the South East, we should not then have had heavy unemployment in Clydeside or Londonderry. So draconian a policy would certainly not be acceptable in Britain, but the extent of the gap between net income when out of work and net income when in work could conceivably become too narrow. We shall return to this point. The migration of workers in order to obtain work should not only reduce unemployment in the assisted areas but increase employment elsewhere. It is necessary to state the obvious in this way because it has sometimes been foolishly implied that any additional manpower employed in the assisted areas by bringing work to these areas would otherwise remain unemployed indefinitely. Thus the whole of the rise in employment in these areas is regarded as a *net* increase. This is not so. Anyone who has ever had any practical experience in assessing the probable effect on local unemployment of the establishment of new projects is well aware that an allowance must be made for a probable decline in outward migration and even for some inward migration.

Migration alone may not suffice, however, to pull down regional unemployment to more acceptable levels, although we cannot, admittedly, be sure about the effect of reducing the obstacles to movement in ways such as those suggested above. Moreover, migration will not raise the regional participation rates, as industrial expansion can be expected to do. There is a further point: industrial advance in the assisted areas may help both nationally and regionally by raising the level and stimulating the future rate of growth of the productivity of those already at work. New factories or expansions of existing ones are, in fact, likely to draw much of their labour from other employments, and the full reduction of unemployment is brought about only after a game of musical chairs, with productivity also increasing. One of the related benefits from industrial expansion of this kind is that it should provide more scope locally for the able and well-trained people who might otherwise leave and thus add to the danger of cumulative decline.

Labour Shortages in Labour Surplus Regions
Regions with relatively high levels of unemployment have long been described as 'labour surplus' regions. This is natural enough, but it will not do to leave the matter there, for it is the case that in these areas where labour appears to be in plentiful supply, labour is often hard to obtain. Although we lack good statistical information, the complaints about labour shortages are far too strong and too persistent to allow them to be dismissed out of hand. Labour surpluses and labour shortages thus appear to exist side by side. This is another delicate issue on which governments have preferred to remain discretely silent, at least in public. To draw attention to these shortages could clearly be embarrassing when public policy aims at industrial development in these areas, primarily in order to absorb surplus manpower. The official reticence may, to this extent, be understandable, but it must also be regarded as unwise and self-defeating. If government is to persist with its interventionist regional policies, the need for a thorough investigation of regional labour markets is apparent.

   With so little definite information available, it behoves us to be careful in speculating both about the scale of this problem and about its causes, but some points can be made. It is often claimed, often without benefit of evidence, that the trouble arises because the unemployed are just as well off as if they were at work. This extravagant claim can be easily and heavily attacked. What cannot be so easily achieved is to show that unemployment pay has no significant effect on the level of structural unemployment. As might be expected, the calculations are somewhat involved. Benefits as a percentage of earned income after tax depend upon the duration of the unemployment, the number of dependents, the take-up of means-tested assistance, the expenses involved in going to work and the possibility that housing may cost more if a change of house has to be made. What may be called the effective marginal tax rate, which includes the loss of benefits, may be quite high. (Great Britain, 1978a, pp. 81–103; Great Britain, 1978b, pp. 114–20). Some examples from the estimates for November 1977 presented by Atkinson and Flemming (1978) are illuminating. About 52 per cent of the unemployed were single and for a single person earning £55 per week the replacement ratios were as follows: for 3 to 28 weeks duration, 70 per cent; for 29 to 52 weeks, 48 per cent; for 53 weeks and over, 47 per cent. For a single person with earning power of £45 per week, the corresponding ratios were 83 per cent, 59 per cent and 59 per cent. For a married man with a wife and two young children earning £55 per week, the replacement ratios would have been: for 3–28 weeks, 101 per cent; for 29–52 weeks, 84 per cent; for 53 weeks and over, 83 per cent. Or, with earning power at £45 per week the average the ratios were: 97 per cent 88 per cent and 87 per cent. (This family type represented 13 per cent of the unemployed.) The detailed estimates presented by the authors show that it was necessary to go down to about £25 per week or to consider bigger families before a large proportion were better off unemployed. This, however, is the wrong test. The real test is whether the prospective *net gain* from working provides so strong an incentive that there is no likelihood of any significant prolongation of the period of job search. In attempting to make such an assessment it is necessary to recall that the means-tested benefits included in the calculations quoted above, are not fully taken up. It is also necessary to observe that these calculations make no allowance for tax rebates and for redundancy payments, and the allowance made for the cost of going to work is only £3 per week.

We can dismiss the complaint that the bulk of the unemployed are better off out of work, although it should be a matter of concern that some should be so—and these not only people with very low earning capacities. We may also regard with some scepticism the view that a substantial proportion are content to remain indefinitely out of work on rather lower incomes. What we cannot dismiss is the possibility that the period of job search is extended because the net gain from working, though usually positive, may be small. Furthermore, in assessing the effect on regional unemployment, allowance must be made for the fact that the earnings available from the jobs on offer in a particular area may well be below the national average. Even if the unemployed move to other areas, they may often lack the skills and experience necessary to obtain employment at the national average. Moreover if getting a job means changing house, then higher rents may well have to be paid—perhaps very much higher when the unemployed family is in rent-restricted privately owned accommodation. The statistical analysis from which the quotations have been derived, illuminating though it is, does not take account of complications of this kind. Unfortunately, there is not even an official regional breakdown of payment for the earnings-related supplement. Indeed, these problems of structural adjustment and mobility have often been completely neglected in studies of the effects of social benefits. It is also worth mentioning that the replacement ratios have already fallen in recent years because, under the Labour Government's legislation, short-term benefits (which include payments to the unemployed) are indexed for rising prices but not for rising wages (as are pensions). As real wages rise in the future, the process will continue. This does not, of course, remove the need for certain reforms in the system or for attempting to raise the earning power of the unemployed by extended training schemes. Nor does it remove the need to reform our housing policy.

There are, of course, other possible explanations of the presence of labour shortages in labour surplus areas. Lack of training, or the wrong training, is an obvious one. Of course, training must be completed 'on the job', but there is also scope for basic training and this is now more fully recognised by government. (It is not so long since we were spending about twenty times as much public money on REP as on training!) Artificial obstacles to entry into certain trades are yet another possible explanation of the paradox with which we are dealing. A drastic reform of apprenticeship arrangements is obviously long overdue in the country as a whole. Manpower is the main asset of the assisted areas, and this asset must be made as valuable as possible both by training and by the removal of artificial obstacles to its effective use. What is also important is to ease or remove some of the deterrents to the use of this asset on the demand side, that is to say, on the part of the employers.

It is generally agreed that in Great Britain as elsewhere it will be difficult to achieve a rise in GNP sufficient to reduce unemployment to a more acceptable level. The problem is made worse because some other factors, as well as rising productivity, may reduce the ratio of increased employment to increased output. The high level of the employer's social security contribution is one example and some reform might be considered here. The severity of the dismissals procedures and the liability to provide redundancy payments mean that an employer is incurring a considerable risk in making any substantial increase in the numbers he employs. As a minimum reform, the responsibility for redundancy payments might be largely transferred to the state.

Fostering Industrial Development

Both subsidies and controls have been used in order to foster the growth of industry in the assisted areas. The use of the Industrial Development Certificate (IDC) has already been discussed (McCallum, chapter 1 of this volume), and it has been suggested that its importance has diminished and may not be restored. From a national viewpoint the waning importance of this form of control may bring some advantages. The uncertainty to which its use can give rise and the delays that it can cause are scarcely desirable at a time when the encouragement of investment on a national scale is generally thought to be essential. Nor is it sensible, at a time when investment in the whole country is lagging, to try to cajole or compel firms, if they are to expand at all, to go to locations not of their choosing. The main benefit from the use of IDC control has been that firms have at least been obliged to look at different locations and may thus have become aware of possibilities that they might otherwise have neglected; it would be over-sanguine to suppose that they could have been induced to consider these possibilities with the same care if reliance had been placed solely on propaganda for the assisted areas. If those who support direct controls tend to press their case on the implicit assumption that the controllers will be exceedingly wise, unbiased and well-informed, the opponents of controls are liable, for their part, to imply that industrial management has at its immediate disposal a fund of knowledge and experience to which no useful additions can be made. A more cautious view that falls somewhere between these extremes would seem to be appropriate. It must be conceded therefore that something may be lost if IDC control continues to weaken; but on balance there could be a net gain, at least from the national point of view.

With the abolition of REP the main subsidies are capital grants, supplementary assistance with capital expenditure and the provision of government factories at subsidised rents. Is this a satisfactory package? Should we mourn the loss of REP? In 1975–76 the REP accounted for about a third of the total amount of public expenditure on regional policies. It is fair to record that this particular form of assistance was strongly supported by a number of economists, partly, it would seem, because its effects were thought to be analogous to those that might be achieved if regions had become nations and had devalued their currencies. To detect an analogy is not to establish a case. The case for REP was particularly weak because its payment was totally unconditional. The subsidy was received by firms that continued to behave precisely as they would have behaved anyway. Perhaps even REP had some very slight effect at the margin, but it is hard to believe that it exerted much influence on decision making about *new* starts or expansions requiring investment, partly because its life was to be short and, even during that short life, it was quite likely that the subsidy would be absorbed in additional labour costs. It is true that REP may have helped existing firms to keep going; but this kind of subsidisation was scarcely likely to foster the dynamic industrial policy that Great Britain is believed to require. It can, of course, be argued that such a dynamic policy is not likely to make much headway when the country as a whole is depressed and investment is stagnant. REP may be a more defensible form of expenditure if the alternative is to spend a comparable additional amount on unemployment pay. In other words, the timing of REP's abolition was not ideal from this point of view, but if a longer view is taken, there is little need to mourn its demise.

There is a different kind of labour subsidy for which a somewhat better case can be made. This is temporary financial assistance during a limited period of, say, two to three years when a newly established factory is coping with the problems of settling down in a new environment. The Canadians used a subsidy of this kind for a time and a similar subsidy was introduced in the Special Development Areas of Great Britain in 1967 but was subsequently withdrawn. (In Northern Ireland assistance of this kind can still be obtained as part of a variable package.) This form of subsidy would not be viewed with favour by the European Community, but the case against it is surely weaker than that against a general unconditional subsidy such as REP; it would be associated with new developments, its period would be limited and its purpose would be to assist in achieving self-sustaining growth.

Capital grants are superior to REP in that changes in a region's industrial capital have to be made before the grants are paid. It is true that some of these changes would no doubt take place anyway, without official assistance, and to this extent the capital grants are also intra-marginal. But the grants are conditional upon change in the sense that investment must take place and can thus exert some marginal effect. One of the objections that has been directed against capital grants is that it is wrong to subsidise capital in labour surplus areas. Better, it is said, to subsidise labour! This is, however, a somewhat odd argument; if labour is in surplus supply and the market is allowed to operate, then labour should already be relatively cheap, but not the capital needed to complement it in production. The argument rests therefore on a (usually implicit) recognition of the fact that regional difficulties are partly caused by national collective bargaining. Even if market forces are thus impeded and labour is not relatively cheap, or only slightly so, it still remains true that investment is required for structural change and improved efficiency. Once again it is a case of subsidising change rather than preserving the *status quo*.

A different objection is that investment grants, unless given with some regard to their probable effect on employment, may subsidise projects that are excessively capital intensive. It may not be unfair to say that this particular objection is likely to weigh too heavily with economists because we have been accustomed by our training to devote so much attention to factor combinations under static conditions! Under dynamic conditions the case looks less strong. Nor can it safely be taken for granted that a marked bias towards the capital intensive has always manifested itself (Chisholm, 1970). The need to prevent such a bias was, however, one of the considerations advanced in defence of REP, which provided an offsetting subsidy to reduce the cost of labour. This was not a wholly reassuring case. If one subsidy is needed in order to offset the ill-effects of another, the implications for public expenditure become somewhat discouraging.

Grants towards the cost of investment can be made in a somewhat more selective way than was the case with regard to the Labour Government's grants introduced in 1966 or the Conservative Government's grants introduced in 1972 (McCallum, chapter 1 of this volume). Under the old Local Employment Acts the second tier of capital assistance was directly related to the increase in employment that could be anticipated. This fact was generally recognised, but it may not always have been understood that even the first tier was not given quite automatically. Some regard was paid to the probable cost per job and thus some check could be imposed in extreme cases, though it was not thought necessary to adopt a rigid formula. Supplementary assistance is still provided on a more generous scale where there is a prospect of increased employment. Would it be sensible to extend this degree of selectivity to the basic investment grants as well? The main objection is that this would greatly complicate their administration and draw out once more the period of negotiation and investigation now greatly reduced from the 18–24 months of the mid-1960s. This is an important point. It is an error to think exclusively about factor endowments and the like and too little about the importance of ensuring that a policy can be implemented easily and quickly. A compromise is, however, possible. Grants could be left conditional only upon investment being undertaken, except in those cases where some specified sum was exceeded over the period of a year or (as a further safeguard) unless they exceeded some specified cumulative amount over a period of, say, three years. Thus only the large projects would need to be investigated and subjected to the employment test or whatever other test was thought to be appropriate. This relatively simple change would have the merit of guarding against any really serious cases of possible oversubsidisation of capital-intensive projects, should these, in fact, be likely to occur.

Apart from any danger of oversubsidising grossly capital-intensive projects, it is necessary to consider the conditions that should be satisfied before a project is deemed to be eligible for assistance. Two questions must then be distinguished: (a) is it right to say that large grants should be confined, as far as practicable, to expenditure that is expected to provide additional employment, or should some other criterion be applied? and (b) should assistance be provided only to incoming firms, not to those already in the assisted areas? It does not follow in principle that an affirmative answer to the first question implies also an affirmative answer to the second. It must be acknowledged, however, that the infant-industry argument applies more strongly in the case of incoming firms unfamiliar with the environment. The Regional Development Grants are, in fact, available to indigenous firms as well as to newcomers, although this was not the case initially and was never the case with the Local Employment Acts. This was the wrong way round! If tests are to be applied, the case for doing so is stronger with regard to indigenous industry. At the present time both the basic grants and discretionary assistance may be obtained by indigenous industry, and this may be all the more important if, in the future, the supply of mobile immigrant industry to a region should prove to be much less than in the past. There is no denying the fact, however, that it is more difficult to present a case, apart from a political one, for assistance to indigenous firms where the infant-industry argument often applies with much less force than it does to newcomers. The case might then have to rest upon there being a scheme for structural change in an indigenous firm so large as to put it, in effect, in an infant-in-dustry position.

Further difficulties are encountered if other criteria, as well as additional employment, are thought to be appropriate. On the face of it, it may seem reasonable enough to say that assistance should be given not only for investment that will create new jobs but for investment that will raise efficiency by assisting with the introduction of new projects or new processes, even if employment is not increased. The introduction of such an additional criterion is bound to impose a severe test on the judgement of those respon-sible for providing the assistance—and a real understanding of the problems of a particular firm and of the industry to which it belongs is not something that can be adequately acquired by reading a few committee papers and talking for an hour or two to some managers!

Firms rarely confine themselves to replacing what is worn out. Replace-ment and modernisation go together and cannot be easily separated. A crude, complicated and incomplete solution might be to deduct the value of any grants provided from the amounts that could subsequently be deducted from tax liability as depreciation. This was, in fact, British practice for many years. The disadvantage was that in order to assess the true value of a grant, as distinct from its nominal value, an involved calculation was required and the appeal of the inducement was liable to be correspond-ingly blurred. It also meant that the cost of regional grants as presented to Parliament was overstated because no deduction was ever made for the subsequent cut in tax allowances. On these grounds the procedure could be legitimately criticised (Wilson, 1964; Northern Ireland, 1965; 1970). The grants were made 'tax-free' in 1972, presumably in order to bring British practice into line with European Community practice. If this change had not been made, less would in fact have been offered in Britain than would have been permissible under the Community rules, which relate to grants that are net rather than gross of tax. There is, however, a further point. The Commission for its part has taken the line that the grants should be so administered as not to provide assistance for mere replacement (MacLennan, chapter 12 of this volume). Whether, in fact, this principle is always observed in practice in the other countries of the Community is not clear. Faced with these difficulties, the best compromise would still appear to be the exercise of discretion with regard to the 'tax-free' grants that are provided for projects above some specified size, as suggested above.

What has been proposed would afford scope for more selectivity but not, some may feel, as much as is required. Moreover, some firms may require advice about how to raise finance and, if they are small, help with some of the problems of management, in particular with marketing. This is an argument for special development agencies. Agencies of this kind might follow a much more selective approach and this approach could be adopted not only within the assisted areas but also, in appropriate cases, in other regions of the country. Thus the awkward question of increasing still more the extent of the assisted areas, which already account for over two-fifths of the population, might be evaded. Here we are touching upon a problem of great difficulty from both an economic and a political point of view. The main criterion for the choice of assisted areas has hitherto been relatively heavy unemployment; but unemployment has increased since the mid-1970s in the nation as a whole and is as heavy in some parts of what were formerly prosperous regions as it is in parts of the assisted areas. Nor is it only a question of unemployment, for some areas, in particular the West Midlands, have had a poor deal from the Exchequer as compared with others such as Wales, Scotland and the North; see Table 4.2 and Figure 4.1.

What then is to be done? One possibility would be to extend the scope of the assisted areas even if this meant that these areas then contained the larger part of the nation's population. The resulting situation would no doubt appear to be absurd to Westminster and the electorate and also to the European Community. Indeed the best that could be said for it would be that it amounted to an explicit recognition of the fact that the South East and some smaller districts here and there in other parts of Britain are carrying a very heavy share of the nation's burdens. Second, the total population of the assisted areas might not be allowed to increase but some new areas might be designated as others were withdrawn. This might make a good deal of sense. Third, it might be held that those parts of the West Midlands now struck so severely with industrial recession have a stronger recuperative power than large parts of the existing assisted areas. When cyclical expansion again takes place, the versatility and experience of their workforces and their range of adaptable and enterprising firms in supporting industries, especially in engineering, will allow them to achieve with reasonable speed and ease the structural adaptation that is required. Meanwhile, can their needs best be met by selective assistance under the Industry Act of 1972?

Although this third possibility seems attractive, there are difficulties. Once again, administrative delays could become a problem, and would indeed be a serious one if any attempt were to be made to canalise the bulk of assistance through development agencies. The assistance provided by them should not generally be regarded as a substitute for grants but rather as complementary to them. There is the further problem that the value of the assistance provided by agencies may be more difficult to assess as, for example, in those cases where some share of capital is acquired. This is relevant, not only from the point of view of the European Community, but also from that of the firms themselves, because it will not be possible to assess in advance the amount of help that they are likely to receive. Questions of equity may also arise: with an agency responsible for selectivity burdened by a multiplicity of cases and obliged to rely, in each case, upon its judgement with regard to a variety of issues, there is an obvious danger that like will not be treated alike. There is yet another basic question. Where does responsibility for a project ultimately rest when an agency is actively involved? To what extent does it rest with the agency or with management? Is there a danger that management will be cajoled or bribed into acting against its better judgement? There is also a somewhat obvious danger that, under political pressure, lame ducks will get assistance on an unwarranted scale from public funds. Although the Industry Act of 1972 lays much stress on efficiency (Cameron, chapter 14 of this volume), it cannot be assumed, unfortunately, that this admirable precept will always be observed. The 'vote' motive can lead to great inefficiency and to great unfairness and is not, to say the least, obviously superior to the profit motive.

The folly of extending extravagant financial help to unsuccessful firms and industries has been stressed on some occasions by commentators in the assisted areas themselves. This was one of the central themes of the Toothill Report (Scottish Council, 1962). The emphasis in that report was placed on measures necessary to facilitate a breakthrough to self-sustaining growth. This can still be regarded as good sense. It can also be regarded, perhaps, as politically naive. For the temptation to help the lame ducks in the assisted areas has been too strong and the tougher policy, however sensible in the long run, has always been represented as inapplicable in particular cases. What was not perhaps anticipated by those in the assisted areas who favoured measures to prop up the inefficient was that similar measures might one day be extended well outside these areas, with a corresponding claim on limited public funds and with harmful implications over the longer run for the national economy and the assisted areas themselves. The car industry is the outstanding example. It would be politically difficult, perhaps impossible, to pour subsidies into Chrysler's loss-making plant in Scotland without also pouring the taxpayer's money into British Leyland plants in the Midlands.

Even if the subsidisation of the incompetent were to be avoided, selectivity would still pose delicate problems. Selectivity is needed if subsidies are to be made as effective as possible, but selectivity must not involve so much investigation, interference and control as to undermine managerial responsibility. A compromise between these conflicting considerations is needed. On balance, one may feel some doubt about the wisdom of placing heavy reliance upon development agencies as the means of achieving selectivity, for the penalty could well be a fudging of managerial responsibility. Responsibility may also be fudged within the official administration itself. The respective roles of the development agency and the government department, or departments, responsible for industry may become confused, with some waste of effort and even some conflict. (There is reason to believe that difficulties of this kind were experienced at one time in Northern Ireland.) Such difficulties might well become serious with legislative devolution in Great Britain. For a single region, there might then be: first, the central legislature and executive at Westminster with responsibility for industry; second, a regional legislature and executive with at least some responsibility and a keen thirst for more; and third, a development agency or perhaps more than one agency.

There is, however, a case for agencies specifically designed to assist small firms to cope with some of the problems that beset them. (The Local Employment Development Unit in Northern Ireland is a good example.) A body of this kind can help with loans or even with equity finance. But its most important role may often be to assist with obtaining advice about marketing, about technical developments in production and so on. It may also seek to ensure that small firms are fully informed about the other sources of financial assistance that are available, both public and private.

Lower taxation

It is now necessary to say a word about a different means of affording assistance: lower taxation. This was the method favoured by the Conservative Government when accelerated depreciation was introduced as a partial substitute for grants in 1971. When accelerated depreciation was extended to the whole of the nation, this particular form of regional assistance lost its edge. The question now is whether corporation tax could be levied at a reduced rate in the assisted areas, as recommended in the past by the Confederation of British Industry in Scotland. Alternatively, there might be a tax holiday for some specified number of years. Such a scheme would be selective, at least to the extent that it increased the net reward for success and left the successful with more funds for further development. The first problem is administrative. In the case of multi-plant firms, is it possible to assign particular proportions of profits to particular areas? Will the scope for tax evasion not be temptingly wide? A possible solution has been suggested by MacKay (1973): profits should be divided among regions in proportion to the labour force employed in the plants located in the respective regions. This, of course, would be a somewhat rough and ready procedure but it could make some sense. It would also have the effect of providing an incentive to embark upon labour-intensive projects in the assisted areas. In newly established plants there might well be no profits for two or three years. If, however, these plants were part of a multi-plant concern, the tax allowance could be set against profits earned elsewhere. A scheme of this kind would not, however, be as attractive to foreign firms with no initial profits in sterling and no anticipation of significant profits for some time. Special grants could, however, be provided in such cases; or they could be given special sterling loans initially in order to reduce the need to bring currency through the exchanges. New firms would also receive no initial assistance from a lower tax rate or a tax rebate and, once more, a special supplementary arrangement would be needed. There is the more general objection that the effectiveness of a reduced rate of corporation tax depends upon profits being sufficiently healthy for a tax remission to be significant; and this condition, as we well know, may not be met. Even if this difficulty does not arise, it remains necessary to ask whether the lower tax rate would have as much effect as a grant on decisions taken at the margin. There is little evidence on this point. Finally, a tax concession of this kind would run counter to European Community policy.

There would not, however, be any Community objection to a lower rate of personal income tax in some regions of the country.[4] If a Scottish Assembly were to be given taxing power, this power could best relate to personal income tax, and it should be possible to use this power to lower the rate, not just to increase it (Firn and Maclennan, chapter 13 of this volume). The implication would be that public expenditure would be correspondingly lower, but it would be reduced from a position where it was high relative to GDP. Some of the lower earners might thus be no longer liable to income tax. Moreover, the rates of tax on high incomes could be reduced and this could be done with little cost to a Scottish government. Such a reduction in the burden of personal taxation might help to keep more able people within Scotland and to tempt able people from outside. And Scotland needs human capital as well as material capital. Whether anything of the kind is ever likely to happen in practice is, of course, another matter! There is the obvious danger that an Assembly would impose a surcharge rather than choose a rate of tax below the national level (Wilson, 1976).

Regional Planning
So far we have been concerned with the means by which work may be brought to the workers or the workers themselves allowed to move to places, within the same region or outside it, where suitable work is more likely to be obtained. As we have seen, a variety of measures may be adopted and, as we have also observed, these measures may well need to be complemented by other measures designed to improve the regional infrastructure. The next step, and it is a rather obvious one, is to bring all these measures together in the form of regional plans. It is necessary, however, to examine what is meant by the term 'plan'. Planning of any

kind requires forecasts but it is more than forecasting. It implies acts of will of a kind appropriate for government to make and possible for government to enforce. Confusion between forecasting and planning is, unfortunately, a common feature of the whole debate. What then is the proper scope for regional planning?

It is appropriate to plan the activities of the many agencies of government itself, not only in order to assess the commitment to future public expenditure but also to ensure that these plans are reasonably consistent in purpose, in amount and in timing. Thus plans for housing, water, sewers, roads, etc. need to be related to each other and to the best assessments that can be made of industrial needs. In principle, this may seem little more than a platitude. In practice, much difficult work is involved in preparing such plans, in ensuring their acceptance and, above all, in monitoring their implementation. All this calls for close interdepartmental cooperation and that is not always easy to achieve. Such planning is quite possible without legislative devolution, and it cannot be taken for granted that plans of this kind will naturally emerge even when there is legislative devolution. With or without devolution, cooperation is needed between government departments and local authorities. Thus detailed urban plans may obviously be required within the wider framework of a regional plan. In some respects the planning of public expenditure appears to have improved over the past decade or so, and might have improved still more had the whole exercise not been so much confused by inflation.

In the mid-1960s it was fashionable to suppose that plans, both national and regional, should contain estimates of GDP for some years ahead and should also contain estimates of the main components of expenditure: private consumption, public consumption, investment, etc. The Northern Ireland plan for 1965–70 (Northern Ireland, 1965) did not contain such estimates and was somewhat criticised for this reason. It is necessary, however, to bear in mind that when the Northern Ireland plan was prepared, no national plan was in existence, and it would have been somewhat meaningless to prepare such a plan for one region *in vacuo*. This was also the case when the Northern Ireland plan for 1970–75 (Northern Ireland, 1970) was being prepared. Perhaps not much was lost, since we may well feel some doubt about the value of such planning or, more accurately, such forecasting. Thus the plan for the Scottish economy for 1965–70 (Great Britain, 1966) was prepared with reference to the National Plan of 1965 (Great Britain, 1965); both sank without trace almost as soon as they were published. Forecasts of GDP can obviously be very helpful (provided they are not absurdly unrealistic) in planning total national public expenditure. But the resources available for public expenditure in a single region viewed in isolation do not depend upon the future growth of GDP in that region. To this extent there is less practical need to perform the forecasting exercise for GDP and its constituents at the regional level.

The quantified programmes discussed so far have related to public expenditure only, set against the background of forecasts of GDP. But much more ambitious suggestions for planning were popular in the mid-1960s. Not only should public expenditure be programmed in this way, but there should be programmes or targets for all the main industries. In the event, the experiments with indicative industrial planning at the national level were not to prove particularly successful and, at the regional level, little was done. Even in France, industrial indicative planning was not translated into detailed industrial plans for the various regions (Allen and MacLennan, 1971).

Detailed industrial plans are one thing. The forecasting of broad trends in sectoral shares is another. In looking towards the future, one of the most important questions is the probable demand for additional labour in manufacturing industry. This is so from a national viewpoint and also from a regional one. The emphasis in regional policies has been placed most heavily on manufacturing industry and, within that total, on mobile manufacturing industry. If there were to be little demand for additional manufacturing labour this would have important consequences for locational policy. We are touching here on such matters as forecasts of the probable rate of growth of GNP, the income elasticity of demand for manufacturing output and the rate of growth of productivity in manufacturing. It would be foolish to resign ourselves too easily to the acceptance of pessimistic forecasts and it would be well to recall how dangerous it is to extrapolate from a phase of the trade cycle. The fate of the Keynes–Hansen prophesy of stagnation should not be forgotten! Moreover, we must allow for the demand for exports of manufactures with rising world output, not just for domestic demand. These warnings are in order; but it would nevertheless be prudent to assess the probable consequences of a gradual but sustained shift in expenditure away from manufactured output. This leads us to an exceedingly important topic which can only be mentioned in passing here: the need for much more work on that miscellaneous group of activities referred to as the service industries.

Conclusions

We have distinguished above between regional assistance in the comprehensive sense and regional assistance in the narrower sense of assistance with regional economic development. According to the MacDougall Report (European Communities, 1977), the interregional transfers made for a wide variety of reasons by the United Kingdom in the early 1970s reduced by about one-third the differences among regional per capita incomes. Massive regional transfers thus take place anyway and will continue to do so. This is the context in which regional-development policies must be judged. These measures account not only for a modest part of total interregional transfers but have the further characteristic of being designed to reduce differences in income per capita by making the less prosperous regions more efficient. If greater geographical equality is to be sought, it is surely better to do so in this way than by simply providing transfer benefits in cash and kind that may bring disposable per capita incomes closer together with little or no effect on the underlying factor incomes. When regional-development policies are seen in context in this light, the positive case in their favour becomes a good deal more convincing from a national as well as a local point of view. But the strength of the case still depends crucially upon the choice of measures adopted and upon the manner in which policies are applied in practice.

Notes

1. It was a Labour Government that was in power in 1947. In 1977 it was again a Labour Government that cut down regional policy by removing REP, itself the child of a previous Labour Government. There is no reason, however, to suppose that its demise caused much grief among the leaders of the Conservative Party! We shall consider this element of instability further, in the course of the chapter.

2. A striking example of the neglect of potentialities and an exclusive concentration on need was afforded by Canadian regional policy in the early 1960s. An area could be designated for assistance only if it had had a sustained record of failure over a prolonged period of years with regard both to unemployment and production. As a consequence, even St. John's, Newfoundland, was deemed to be ineligible and, for a still longer period, even Halifax, Nova Scotia, was excluded. This was a recipe for failure. A quite different policy was subsequently adopted.

3. Officially built advance factories also involve a gamble on the part of government, though it may be one that has not often involved much loss.

4. This power was accorded to the Government of Northern Ireland by the Government of Ireland Act, 1920. The power was never used.

References

Allen, K. J. and MacLennan, M. C. (1971) *Regional Policies in Italy and France*. London: Allen and Unwin.
Atkinson, A. B. and Flemming, J. S. (1978) 'Unemployment, Social Security and Incentives', *Midland Bank Review*, Autumn, pp. 6–16.
Brown, A. J. (1972) *The Framework of Regional Economics in the United Kingdom*. Cambridge: Cambridge University Press.
Brown, A. J., Lind, H. and Bowers, J. (1967) 'The "Green Paper" on the Development Areas', *National Institute Economic Review*, No. 40, pp. 26–33.
Chisholm, M. (1970) 'On the Making of a Myth? How Capital Intensive is Industry Investing in the Developing Areas?', *Urban Studies*, Vol. 7, pp. 289–93.
European Communities (1977) Commission. 'Report of the Study Group on the Role of Public Finance in European Integration', Brussels.

Finer, S. E. (ed.) (1975) *Adversary Politics and Electoral Reform*. London: Wigram.
Great Britain (1963) National Economic Development Council. *Conditions Favourable to Faster Growth*. London: HMSO.
Great Britain (1965) Department of Economic Affairs. *The National Plan*. Cmnd. 2764. London: HMSO.
Great Britain (1966) Scottish Office. *The Scottish Economy 1965 to 1970: A Plan for Expansion*. Cmnd. 2864. Edinburgh: HMSO.
Great Britain (1967a) Department of Economic Affairs. *The Development Areas. A Proposal for a Regional Employment Premium*. London: HMSO.
Great Britain (1967b) Department of Economic Affairs. *The Development Areas. Regional Employment Premium*. Cmnd. 3310. London: HMSO.
Great Britain (1973a) Royal Commission on the Constitution. *Report*. Vol. 1. Cmnd. 5460. London: HMSO.
Great Britain (1973b) House of Commons. Expenditure Committee (Trade and Industry Sub-Committee) Session 1973–74. *Regional Development Incentives: Report*. House of Commons Paper 85. London: HMSO.
Great Britain (1975) House of Commons. *Official Report*, Fifth Series. Parliamentary Debates, Vol. 901, col. 478. London: HMSO.
Great Britain (1976) The Treasury. 'The North Sea and the Balance of Payments', *Economic Progress Report*, No. 71, pp. 1–3.
Great Britain (1977) The Treasury. 'The North Sea and the UK Economy', *Economic Progress Report*, No. 89, pp. 3–5.
Great Britain (1978a) Royal Commission on the Distribution of Income and Wealth. *Lower Incomes*, Report No. 6. Cmnd. 7175. London: HMSO.
Great Britain (1978b) Department of Health and Social Security. *Social Assistance*. London: Department of Health and Social Security.
Kemp-Smith, D. and Hartley, E. (1976) 'United Kingdom Regional Accounts', *Economic Trends*, No. 277, pp. 78–90.
McCrone, G. (1969) *Regional Policy in Britain*. London: Allen and Unwin.
MacKay, D. I. (1973) *A New Approach to Regional Policy*. Poland Street Paper, No. 1. London: PEST (Progressive Tory Pressure Group).
MacKay, D. I. and Reid, G. L. (1972) 'Redundancy, Unemployment and Manpower Policy', *Economic Journal*, Vol. 82, pp. 1256–72.
MacKay, R. R. (1974) 'Evaluating the Effects of British Regional Policy—A Comment', *Economic Journal*, Vol. 84, pp. 367–72.
Moore, B. and Rhodes, J. (1973) 'Evaluating the Effects of British Regional Economic Policy', *Economic Journal*, Vol. 83, pp. 87–110.
Moore, B. and Rhodes, J. (1975) 'The Economic Exchange Implications of British Regional Policy' in J. Vaizey (ed.), *Economic Sovereignty and Regional Policy*. Dublin: Gill and Macmillan.
Northern Ireland Government (1965) *Economic Development in Northern Ireland*. Cmd. 479. Belfast: HMSO.
Northern Ireland Government (1970) *Northern Ireland Development Programme, 1970–75*. Belfast: HMSO.
Northern Region Strategy Team (1976) 'Public Expenditure in the Northern Region and Other British Regions 1969/70–1973/4', Technical Report, No. 12, Newcastle.
Oates, W. E. (1972) *Fiscal Federalism*. New York: Harcourt Brace Jovanovich.
Scottish Council (Development and Industry) (1962) *Report on the Scottish Economy*. Edinburgh: Scottish Council (Development and Industry).
Wilson, T. (1964) *Policies for Regional Development*. University of Glasgow Social and Economic Studies, Occasional Paper, No. 3. Edinburgh and London: Oliver and Boyd.
Wilson, T. (1968) 'The Regional Multiplier—A Critique', *Oxford Economic Papers*, New Series, Vol. 20, pp. 374–93.
Wilson, T. (1976) 'Devolution and Public Finance', *Three Banks Review*, No. 112, pp. 3–29.

PART II

The Changing
Economic Environment

Part I of this volume directed attention to the conventional assumptions, general strategies and economic justifications of regional policy, and past policies were analysed and discussed. From time to time, allusion was made to the changing fortunes of the national economy that was the setting for regional policy. The national economic performance in the 1970s has been disappointing, to say the least. A depreciating currency, a very high and sustained rate of price and wage inflation and high unemployment rates, in relation to the rest of the post-war period, have been characteristic of the economy since 1972. Furthermore, in the mid-1970s the rate of investment has been extremely low and the economy has tended to stagnate, with decreases in real output during certain periods. This relative decline in national economic prosperity has been accompanied by two developments that have important implications for regional policy. First, the government has attempted to improve macro-economic performance by reducing the share of national resources appropriated by the public sector. As a result, the efficacy of public expenditures, including those on regional policy, is now subject to closer economic scrutiny. Second, it is becoming increasingly apparent that many of the assumptions and erstwhile empirical regularities on which regional policy has been traditionally based are no longer valid. There is a danger that regional policy may well have become a collection of policies designed (sometimes imperfectly) in the past to deal with problems as they then were. It is entirely an open question whether such policies are appropriate for solving the regional question as it now exists.

The slow, and occasionally negative, rate of real economic expansion has had an obvious and direct effect on policies. Regional policies have been largely directed at the diversion of expanding or new plants from the non-assisted areas to the assisted areas. Clearly, in a period of low rates of investment and growth, the supply of investment projects suitable for diversion is reduced and regional-policy measures, as they presently exist, may be relatively ineffective. Poor national economic performance has an even more important, if less direct, effect on regional policies. This relates to the marked change in the regional distribution of unemployment in Great Britain and the emergence of extensive sub-regional clusters of high unemployment within previously prosperous regions. For many years, there existed a fairly well-defined pattern of high (and above-average) unemployment rates in the problem regions and low rates of unemployment in the prosperous regions. While elements of this pattern are still visible, the situation has altered. The national rate of unemployment is now at a much higher level and there has been a convergence in unemployment rates among regions. This has been brought about by increases in unemployment rates in problem regions being accompanied by much greater relative increases in unemployment rates in the prosperous regions. To some extent, at least, this may have been the result of the operation of regional policy. There has also been a general marked increase in unemployment rates in the metropolitan areas in both the problem regions and the prosperous regions. This latter change is in part due to the changing structure of metropolitan development, but again may be also due to the operation of government policies. The general effect of these changes has been a blurring of the regional problem, as traditionally defined. The former willingness of the prosperous regions to have regional policy operated to their immediate disadvantage seems to have disappeared. As a result of these changes, it may no longer be possible to sustain a strong diversionary element of regional policy, either on the grounds of interregional equity or in terms of political feasibility.

The discovery and exploitation of North Sea oil has been the single major factor conducive to national economic development in the 1970s. The exploration and exploitation activities, which have had an unequal regional impact, have undoubtedly been responsible for the redefinition of the regional problem in relation to income levels and unemployment rates. Indeed, in the 1970s onshore oil activities may have contributed as much to the improvement of the unemployment relatives in regions such as Scotland and the North as the traditional regional policies. Although the direct effects of oil development have an important bearing on regional disparities, the major effects of North Sea oil on regional development may well stem from future decisions regarding the use of revenues from North Sea oil and the extent to which these oil revenues can restore growth and relative prosperity to the national economy. Thus, whether attention is directed to the current problems in regional development in Great Britain or to the more encouraging prospects for the future, it becomes fairly obvious that the environment within which regional policy is required to operate has undergone a significant transformation within the last ten to fifteen years.

CHAPTER 5

The Changing Nature of the Regional Economic Problem since 1965

-? 133

J. N. Randall*

Introduction

It has recently been suggested that there is a need for a basic reinterpretation of Britain's regional problems (Manners, 1976) and the policies that are now appropriate (Chisholm, 1976). This chapter sets out to consider the nature of the regional economic problem in Britain in the late 1970s and the extent to which fundamental changes have occurred over the last ten years or thereabouts. The year 1965 provides a convenient starting point for a number of reasons: it coincides with the publication of the National Plan (Great Britain, 1965), which contained a clear statement of the manner in which the regional problem was viewed by the government at that time; the year 1965 also marks the start of a new and strengthened approach to tackling regional problems introduced by the 1966 Industrial Development Act; and it allows data on the main regional economic indicators to be examined over a complete ten-year period up to 1975. The term 'regional economic problem' can cover a wide range of issues. For the purpose of this paper it is taken to signify the existence of disparities in the level of economic prosperity between regions of Great Britain on a scale that is a matter of public and political concern. Defined in this way, it is clear that there has been throughout the last ten years something that can be called a regional economic problem. However, the problem will tend to be different according to the viewpoint taken. From an overall national economic perspective, for example, it is not self-evident that disparities in regional welfare constitute an economic problem, and it is necessary to identify the specific circumstances in which public intervention to bring

* Scottish Economic Planning Department, Scottish Office, Edinburgh. The views expressed are those of the author, and do not necessarily reflect the views of the Department. This chapter has benefited from the comments received from many people, too numerous to mention individually, in government (particularly in the Scottish Economic Planning Department and the Department of the Environment) and in regional-planning organisations. The author expresses his thanks to them all for their constructive advice. The responsibility for any remaining errors of fact or judgement remains, of course, with the author.

about a more even distribution is justified. To the resident or politician
in an individual region with below-average income and above-average
unemployment, however, the regional problem will be immediately recognis-
able, and it will be possible to point to particular economic issues that
are of concern to that region. The same will also be true, of course,
in the case of regions such as East Anglia or the South East with below-average unemployment, but their regional economic problems are not discussed
in any depth here.

The notion of a regional economic problem is thus both complex and
elusive, and the fundamental distinction between the problem as seen at
the national level and from the viewpoint of a problem region runs through
the remainder of this chapter. It follows that the nature of the regional
problem, and the extent to which this has changed since 1965, is also
capable of more than one interpretation. In addition, there is the choice
between examining the symptoms of a regional economic problem at a
fairly superficial level or attempting to evaluate the more basic causes
and processes at work. In the sections below an attempt is made to look
at the way in which three elements of this multi-sided problem seem
to have changed since 1965: changes in the underlying national context
and circumstances within which the regional problem is set; changes in
the relative economic standing and performance of regions on a number
of conventional indicators of the regional economic problem between 1965
and 1975; and changes that have occurred in the diagnosis of the regional
problem since 1965, due to changes either in the fundamental nature
of the regional economic problem over this period, or in the way in which
the same problem is interpreted. In the final section the strands are drawn
together and an assessment offered of the nature of the regional economic
problem facing Britain in the late 1970s.

Changes in the National Context

The underlying assumptions that influenced the way in which the regional
problem was generally viewed in the mid-1960s can be illustrated by reference to the National Plan (Great Britain, 1965). Because it made these
assumptions explicit, it is easier than in most documents of the period
to identify where subsequent trends departed from them; in drawing attention to these differences the purpose is not to criticise the National Plan
per se, but simply to show how the assumptions and expectations fairly
generally held at this time (Beckerman and Associates, 1965) measure
up to subsequent changes. In the mid-1960s the existence of regional disparities in unemployment rates and activity rates was regarded as a problem
likely to hinder the achievement of faster national economic growth. The
contribution that regional-policy measures could make to national economic
objectives through bringing unused labour resources into production had

received official emphasis in 1963 (Great Britain, 1963) and this approach was supported in the National Plan. It was also argued that a more even spread of employment throughout the country would help to avoid regional pockets of excess demand that would tend to drive up costs and prices. The background was an expected slowing down in the rate of growth of the working population in the Plan period (1964–70), and a projected manpower shortage of some 400,000 by 1970 compared with estimates of the demand for labour at that date. In this situation vigorous action to mobilise the labour reserves in the less prosperous regions and to reduce labour market pressures in the low-unemployment regions was thought essential, and the Plan concluded that regional-policy measures to reduce unemployment rates and raise activity rates in the less prosperous regions towards the national average could bring an additional 150–250,000 people into production by 1970. Even with strengthened policies, therefore, the prospect was one of tight labour markets and a manpower shortage.

It is instructive to compare the assumptions and projections that under-pinned the official approach to the regional problem in the mid-1960s with the actual experience of the succeeding years. For example, the National Plan was geared to a target increase of 25 per cent in the Gross National Product (GNP) of the United Kingdom between 1964 and 1970 (an average growth rate of 3.8 per cent per annum), with particularly rapid rates of growth planned for investment (+38 per cent in 1964–70) and exports (+36 per cent). In fact the increase in GNP achieved between 1964 and 1970 was approximately 14 per cent, only a little over half the projected figure, and while the objectives for exports (which increased by 37 per cent in value, slightly more than planned) and the balance of payments were largely achieved through devaluation and the financial 'squeeze' of the late 1960s, the other categories of expenditure fell well short of the target (Great Britain, 1974a). For example, investment increased by only about 23 per cent over the period, and personal consumption (which had been projected to grow by 21 per cent) by only 11 per cent. Moreover, it is worth emphasising that the national economic performance since 1965 has been unsatisfactory not only in relation to the targets of the National Plan, but also compared with almost all other Western European countries. Relatively slow economic growth was associated with a gently falling trend in the long-run demand for labour. Instead of a projected growth in employment of 3.1 per cent between 1964 and 1970, a fall of −1.5 per cent was recorded in the number of employees in employment. While the number of employees in employment in the United Kingdom increased between 1970 and 1974, this was insufficient to offset the earlier losses, and over the whole period 1964–74 a slight fall of under 1 per cent was recorded (Great Britain, 1975). Apart from peak years of the economic cycle (e.g., 1973–74), labour markets have been much slacker than expected and national unemployment has shown a secular increase (under 2 per cent for most of the first half of the 1960s, between 2 and 3 per cent for most of the second half of the decade and well over 3 per cent for most of the 1970s to date).

Turning to the industrial structure of employment, the rate of change appears to have been less favourable than expected in each of the primary, manufacturing, construction and service sectors. More rapid declines than projected took place between 1964 and 1970 particularly in the Agriculture, Mining, Shipbuilding, and Clothing Orders, less rapid increases than projected in the Engineering and Paper Orders, while in the case of Metal Manufacture, Timber, Construction, Public Utilities, Distribution, and Miscellaneous Services Orders a decline occurred instead of a projected increase. On the other hand, employment change was more favourable than expected in the Food, Chemicals, Vehicles, Leather, Transport, Insurance, Professional services and Public Administration Orders, particularly the latter three. Over the period 1964–74, the manufacturing sector declined by 7 per cent, the largest absolute losses occurring in the following Orders: Textiles ($-180,000$), Metal manufacture ($-133,000$), Mechanical engineering ($-99,000$), Clothing ($-87,000$) and Vehicles ($-71,000$). Some of these industries (e.g., Vehicles, Clothing) were not disproportionately located in the assisted Areas. While the service sector increased over the period by over 11 per cent, much of the more recent rise comprised an increase in the number of part-time females and it has been argued that the period of most rapid employment growth in services is over, now that this sector, like the rest of the economy, has become heavily influenced by the forces of technology and organisational change, bringing about major improvements in labour productivity (Harris, 1976).

There are several implications from this unsatisfactory economic performance for the nature of the regional problem. First, the low rate of economic growth means that industrial establishments have had less incentive to expand, have been faced less frequently with capacity constraints (particularly in terms of labour) and are therefore less likely to have been forced to consider movement. When firms have needed to move, the increased availability of labour throughout the economy has reduced the relative advantage offered by the assisted areas. Employment generated by interregional and overseas moves to assisted areas, which was comparatively high between 1960 and 1965, has fallen in the succeeding five years and again more steeply in the first half of the 1970s. Second, the fairly wide range of industries in which employment decline has occurred (and the fact that some of them were not concentrated in assisted areas) has meant that structural problems have been experienced by a rather larger number of regions than in the past. Third, higher rates of unemployment nationally and in the non-assisted areas appear to have weakened one of the main economic justifications for regional policy advanced in the mid-1960s (since the national resource gain from additional jobs in the assisted areas is probably smaller now that there is less than full employment), while at the same time tending to reinforce the misgivings of those resident in the non-assisted areas. Fourth, the growing recognition of the magnitude of the national economic problem, marked by the emphasis now placed by the Government on a national industrial strategy, must place the regional problem in a different (although not necessarily less important) setting. A final implication of the unsatisfactory economic performance is the need to restrain public expenditure in support of the national strategy, and this could have important consequences for many regions, not only through the specific effect on regional-policy expenditure but more widely.

A number of other important changes have taken place in the national context within which the regional problem must be assessed. National and international rates of price inflation have been far higher in the period since 1970 than at any time for decades, despite the rise in unemployment. The cause of high rates of inflation is the subject of considerable debate and controversy, but it is clear that the emphasis placed in the 1960s on the regional problem as a contributory factor to national inflation is out of balance when seen against the high rates of recent years. A further important change has been the major downward revisions made to national population projections by the Registrar General in the last ten years (Chisholm, 1976; Manners, 1976). In contrast to projections prepared at the time of the National Plan when a population of over 60 million was estimated for Great Britain in 1981 (an increase of over 7 million compared with 1964), the official 1974-based projection suggests a population of only 54.7 million (within a range from 54.3 to 55.4 million) at this date (Great Britain, 1976a). In the longer term, total population now seems likely to increase only very slowly, if at all.

Again there are implications for the manner in which the regional problem is viewed. The emphasis placed in the latter half of the 1960s on identifying areas suitable for large-scale development (Humberside, Severnside, Tayside, etc.) now appears misplaced. Similarly, the lower population projection has been an important factor leading to a re-examination of the feasible rate of growth in several New Towns (and to the abandonment of plans for Stonehouse New Town). On the other hand, the prospect of little or no population growth nationally brings with it (for the first time in many years) the likelihood of significant declines in the population of some regions, and increases the danger that current migration patterns could involve resource losses through the need to provide additional infrastructure (particularly housing) in the growing regions when equivalent facilities are underutilised in other regions. The validity of this argument depends on a number of factors, such as the quality of infrastructure in the regions of population decline, and the extent to which resource losses result mainly from intraregional rather than interregional flows of population.

The emergence of and greater attention to urban economic problems in the last few years is an important development (Hughes, chapter 8 of this volume). Between 1961 and 1971 employment in all seven of the Census conurbations in Great Britain declined significantly (from −2.0 per cent in the case of the West Midlands to −9.0 per cent in the case of Greater London) compared with a growth of 7.9 per cent in the rest of Great Britain (Corkindale, 1976), and the rate of population and employ-ment decline of the inner parts of the conurbations has been exceptionally rapid. In most conurbations concern has switched from one of providing sufficient opportunities for population and industrial movement from the congested cities to overspill locations such as New Towns in the region (see, for example, Great Britain, 1969) to one of alarm at the rate of urban decline and the possibly unfavourable effects that the new centres may have on the core cities. In assisted areas, urban problems tend to be superimposed on existing regional problems, but in London or Birming-ham the measures needed to deal with urban problems may conflict with those designed to help the regional problem.

The political context of the regional problem has also changed since 1965. The British entry into the European Community in 1973 has served to place the scale and nature of Great Britain's regional problem in a wider perspective. For example, the South East with the highest Gross Domestic Product (GDP) per capita in the United Kingdom (16 per cent above average) ranked only 17th on this indicator in 1970 out of 49 European regions studied (Great Britain, 1976d), although differences in purchasing power also need to be taken into account. Furthermore, the gradual reduction of tariff barriers among the countries of the European Community will influence the location of new investment and the relative competitiveness of existing firms. On the one hand, British industry is faced with stronger competition, and new investment may increasingly tend to favour locations near to the centre of the European market rather than more peripheral regions such as Scotland. On the other hand, entry into the European Community opens up a wider potential market for British industry and may make British locations more attractive than in the past for overseas investment (which has been particularly important in Scotland), while the European Community's own measures of assistance to help regional problems (notably the European Regional Development Fund) offer a supplementary source of finance (MacLennan, chapter 12 of this volume). Within Great Britain, steps to increase the administrative or legislative devolution of powers to Scotland and Wales represent another important change in the political context of the regional problem. The administrative powers of the Scottish and Welsh Offices over industry were strengthened in 1975 by their taking over responsibility for selective financial assistance under Section 7 of the 1972 Industry Act and by the setting up of the Scottish and Welsh Development Agencies. Control by a Scottish Assembly over the allocation of substantial public expenditure in Scotland as well as over the Scottish Development Agency would mark a further move in the direction of more local control to deal with regional problems, although within the framework of continuing macro-economic planning for the nation as a whole (Firn and Maclennan, chapter 13 of this volume).

Changes in the Indicators of the Regional Problem

The absence or limitations of data on many of the most important indicators of regional economic performance in Great Britain is well known, although there have been some notable improvements in recent years. One useful indicator of economic performance is the GDP per capita in each region, and a series of estimates for each region relative to the national performance is now available for each year over the period 1966–74; see Table 5.1.

TABLE 5.1
Per capita gross domestic product by region at factor cost, 1966–74

Region	1966	1967	1968	1969	1970	1971	1972	1973	1974
North	84.1	83.8	83.8	84.4	85.9	86.1	87.8	88.8	90.1
Yorks. & Humberside	96.7	95.6	94.4	94.7	94.8	92.2	91.9	91.5	93.0
East Midlands	96.5	96.9	95.7	96.5	96.1	95.4	96.8	96.9	95.6
East Anglia	96.0	96.2	96.5	95.4	96.1	93.0	91.3	93.1	93.4
South East	114.7	115.1	116.0	115.7	115.1	116.1	116.2	115.8	116.6
South West	92.0	92.7	91.7	91.9	91.1	92.6	93.1	91.7	93.1
West Midlands	108.2	106.0	105.9	105.1	105.2	102.1	100.3	100.2	99.3
North West	95.7	95.4	95.2	95.7	95.5	95.8	96.2	95.9	94.5
Wales	84.2	85.5	84.8	84.0	85.1	87.1	87.6	87.0	83.9
Scotland	89.1	89.5	89.7	89.6	90.4	91.1	90.9	92.8	93.4

Note: United Kingdom = 100. Owing to refinements in the methods from 1971 onwards there is a break in the time series between 1970 and 1971. Due to changes in the definition of Economic Planning Regions following local-government reorganisation, the 1974 figures for the North, Yorkshire and Humberside, East Midlands, South East, South West and North West are not strictly comparable with those for earlier years (McCallum, chapter 1 of this volume, Figure 1.1). These differences are thought unlikely to distort the broad regional comparisons.

Source: Kemp-Smith and Hartley (1976, Table 1A).

It should be noted, however, that measures of GDP per capita will be affected by demographic differences between regions, particularly the population in the working age groups, and this could alter both the range about the national average and the ranking of regions in some cases, e.g., the South West. The national average GDP per capita is heavily weighted by the very high figure recorded for the South East (over 16 per cent above average in 1974), all the remaining regions having below-average indices in 1974. Looking at the broad ranking of British regions over time a considerable consistency is revealed. In 1966 two regions (South

East and West Midlands) had an estimated GDP per capita well above average, followed by an intermediate group (Yorkshire and Humberside, East Midlands, East Anglia and the North West) with an index close to 96–97 and two groups with low figures (the South West and Scotland with an index between 89 and 92, and Wales and the North around 84, although in the case of the South West the high proportion of retired people is an important factor). By 1974 the South East and West Midlands still had an estimated GDP per per capita well above any other regions (although West Midlands had fallen considerably relative to the South East), followed by a large group of regions with an index in the range 93–96 and (still at the bottom) the North and Wales. This greater clustering of regions around the 93–96 index is evidence of some reduction in the scale of regional disparities. The most noticeable changes in the relative performance of individual regions—the faster than average growth in GDP per capita in the North, Scotland (which improved its ranking from 8th to 5th over the period) and (until 1973) Wales, and the less rapid growth in the West Midlands and Yorkshire and Humberside—also reinforce the general trend.

The traditional and still most commonly used indicator of the regional problem is the regional unemployment rate compared with the Great Britain average. Table 5.2 sets out the regional unemployment rates expressed as a percentage of the Great Britain rates for 1965, 1970 and 1975. Unemployment rate relatives of this kind can be distorted because of cyclical factors, while for some purposes it is more appropriate to consider the absolute difference in unemployment percentage points rather than the percentage, but as a broad overall guide to the relative economic standing of regions at different points in time the data in Table 5.2 are useful.

TABLE 5.2
Regional unemployment rates relative to Great Britain (annual average numbers unemployed)

Region	1965	1970	1975[a]
North	179	188	144
Yorkshire & Humberside	79	116	98
East Midlands	64	88	88
East Anglia	93	84	83
South East	57	64	68
South West	107	112	115
West Midlands	50	80	100
North West	114	108	129
Wales	179	156	137
Scotland	207	168	127

[a] See second part of 'Note' in Table 5.1.

Note: Great Britain = 100.

Source: data supplied by the Department of Employment.

There are clearly similarities between the regional relatives when measured by unemployment rates and by GDP per capita. Thus, the six regions with unemployment rates higher than average in 1970 (the North, Scotland, Wales, Yorkshire and Humberside, South West and North West) were also the regions with the lowest estimated GDP per capita in that year. There is also a broad consistency in the regional unemployment rate relatives over time, since the same five regions recorded levels above the Great Britain average in both 1965 and 1975. But closer inspection also reveals some significant differences between these two dates. Most noticeable is the major improvement in the relative position of the three regions of highest unemployment (Scotland, the North and Wales) over the period, and the deterioration in the position of the West Midlands, which in 1965 had the lowest unemployment rate for any region. Other regions have also recorded changes but they are less marked. The result is that the range of regional unemployment relatives in 1975 (from 68 to 144) is much narrower than in 1965 (from 50 to 207). This partly reflects the increase in the level of the average unemployment rate over the period from 1.4 per cent to 4.1 per cent; if the absolute difference between the regional and Great Britain rates is taken, the differential has actually increased slightly in the North and Wales despite the big fall in the unemployment relative.

It is important to make allowance for special factors that have influenced the position in an individual year but may not continue to do so to the same extent in future. For example, the improvement in Scotland's unemployment rate relative since 1965 and particularly since 1970 reflects North Sea oil related employment, as well as the effects of regional policy (Moore and Rhodes, 1974), and it is unrealistic to expect oil-related employment to continue to increase at the rate recorded during the first half of the 1970s. In the case of the West Midlands, the figure for 1975 may be distorted because of the deep recession in the car industry at this time; it is noteworthy that this region's unemployment rate relative to Great Britain also deteriorated (to an index of 97) at the time of the 1972 recession but recovered thereafter, and a similar improvement to a better than average position seems likely in the future. The big improvement in the North's relative position has taken place only since the second half of 1974 in response to factors such as a large increase in public sector employment, a national shift in the industrial and occupational composition of earnings in favour of certain (mainly manual) industries and occupations heavily represented in the region, and cyclical factors; while a return to the high unemployment rate relative of 1970 is not expected, there could be some deterioration in the relative position over the next one or two years (Northern Region Strategy Team, 1976a). These considerations suggest caution in attaching too much weight to what could be temporary phenomena, but nonetheless the figures (taken together with the GDP per head data in Table 5.1) suggest that, within a broad pattern of considerable consistency in the ranking of regions, some regions have experienced a significant change in their relative economic fortunes.

Unemployment rate changes result from an imbalance in the changes between the supply of and demand for labour. Some further light is shed on the trends revealed in Table 5.2 by an examination of comparative regional rates of change in population (which is likely to bear a broad but not precise relationship to labour supply because of changes in activity rates) and employment between 1965 and 1975. Table 5.3 ranks the various regions according to their rates of growth of population and employees in employment in each of the sub-periods 1965–70 and 1970–75, as well as for the period as a whole. Regional changes in population and employment are interrelated in a complex way. On the one hand, population growth will tend to encourage employment growth both through an expanding market (particularly for local services) and through the ready availability of a local supply of labour, although interregional travel-to-work flows will of course distort this relationship. Population decline will tend to have the opposite effect. On the other hand, expanding employment opportunities will tend to raise activity rates and attract migrants from other regions and so increase local population growth, while a rate of job growth below the growth of the local labour supply is likely to lead to outmigration and less rapid population growth. Although the causal relationships are complex and the time lags involved uncertain, and although population may not be a direct reflection of changes in labour supply, we would expect at least a broad consistency in the relative performance of regions in terms of population and employment change over a period of ten years.

Table 5.3 reveals a fair degree of consistency, both in terms of the ranking of different regions on the population or employment indicator over time, and in the relationship between the two. Looking at population changes, the same three regions (East Anglia, the South West and East Midlands) recorded the most rapid growth both in 1965–70 and 1970–75, while the North West, the North and Scotland had the least rapid growth (or largest decreases) in both periods. Compared with other regions the biggest changes over time were the faster population growth of Wales and the slight decline of the South East in the second sub-period. In the case of relative employment change there was less consistency in the ranking of regions, although a broad similarity was still retained; the most noticeable changes were again a big improvement in the ranking of Wales and a big deterioration in the ranking of the South East, while Yorkshire and Humberside (improvement) and the East and West Midlands (deterioration) also recorded changes in their ranking between the two sub-periods. Turning now to the rankings of regions on the population and employment indicators for the period as a whole (the final two columns of Table 5.3), we see that East Anglia, the South West and East Midlands

TABLE 5.3

Rates of change of population and employees in employment by region, 1965–75

Rank	1965–70 Percentage population change	1965–70 Percentage change in employees in employment	1970–75[a] Percentage population change	1970–75[a] Percentage change in employees in employment	1965–75[a] Percentage population change	1965–75[a] Percentage change in employees in employment
1	East Anglia +7.1	East Anglia +5.6	East Anglia +7.0	East Anglia +7.7	East Anglia +14.6	East Anglia +13.7
2	South West +4.6	East Midlands −0.8	South West +4.3	South West +6.5	South West +9.1	South West +4.8
3	East Midlands +4.0	South West −1.6	East Midlands +3.4	Wales +3.2	East Midlands +7.5	East Midlands +2.2
4	West Midlands +3.7	South East −2.0	Wales +1.8	East Midlands +3.1	West Midlands +5.5	North −0.3
5	South East +2.1	Scotland −2.7	West Midlands +1.6	North +2.7	Wales +2.9	Scotland −1.9
6	Yorks. & Humberside +1.3	North −2.9	Scotland +0.8	Scotland +0.9	Yorks. & Humberside +2.2	South East −1.9
7	Wales +1.2	West Midlands −3.6	Yorks. & Humberside +0.8	Yorks. & Humberside +0.8	South East +2.0	Wales −2.9
8	North West +1.1	North West −4.7	South East −0.2	South East +0.1	North West +0.9	Yorks. & Humberside −4.2
9	North +0.3	Yorks. & Humberside −5.0	North West −0.2	North West −1.3	North 0	West Midlands −5.1
10	Scotland +0.1	Wales −5.9	North −0.3	West Midlands −1.6	Scotland −0.1	North West −6.0

[a] See second part of 'Note' in Table 5.1.

Note: bracket indicates equal ranking for the regions concerned.

Source: Great Britain (1976b; 1976c).

head the table on both counts while Wales, Yorkshire and Humberside, the South East and North West have roughly similar rankings. The three outstanding cases where regions occupy significantly different rankings according to the population and employment indicators are Scotland and the North (which had the lowest rankings for population change of any region but intermediate rankings for employment change) and the West Midlands with the fourth most rapid increase in population but the second most unfavourable employment growth. This somewhat unusual relationship also holds true for these regions in both of the sub-periods.

Given the qualifications that must be attached to this analysis, particularly the simplifications introduced by the use of rankings rather than a comparison of changes in the absolute numbers of population and employment in each region, the imprecise relationship between changes in population and labour supply, and the use of regional data, which may conceal different sub-regional trends, it would clearly be wrong to reach firm conclusions. But is is interesting to note that the three regions where relative population and employment changes appear to be most out of line between 1965 and 1975 have all recorded shifts in their unemployment rates relative to Great Britain over the same period, and in the expected direction (an improvement in the case of Scotland and the North where the employment change ranking is more favourable than that for population change, and a deterioration in the case of the West Midlands were the opposite applies). For Wales an improvement in the unemployment relative occurred despite a more favourable ranking on the population than on the employment indicator, although since 1970 employment increased more rapidly than population in Wales. In general, Table 5.3 suggests that some part of the change in regional unemployment relatives could well lie on the labour supply side as well as on the labour demand side, which has received more attention from economists.

Changes in the Diagnosis of the Regional Problem

In the second section some of the changes in the national context within which the regional problem is set were discussed, while in the previous section, changes in the main indicators of the regional problem were described. In this section an attempt is made to look at the more fundamental causes of the regional economic problem, with particular reference to those assisted areas such as Scotland and the North that have for many years experienced above-average unemployment and below-average incomes and GDP per capita. In what respects is the diagnosis of regional problems today different from that current in 1965, and how far does this reflect a change in the basic nature of the problem? The discussion is grouped under the following seven major headings: the timescale and dynamic nature of regional problems; the importance of labour demand deficiency and labour supply factors to regional problems; the importance of industrial structure and other factors; the significance of economic function and type of employment; the distinctive nature of problems in particular regions; intraregional differences; the relevance of public expenditure and wider political issues.

The Timescale and Dynamic Nature of Regional Problems

Most analysts of the regional problem today are less sanguine than ten years ago about the possibility of eliminating differences in regional economic prosperity in the short or medium term. The introduction of the Regional Employment Premium in 1967 was expected to halve the difference between unemployment rates in the assisted areas and elsewhere over a period of years—by implication about five years (Great Britain, 1967). Even at the end of the 1960s it was possible for the Hunt Committee to talk abour 'breaking the back' of the regional problem and 'finishing the job', concluding that '... it may be reasonable to hope that by the mid 1970s the major problems in many parts of the development areas will have been largely overcome, at least so far as unemployment is concerned' (Great Britain, 1969, p. 39). The more realistic assessment of the long time-scale needed to solve regional problems stems from an improved understanding of the dynamic nature of the processes that create and sustain high rates of unemployment in some regions. At the time of the National Plan there was a tendency to think in terms of a 'once-and-for-all' effort to bring unused labour reserves into use and to transform the industrial structure of the problem regions. More recent work emphasises the strength of the forces that perpetuate regional disparities and hinder adjustments: (a) the need for regions with an unfavourable industrial structure to sustain a higher level of investment than nationally even though the main influence on investment in the region is the macro-economic climate of the country as a whole (McCrone, 1975; (b) a positive association between rapid growth in output and productivity and the institutional factors that prevent wage levels in regions of low productivity adjusting to allow greater regional competitiveness (Kaldor, 1970; Cameron, 1971); and (c) the various kinds of short-run and long-run regional multiplier mechanisms that make regional economic growth or decline to some extent self-reinforcing (Brown, 1972). The regional problem and regional policy are now seen as long term and continuous in nature; in this respect we can conclude that it is our understanding of, rather than the fundamental nature of, the problem that has changed.

The Importance of Labour Demand and Labour Supply Factors

Higher than average unemployment rates in regions such as Scotland or the North have conventionally been attributed to a deficiency in the regional demand for labour. This interpretation would be accepted as broadly valid today but there is now a greater recognition that factors on the labour supply side may have at least a subsidiary part to play in some regions. The relatively small amount of research devoted to regional variations in the growth of labour supply is drawn attention to by Law (1975), who argues that the relatively high birth rates in the Republic of Ireland, Northern Ireland, Scotland and Wales may be equally as important in explaining high outmigration or unemployment in these areas relative to England as are differences in the rate of employment growth. The same factor is probably also important in parts of England (e.g., North Humberside). The possible importance of supply side factors has already been mentioned in the discussion in the previous section of this chapter. Qualitative aspects of the labour supply (e.g., age structure and socio-economic structure) have also been emphasised in recent analyses of urban unemployment rates (Metcalf, 1975) and it seems likely that at a very small scale of analysis, supply factors are the major determinants of variations in local unemployment rates; even at a regional scale, however, areas with higher than average unemployment may have a relatively high proportion in socio-economic groups such as the unskilled who tend to be more liable to unemployment irrespective of location. A further indication of the significance of supply factors was the fairly widespread occurrence of shortages of skilled labour at the height of the economic cycle in 1973-74 even in areas with relatively high unemployment. We should not get supply side factors out of perspective; many of the qualitative problems mentioned above can be attributed to the long-run effects of many decades of deficient labour demand in the problem regions. But regional differences in the growth and quality of labour supply would seem to have a bigger part to play in explaining the regional economic problem than previously recognised.

The Importance of Industrial Structure and Other Factors
Accepting that labour demand deficiency is the major determinant of high regional unemployment rates, a substantial literature has been devoted to an investigation (using shift-share analysis and other techniques) of how far an unfavourable industrial structure and/or other factors (particularly the tendency for particular industries to grow more or less rapidly than their counterparts elsewhere) are the major explanation; see, for example, the bibliography in Randall (1973). In general, the results of this work support the conventional explanation that in most assisted areas the problems are largely structural in origin. Notwithstanding this broad conclusion, there has been a tendency in the last ten and especially the last five years to place greater stress on factors internal to a region as major causes of economic problems (West Central Scotland Plan, 1974; Northern Region Strategy Team, 1977). In particular, attention has been drawn to the need to improve the efficiency and competitiveness of industry

and to a relative lack of success by some of the regions' existing industries in adapting to growing but changing markets within their industries, and in generating new and different activities as the traditional ones declined (Segal, chapter 10 of this volume). Significantly, the Industrial Strategy is now concerned with similar problems of how to improve competitiveness and diversify into new opportunities at a national level (Cameron, chapter 14 of this volume). The limited level of new-company formation in some assisted areas, which has been studied by Firn (1974), may not of course be unconnected with the region's industrial structure; in the case of the North, for example, Segal (chapter 10 of this volume) argues that the nature of the region's traditional products (heavy, large-scale goods, highly cyclical in demand), traditional firms (high degree of vertical integration, large size, paternal management style) and geographical settlement pattern (dispersed labour markets often dominated by single employers) all militate against entrepreneurship and professional skills.

In 1969 the Hunt Committee (Great Britain, 1969) referred to the attraction of new industries to assisted areas as 'the key to their future'. The shift in thinking described above (together with the reduced levels and prospects for mobile industry) has led to a much greater emphasis than in the past on the need for development from within the problem regions, both by the diversification and growth of existing companies and by the establishment of new enterprises. The setting up of the Scottish and Welsh Development Agencies with powers to give both financial and other assistance to companies in their areas and in some circumstances to take share capital or to start new companies can be seen as some reflection of this change in emphasis. Again, it is important to place more recent developments in perspective. The problem regions continue to need both new mobile industry and more rapid growth from existing industry. To some extent the success of regional policy in attracting new companies (often in new industries and with different management approaches) makes the emphasis on development from within a region more feasible.

The Significance of Economic Function and Type of Employment
We have already seen that the longer time-scale within which the solution to regional problems is now conceived reflects a better understanding of the dynamic processes that perpetuate regional disparities. There has also been greater attention in recent years to the functions that establishments in particular regions tend to fulfil in relation to their own industrial organisation and the national economy, and to the qualitative problems of the type of jobs available in assisted areas that this may produce. For example, there has been criticism that regional-policy measures have largely resulted in the attraction of branch plants to the assisted areas, carrying out routine production functions with relatively low-status jobs, while top management and decision making (on financial and marketing policy, for example)

and often also research and development activities are located outside the region, usually in London or the South East. The high and apparently increasing level of external ownership of manufacturing industry in Scotland (Firn, 1975), for example, is sometimes held to result in a limited range of job opportunities in Scotland and a continued need for the more skilled or ambitious to emigrate once they have achieved a certain status in their company's organisational structure. There may also be long-run effects on a region's ability to generate new enterprises and opportunities from within. The importance of the type as well as the number of jobs available in the regions has been stressed in a number of contexts in recent years; for example, the campaigns by several regions to attract more office jobs including top decision-taking Civil Service jobs following the Hardman Report, and the possibility of giving additional assistance to encourage companies to establish operations in the regions carrying out a wider range of functions other than production, in order to diversify the occupational structure (Northern Region Strategy Team, 1977).

The Distinctive Nature of Regional Problems

Another theme that may be detected over the last decade or so is a growing awareness of the distinctive nature of problems in particular regions, and the need for a more sensitive locally based analysis and response to them. Again this follows from the numerous studies and plans produced for particular regions. In the North West, for example, there is now a clearer understanding that the most distinctive problem is one of a general obsolescence in much of the region's infrastructure and environment. Despite the improvements that have been made in the last ten years, particularly in communications, the essential nature of the problem remains unchanged; while the early regional studies of the North West in the mid-1960s drew attention to the poor facilities for education and other services, and the Hunt Committee report stressed environmental factors, it was only with the *Strategic Plan for the North West* (Great Britain, 1974b) that these problems were crystallised and brought together under the general heading of obsolescence. Other regions have their own distinguishing characteristics, problems and opportunities. For example, the greater proximity of South Wales to the major markets of the South East and West Midlands affords different opportunities for industrial growth from those in Central Scotland, for example.

Intraregional Differences.

The official regions of Great Britain are relatively large, and conceal a considerable measure of internal diversity, which has again been given more attention in recent years. Perhaps the extreme example is Scotland, an area accounting for approximately one-third of the land surface of Britain and containing sub-regions that are experiencing very different types of economic problem (e.g., Clydeside, the Borders, Edinburgh, North

East Scotland, the Highlands, Shetland). Following a series of sub-regional planning studies for different parts of Scotland and the discovery of North Sea oil, which tended to reinforce the disparities between West Central and Eastern Scotland, more attention is now being given to understanding and meeting the specific requirement of different areas. To some extent this reflects the improvement in Scotland's overall unemployment rate relative to Great Britain. The introduction of Regional Reports in 1975, in which the new regional local authorities were asked to submit to the Scottish Office an overview of their major problems and priorities for future action, marks a big step forward in this respect. Other major intraregional differences (and moreover ones that have changed over time) are apparent in other regions. In the North West, for example, the economic problems of Merseyside now dominate the overall regional prospect in a way that appeared very improbable at the end of the 1960s—the Hunt Committee (Great Britain, 1969) reported that Merseyside was increasing employment rapidly, while the remainder of the North West was generally sluggish, and recommended the downgrading of the then Merseyside Development Area. We have already noted the development of urban problems in recent years, and these are a major source of intraregional differences in several regions.

The Relevance of Public Expenditure and Wider Political Issues
The regional problem can no longer be viewed in a relatively self-contained framework. The effect of the planned devolution of powers to Scotland and Wales and of the greater insight into the incidence of public expenditure between regions (Northern Region Strategy Team, 1976b) has been to break down the barriers between the regional problem and other policy issues. Analysis of the regional problem in the mid-1960s was concerned primarily with the prospects for private industrial investment and for public expenditure under the specifically regional-policy programmes; only gradually with work by regional planning teams and better estimates of the regional breakdown of public expenditure was it appreciated that both the total level of public expenditure in a region and its allocation between services are an important contributory factor to the relative prosperity of different regions and potentially a powerful instrument for influencing regional change. Similarly, the movement towards devolution of powers to Scotland and Wales has opened up questions about the extent to which regional problems reflect the structure of government in Britain, and the extent to which different regions might fare better or worse under alternative arrangements. As with most of the issues discussed in this section, these new dimensions of approach to the regional economic problem stem not from fundamental changes in the causes or incidence of regional disparities since 1965 but much more from a better understanding of the problem and of the context within which solutions must be sought.

Conclusions

This chapter has reviewed the changes that have occurred since 1965 in the nature of the regional economic problem in Britain, whether the problem is viewed from a national perspective or from the viewpoint of the regions with below-average economic welfare, as indicated, for example, by relatively high unemployment rates. We have seen that some significant changes have occurred in the national context within which the regional problem is set, particularly because of the much lower rate of economic growth, higher rate of inflation and lower growth of national population that have occurred or are now in prospect compared with the assumptions current in 1965. Changes have also occurred in the political context as a result of entry into the European Community and the plans for devolution of power within Great Britain. At the same time there have been shifts in the relative economic standing of some regions (even if the ranking of regions according to unemployment rates and other indicators remains broadly similar in 1975 to that in 1965), and a tendency towards the narrowing of regional economic disparities as measured by the conventional indicators (although there is a risk of attaching too much emphasis to relatively short-run phenomena and to changes in relative unemployment rates expressed as percentages rather than absolute differences). As regards the basic nature of the economic problem facing the less prosperous regions, there have been several important changes in the last ten years in the diagnosis of these problems, particularly in the emphasis now placed on the long-run dynamic nature of the problem and the need for innovation and adaptation by the regions' existing industries. However, these changes in interpretation largely reflect a better understanding of (as much as a fundamental shift in) the underlying nature of the problem.

What are the implications for the nature of the regional economic problem facing Britain in the late 1970s? From a national viewpoint, a number of factors suggest that the scale of the problem may appear to be of less concern than in the past. First, the size of (and priority given to) the national economic problem now tends to dominate the specifically regional problem, particularly at a time when there has been some narrowing in the regional differentials (partly reflecting higher national unemployment). Second, at a time of high national unemployment and high rates of inflation, the economic gains envisaged in 1965 from tackling the regional problem seem to be smaller, at least in the short run. While the prospect of declining population in several regions suggests that existing infrastructure may be less fully utilised than in the past, involving resource losses through its replacement elsewhere, the greater part of population movements takes place within particular regions and points to the need for urban as well as regional policies. Third, the need for restraint in the growth of public expenditure gives a special importance to approaches that do not require large-scale financial inducements.

To set against these factors, the analysis carried out over the last ten years does not suggest that regional problems are in sight of early solution. There is a better understanding that regional problems tend to be sustained by dynamic processes, and that the problems of the less prosperous regions are often the problems of the nation in more acute form. It is significant that the emphasis placed by recent regional plans on improving the competitiveness of existing industry and on seeking out new market opportunities at industry and plant level are to a large extent the same issues that dominate the national industrial strategy. This points to the complementarity of regional and national requirements and suggests that (as in the mid-1960s, though in a different way) a strong attack on regional problems has an important contribution to make to overcoming national economic problems. Recent moves to increase the powers available at regional level to tackle regional problems, partly in recognition of the distinctive nature of some of these problems, are also in line with greater emphasis on a 'grass-roots' approach to national problems.

It can be concluded, therefore, that significant regional problems remain. There have been notable shifts over the last ten years in the relationship with national problems, in our understanding and diagnosis of the nature of regional problems, and to a lesser extent in the relative standing of particular regions; but it remains true that a stronger national economy will both require and assist improvements in regional performance. Of course, it is possible that conflicts may arise between efforts to tackle national, urban and regional problems. For example, the emphasis placed by the emerging national Industrial Strategy on the regeneration of manufacturing industry (and, within this, selected sectors in engineering and vehicles) could be of particular benefit to regions such as the West Midlands that, despite a deterioration in their unemployment rate relative to that for Great Britain during the recent recession, still compare favourably with the assisted areas. The stress on manufacturing could also run counter to the importance placed by several recent regional plans on developing the service sector and diversifying the occupational structure of their economies. But such conflicts may not be inevitable. Several areas in the less prosperous regions (e.g., the Strathclyde Region of Scotland) have an industrial structure weighted in favour of those industries that can expect to receive priority in the Industrial Strategy, while a more competitive manufacturing sector would probably involve a greater proportion of scientific and more skilled jobs. Similarly it should be possible to help ease the urban problems of cities such as London and Birmingham by devising policies that would not adversely affect regions such as the North and Scotland (with their own urban problems). Given the active involvement of the established regional-planning machinery in Britain, the improved regional prospects in many areas brought about by the success of regional policy in the past, and the better understanding of regional problems that has resulted from over a decade of active interest and research, it seems possible that the new approaches to national and regional economic problems can develop in a consistent and reinforcing way. The need is to ensure that efforts to improve the national (and urban) economy build on the policies required to tackle the changing nature of regional problems.

References

Beckerman, W. and Associates (1965) *The British Economy in 1975*. Cambridge: Cambridge University Press.

Brown, A. J. (1972) *The Framework of Regional Economics in the United Kingdom*. Cambridge: Cambridge University Press.

Cameron, C. C. (1971) 'Economic Analysis for a Declining Urban Economy', *Scottish Journal of Political Economy*', Vol. 18, pp. 315–45.

Chisholm, M. (1976) 'Regional Policies in an Era of Slow Population Growth and Higher Unemployment', *Regional Studies*, Vol. 10, pp. 201–13.

Corkindale, J. (1976) 'Employment in the Conurbations', paper presented to the Inner City Employment Conference at York University, September 1976.

Firn, J. (1974) 'Indigenous Growth and Regional Development; the Experience and Prospects for West Central Scotland', University of Glasgow, Urban and Regional Studies Discussion Papers, No. 10.

Firn, J. (1975) 'External Control and Regional Policy' in G. Brown (ed.), *The Red Paper on Scotland*. Edinburgh: Edinburgh University Student Publications.

Great Britain (1963) National Economic Development Council. *Conditions Favourable to Faster Growth*. London: HMSO.

Great Britain (1965) Department of Economic Affairs. *The National Plan*. Cmnd. 2764. London: HMSO.

Great Britain (1967) Department of Economic Affairs. *The Development Areas: A Proposal for a Regional Employment Premium*. London: HMSO.

Great Britain (1969) Department of Economic Affairs. *The Intermediate Areas*. Cmnd. 3998. London: HMSO.

Great Britain (1974a) Central Statistical Office. *National Income and Expenditure 1963–73*. London: HMSO.

Great Britain (1974b) Strategic Plan for the North-West Joint Planning Team. *Strategic Plan for the North-West*. London: HMSO.

Great Britain (1975) Department of Employment. *Department of Employment Gazette*, Vol. 83, pp. 1030–6.

Great Britain (1976a) Central Statistical Office. *Social Trends*, No. 7, p. 64.

Great Britain (1976b) Office of Population Censuses and Surveys. *Population Trends*, Vol. 5, p. 45.

Great Britain (1976c) Department of Employment. *Department of Employment Gazette*, Vol. 84, pp. 839–50.

Great Britain (1976d) South-East Joint Planning Team. *Strategy for the South East: 1976 Review*. London: HMSO.

Harris, D. F. (1976) 'The Service Sector: Its Changing Role as a Source of Employment', paper presented at the Centre for Environmental Studies seminar on Employment in the Inner City, York, January 1976.

Kaldor, N. (1970) 'The Case for Regional Policies', *Scottish Journal of Political Economy*, Vol. 17, pp. 337–48.

Kemp-Smith, D. and Hartley, E. (1976) 'United Kingdom Regional Accounts', *Economic Trends*, No. 277, pp. 78–90.

Law, D. (1975) 'The Economic Problems of Ireland, Scotland and Wales' in J. Vaizey (ed.), *Economic Sovereignty and Regional Policy*. Dublin: Gill and Macmillan.

McCrone, G. (1975) 'The Determinants of Regional Growth Rates' in J. Vaizey (ed.), *Economic Sovereignty and Regional Policy*. Dublin: Gill and Macmillan.

Manners, G. (1976) 'Reinterpreting the Regional Problem', *The Three Banks Review*, No. 111, pp. 33–5.

Metcalf, D. (1975) 'Urban Unemployment in England', *Economic Journal*, Vol. 85, pp. 578–89.

Moore, B. and Rhodes, J. (1974) 'Regional Policy and the Scottish Economy', *Scottish Journal of Political Economy*, Vol. 21, pp. 215–35.

Northern Region Strategy Team (1976a) 'Causes of the Recent Improvement in the Rate of Unemployment in the Northern Region Relative to Great Britain', Technical Report, No. 11, Northern Region Strategy Team, Newcastle.

Northern Region Strategy Team (1976b) 'Public Expenditure in the Northern Region and other British Regions 1960/70–1973/74', Technical Report, No. 12, Northern Region Strategy Team, Newcastle.

Northern Region Strategy Team (1977) *Strategic Plan for the Northern Region*, Vol. 2 (Economic Development Policies). Newcastle: Northern Region Strategy Team.

Randall, J. N. (1973) 'Shift-Share Analysis as a Guide to the Employment Performance of West Central Scotland', *Scottish Journal of Political Economy*, Vol. 20, pp. 1–26.

West Central Scotland Plan (1974) *The Regional Economy*. Supplementary Report, No. 1. Glasgow: West Central Scotland Plan.

CHAPTER 6

Changing Metropolitan Structure

P. A. Stone*

Introduction

Over the last two decades the perspective for population, employment, output and welfare in Great Britain has changed in a number of ways. This changed perspective can be viewed in terms of national aggregates and interregional distributions.

Population Trends

Nationally, birth rates peaked in the late 1940s, declined until the early 1950s and then increased continuously until the mid-1960s, since when they have continued to decline steeply. Now, despite a much larger population, live births are fewer than in the mid-1930s. By contrast, death rates have remained within narrow limits. Population increased substantially until the mid-1960s, and since then the rate of increase has been slowing down and is now about zero. Population projections have also varied during the last two decades. Until the mid-1960s it was expected that the population would continue to increase. Now, however, even the more optimistic projections suggest only a moderate increase in population to the end of the century and some indicate relative stability.

British experience is far from unique. Birth rates have followed a broadly similar pattern in most countries of Western Europe, displaying a steep decline since the mid-1960s. Again, death rates have remained reasonably steady. The expectation for the future is for stable or falling birth rates and for stable or slightly rising death rates. Since external migration is not expected to influence national population significantly, the expectation for West European countries is for limited growth, with stability or even decline in some cases. The similarity of demographic experience in West European countries, despite widely differing economic experience, suggests that future population experience in this country may not be affected even by radical changes in the economy.

The declining rate of growth in national population is reflected in

* *Director General's Department, Greater London Council. This chapter represents the views of the author and does not necessarily reflect those of the Greater London Council.*

the rates of growth in the regions, but the pattern is overlaid by the effects of interregional migration. Broadly speaking, over the last fifteen years, population has increased most rapidly in the South and Midlands, and least rapidly in the North and West. Growth has been most steady in East Anglia and the South West. In the other regions (the South East, West Midlands and East Midlands) there was a substantial rate of growth in the early 1960s, but subsequently the rates of growth have declined steeply.

Perhaps more striking than the regional changes in population growth are the intraregional changes. These can be expressed most clearly in terms of the experience of the metropolitan areas as compared with that of the remainders of the respective regions and of regions with no metropolitan areas. Such changes parallel those in the Standard Metropolitan Labour Areas analysed by Hall et al. (1973) and Goddard and Spence et al. (1976). In regions containing metropolitan areas, population has increased relatively slowly. While all metropolitan areas have lost population in the five years 1971 to 1976, and several have been losing population since 1961, the remainders of their respective regions have gained population over the fifteen years 1961 to 1976, as have other regions. This reflects the movement of population out of the urban cores to the smaller towns around them. The current annual rate of population decline from the most affected metropolitan areas (London, Merseyside and Clydeside) is about one per cent.

Changes in Distribution of Employment

The movement of population is naturally mirrored by the movement of employment. People initially move out of the urban cores in search of a better environment for living, where housing is of a higher standard, cheaper and more attractive. At first, they may travel back to the urban core for employment. However, as the number of people in the growth areas around the core increases, the areas attract more firms, employment opportunities grow, attracting yet more residents. The metropolitan areas that have had the greatest net losses of population have lost the most employment in manufacturing and non-growth services and have gained the least in the Growth Services (to be defined later).

Decline of Metropolitan Areas and the Operation of Public Policy

It is apparent, therefore, that over the last two decades a new regional dimension has developed. While the pattern of declining regions, mainly in the North and West of the country, remains, this pattern has been overlaid by the decline of the metropolitan areas. This has affected metropolitan areas within regions of growth as well as those in regions of decline. In fact, as will be shown later, even in the regions of decline, the decline has been confined to their metropolitan parts; their remaining parts have shown a rate of population and employment growth greater than or not far short of the national average.

To some extent at least, the decline of the metropolitan areas is a product of government policies, which have aimed on the one hand at redressing regional imbalances between prosperous and less prosperous areas and, on the other hand, at reducing the congestion of large urban concentrations. Both groups of policies originated with the Barlow Report (Great Britain, 1940). These policies have attempted to divert the growth potential of the prosperous areas to develop the economies of the less prosperous regions and to divert potential population growth from the large urban concentrations to New Towns and other outlying centres.

Regional policy has operated with varying intensity throughout the post-war period (McCallum, chapter 1 of this volume). Its object has been to generate industrial growth in the less prosperous regions by offering financial and fiscal inducements to firms to locate or expand within these regions. Originally, such inducements were confined to manufacturing industry but they are now available to certain service activities. The areas in which these benefits are payable have gradually been extended so that they now include more or less the whole of Great Britain other than the Midlands and the South (McCallum, chapter 1 of this volume, Figure 1.2). The positive policy instruments of inducement are supported by negative instruments of constraint. These make it necessary to obtain an Industrial Development Certificate (IDC) or Office Development Permit (ODP) before seeking planning permission to develop, redevelop or extend any but the smallest factories and office buildings. Such regulations have applied with differing degrees of stringency to the South East and the West Midlands and at times to adjacent regions. Generally, the policies have been applied far less strictly outside the metropolitan areas, particularly in the New Towns and expanding towns.

Policies directed towards the easing of congestion in large urban concentrations have included both positive and negative features. On the positive side there has been the creation of New Towns under the New Towns Acts, town expansion schemes under the Town Development Act and the acceptance of the growth of other towns. On the negative side there has been the Green Belt policy, which limits physical expansion of the large cities (in some cases expansion is limited physically by the urban development on the city boundary), and the control on development in certain regions through IDC and ODP policy. Furthermore, since the capital resources and finance available nationally, both from public and private sources, are limited, the siphoning-off of large amounts, to finance the development of New Town, other growth areas and the assisted areas, reduces the availability of resources for the rest of the country, particularly Greater London and the West Midlands Metropolitan Area, the only two metropolitan areas lying outside assisted areas.

The Effects of Decline in Metropolitan Areas

The decline in population and employment (a rough measure of economic activity) of the metropolitan areas is accompanied by a decline in the relative well-being of the inhabitants and of the infrastructure of these areas. The range of well-paid employment opportunities in metropolitan areas is declining, the levels of unemployment are increasing relative to elsewhere, relative earnings and household incomes are falling, and there is relatively less private and public wealth to sustain the quality of the infrastructure and environment. As conditions in the metropolitan areas decline and the relative attractions of the growth areas increase, households and firms decline in the former (particularly in the inner-city areas) and increase in the latter. Clearly, there is a danger that the cycle of decline and deprivation in the metropolitan areas will be self-perpetuating and that the welfare of their inhabitants (particularly those of the inner city) will deteriorate.

In this chapter the changing metropolitan structure and its consequences will be explored. Consideration will be given initially to changes in London and the South East for which more comparative intraregional data are available than for elsewhere and which have been the most researched. Decentralisation will then be considered in other regions and comparisons made with the South East. Finally, attention will be directed to the consequences of change for the metropolitan areas and to the action that might be taken to revive them and to prevent a self-perpetuating cycle of deterioration and deprivation.

Decentralisation and Change within the South East

Population and Employment Changes

By 1961 the population of Greater London had already fallen from a peak of 8.5m to 8.0m. It continued to fall (until recently at an accelerating rate) to reach about 7.0m in 1976 (Table 6.1); most of this change related to the outward flow of people, which exceeded the inward flow by about 1m. Projections suggest that by 1986 the population of Greater London may have fallen to between 5.8m and 6.3m. By contrast, the population of the rest of the South East (ROSE) increased from 8.1m in 1961 to 9.9m in 1976. The population of the rest of Great Britain has also increased but not as fast as for ROSE.

At the sub-regional level, economic activity can best be measured in terms of employment, changes in which are closely related to changes in population. As population migrates from London, it increases the labour force available in other areas, which then become more attractive to firms and other employers. The movement of firms out of London is encouraged by the reduced availability of labour there and its improved availability in other areas. The resulting decline in jobs in London and the expansion

TABLE 6.1

Population changes in the South East (in thousands)

Year	Greater London	Rest of the South East	Rest of Great Britain[c]
1951[a]	8,197	6,930	33,727
1961[a]	7,992	8,279	35,014
1961[b]	7,977	8,094	35,309
1966[b]	7,810	8,909	36,306
1971[b]	7,441	9,553	37,078
1976[b]	7,028	9,865	37,454

[a] Derived from Great Britain (1966) and referring to the enumerated population for areas defined prior to 1974 in England and Wales and prior to 1975 in Scotland.
[b] Derived from the mid-year estimates of the Registrars General and referring to current areas.
[c] Total for Great Britain minus total for the South East.

elsewhere further stimulate migration from London. The underlying rate of movement is affected by the state of the national economy, with a tendency to accelerate when the economy is buoyant and to slow down (overall movement being still considerable) under conditions of stagnation.

The number of jobs in London declined from 4.39m in 1961 to 3.99m in 1974 (Table 6.2), the rate of decline being particularly rapid between 1966 and 1971 (Table 6.3). Over the period 1961–74, employment was

TABLE 6.2

Employment by major sector, 1961 and 1974

Sector	Number (thousands)			Percentage of total		
	Greater London	Rest of the South East	England and Wales	Greater London	Rest of the South East	England and Wales
Manufacturing:						
1961	1,429	990	7,626	32.6	30.5	36.5
1974	940	1,194	7,248	23.6	28.8	32.7
Growth services:						
1961	1,190	826	4,266	27.1	25.5	20.4
1974	1,528	1,238	6,061	38.3	29.8	27.3
Other industries and services:						
1961	1,767	1,424	9,021	40.3	44.0	43.1
1974	1,522	1,717	8,877	38.1	41.4	40.0
Total:						
1961	4,386	3,240	20,913	100.0	100.0	100.0
1974	3,990	4,149	22,186	100.0	100.0	100.0

Note: sectors are defined in the Note to Table 6.4.

Source: Great Britain (1966), corrected for bias; Great Britain (1975a), adjusted to Census of Population equivalent on the basis of 1971 data from both sources.

TABLE 6.3
Average annual percentage change in employment by major sector

Sector	Percentage change		
	Greater London	Rest of the South East	England and Wales
Manufacturing:			
1961–66	−1.68	+3.07	+0.58
1966–71	−3.30	+1.02	−1.03
1971–74	−4.67	−0.17	−0.88
1961–74	−2.63	+1.58	−0.38
Growth services:			
1961–66	+2.57	+3.08	+3.17
1966–71	+1.31	+3.44	+0.92
1971–74	+2.26	+3.61	+3.70
1961–74	+2.18	+3.83	+3.23
Other industries and services:			
1961–66	+0.16	+3.60	+1.14
1966–71	−2.44	−1.13	−1.93
1971–74	−0.09	+2.82	+1.01
1961–74	−1.06	+1.58	−0.12
Total:			
1961–66	+0.21	+3.32	+1.35
1966–71	−1.56	+0.66	−0.68
1971–74	−0.77	+2.13	+0.97
1961–74	−0.69	+2.15	+0.46

Note: sectors are defined in the Note to Table 6.4.

Source: Great Britain (1966; 1967; 1975b); Great Britain (1975a) adjusted to Census of Population equivalents on the basis of 1971 data.

falling at an average of 0.69 per cent per annum in London, while rising at 0.46 per cent in England and Wales and 2.15 per cent in ROSE (Table 6.3).

Changes in Employment Structure

Both industrial and occupational structures are changing nationally and this is reflected in the structure of employment. Manufacturing employment is declining, while employment in Growth Services (financial and business services, professional and scientific services, public administration and some branches of communications) is increasing (Table 6.3). Employment in Other Industries and Services is declining, although less rapidly than in Manufacturing. In terms of occupations, office work is increasing in all industries, mainly at the expense of operative work.

These national trends are modified in the case of London, partly as a result of local conditions (including the effect of changes in the distribution of population) and partly as a result of regional policy. As a result of changes in the industrial structure in London, there are mismatches between the supply of and demand for labour, reduced job choice and security and relatively lower growth in earnings and in household incomes.

In London the major decline in employment occurred in Manufacturing, in which the number of jobs fell from 1.43m in 1961 to 0.94m in 1974, a decline of 34 per cent, the rate of decline accelerating over the period (Tables 6.2 and 6.3). The average rate of decline over the period was nearly seven times as great in London as in England and Wales. By contrast, there was considerable growth in ROSE. In the case of Growth Services, employment grew both nationally and in London. In London the increase was from 1.19m in 1961 to 1.53m in 1974 (Table 6.2). The average annual rate of increase in London was 2.18 per cent, that in England and Wales was 3.23 per cent, while in ROSE it was 3.83 per cent (Tables 6.2 and 6.3). Inevitably, as population and economic activity decline, fewer workers are required to man the Other Industries and Services; further, the rate of decline in London has been increased as a result of national changes in these industries. As a consequence, the number of the workers in this sector in London has declined from 1.77m in 1961 to 1.52m in 1974 (Table 6.2). The average annual rate of decline was 1.06 per cent in London as against 0.12 in England and Wales (Table 6.3). By contrast, in ROSE there was a substantial rise of employment in this sector, averaging 1.58 per cent a year.

The poor experience of London industry overall was shared by nearly every individual industry. In Manufacturing, every industrial group in London, with the exception of textiles, declined in employment terms more than it would have done had it followed the national trend. Over the period 1961–71 the number of jobs in Manufacturing in London fell by 335,190 whereas, had it followed national trends, there would have been an increase of 13,140 jobs (Table 6.4). The positive 'structural component' of +13,140 was thus more than offset by a negative 'local component' of −348,330, reflecting the generally poor growth performance of individual industries in London relative to their respective counterparts in the nation as a whole. The sum of the structural component and the local component yields the overall change, which in this case was −335,190. In the case of Growth Services it was only in public administration that London gained more jobs than it would have done had it followed the national trend. Overall, London gained 240,590 jobs in Growth Services, the positive structural component of +360,420 being offset by a negative local component of −119,830. For Other Industries and Services the number of jobs in London declined over the period 1961–71 by 233,960, whereas had national trends been followed the decline would have only been 17,630.

The Changing Economic Environment

TABLE 6.4

Analysis of employment changes for London and Rest of South East, 1961–71

| Sector | Employment in 1961 | Change, 1961–71 | | | Local component as a percentage of 1961 employment |
		Total	Structural component	Local component	
Manufacturing:					
Greater London	1,428,490	−335,190	+13,140	−348,330	−24.4
Rest of the South East	990,640	+209,610	+230	+209,380	+21.1
Growth services:					
Greater London	1,190,650	+240,590	+360,420	−119,830	−10.1
Rest of the South East	813,860	+303,060	+232,190	+70,870	+8.7
Other industries and services:					
Greater London	1,741,660	−233,960	−17,630	−216,330	−12.4
Rest of the South East	1,422,030	+131,790	−630	+132,420	+9.3
All sectors:					
Greater London	4,360,800	−328,560	+355,930	−684,490	−15.7
Rest of the South East	3,226,530	+644,760	+231,790	+412,670	+12.8

Note: Manufacturing comprises the 1968 sics 3–19; Growth Services comprise the Air Transport, Posts and Telecommunications, and Miscellaneous Transport parts of sic 22 (i.e., mlh 707–709) and sics 24, 25 and 27; Other Industries and Services comprise all activity not included in Manufacturing or Growth Services. The employment figures for Greater London and the Rest of the South East in this table differ slightly from those in Table 6.2; the discrepancy is attributable to persons listed in the Census under 'Industries Inadequately Described'.

Source: Great Britain (1966), corrected for bias; Great Britain (1975b).

A comparison by Townsend (1976) by separate services (Minimum List Headings) over the period 1971–74 showed that for 80 per cent of the services, the percentage decreases in employment in London were greater than in the United Kingdom as a whole, while the percentage increases in London were lower than in the United Kingdom.

The Decline of Manufacturing Industry in London
An examination of the decline in manufacturing employment in London indicates that the decline is more the result of closures and run-down of plants than of transfers of plants. Over the period 1966–74, Dennis (1978) estimates the loss in manufacturing employment for London to

be 390,100 (Table 6.5). It will be seen that only about 9 per cent of the decline in jobs was a result of moves to the assisted areas. More significant were moves to London overspill towns and to other locations outside London (primarily moves to locations within the South East and East Anglia), amounting together to 18 per cent. Thus twice as many jobs were lost by Greater London to ROSE and (to a lesser extent) other non-assisted areas as were lost to assisted areas. Hence, assistance to manufacturing industry leaving London had less impact on the assisted areas than on other areas. The remainder of the jobs lost in London, 284,800 (73 per cent), was due to closures and shrinkage at the remaining plants. While many of these losses represent national losses as well as London losses, some may be due to multi-plant firms closing or running down plants in London and making up production at plants in other

TABLE 6.5
Components of industrial decline in Greater London, 1966–74

Job loss due to movement to assisted areas:		
Transfers to assisted areas	22,100	
Plus notional loss through creation of branches in the assisted areas	+ 14,100	
	36,200 (9%)	
Job loss due to movement to overspill towns:		
Transfers to planned London overspill towns	26,400	
Less notional *increase* through creation of branches in the New Towns and expanding towns	− 400	
	26,000 (7%)	
Job loss due to movement elsewhere:		
Transfers to other locations outside London	48,600	
Less notional *increase* in employment due to creation of branches elsewhere	− 5,500	
	43,100 (11%)	
SUB-TOTAL (job loss due to movement from London)		105,300 (27%)
Net job loss due to difference between openings and complete closures:		
Total complete closures	183,200	
Less opening of enterprises new to manufacturing	− 9,900	
Less new branches established in London	− 3,300	
	170,300 (44%)	
Estimated decline in firms employing under 20 people:		26,000 (7%)
Residual Shrinkage:		88,500 (23%)
TOTAL DECLINE IN MANUFACTURING EMPLOYMENT IN LONDON		390,100 (100%)

Source: Dennis (1978).

parts of the country, and some may be due to a shift of business to out-of-London firms. The indications are that the proportional loss of jobs was little greater in Inner London than in Outer London but that whereas 66 per cent of the loss from Inner London was due to closures and shrinkages, this figure was 58 per cent for Outer London.

A large proportion of the 284,800 jobs lost and not attributed to moves out of London results from total closures. As noted earlier, London has a relatively favourable structure of manufacturing industries which, if they had individually followed the national trends, would have resulted in London producing a net gain in manufacturing employment over the period 1961–71, even when there was a net decline in all manufacturing nationally. The large loss of jobs in London due to closures and shrinkages, particularly in industries that were growth industries nationally, indicates a loss of productive capacity that could make an important contribution to the objective of national industrial revival and might have implications for the balance of payments. Some of the firms reducing or eliminating production in London are likely to be multi-national firms and may be moving their activities abroad. There is a need that extends beyond London's interest to consider the part played by regional policy, direct and indirect, in creating the climate which gave rise to these closures and shrinkages, and also the part that national policies could play in alleviating such decline.

Some of the manufacturing industries that experienced an above-average rate of decline due to the local factor were among the largest in London. There is the obvious danger that the industrial decline might have an adverse effect on the structure of London manufacturing. The viability of London manufacturing industry is also endangered because firms moving out or expanding activities outside London are likely to be the more progressive and the more likely to expand. Neither these firms nor the firms closing in London are being replaced by new firms because of the factors that militate against entry. Moreover, the closure and contraction of manufacturing firms in London has an adverse effect on dependent firms in transport, supplying industries and other services.

Changes of Employment in the Rest of the South East (ROSE)
In contrast to the London experience, ROSE gained 209,610 jobs in manufacturing industry over the period 1961–71, whereas had its industries followed national trends they would have gained only 230 jobs (Table 6.4). In Growth Services the gain in jobs in ROSE was 303,060, whereas on the basis of national trends it would have gained 232,190 jobs. In the case of Other Industries and Services the gain of jobs in ROSE was 131,790 whereas on the basis of national trends it would have lost 630 jobs. Thus ROSE gained jobs on a considerable scale against the national trend, while London lost.

Changes in Occupational Structure

The changes in the industrial structure of London, together with the changes in occupational structure of each industry nationally, have resulted in significant changes in the occupational structure in London. Operative employment, which in 1971 accounted for 28.4 per cent of total employment, is provided mainly by Manufacturing, which employed 53.7 per cent, with Growth Services employing only 10.6 per cent. On the other hand, office work, which in 1971 accounted for 37.4 per cent of total employment, is provided mainly by the Growth Services, which employed 51.2 per cent of all office workers. The combined effect of changes in industrial structure and in the occupational structure of industries over the period 1961–71 was to reduce substantially the absolute and relative importance of operative work and to increase the importance of office work. If these trends continue the occupational structure will be changed even more radically. In particular, the number of operative jobs in manufacturing might be more than halved over the period 1961–81, with the other 90 per cent of jobs divided more or less equally between office and other workers.

The size of the shift from manufacturing to service industries creates an unstable employment base in London and a threat to future employment and the London economy. If present trends continue, only a fifth of employment would be in Manufacturing and over two-fifths in Growth Services by 1981, creating a situation of overdependence on a few service industries and routine office work. A reversal in the relatively favourable conditions of the past for office employment in London would affect large numbers of people. Routine office work might contract in London as a result of changing methods or because it might be induced to move out of London. Professional and scientific services, which have had the largest rate of growth and account for one eighth of London employment, consist mainly of public services such as education and health—services more likely to be reduced than expanded, given the Government's intention to reduce resources for public expenditure in favour of manufacturing industry. Moreover, the continued decline in births reduces the need for such services as education. Jobs in Other Industries and Services will contract as population and the activities to be serviced decline, particularly if, as an instrument of national policy, services are reduced to provide more resources for manufacturing industry. This would particularly affect London, which provides regional and national services as well as local ones. Moreover, this would not be compensated for by an increase in the growth of invisible exports, since relatively little additional employment would be created as a result of such expansion.

The changing structure of employment also narrows occupational choice, especially the option to use a manufacturing skill. The balance of employment is being shifted both away from manual work and away from better-paid manual work. An analysis of the New Earnings Surveys for 1971 and 1974 indicates that London's proportion of the South East Region's better-paid manual work (mainly in manufacturing industry) is declining more rapidly than the less well-paid manual work in other industrial sectors. Moreover, the average weekly earnings of manual workers in London (relative to ROSE) are declining faster in non-manufacturing industries than those in manufacturing industries. Thus the shift out of manufacturing poses a threat to earnings in London relative to those in ROSE. The position of resident Londoners is even less favourable than that implied by the above comparisons, which relate to workers employed in London. This arises because those commuting into Greater London from outside (about a tenth of the total working there) tend to be the more highly paid professional groups. London's share of the region's male workers fell by 12.7 per cent between 1961–71; the share of the more highly skilled groups fell faster than average, while the share of the less skilled groups fell less rapidly than average. Some of the decline of employment in London can be attributed to a continuing shortage of skilled workers, bringing in its wake a reduction in opportunities for the less skilled workers. Generally, the position for ROSE is the reverse of that for London. This can be traced back to the changes in the employment pattern. Over the period 1961–74 the proportion in Manufacturing declined little (less than nationally), while the decrease in Other Industries and Services was only a little higher than elsewhere (Table 6.2).

Unemployment and Vacancies
Unemployment has a number of effects including interrupted earnings, longer journeys to obtain similar jobs and hence greater expenses, acceptance of lower-grade and lower-paid employment, greater job uncertainty and instability of career prospects, particularly for young people. The rate of unemployment among resident males[1] over the period April 1971 to October 1976 has increased faster in the South East (1.89 times) than in Great Britain (1.68 times); see Table 6.6. The increase in the South East has been the result of a large increase in London (2.04 times); the increase in ROSE (1.71 times) was about the same as in Great Britain. In fact, the rate of increase in Outer London (2.05 times) has been greater than in Inner London (2.00 times), but in October 1976 the level of male resident unemployment in Inner London was 1.85 times that in Outer London. The level of unemployment in Inner London in October 1976 was 1.16 times that of Great Britain. There was a high level of unemployment in each of the Inner London sectors and about a third of the employment office areas in London have recently had rates equal to or greater than the Great Britain average, with some having rates fifty per cent greater than the Great Britain average.

TABLE 6.6

Male resident unemployment rates in April and October, 1971-76

Area	April 1971	Oct. 1971	April 1972	Oct. 1972	April 1973	Oct. 1973	April 1974	Oct. 1974	April 1975	Oct. 1975	April 1976	Oct. 1976
Inner London[a]	3.6	3.6	4.3	3.7	3.3	2.4	3.0	3.0	4.4	5.7	7.1	7.2
Outer London	1.9	2.1	2.4	2.0	1.8	1.3	1.6	1.6	2.4	3.3	3.9	3.9
Greater London	2.7	2.8	3.2	2.8	2.5	1.8	2.3	2.2	3.3	4.3	5.4	5.5
Rest of South East[b]	2.4	2.4	2.7	2.1	1.9	1.5	1.9	1.9	2.9	3.5	4.1	4.1
South East	2.5	2.6	3.0	2.4	2.1	1.6	2.1	2.0	3.1	3.8	4.6	4.7
Great Britain[c]	3.7	4.1	4.7	3.9	3.5	2.6	3.7	3.2	4.6	5.5	6.1	6.2

[a] Inner London consists of the North East Sector, the South Sector and the North West Sector. The Central Sector is omitted since this area is seriously affected by the registration of the unemployed elsewhere.
[b] The figures for Rest of the South East have been adjusted to take account of changes to the South East Region from October 1974 (McCallum, chapter 1 of this volume).
[c] The figures for Great Britain include males registered at both Employment Services Agency offices and at Careers Offices.

Note: the unemployment rate = (number of males registered unemployed at Employment Services Agency Offices)/(estimated resident economically active males aged 16 and over). Males registered at Careers Offices are excluded because the areas covered are different.

Source: data on the number of unemployment are taken from various issues of the *Department of Employment Gazette* and from unpublished local office returns. Data on economically active males are based on Great Britain (1975a; 1975b) and the mid-year estimates of the Registrars General.

The higher unemployment rates in Inner London relative to those in Outer London are to some extent explained by the relatively large proportion of unskilled workers in the residential labour force in Inner London. However, in March 1975 the actual unemployment in Inner London was far higher than that which would have been expected, given the socio-economic structure of the resident labour force. One important contributory factor behind this may have been the low or intermittent local demand for labour. In Outer London, actual and expected rates were similar and the unemployment problem at that time was largely the problem of the employment of the unskilled. Again, in ROSE, where the unemployment level was relatively low compared with London, it was mainly the problem of the unskilled.

Turning to the rates of unemployment registration, these tend to be particularly high in Inner London, especially for the younger people. The median duration of unemployment is less variable over London and is lowest for the younger group, indicating rapid job changes by this group. Analysis of data over a number of years suggests that the differences are

TABLE 6.7

Unfilled vacancies and unemployment among males in London and Rest of the South East, March 1974

	Number of unfilled vacancies (male)	Number of unemployed (male)	Ratio of vacancies to unemployed
Greater London:			
Skilled	8,171	7,628	1.07
Semi-skilled	2,705	3,837	0.70
Unskilled	3,045	16,194	0.19
All operatives	15,048	30,197	0.50
Office workers	8,056	9,461	0.85
Others	11,220	11,595	0.97
Total	34,324	51,253	0.67
Rest of the South East:			
Skilled	13,096	6,875	1.91
Semi-skilled	3,768	3,274	1.15
Unskilled	5,278	15,829	0.33
All operatives	23,967	27,486	0.87
Office workers	8,040	14,464	0.56
Others	9,088	8,316	1.09
Total	41,095	50,266	0.82

Note: recorded vacancies are thought to be about one-third of the actual number, so that the real ratios of vacancies to unemployment are likely to exceed 1.00 for all groups except unskilled operatives.

Source: data on unfilled vacancies and unemployment (EDS 68) supplied by the Department of Employment.

likely to persist. It is worth pointing out that registration rates decline with age and only rise slightly for the over 60s. Youth Unemployment is now common in most Western economies, but the form it takes varies. In the South East, youth employment is unstable and at a low level in the inner city.

Vacancies[2] are generally greater in ROSE than in London, while unemployment tends to be greater in London than ROSE. The ratio of vacancies to unemployed is less in London than in ROSE (Table 6.7), the vacancy–unemployed ratio being less in ROSE than London only for office jobs. For operatives in the region as a whole the ratio of vacancies to unemployed declines with skill, the ratio being about five times as great for skilled as unskilled. Unskilled operatives form the largest class of unemployed, but no more than a third of the total. Skilled workers are able to obtain new jobs with rather less difficulty than unskilled workers and hence tend to be unemployed for shorter periods.

It is likely that in London many unemployed workers, particularly those without a skill or a skill now in demand within manufacturing industry, take up employment in service industry, often in less well-paid employment and possibly with a longer journey to work. On subsequent unemployment they are, of course, registered as service workers rather than manufacturing workers. In considering the importance of the decline in manufacturing as a factor in unemployment, it must be recognised that, to the extent that the service sector is servicing manufacturing industry, a decline in the latter in itself is a contributory cause of unemployment in the service sector.

Earnings and Incomes
Data on earnings provide a measure of the level of earnings of those in gainful employment, while data on incomes provide a measure of total purchasing power. Clearly, the data only have meaning when allowance is made for the occupation structure of the labour force, the cost of living, comparability with other areas and the number of people to be supported by the income. Average levels of earnings reflect both individual earnings and the proportion of workers at each level. In 1974–75 men resident in London earned on average less than those in ROSE, while married women and other women earned more, but at best the excess did little more than make up for the higher cost of living in London (Table 6.8). All three groups earned on average more in London than those in Other Regions but the excess for men was hardly sufficient to make good the higher cost of living.[3] The earnings of all workers in Inner London outside the Central Sector were only marginally greater than those in Other Regions and again by no means sufficient to offset the higher cost of living (Great Britain, 1974). The range of earnings of residents of the Central Sector of London is very wide. For men the lower-quartile figure is substantially

TABLE 6.8

Average employment earnings by area of residence, 1974–75

	Average annual earnings (in pounds)			
Area	Men	Married women	Other women	All employees
Central Sector	2,570	1,341	1,741	2,142
Other inner sectors	2,486	1,236	1,590	1,980
Outer sectors	2,878	1,264	1,695	2,257
Greater London[a]	2,694	1,259	1,648	2,143
ROSE	2,751	1,077	1,487	2,152
Other regions	2,437	1,011	1,319	1,913
Great Britain	2,524	1,054	1,402	1,986

[a] Includes those whose sector of residence was unknown.

Note: the figures are based on a sample of virtually all employed persons aged 18 and over who had PAYE earnings on which graduated contributions were paid during the tax year.

Source: data supplied by the Department of Health and Social Security.

lower than in Other Regions; only the upper-quartile figure is higher and that is less than for ROSE.

Separate figures for those in full-time employment by place of employment (as distinct from residence) are available for 1975. These indicate that, on average, earnings for all full-time workers in 1975 in London exceeded those for ROSE by a percentage about equal to the difference in the cost of living. Nevertheless, the earnings of London male manual workers, except for those in construction, were certainly not enough (by comparison with the same group in ROSE) to offset the higher cost of living (Great Britain, 1974). The earnings of male clerical and sales workers were similarly inadequate. The three groups (manual, clerical and sales workers) comprise two-thirds of the male workers in London.

The difference between the averages for all residential workers and the average for full-time workers employed in London can be attributed to a number of causes. As was pointed out earlier, many of the better-paid workers in London are commuters. The difference may also reflect a greater incidence of part-time employment in London and a greater number of workers unemployed for a part of the year, as compared with ROSE. The level of resident earnings is reflected in household incomes. These have been rising faster in ROSE and nationally than in London. This is true for each quartile level, and an actual decline in terms of real values has occurred in the lowest quartile of London incomes. These incomes in London are now exceeded by those in ROSE despite the higher cost of living in London (Great Britain, 1974).

The factors causing the faster rates of increase in household incomes in ROSE as compared with London are likely to include the relatively rapid growth of highly paid workers living in ROSE and the relative growth of female activity rates in ROSE, as compared with London. It is also possible that the relatively rapid decline of male workers in manufacturing compared with other industries in London contributed to the lower-quartile differential. The lower-quartile figures may also be influenced by changing household size. In general, therefore, the slower rate of increase in household incomes in London compared with ROSE is associated (as are the higher local rates of unemployment) with higher rates of net migration of firms and people from London. At the same time the actual differences in household incomes between the two areas do not offset the differences between them in terms of the cost of living.

Decentralisation and Change in Other Regions

It is not possible to provide the equivalent range of statistical indicators of the extent and effect of decentralisation in regions other than the South East. Because these regions are so much smaller, separate figures for the metropolitan areas and the remainders of their respective regions do not generally exist. Nevertheless, the data that are available indicate that decentralisation has occurred in all metropolitan areas to a varying extent and for different reasons, but with similar relative declines in welfare.

Population Changes
The success of the policies aimed at reducing congestion in the conurbations (broadly the same as metropolitan areas), together with the effect of other factors, can be seen from Table 6.9. Against a rising national population, Greater London, Tyne and Wear and, to a smaller extent Merseyside and Central Clydeside lost population over the period 1961–66. In the quinquennium 1966–71, these areas were joined by Greater Manchester, and the rate of loss of population was much greater, particularly in the case of Greater London, Merseyside and Clydeside. The two Yorkshire conurbations and West Midlands joined the losers in the quinquennium 1971–76 and the rates of population losses all increased. By contrast, the populations of the remainders of the respective regions and of regions with no conurbations increased, although some at a declining rate in accordance with national trends.

Intraregional Changes in Employment
Over the period 1966–71, employment fell in Great Britain as a whole, but this fall reflected cyclical movements rather than a long-term trend.

TABLE 6.9
Population changes, 1961–76

Area	Percentage change 1961–66	Percentage change 1966–71	Percentage change 1971–76	Population in 1976 (thousands)
Tyne and Wear Met. County	−1.2	−1.4	−2.2	1,182.9
Rest of the North	+1.4	+1.5	+0.6	1,939.2
South Yorkshire Met. County	+1.6	+0.1	−0.2	1,318.3
West Yorkshire Met. County	+2.6	+1.1	−0.2	2,072.5
Rest of Yorks. & Humberside	+4.3	+2.4	+2.0	1,501.6
Greater Manchester Met. County	+1.1	−0.2	−1.8	2,684.1
Merseyside Met. County	−0.8	−2.6	−4.6	1,578.0
Rest of the North West	+5.7	+5.4	+3.5	2,291.9
West Midlands Met. County	+1.1	+1.4	−1.8	2,743.3
Rest of the West Midlands	+7.6	+6.2	+4.0	2,421.8
Greater London	−2.1	−4.7	−5.6	7,028.2
Rest of the South East	+10.1	+7.2	+3.3	9,865.4
Central Clydeside Conurbation	−0.1	−1.5	−3.8	1,807.0
Rest of Scotland	+0.6	+1.4	+1.9	3,396.0

Note: 1976 figures for England and Wales are provisional; figures for Scotland have been projected from the 1971–75 change.

Source: mid-year estimates of the Registrars General of the Home Population.

It is notable, however, that the decline in the conurbations was greater than in Great Britain as a whole as well as in the remainders of the regions containing the conurbations (Table 6.10). The highest rates of decline in employment occurred in the two conurbations in the North West and in Greater London. The rates of decline in employment were generally faster than the rates of decline in population.

Changes in Employment Structure
The rates of decline in employment were particularly rapid for manufacturing industry. Nationally, manufacturing employment declined only marginally faster than total employment but the rate of decline per annum was substantially faster within the conurbations. For the conurbations in which Manufacturing fell the least, the Merseyside, Tyneside and West Midlands conurbations, the average annual rate of decline was about 2 per cent compared with 1 per cent for Great Britain. In the worst hit conurbation, Greater London, the rate of decline was over 3 per cent a year. The situation for employment in the Growth Services is naturally different from that for manufacturing industry, since by their nature most

TABLE 6.10
Employment changes by major sector, 1966–71

Area	Employment in 1971 as a percentage of employment in 1966			
	Manufacturing	Growth industries and services	Other services	Total employment
Greater London	83	107	88	92
Rest of the South East	105	117	94	103
Merseyside conurbation	91	109	82	91
South East Lancs. conurbation	86	113	89	92
Rest of the North West	97	115	92	98
Tyneside conurbation	91	114	85	93
Rest of the North	105	112	86	97
West Yorks. conurbation	87	113	91	93
Rest of Yorks. & Humberside	96	114	89	96
West Midlands conurbation	90	114	89	93
Rest of the West Midlands	98	113	92	98
Central Clydeside conurbation	86	112	87	95
Rest of Scotland	102	112	88	97
Great Britain	95	111	90	96

Note: sectors are defined in the Note to Table 6.4.

Source: Great Britain (1967), corrected for under-enumeration; Great Britain (1975b).

of the Growth Services congregate in cities, and hence conurbations would expect to do better than with Manufacturing. In fact, employment in Growth Services has grown in all the areas for which an analysis has been made (Table 6.10). Growth has equalled that in Great Britain and slightly exceeded it in all the conurbations except Merseyside and Greater London, where it has fallen short of the national growth rate of 11 per cent over the period 1966–71, increasing by only 9 per cent and 7 per cent, respectively. In most cases the Growth Services have increased by nearly as much (or a little more) in the conurbations as in the remainders of their respective regions; the exceptions are Greater London where the increase was 7 per cent, as against 17 per cent in ROSE, and Merseyside where the increase was 9 per cent, as against 15 per cent in the rest of the North West (Table 6.10). Other Industries and Services have declined nationally and in all the areas analysed (Table 6.10), but with exception of the West Yorkshire conurbation the rate of decline has been greater in the conurbations than in the remainders of their respective regions. Merseyside and Greater London have had the greatest declines in employment relative to the remainders of their regions, while Merseyside has had the greatest decline in Great Britain.

The overall picture thus reflects not only the high rate of population decline in the conurbations as against increases elsewhere but comparatively high rates of decline in employment in the conurbations, particularly for manufacturing employment. Rates of decline tended to be more rapid than the rates of decline in population. The rates of decline during the period considered were particularly great for the Merseyside, Greater London, South East Lancashire and Tyneside conurbations. High rates of decline have also been experienced by Central Clydeside. It can be seen from Table 6.11 that in 1971 the conurbations, other than Greater London, still had a greater proportion of their employment in Manufacturing than the rest of Great Britain but a smaller proportion in Other Services—a category that includes the Growth Services of Tables 6.10 and 6.4. The West Midlands, West Yorkshire and South East Lancashire conurbations depend particularly heavily on Manufacturing and have comparatively low proportions of employment in Other Services (Table 6.11).

The changes over the period 1966–71 are part of a long-term trend. An analysis of trends over the period 1951–71 by Corkindale (1976) for the English conurbations indicates the extent to which the employment structure changed in relation to the national trend. This analysis is summarised in Table 6.12. Here the expected employment in 1971 for a particular sector represents the level of employment that would have been attained in 1971 if the sector had grown at the national rate over the period 1951–71. The residual item for a particular sector represents the difference between the actual employment in 1971 and the expected employment in 1971 and thus comprises the local factor, reflecting the overall growth performance of that sector within the conurbation. In the case of Manufacturing, the residuals for all the conurbations are negative, indicating in each case that the industrial structure of the conurbation (the structural factor) was favourable, but that this effect was more than offset by poor growth performance (the local factor). This was especially true for the conurbations of Greater London, South East Lancashire and West Yorkshire. It will be recalled that Table 6.4 also showed a similar pattern for Greater London over the period 1961–71.

In the case of Public Utilities, Transport and Distribution, actual employment in 1971 was below the expected level on the basis of the 1951–71 trend, except for the West Midlands (Table 6.12). Such a tendency is to be expected since the demand for such services decreases with declines in population and activity. For Other Services, only Greater London and Merseyside had expected changes above the actual changes (Table 6.12). This group includes the Growth Services and it is likely that the other conurbations, particularly the West Midlands (which had not suffered much population and employment decline by 1971), gained more employment from the expansion of Growth Services than they lost from the decline in demand as population and economic activities fell.

TABLE 6.11

Composition of employment in the conurbations, 1971

Percentage of employment

Sector	Greater London	Central Clydeside	Mersey-side	South East Lancashire	Tyneside	West Midlands	West Yorkshire	Rest of Great Britain
Primary	0.2	0.6	0.2	0.6	2.4	0.2	1.3	6.6
Manufacturing	26.8	38.3	33.4	43.1	36.6	53.3	44.9	33.4
Construction	6.1	7.7	7.2	6.2	7.0	5.7	5.8	7.4
Public utilities, transport and distribution	25.2	23.2	27.2	22.2	21.7	16.8	20.2	19.5
Other services	40.3	29.8	31.3	27.3	31.9	23.2	27.5	32.4
Total employment[a]	100.0	100.0	100.0	100.0	100.0	100.0	100.0	100.0

[a] Columns do not add to 100 because persons with workplaces outside Great Britain and workers who inadequately describe their industries are included in the employment totals.

Source: Corkindale (1976).

TABLE 6.12

Actual and expected employment in 1971 by major sector in the English conurbations

Sector	Employment in 1971 (in thousands)					
	Greater London	Mersey-side	South East Lancashire	Tyneside	West Midlands	West Yorkshire
Primary:						
Actual	10	1	6	9	2	11
Expected	10	2	9	10	4	12
Residual	0	−1	−3	−1	−2	−1
Manufacturing:						
Actual	1,093	188	484	139	638	362
Expected	1,486	200	665	146	675	454
Residual	−393	−12	−181	−7	−37	−92
Construction:						
Actual	250	41	70	26	68	47
Expected	340	45	73	25	63	47
Residual	−90	−4	−3	+1	+5	0
Public utilities, transport and distribution:						
Actual	1,032	153	249	82	201	163
Expected	1,153	205	267	113	199	169
Residual	−121	−52	−18	−31	+2	−6
Other services:						
Actual	1,647	177	306	121	278	223
Expected	1,851	303	303	115	244	209
Residual	−204	−126	+3	+6	+34	+14

Source: Corkindale (1976).

Unemployment

Unemployment rates published by the government underestimate unemployment in the conurbations because they are not resident-based; see Note 1. Unemployment rates based on Census of Population figures do not suffer from this disadvantage, although they tend to be higher than those based on people registering as unemployed. In the case of all six regions with conurbations, the male unemployment rates for the conurbations compared more unfavourably with those for the remainders of their respective regions in 1971 than in 1966. In some cases the comparative rates changed from being more favourable to the conurbations in 1966 to being less favourable to the conurbations in 1971, while in other cases an already unfavourable situation deteriorated. Residential unemployment rates for 1976 are only available for the South East. These show the metropolitan-area figure substantially above the regional figure (Table 6.6). Employment area based figures for the other regions with conurbations indicate that residential-based indicators would confirm that unemployment rates in the conurbations were higher in August 1976 than those for their respective regions. Within the conurbations, unemployment is particularly heavy within their inner areas.

Metropolitan Areas in Decline

The changing patterns of employment and population within British regions since the early 1960s have been analysed in the previous section. In addition to these changes, regional policy, over the same period, has generally favoured the northern and western regions of Great Britain, probably at the expense of the southern regions, which contain major metropolitan areas. Discussions of these changes are provided by McCallum and Randall (chapters 1 and 5 of this volume). The net effect of decentralisation tendencies on the one hand and regional policy on the other has been to reduce considerably the volume of population and employment in the metropolitan areas, while stimulating both in the parts of the regions outside the metropolitan areas and in regions with no metropolitan areas. At the same time the volumes of population and employment have been stimulated in the western and northern regions at the expense of the southern and midland regions. The effect on the interregional distribution of population and employment has been less than on the intraregional distribution in regions with metropolitan areas, into which category all the northern regions fall. The effect in these regions has been dampened because there has not been the stimulus necessary to reveal the relative disadvantages of the metropolitan areas in competition with the new and expanding towns in these areas.

The metropolitan areas, and particularly the inner cities, have been in decline everywhere. The non-metropolitan parts of the regions have had population gains and at least relative employment gains, but those in the West and North have fared less well than the rest of the South East and West Midlands regions. The changes in population and employment have been associated with changes in living conditions and welfare. The growth of population and employment in the non-metropolitan areas has been associated with a better employment situation, relatively more opportunities for skilled and professional workers, relatively lower unemployment, faster growth in earnings and incomes, better housing opportunities and a generally superior environment for living and working. Broadly speaking, the metropolitan areas, and particularly the inner cities, have suffered relative declines in all these respects, while the non-metropolitan areas have gained through the growth and development of New Towns and expanding towns. The stimulus to development provided by regional policy in the assisted areas and the curbs on development in some other areas appear to have just more than offset the balance of advantage otherwise enjoyed by the non-assisted areas. The percentage increases in the number of unemployed in recent years in the various types of assisted areas and in the non-assisted areas are roughly inversely related to the assistance provided (McCallum, chapter 1 of this volume, Table 1.7). Within the assisted areas, as outside them, the metropolitan areas have not been able to compete with the New Towns and expanding towns.

It is necessary to consider whether the interregional and intraregional changes that are taking place are in the national interest and whether the resources used to stimulate such movements are justified. While the development in the New Towns and expanding towns provides an attractive environment for living and working, the existing built environment of the metropolitan areas is deteriorating and some of it is becoming derelict. Although much of this needs to be rehabilitated and some rebuilt, such renovation requires fewer resources than development with complete infrastructure on greenfield sites. To a large extent, development in New Towns and expanding towns duplicates facilities already available in the metropolitan areas. Population migrating from the metropolitan areas tends to reduce the need for facilities and services only marginally in each area, since migration takes place from dispersed locations. However, migration to the new areas is generally concentrated and additional facilities and services need to be provided in order to accommodate it. In addition to the resources needed to develop and service the migrants, more land needs to be taken from agriculture, reducing the potential for growing food at home; in the meantime, land becomes vacant and derelict in the metropolitan areas.

About half the finance used to develop the growth areas is provided by the public sector out of taxation and borrowing. Public finance is also provided to develop the additional public services, and used to provide the grants and subsidies to stimulate development in the assisted areas. In 1975–76 Regional Development Grants amounted to £325m and the Regional Employment Premium (now phased out) amounted to £213m;

in addition, regional selective financial assistance was about £50m. The need for these various types of grants and subsidies provides a measure of the extent to which industry would not otherwise have developed and remained in the assisted areas. Insofar as industry was successfully diverted from regions with greater levels of productivity, national output levels would tend to be depressed unless offset by reduced unemployment; Gross Domestic Product per head is about two-fifths greater in the South East region than in Wales, the regions having the highest and lowest level of Gross Domestic Product.

Dispersion policy and regional policy were developed in a period when population was expected to expand at a high rate—when the expectation was for substantial annual increases in productivity and when the metropolitan areas had populations much larger than today. Now, population growth is slowing down and national population may become static; the national economy is at best static and its future growth is likely to be low; and all the metropolitan areas have lost considerable population and economic activity. Dispersion policy and regional policy and their effects on productivity and costs need to be re-examined. In future, policies need to be orientated to produce the maximum output of goods and services for the minimum input of additional resources. Industry needs to be developed where the net gain to the nation is the greatest, taking into account additional public and private resources—direct as well as indirect. While development in new areas may result in higher net productivity for the individual establishment, it may help to destroy the viability of other establishments in the areas from which industry has been diverted, thereby reducing national output and wasting national resources, and at the same time resulting in the duplication of public and private services. If the fullest use is to be made of the potential of existing national resources and efficient use made of additional resources, greater attention needs to be given to utilising the potential of the existing built environment. Before settlements are further expanded or new ones developed, it is necessary to compare the level of resources required with that required to make existing developed areas viable for industry.

While there may be a case for continuing to subsidise industry in certain regions, this does not also justify the development of new settlements to house them. Rather, it only justifies efforts to replace dying industries with firms with growth potential in existing areas of development. The deprived areas, mainly the inner cities within the metropolitan areas, have proven unable (given the restrictions imposed on them) to compete with the New Towns and expanding towns in the rest of their regions. Metropolitan areas with assisted-area status have done less well than other areas with such status. If the development potential already available within the metropolitan areas is to be utilised, it will be necessary to rehabilitate such areas and to take measures to enable firms located there to maximise their productivity, perhaps granting them some temporary assistance. If nothing were done to reverse the balance of advantage against the metropolitan areas, it would be necessary to consider how they might be run down in an orderly way, so that neither the people nor the firms remaining in deprived areas would be unduly penalised. This would involve sustaining the viability of firms in deprived areas until they could be closed and their work transferred to growth areas, and maintaining the environment and level of services without excessive local taxation until the inhabitants could be persuaded to migrate. It is not clear how such objectives could be achieved without creating excessive national costs and redirecting national production.

Notes

1. The unemployment rate published by the government uses as the denominator those employed in the area, as distinct from those resident in the area, and thus understates (because of the level of commuting) the rate for Greater London and overstates it for ROSE. Female unemployment rates are unreliable because many do not register when unemployed.

2. For some classes of jobs, particularly female office jobs, many vacancies are not reported to the employment offices.

3. The difference between London and elsewhere was estimated by the Pay Board to have been 14 per cent (Great Britain, 1974).

References

Corkindale, J. T. (1976) 'Employment in the Conurbations', paper presented to the Inner City Employment Conference at York University, September 1976.

Dennis, R. D. (1978) 'The Decline of Manufacturing Employment in London' *Urban Studies*, Vol. 15, pp. 63–73.

Goddard, J. and Spence, N. *et al.* (1976) 'Urban Change in Britain', Department of Geography, London School of Economics, Working Paper, No. 34.

Great Britain (1940) Royal Commission on the Distribution of Industrial Population. *Report.* Cmd. 6153. London: HMSO.

Great Britain (1966) Registrars General. *Census of Population 1961.* London and Edinburgh: HMSO.

Great Britain (1967) Registrars General. *Sample Census of Population 1966.* London and Edinburgh: HMSO.

Great Britain (1974) Pay Board. *Advisory Report, No. 4.* Cmnd. 5660.

Great Britain (1975a) Department of Employment. 'Annual Census of Employment: June 1974', *Department of Employment Gazette*, Vol. 83, pp. 643–9.

Great Britain (1975b) Office of Population Censuses and Surveys; Registrars General. *Census of Population 1971.* London and Edinburgh: HMSO.

Great Britain (1977) Department of the Environment, Scottish Office and Welsh Office. *Policy for the Inner Cities.* Cmnd. 6845. London HMSO.

Hall, P., Gracey, H., Drewett, R. and Thomas, R. (1973) *The Containment of Urban England.* London: Allen and Unwin.

Townsend, A. R. (1976) 'The Relationship of Inner City Problems to Regional Policy', paper presented to the Inner City Employment Conference at York University, September 1976.

CHAPTER 7

Regional Development and North Sea Oil and Gas

G. A. Mackay*

Introduction

It is undeniable that one of the few bright features of the British economic
scene in recent years has been the discovery of North Sea oil and gas.
Although oil production from the North Sea has only recently commenced,
the likelihood of substantial domestic production and government revenue
has made overseas borrowing much easier and current economic problems
have been accordingly less severe. By the end of 1976 there had been
fourteen commercial discoveries of oil on which development was under
way. Of these, six fields were producing by the end of the year and
a further six fields were producing by the end of 1978. In addition, by
the end of 1976 there had been thirty other potential commercial discoveries
and it is possible that one-half to two-thirds of these could eventually
be developed as worthwhile commercial propositions. Also, there are bound
to be further discoveries in the North Sea and the other United Kingdom
waters, although on present evidence these are likely on average to be
smaller and less frequent than has been the case with discoveries over
the last decade. Throughout this chapter the term 'North Sea oil' should
be taken to include both oil and natural gas, except where a clear distinction
has been made.

The fourteen known commercial finds have estimated recoverable
reserves of oil of around 10,000m barrels and recent Department of Energy
estimates (Great Britain, 1976a) put likely total reserves in British waters
as approximately 34,000m barrels or 4,500m tonnes. Domestic consumption
in 1976 was approximately 80m tonnes. The known reserves are thus equivalent to approximately fifteen years' consumption at the present levels and

* Institute for the Study of Sparsely Populated Areas, University of Aberdeen. This chapter is based
largely on work undertaken in the course of a study for the Scottish Office on the economic impact
of the North Sea oil and gas developments. I am grateful, therefore, for the help and advice given
by my colleagues on that study, Max Gaskin, Donald MacKay, Alison Marr, Anne Moir and Niall
Trimble. The views expressed in this chapter do not necessarily represent those of the Scottish Office
or those of my colleagues.

159

the estimated total reserves to roughly fifty years. In the case of gas, there are nine known commercial discoveries, some of which have been producing since the late 1960s, and twelve other commercial possibilities discovered by the end of 1976. Although still important, the gas discoveries have not been on the scale of the oil discoveries and have consequently attracted relatively little attention. As well as wholly gasfields, there have been significant discoveries of associated gas in oilfields such as Brent and Ekofisk. The recent Department of Energy estimates for proven reserves of gas remaining at the end of December 1975 were 815,000m cubic metres, and the total possible reserves could be as high as 1,430,000m cubic metres (Great Britain, 1976a). In 1976 natural gas production amounted to over 14,000m therms, nearly 18 per cent of total domestic energy consumption (on a primary fuel input basis). This share should rise to between 23 per cent and 25 per cent of total energy consumption by the end of the decade.

These discoveries will be of substantial benefit to the national economy as a whole. Regarding the balance of payments, for example, North Sea oil and gas will make a positive contribution to the current account from 1977 onwards and should be contributing around £4,500m per year by 1980. In time the discoveries will obviate the need for heavy borrowing to meet the balance of payments deficit, which has been growing rapidly since the rise in oil prices in the winter of 1973–74. The other major benefit would be the increase in government revenue, from royalties and taxation. MacKay and Mackay (1975) have estimated that the government 'take' in 1975 prices from the North Sea finds will be around £2,150m in 1980 and over £2,500m per year from 1984 onwards until production starts to decline. The significance of these revenues is discussed in more detail below. It should be clear therefore that the benefits (or, more precisely, the potential benefits) offered by the North Sea discoveries are substantial and will make a noticeable difference to the national economy. A growing economy and a government with substantial offshore revenues should ensure an active regional policy for many years to come, for it is generally accepted that regional policies are more successful in times of expansion than recession. Nevertheless, this present chapter intends to look at the implications for regional development in a different light, firstly by considering the present direct regional impact of the North Sea developments, secondly by considering the differences between the direct and indirect effects, and thirdly by looking at the possibilities for using some proportion of the oil revenues explicitly for regional development.

Regional Impact to Date

Of greater interest in the recent past has been the direct effect on certain parts of Great Britain, particularly Scotland. To date, all the gas and oil discoveries in United Kingdom waters have been in the North Sea, the gas discoveries mainly off the coast of East Anglia and the oil discoveries off the east coast of Scotland. Many of the former were discovered in the mid-1960s and the first British natural gas production from the North Sea began in March 1967. There are now three onshore terminals taking gas from the southern North Sea: Bacton in East Anglia, Theddlethorpe and Easington in Yorkshire. Exploration activity moved further north and, after a disappointing period, oil was first discovered in the Norwegian sector (the Ekofisk field) in 1968. In the British sector the first discoveries were Montrose (September 1969) and Forties (November 1970), both in what could be regarded as the middle North Sea. More recently, all the major oil discoveries and some gas discoveries have been made off the east coast of Scotland in the northern North Sea, most of them in the East Shetland basin.

Therefore the direct effects of offshore exploration, development and production have been felt very largely on the east coast of Britain, particularly the north and east of Scotland. Because of the physical problems of crossing the Norwegian Trench, the pipeline from the Ekofisk field has been laid to a terminal at Teesside in North East England; the onshore terminal for the Forties field is at Cruden Bay, just north of Aberdeen in Scotland; and two other large terminals have been or are being constructed at Flotta in the Orkney Islands and Sullom Voe in the Shetland Islands. Of the four large steel production platform yards in Britain, one is at Graythorpe in North East England and the other three are in Scotland: at Methil in Fife, Ardersier near Inverness and Nigg near Invergordon. The four large concrete platform yards are all on the west coast of Scotland where there is sufficient depth of water.

Taking Scotland first, it is clear that the discoveries have made a major contribution to the improved performance of the Scottish economy relative to that of the nation as a whole. In the late 1950s and early 1960s Scotland was economically one of the weakest of the Standard Regions. Unemployment averaged more than twice the British figure. Net emigration per year from Scotland averaged almost 37,000 from 1960 to 1968 and over the period 1965–67 was so heavy that the total population actually declined. Even with this high rate of outmigration, per capita incomes (by any measure) lagged appreciably behind the national average. From the mid-1960s the slow recovery began, helped initially by a more active and more generous regional policy. As national employment fell from its peak in 1966, the Scottish economy rode the recession more easily. For example, over the period 1965–73 Scottish GDP rose by approximately 24 per cent, compared with 22 per cent for the nation as a whole. From 1964 there was a marked fall in the Scottish/British unemployment relative: from around 2.0 in 1964 to 1.6 in 1966, remaining at that level until 1973 before falling steadily to as low as 1.2 in early 1976—the most favourable relative position recorded since the commencement of the modern series of unemployment statistics in 1924.

Regarding population, the improvement in Scottish employment and incomes relative to that of the rest of the nation is reflected in population movements from 1967 onwards. Net outmigration, which reached a peak of 43,000 in 1966–67, fell rapidly over the next two years, levelled off at a plateau in the region of 20,000 and then fell sharply again from 1972, although in 1974–75 the loss again approached the level of the early 1970s. There were two major causes of this improvement in Scotland's overall position from the mid-1960s: first, the introduction and gradual strengthening of an active regional policy designed to shift the pattern of economic activity in favour of the areas of high unemployment; and second, the impact of the North Sea oil and gas discoveries, which became increasingly important from 1970 onwards. The latter has been the more spectacular effect and is often considered to hold out substantial promise for the future. However, the first improvement in Scotland's relative position pre-dates any impact of North Sea oil and the evidence suggests that a more active regional policy pursued from 1963 may have made the major contribution to strengthening the competitive position of the Scottish economy.

This is not the place to examine the details of regional policy, but the level of expenditure in Scotland on regional aids of different kinds clearly reflects its increasing importance, rising from £7.9m in 1963–64 to £80m annually in the early 1970s, and rising again to almost £150m in 1974–75. These figures are based on work carried out at the Department of Economics, University of Dundee (Great Britain, 1976b, p. 21). It is impossible to determine precisely the employment creation that may have resulted from these expenditures, but it has been suggested by Moore and Rhodes (1974) that over the period 1960–71 regional policy might have created some 70–78,000 jobs in Scotland over and above the level of job creation that would have been expected in its absence. These authors argue that the persistent high unemployment in Scotland was due to labour supply responses that prevented regional job creation from being fully reflected in unemployment statistics. However, there is a further reason for expecting a long time lag before a more active regional policy is reflected in labour market indicators such as employment and unemployment. In brief, regional policy is dependent for its effectiveness on improving the economic efficiency of the assisted area rather than subsidising inefficient activities within that area. To the extent that the former occurs, the process is necessarily long term, and improved efficiency may even involve some initial reduction in employment—for example, if additional capital investment as a result of regional policy is capital deepening rather than capital widening, then the initial result of the more active policy will be higher unemployment, although it is extremely unlikely that this will be the long-term result.

While regional policy appears to have been the single most important factor in the relative improvement of the Scottish economy, the impact of the North Sea oil and gas activities has been the dominant influence in the further improvement observable in the 1970s. In mid-1971 no more than 500 persons were employed in all North Sea oil and gas activities in Scotland, but from then onwards the numbers grew rapidly and by mid-1972 exceeded 2,500. From 1973, official estimates of employment in wholly related companies (i.e., companies wholly engaged on North Sea oil work) are available. These show that in May 1973 some 5,100 persons were employed in such companies; a year later the figure was 15,000; and in May 1976 it reached 25,500. Since these figures refer only to wholly related companies, the total level of job creation has certainly been in excess of these estimates and is now likely to be in the region of 45,000. Taking into account the usual multiplier effects, this would represent a gross increase of employment of between 60,000 and 70,000. A recent Scottish Office study (Great Britain, 1976b) has suggested a slightly lower overall range of 55,600 to 64,800. A substantial proportion, perhaps a quarter, of this employment is in exploration, drilling, pipelaying and other offshore installation operations where much of the employment and income accrues to foreign nationals with no direct impact on Scotland. Nevertheless, it is clear that the North Sea oil discoveries have been a major stimulus to the Scottish economy in the 1970s.

It is also worth pointing out that these increases in employment are themselves highly concentrated geographically within Scotland, with about 40 per cent of the direct employment being in the Grampian Region (mainly in Aberdeen and Peterhead), which has a 8.5 per cent share of total Scottish employment and population, and about 15 per cent in the Highland Region, which has a 3.5 per cent share of total Scottish employment and population. Other relatively large and growing concentrations are located in the Orkney and Shetland Islands; consequently the proportion of oil-related employment in the Central Belt, which contains 75 per cent of Scotland's population and over 80 per cent of the unemployed, is relatively small. To a large extent the oil developments have occurred in the more sparsely populated parts of Scotland, with limited manufacturing bases and limited infrastructure, and this has generated a large number of problems, some of which are mentioned below. To a lesser extent, though still important, similar developments have occurred on the east coast of England. East Anglia, for example, is the major centre for the southern North Sea gasfields, with Great Yarmouth as the major supply base and the Bacton terminal taking most of the gas from the producing fields. Total direct gas-related employment is probably around 10,000 at the present time, most of which is involved in the production phase, since exploration activity has fallen off sharply. Another large concentration of activity and employment is in the North East region of England, centred principally on the Ekofisk oil terminal and the steel platform yard at

Graythorpe. Here, direct employment is probably in the range 15,000–20,000, and there have been a significant number of downstream and other related developments. As in Scotland, much of the relative improvement in the North East's economic performance in the 1970s can be attributed to the North Sea oil and gas developments.

Prospects for oil development now exist on the west coast, principally off North West England around the Isle of Man and off Wales in the Celtic Sea, and the recent fifth licensing round has designated blocks off the South West Region. Exploration results in these areas have been disappointing to date, and hence onshore activity has been very limited and on nothing like the scale in Scotland, but the possibility of commercial discoveries cannot be ruled out. Again, it is coincidental that the offshore activities on the west coast are mainly taking place off the less prosperous regions of the nation.

Direct and Indirect Effects

The North Sea developments have generated a large number of social and economic effects within the nation. For present purposes it is possible to divide these into two broad groups: the direct effects and the indirect effects. The former can be taken as including the increases in employment and income attributable to the North Sea activities, and these have arisen largely on the east coast of Britain. As was shown in the preceding section, the largest beneficiary to date has been Scotland with over 60,000 jobs (including those generated by the multiplier process), followed by North East England with 15,000–20,000 and East Anglia with around 10,000. The direct impact has certainly made a significant improvement in Scottish economic fortunes and a lesser impact in the other regions affected.

Without doubt, however, the main beneficiary is the national economy as a whole, because of the great magnitude of the indirect benefits. The major economic benefits are the improvements that the North Sea discoveries will bring to the balance of payments and to the government in the form of revenues from royalties and taxes. The main point to be made is that the indirect effects are much greater than the direct effects and therefore the long-term direct benefits to a region such as Scotland are relatively small. A simple example should suffice to demonstrate this point. It may be assumed that North Sea oil sells at $14 per barrel and that, on average, the capital and operating costs are at present around $4 and $1, respectively. In the case of capital expenditures there is a high propensity to import (around 0.5 for the nation as a whole) and from the viewpoint of Scotland, for example, there is a high propensity to import from the rest of the nation. In rough terms, we can assume that only 25 per cent of the required equipment, materials etc. is produced in Scotland and this is the proportion that determines the direct increases in employment and incomes. With operating expenditures, the propensity to import is lower and we can assume that around half of the equipment, materials etc. is produced in Scotland. Adding the two together gives a direct impact in Scotland equivalent to around $1.5 per barrel. Let us then assume that, of the remaining value added, $1 goes to the oil companies by way of profit and the remaining $8 to the government in the form of royalties and taxes. Thus the indirect effects accruing to the nation are equivalent to around $8 per barrel, compared with the direct effects in Scotland of around $1.5 per barrel. In other words, the indirect effects are five or six times as great as the direct effects.

This difference is so substantial that minor adjustments to the cost or to the import propensity estimates would not affect the basic argument. Also, it is one that will apply to the offshore developments in any region of the nation; indeed, the propensity to import for Scotland may be less than in any other region. The underlying explanation is the fact that since the oil price rises in the winter of 1973–74 and subsequent increases, the selling price of North Sea oil (and, to a lesser extent, gas) has been substantially above the production cost and, given that North Sea oil will sell at world market prices, there has been a tremendous addition in value added. Consequently, the distribution of the economic benefits from North Sea oil depends on the political framework in which they are set and on the priorities and preferences of those who manipulate that framework. A similar comment could be made of any industry but it has a special force when applied to North Sea oil. The difference is so substantial that it amounts to a difference in kind rather than of degree, and an understanding of the nature of this difference is vital.

Oil Revenues and Regional Development

Should some proportion of the oil revenues be earmarked explicitly for regional development in Scotland or any other part of the nation? This is the crucial question running through this chapter, and the answer is a difficult one since it involves both political and economic judgements. The political aspects are not considered here in any detail because they are examined in more detail by Firn and Maclennan (chapter 13 of this volume). The case for revenues being used as an element of regional policy appears to be twofold: (a) as compensation for the detrimental effects of the direct impact; (b) as a means of maintaining in Scotland some of the value added that oil and gas developments are creating in the region.

Taking the compensation argument first, there is the simple point that the appropriateness of policies and the assessments of their success depend largely on the particular viewpoint from which such policies are considered. In the present context a distinction can be made among the national,

Scottish, and local-community viewpoints. It is to be expected that some conflicts of interest will occur because it would only be in the hypothetical world that these three viewpoints always coincided. Inevitably, some policies implemented by the national government will not be in the best interests of Scotland; some Scottish policies will not be to the liking of local communities, such as Orkney and Shetland; and some policies of local communities will appear selfish when looked at from a Scottish or national standpoint. An example is the optimum level of oil output from the British sector of the North Sea: from the national viewpoint the peak level of around 150m tonnes per year (in the mid 1980s) appears to be an acceptable level of production. However, if Scotland were independent, probably about 50m tonnes per year would be more appropriate; and, in contrast, Norway is planning for peak production of around 90m tonnes per year, probably by the 1990s. Some conflict of interest must be accepted as inevitable and any disagreements should be seen in that light. This might sound obvious but it is surprising how often it is forgotten.

In the case of direct effects, one obvious conclusion is that the magnitude of these effects will diminish over time as production activities become dominant and the development phase becomes less important. This is really an inexorable conclusion, although it is perfectly possible to hold different views about the timing of the decline or its eventual scale. The development phase is much more labour intensive than any other phase in the life of an oilfield, and after this phase is completed employment will decline rapidly as production commences. There are signs of this occurring in Scotland already. It should therefore be obvious that it is very unlikely that the direct income and employment effects will be sufficient to bring a major and permanent change in Scotland's economic prospects, or those of any other region similarly affected. Rather, they have provided a once-and-for-all increase in activity that has offered something of a breathing space during which the more fundamental long-term problems can be tackled.

The eventual decline in employment will obviously affect some areas more than others and the areas worst affected will generally be those concentrating on development work such as platform and module construction. A distinction can be drawn between two types of problem area: (a) those where expectations of long-term permanent employment are not likely to be met, e.g., East Ross, South Argyll and Fife; (b) those where the establishment of permanent facilities requires construction labour forces substantially in excess of the permanent labour forces, e.g., Orkney, Shetland and Peterhead. Communities of the latter type are the ones bearing the greatest costs of the policy of rapid exploration and development, and there appears to be a strong case for special assistance for the areas in question. A possibility is the earmarking of a proportion of government oil revenues for the provision of alternative employment opportunities.

This is not novel insofar as it has already occurred in Orkney and Shetland by way of special agreements negotiated by the local authorities with the oil companies. Because of the sparse populations and limited facilities available in the islands, incoming oil-related and construction companies have had to depend very heavily on migrant labour. Nevertheless, even the movement of a relatively small number of local people from their existing occupations to oil-related activities has created substantial problems for local industries, both in the manufacturing and service sectors. An added complication in Shetland was that at the time of the advent of oil, the local fish-processing and knitwear industries were performing poorly and there were widespread fears that labour losses in indigenous industries would be not only harmful but completely destructive. Given that the permanent labour forces of the oil terminals in Shetland and Orkney will be only a small proportion of the construction labour forces required, the local authorities were determined to do all they could to help maintain indigenous industries until such times as the construction work was largely completed. The funds established with the income from the oil companies are intended for this purpose, although it is a very difficult task to disperse the income appropriately.

The argument that Orkney and Shetland are special cases is very tenuous and there is surely a case for applying the same principle to other parts of Scotland. Virtually all the local authorities have had to expend a great deal of money on providing houses, schools, roads and other infrastructure for the incoming migrant labour and oil-related companies, and special assistance from central government has been very small. Future income from increased rates will not be sufficient to offset these additional costs. It could well be that all the local authorities so affected could negotiate separate agreements with the oil companies involved (although in many cases there is a problem of identifying the appropriate companies), but a centrally coordinated disbursement of funds would have some advantages, given the similarity of many of the problems and the authorities' lack of expertise in development matters. A possibility could be the allocation of some oil revenues to the Scottish Development Agency, for example, which could supplement the local expertise and understanding required.

Turning to the more general second point made above, the oil and gas industry has been one of the few growth industries in Scotland. It has long been a recognised objective of regional policy in Scotland to attract and encourage such industries because of the high value added that they generate, and the oil industry clearly falls into this category. However, it has been decided that the value added by such activities is so great that it is necessary to impose certain additional taxes (the Petroleum Revenue Tax and royalties) in order to divert the additional revenue to the central government. It has to be recognised that, in relation to virtually every other industrial activity in the country, this is a most unusual approach, and although this tax regime in principle applies throughout the nation, it discriminates strongly in practice against Scotland and North East England, because virtually all of the major activity is located there. This is not to say that the introduction of special taxes was not necessary, but to point out that in comparison with all other activities it is a discriminatory approach, which adversely affects the generation of value added in Scotland. *A priori*, a case therefore exists for at least a proportion of the value added remaining in Scotland or being returned to Scotland if the tax system is to remain unchanged. This happens in many other countries, particularly those with federal systems of government. The best example is probably Canada where, according to Crommelin, Pearse and Scott (1976, p. 6),

> the constitution vests ownership of the natural resources largely in the Provinces, but legislative authority is divided: essential powers relating to the management and sale of oil and gas rest with Alberta, while the Federal Parliament can exercise important controls over the trade and commerce, inter-provincial pipelines and taxation.

The fundamental issue is the ownership of property rights. As Ditwiler (1975, p. 665) has pointed out,

> although economics has traditionally abstracted from the complexity of property rights, such rights constitute a fundamental underpinning of economic activities. Property rights confer a capacity to participate in economic decision-making and activity. This capacity is defined in terms of relative rights over inputs and outputs as well as a coercive power over others to reap benefits and impose the burden of costs.

Thus the problems generated by a national policy of a rapid rate of depletion and the costs consequently imposed on local communities derive from the fact that the appropriate decisions are made centrally. It may well be the case that this institutional framework is not capable of maximising the indirect benefits and that an alternative would be more efficient. If property rights were vested in regional or local authorities, this would have far-reaching implications for regional development and policy. At least for the industries or resources concerned, these authorities would have considerable powers over the level of development and the distribution of value added. By contrast, the role of central government would be correspondingly reduced. This arrangement is common in many countries but not in the United Kingdom.

North Sea oil and gas discoveries are of great significance in two respects. First, they constitute the resource that in present circumstances most clearly illustrates the divergence between direct and indirect benefits and the inherent conflict between central and local authorities. Second, the financial sums involved are sufficiently large to enable an alternative system to work, which may not be the case with the other resources (coal, timber, etc.) found in the less prosperous regions of the country. Thus it may well be that the North Sea discoveries will act as a catalyst in changing the administrative framework within which most economic developments occur. While this is not the place to discuss political issues in detail, there are signs, in Scotland at least, that pressures generated by North Sea oil may bring about changes in the institutional framework in which such decisions are made. Given the current political situation in Scotland, particularly the recent growth of the Scottish National Party, it is not surprising that attention has been given to the use of oil revenues for purely Scottish rather than British purposes. This should not be construed as arising from the type of argument outlined above: it is in part a reaction to the continuing disparity in economic standards between Scotland and much of England. In any case, the rise of the Scottish National Party has forced the other political parties to offer alternative suggestions as to the use of the North Sea oil revenues, some of which are close to the arguments presented in this chapter.

The case should not be argued solely on grounds of Scottish politics, because if accepted it must apply equally to all regions. A common suggestion is that a proportion of the oil revenues should be earmarked for industrial development. In the first instance, there are many opportunities in the oil-related sector, both for the North Sea and other offshore areas, but this need not be a major target for investment. It is not necessary at this juncture to examine in detail the opportunities for disbursement of such funds but rather to consider the idea *per se*. The Scottish Development Agency and the Welsh Development Agency have been established already with funds from central government but with considerable discretion over their use. In many respects they operate as the regional counterparts of the National Enterprise Board. It would therefore be a simple matter in the Scottish case to replace funds from Westminster by funds from North Sea oil revenues, possibly increasing the total Scottish Development Agency budget by so doing. In the long run, this would give Scotland and Wales much greater control over the exploitation of their natural resources and over the funds available for regional development. Central-government funds could then be applied more intensively to those problem regions lacking in natural resources such as oil and gas or deficient in other respects which have formed the rationale for regional policy in the past.

References

Crommelin, M., Pearse, P. H. and Scott, A. (1976) 'Management of Oil and Gas Resources in Alberta', University of British Columbia, Department of Economics, Resources Paper, No. 1.

Ditwiler, C. D. (1975) 'Water Problems and Property Rights—An Economic Perspective', *Natural Resources Journal*, Vol. 15, pp. 663–80.

Great Britain (1976a) Department of Energy. *Development of the Oil and Gas Resources of the United Kingdom*. London: HMSO.

Great Britain (1976b) Scottish Office. *Scottish Economic Bulletin*, No. 9, pp. 14–21.

MacKay, D. I. and Mackay, G. A. (1975) *The Political Economy of North Sea Oil*. London: Martin Robertson.

Moore B. and Rhodes J. (1974) 'Regional Policy and the Scottish Economy', *Scottish Journal of Political Economy*, Vol. 21, pp. 215–35.

PART III

Neglected Aspects in Regional Policy

It was argued earlier that in spite of changes in overall economic conditions, there has been a remarkable constancy in the spirit and general thrust of regional policy. This is, of course, true of many facets of public intervention. A familiarity and expertise are acquired during the initial phases, a fund of conventional wisdom is built up and organisational structures become established. This all tends to condition the scope and nature of subsequent policy. In the same way that one may discern common threads and even biases within regional policy, so it is possible to identify aspects of policy that have been consistently neglected or been given inadequate attention. This applies not only to the general conception of regional policy but to the assumptions upon which detailed policy is based and the instruments used in the implementation of policy.

The urban dimension of the regional problem and the lack of explicit recognition given to this in regional policy is a fairly obvious case in point. Except for fairly brief periods when attention was focused on relatively small problem areas, the general spatial framework for policy has been the Economic Planning Region, or before 1964 the Standard Region. It is questionable, in a highly urbanised nation, whether this is an appropriate perspective. The metropolitan area, together with its wider sphere of influence, perhaps represents a more meaningful focus. Furthermore, the overwhelming bulk of the regional problem, with respect to high unemployment and problems of economic decline, is localised to a large extent within the metropolitan areas, and within any problem region there are many areas in which the problems have not reached serious levels.

If, however, policy is to be conceived in terms of the region, then the region needs to be regarded as something more than a sub-national entity or building block. The region has its own internal structure, whether this is viewed as a system of interrelated urban centres or a pattern of spatial linkages. Many of the problems of regional economic adjustment can be usefully viewed in terms of such a structure. Indeed, this structure might contribute to the economic malaise of a problem region and it is a feature of the economy that is often overlooked in the implementation of regional policy. There is, of course, an official awareness that particular problem regions are not homogeneous, but all too frequently the individual region tends to become divided into areas with pressing problems and areas that are reasonably *prosperous. While this type of differentiation may represent a pragmatic response to pressures for rapid implementation of policy, it is an inadequate characterisation of regional spatial structure and cannot therefore cast light on the relationship between spatial structure and economic performance.*

This brings us to the question of firm behaviour and the assumptions usually employed in this connection in the implementation of public policy. It can be reasonably claimed that in trying to revitalise the economies of problem regions, far too little is known of the behaviour of firms and their role in the regional-development process. The firm is, after all, the locus of decision making in the private sector of the economy. In the past, regional policy has paid insufficient attention to the organisational structure of the firm. Two interrelated problems of present regional policy are singled out for attention.

The first is that regional policy might have encouraged the movement (to assisted areas) of plants whose organisational status limits future economic growth. A preoccupation of regional policy has been the emphasis on manipulating mobile industry, to the neglect of stimulating regionally based indigenous development. It has been the contention of many that the former approach runs the risk of creating an ill-balanced economic and occupational structure and pushing the region well along the road to a branch-plant economy in which many of the decisions relating to innovation, production and the disposal of surpluses are taken outside the region. This could give rise to a situation in which the region is denied the ability to pursue a range of rational market adjustments, with the possible result that the support given by regional policy could only be removed with great difficulty. It would probably be unrealistic to argue in favour of the abandonment of the policy of industrial migration, but the case for encouraging regionally based development ought to be examined more carefully.

The second problem is that the performance of firms depends crucially on entrepreneurship—on the quality of managerial decision making. Recent work has suggested that the problems of at least some assisted areas might be due more to inefficient management than to unfavourable industrial structure or geographical location, and in the past this has received insufficient consideration in regional policy. For a regional economy to be competitive in the long run, it must be able to adapt to economic change. However, the nature of policies necessary to ensure such regional adaptability in the British economy, with its high level of integration and high concentration of ownership, is not immediately apparent. At present, the balance of evidence seems to suggest that regional policy cannot be treated independently of national industrial policy—a theme that will also be examined in Part IV of the volume.

CHAPTER 8

An Urban Approach to Regional Problems

J. T. Hughes*

Introduction

Regional policy in Great Britain for the past forty years or so has been divided into two administrative compartments which, although not water-tight, have operated with independent goals and objectives (McCallum, chapter 1 of this volume). First, a set of policies, initiated before the Second World War, has been concerned with the geographical distribution of industry. Second, the 1947 Town and Country Planning Act consolidated the emergent power of local authorities in community planning and land use control. It also placed responsibilities on these authorities to prepare development plans which regulated town development and segregated land uses into zones that were compatible with the abolition of the social and environmental problems that had emerged with urban development in the nineteenth century. Regional or distribution-of-industry policy instruments has undoubtedly been effective in changing the location of jobs associated with new investment in manufacturing (Moore and Rhodes, 1973). However, the principal concern of this chapter is that this policy, by its concentration on broadly defined regions, has ignored the changing spatial dimension of population and industrial change. The emerging economic problem of urban areas has become a more dominant source of spatial imbalance and inequality; but it has tended to fall into a policy 'gap' caused by the separation of 'industrial' (economic) and 'physical planning' policies.

At first sight this change may seem surprising since an integral part of the distribution of industry policy was the control over land use, made possible by the Town and Country Planning Act. An Industrial Development Certificate (IDC) was required if planning permission were to be granted to new factories or extensions; these were not granted for major projects (the limiting size has been varied by successive changes of policies) in

* Highlands and Islands Development Board, Inverness. The views expressed in this chapter do not necessarily reflect those of the Board.

the South and Midlands unless it could be demonstrated that special difficulties would result from refusal to grant permission. Many commentators have laid considerable stress on the importance of this so-called 'stick', as compared to the 'carrot' of financial incentives. However, although the incentives have been graduated among areas of greater or lesser need, such as Special Development Areas and Intermediate Areas, it would appear that neither these incentives nor IDC policy have paid adequate attention to the most serious spatial disparities of income and employment opportunities. The focus of the distribution of industry policy was firmly on the official Standard Regions, (Economic Planning Regions after 1964) or, to adopt the terminology common in East European spatial planning, 'macro' regions.

This chapter is concerned to contrast this 'regional' approach of existing policy with the emerging 'urban' nature of the spatial disparities in employment and income opportunities. It is argued that it is possible to develop a more effective policy for the distribution of employment by taking account of the trends and causal factors involved in 'micro' regional employment change. In addition to the 'need' illustrated here and in Stone (chapter 6 of this volume), such a revision of policy would have to take into account the current effectiveness of regional policy and the problems of redirecting a policy for economic planning into a sub-regional framework.

Why Regional Policy?

Part of the reason why the spatial structure of regional policy has escaped a more radical re-examination is that the definition of administrative regions has remained relatively constant in Great Britain (McCallum, chapter 1 of this volume). Many regions have an obvious geographical integrity related also to cultural and quasi-national factors. Administratively, the regions were legitimised by their designation for decentralised autonomous government in the event of civil disturbance or war. Later the flow of statistics that followed upon the acceptance of the Standard Regions increased their use as the obvious units for spatial analysis. There was very little discussion of the appropriate units for the application of policy decisions or the statistical monitoring of effects. Had there been, the official attitude would probably have regarded it as liable to delay the implementation of policy and/or to involve an administratively impractical solution. In 1960 the intentions of the Local Employment Act were to introduce a degree of geographical selectivity but the experiment was short-lived. The reasons are more fully discussed in McCallum (chapter 1 of this volume) but, although based on groups of local employment exchange areas that approximated travel-to-work areas, the spatial basis was determined by the administrative structure of the Department of Employment. The limitations created by this structure were added to by the wide use of unemployment as the measure of need and by the conflicts that arose between the demands of efficient relocation and the implicit aims of solving local unemployment within local-area boundaries.

To some extent the regional focus of the distribution-of-industry policy mirrored the development of regional economics although interregional trade theory has not proven a useful basis for policy because of the lack of information about trade flows and the lack of comparative measures of cost and efficiency. Other analytical methods, which have included the use of location quotients (Mattila and Thompson, 1955; Mayer and Pleeter, 1975), the identification of growth industries (Scottish Council, 1962; Humphrys, 1962), and shift-share analysis (Perloff *et al.*, 1960), concentrate on regional variations from the national average.

There were other obstacles to the realignment of policy. The effects of the distribution-of-industry policy were not only spatial ones. Part of its purpose was to channel funds and liquidity to the corporate sector of manufacturing industry. Although the incentives were available in the assisted regions, they contributed to the general financial stability of many firms that had branches and subsidiaries in several regions. If they became more geographically selective, their incidence would be more arbitrary, as far as the corporate sector as a whole was concerned. It is possible to conclude, bearing in mind the necessary pragmatic strength of a successful policy, that regional policy has been responsible for relocating a substantial number of jobs from the 'pressure' regions in the South and Midlands to regions where the social need for additional employment opportunities was combined with the economic advantages of higher utilisation of capacity over the economy as a whole. Brown (1972), Moore and Rhodes (1973) and others have argued that regional incentives have created thousands of additional jobs in the assisted areas at a low opportunity cost to national economic growth and efficiency and in certain periods of high national unemployment at a low cost to the national Treasury.

The Urban Dimension

In this section we shall argue that there has been an opportunity cost of regional aid in that it could have been redistributed in a way that recognised that the areas of greatest need are concentrated in older urban areas and that many of these areas exist within the prosperous regions. Holmans (1964) argued that small towns and semi-rural areas of Kent were less well off than parts of Scotland, but the main conurbations in both prosperous and depressed regions were at that time subject to policies of restraint or containment. Yet the large metropolitan areas and especially the cities that formed their nuclei were experiencing either a low rate of population growth or substantial population decline. Insofar as these

TABLE 8.1

Population change in British Metropolitan Areas, 1951–66

	Percentage annual population change			
	Metropolitan areas		Central cities	
Population size class	1951–61	1951–66	1951–61	1961–66
Over 1,000,000	+0.27	−0.41	−0.32	−1.23
500,001 to 1,000,000	+0.61	+0.46	+0.15	−0.06
250,001 to 500,000	+0.65	+0.64	−0.05	−0.24
100,000 to 250,000	+0.75	+0.93	+0.65	−0.50

Source: Service Industries in Metropolitan Areas Project, Department of Social and Economic Research, University of Glasgow.

trends were appreciated, they could well have been regarded as reflecting the success of policies to restrict development and congestion in the urban centres and of urban redevelopment (mainly housing) in the inner areas, which was reducing residential densities.

Just as the support for regional policy was assisted by a widely agreed definition of regions, an urban approach has to clarify the meaning and definition of urban regions. The British concept of conurbation has been based to a large degree on the extent of a built-up area. With the greater freedom in locational choice created by the car in the twentieth century, it has been necessary to add the 'separated' communities that are linked to the urban centre by travel-to-work and other mobility patterns. In Tables 8.1 and 8.2, two alternative definitions of urban regions in Great Britain are employed.[1] By 1967 when the population tabulations of the 1966 Sample Census of Population were available, two trends in Table 8.1 should have been visible. First, the central cities of the larger Metropolitan Areas (MAS) were suffering marked losses of population. Second, in some cases these were being translated into modest declines in the overall MA populations. Population was decentralising from the central cities of

TABLE 8.2

Population and employment change by urban zone in Great Britain, 1951–71

	Percentage change			
	Population		Employment	
	1951–61	1961–71	1951–61	1961–71
Urban core	1.9	−2.8	6.7	−3.1
Metropolitan ring	13.3	17.2	6.6	15.0
SMLAS	5.7	4.4	6.7	1.4
Outer metropolitan ring	3.1	9.8	−0.4	3.9
MELAS	5.3	5.2	5.6	1.8

Source: Great Britain (1976, p. 10).

most MAS, even in medium-sized (250,000–500,000 population) and small (100,000–250,000 population) MAS. Population was also draining from the larger MAS. Although part of the reason for the trend may be definitional, that is to say, the larger MAS tended to be 'underbounded', there was a significant negative correlation between population size in 1951 and the growth of population.

If the results of the 1966 Sample Census were accepted with some reserve, the 1971 Census fully confirmed and amplified the evidence. The growth of the metropolitan ring and especially the outer metropolitan ring has accelerated in the period 1961–71, whereas the urban core has slipped into absolute decline on both the population and employment fronts (Table 8.2). In Table 8.3, the decline of the urban core is seen to exist in various types of region. The remarkable change in fortune for the metropolitan-ring area in both the regions containing assisted areas can be interpreted as the area within which regional policy was having its principal effect in creating new manufacturing in peripheral urban sites.

A number of conclusions can be drawn from these estimates and the detailed analysis of employment trends from estimates of insured employees.[2] Decentralisation from the central cities, as measured by the net shift of employment (i.e., the declining share of the central city in total employment), was well established in the period 1959–68. It was concentrated largely in the manufacturing sector but it is difficult to attribute it to the decline of that sector *per se*. It was observed that the highest net shift away from central cities of MAS took place in the industries that experienced a high rate of employment growth nationally and in the industries that experienced a high rate of employment decline. The industries in which employment did not change or grew only slightly exhibited the lowest value of net shift (Hughes and Firn, 1973). Although the detailed analysis of the Clydeside conurbation did not entirely bear out the hypothesis, one conclusion of this work was that where an industry experiences a period of industrial and corporate change, location is likely to be considerably revised. Once this reorganisation is carried out, it is clear to the firms involved, in a high proportion of cases, that their manufacturing establishments (having existed for decades in older areas or having originally been attracted there by the availability of industrial premises) are too centralised, given modern techniques of production and distribution. In addition, a period of either growth or decline may be associated with a higher level of competition, which drives out: (a) the smaller units; and (b) the less efficient units. There is certainly a higher proportion of category (a) and, more arguably, a higher proportion of category (b) in the central cities or urban cores.

The other dimension of change in the urban system is the decline in the relative share of the largest MAS in total employment. Most of

TABLE 8.3

Population and employment change by urban zone in selected Economic Planning Regions, 1951–71

Percentage change

	South East		West Midlands		North West		Scotland	
	1951–61	1961–71	1951–61	1961–71	1951–61	1961–71	1951–61	1961–71
Population:								
Urban core	2.1	−2.0	4.1	−1.2	−2.4	−8.1	0.4	−6.5
Metropolitan ring	16.1	14.5	16.9	22.6	9.9	20.4	13.3	17.1
Employment:								
Urban core	8.6	−2.5	8.4	−3.4	1.5	−8.3	1.9	−7.0
Metropolitan ring	13.5	19.4	10.9	18.8	−1.5	10.2	−0.3	13.1

Source: Great Britain (1976, p. 38).

the large MAS are based on the Census conurbations and we can follow
the sectoral changes in these areas from 1966 to 1971 in Table 6.10 of
Stone (chapter 6 of this volume) which is taken from Stone (1975). The
conurbations are holding their share of employment growth in the service
sector to a much greater extent than in manufacturing; the generalisation
seems to hold true for both 'growth' and 'non-growth' sectors. As with
decentralisation from central cities, it is difficult to place these changes
in the context of broader industrial and sectoral changes which will allow
one to judge whether they are 'expected' or a result of national trends.
Shift-share analysis is derived from the postulate that an area's economic
fortunes derive either from its industrial structure or from some other
cause (Perloff *et al.*, 1960). In Table 8.4, this methodology is applied
to the metropolitan hierarchy. At the beginning of the period studied,
the larger MAS did not have industrial structures with markedly worse
growth prospects than smaller MAS. The main structural decline took place
in the manufacturing sector which comprised Minimum List Headings
(MLH) 211–499. This decline affected all sizes of MA, although the structural
handicap of non-metropolitan Great Britain was relatively lower. The non-
structural component of change, however, varied systematically in that
there were large differential 'losses' of employment in both manufacturing
and services in MAS with a population of more than 1m. These losses
reduced and changed to 'gains' as the size of MA fell, the principal exception
being the surprisingly 'good' performance in the manufacturing sector
of MAS with populations in the range 250,000–500,000. Non-metropolitan
areas are prosperous by any standard of comparison.

Normative judgement about the implications of these comments has
been implicitly reserved by the use of quotation marks in the last paragraph.
A number of commentators would claim that, by a process of spatial
competition, the areas with positive differential components are competing
employment away from other areas. In view of *prima facie* evidence of
the imperfections in the operation of markets, and the land market in
particular, such conclusions are unwarranted. The causes of the shifts of
employment are complex and beyond the analysis possible in this chapter,
but the trends are unmistakable. The symptoms generally accepted of
regional decline, the shift of population and employment away from the
area in question, are widely observed in the urban system and affect
central cities and the larger metropolitan areas. The result has been that
there is a growing unemployment (one of the short-term measures of economic malaise) in inner areas and wider parts of the central city.

An Urban Economic Policy

There are, however, several further steps to be taken in the argument
that future regional policy should have a greater urban bias. In the first

TABLE 8.4
Analysis of Metropolitan Area employment, 1959–68

ALL SECTORS:

Area[a]	Minimum List Heading	Change	Structural component	Local (non-structural) component	Total[b] employees in 1968
All MAS including London	001–109	−297,232	−309,979	+12,747	17,000,000
	211–499	−416,540	−116,555	−299,985	
	500–906	+429,846	+597,734	−167,888	
All MAS excluding London	001–109	−281,546	−292,195	+10,649	11,400,000
	211–499	−200,859	−224,619	+23,760	
	500–906	+279,479	+301,602	−22,123	
Over 1m	001–109	−99,031	−83,718	−15,313	5,200,000
	211–499	−232,815	−123,054	−109,761	
	500–906	+52,673	+147,780	−95,107	
500,000–1m	001–109	−70,416	−70,463	+47	2,200,000
	211–499	−10,675	−6,758	−3,917	
	500–906	+80,267	+62,647	+17,620	
250,000–500,000	001–109	−50,701	−45,229	−5,472	1,800,000
	211–499	+51,889	−42,681	+94,570	
	500–906	+42,605	+36,554	+6,051	

Area		Change	Structural component	Local (non-structural) component	Total employees in 1968
100,000–250,000	001-109	−61,398	−92,784	+31,386	2,200,000
	211-499	−9,269	−52,127	+42,858	
	500-906	+103,928	+54,624	+49,304	
Non-metropolitan Great Britain	001-109	−352,343	−339,604	−12,739	6,100,000
	211-499	+246,002	−53,889	+299,891	
	500-906	+356,226	+187,457	+168,769	

SERVICE SECTOR:

Area[a]	Change	Structural component	Local (non-structural) component	Total[b] employees in 1968
Non-metropolitan Great Britain	+356,000	+187,000	+169,000	6,100,000
MAS 100,000–250,000	+104,000	+55,000	+49,000	2,200,000
MAS 250,000–500,000	+43,000	+37,000	+6,000	1,800,000
MAS 500,000–1m	+80,000	+63,000	+18,000	2,200,000
MAS Over 1m excluding London	+53,000	+148,000	−95,000	5,200,000
London MA	+150,000	+296,000	−146,000	5,600,000

[a] Population in 1961.
[b] All sectors.
Source: Service Industries in Metropolitan Areas Project, Department of Social and Economic Research, University of Glasgow.

instance an argument based on 'need' is a necessary but not a sufficient step in justifying a change in policy. The previous section has presented evidence that suggests that there are significant changes in the locational preferences of (or constraints on) manufacturing industry in particular, but by the statistical nature of the areas defined and in view of the very few years since their establishment, it is not possible to derive a broader range of economic series. However, from the evidence it would appear that the changes underlying the observed shifts are not marginal nor is there any evidence that they are moderating or have run their course. A second important point of clarification is that an urban-oriented policy is not necessarily in direct opposition to a regional economic policy; indeed we shall argue next that in some respects the urban orientation may make aid to the regions more effective by concentrating it on a geographically more selective basis. However, without doubt, assuming an overall limitation on the public finance and resources available for a policy or policies to correct spatial imbalance, there will be a diversion of aid to the metropolitan areas in the 'prosperous' regions at the expense of parts of the areas currently assisted. There will, therefore, be a sharp trade-off in the operation of new policies between the 'withdrawal symptoms' associated with reducing funds as well as the favoured-area treatment of certain parts of the regions, and the social and economic benefits to be gained from the new directions of expenditure. One cannot envisage a radical public reshaping of regional policy in the immediate future by any government that is aware of the votes to be lost in the regions currently aided, not to mention the opportunities presented to the separatist movements. The change will no doubt, be incremental but with the danger that it will end up with the worst of both policies.

On the urban side, there is a danger that unless economic policies are on a sufficiently large scale (and integrated with other social and physical-planning policies), they will end up placing funds and resources in areas where the continuing forces of change will swamp them. The lessons of the Equal Opportunity Program in the United States may have to be relearned in Great Britain. Many of these programmes failed because they were directed towards characteristics of the poverty problem in urban areas that were symptoms of more general underlying social difficulties and because they were the products of a great deal of 'instant analysis'. In the foreseeable future in this country, it is difficult to see a large enough shift of public resources to generate a significant change in the trends which, as we have argued above, are long established. There may also be an operational constraint in that a central-government policy would need to have regard for the rights and duties of local authorities. The Northern Region Strategy Team did not deal with some of the implications for the physical structure of the region for reasons that included a desire not to impinge upon the planning responsibilities of local authorities. On the other hand, the West Midlands Metropolitan County has developed a strong interest and expertise in economic policy, which in many respects would take them into an area of policy that would overlap with an 'urban' regional policy. Ultimately, such an integration between the policies of the 'regional' arm of local government and decentralised regional policy of central government is desirable but the tensions should not be underestimated.

Equally, there are non-urban parts of the country where there are continuing difficult economic problems. These areas will require continuing support, perhaps through multi-purpose regional agencies such as the Highlands and Islands Development Board (House, 1976).

Economic Theory and Analysis for an Urban Economic Policy

Earlier in this chapter it was stated that one of the drawbacks to regional policy, as it has operated, is that it is difficult to establish empirically the effects of alternative locations on the economics of industrial production and on the competitiveness of particular sectors or firms. The most generally applicable theory is Weberian, which relates the location of a firm to the location of raw materials, other inputs and markets in relation to the 'transportability' of the product. The main criticisms, that it is mechanistic and simplistic in assumptions of 'point' locations rather than 'extensive' market areas and supply areas (from which inputs are drawn), can be met to some extent by the adaptations proposed by Hoover. However, probably the most fundamental weakness is the effect of external economies in agglomerations and the extent to which internal economies of scale may be limited by, for example, labour supply constraints in smaller communities. Frequently, the most successful of these applications have used input–output or industrial-complex analysis, which do not in themselves have the capacity to be highly spatially discriminating (Parr, chapter 9 of this volume). Many other attempts to identify the effects of regional variables and relative wage rates in econometric analysis (Tooze, 1976; Dixon and Thirlwall, 1975) have been indecisive in conclusion, certainly from the point of view of policy making. In the face of these limitations, recent developments in regional growth theory have introduced agglomeration effects into a regional model (Richardson, 1973).

One cannot argue convincingly that urban economic theory, as developed for example by Wingo (1961) and Alonso (1964), is a suitable alternative vehicle to support a pragmatic policy. Although the basic model of trading off accessibility to the city centre for the additional rent payable for sites closer to the centre is generally acceptable, there are two principal problems in applying that model to many types of economic activity. First, the centres of cities have lost the attribute of being the most accessible area in the distribution of numerous materials and final products and even in the performance of certain services. Whereas formerly the centre of a city combined access via rail to other cities and regions with radial access by rail and road to the surrounding local areas, the advent of road, air and specialised rail facilities has broken that monopoly. Accessibility is now much more diffused and complex for many establishments, involving a choice that is dependent upon the organisation of alternative modes of transport. Second, until it was possible to assess the importance of this partial model (partial in the sense that it did not embrace all the parameters of a firm's equilibrium) in the overall strategic decisions of a firm, it was impossible to predict the sensitivity of firms to changes in locational conditions. As was argued above, a locational decision was likely to be reappraised only if and when the firm's equilibrium was seriously disturbed, frequently by changes that may not be directly related to location.

Richardson (1973) recognised the interrelationships between spatial levels in analysing the growth process: (a) national growth is associated with dispersion or 'spread' (in Myrdal's terminology) from leading to lagging regions; (b) regional growth involves spatial concentration and urbanisation; (c) metropolitan growth is accompanied by decentralisation. Thus the same process entails decentralisation or centralisation, depending upon one's vantage point. The process of urban change, which has been outlined earlier in this chapter, and which is receiving increased public attention, is one that involves the urbanisation of formerly small towns and rural areas. This is a useful perspective but like so many integrative steps it is at the cost of not (as yet) specifying the theoretical relationships between the process of national growth and the spatial and industrial structure at the regional and at the urban level. It is not, therefore, possible to examine closely what effects alternative national growth strategies will have on the process of urban change. It is certain, however, that the factors causing the change are of long standing. The integrative perspective is also useful when we turn to policy and the question of what model is perceived as a desirable goal. Are we postulating a uniform distribution of population and jobs from London Wall to Cape Wrath? Obviously not, but the desirable degree of concentration can only be set in relation to a concept of the efficient urban area. Here we return to adaptations of the Alonso (1964) and Wingo (1961) models. Mills (1974) reached admittedly tentative conclusions that the urban structure was relatively insensitive to changes in transportation costs and technology. The spatial structure is the product of fundamental industrial and social changes.

There have, however, been several empirical studies of the industrial composition of urban change, which may allow some generalisations about the nature of urban economic change. Keeble (1965; 1968) presented detailed studies of industrial relocation from London. Later, more comprehensive studies of the industrial structure at the level of individual establishments clarified the nature of industrial change in urban areas (Firn, 1976; Lloyd and Mason, 1976). Most industrial 'relocation' does not take the form of transfer of establishment; rather, the important factor is the rate of births and deaths in the establishment population. Typical information from such studies is presented in Table 8.5: (a) the largest component of net change is the rate of net closures; (b) relocations or transfers are a relatively small part of the loss to the central city, but more significant in the growth of the periphery; (c) although small in net terms, employment change by establishment *in situ* is large.

TABLE 8.5
Components of manufacturing employment decentralisation, 1958–68

	Glasgow		Periphery		Total
	Number	Percentage	Number	Percentage	Number
Stock Changes:					
New firms	+8221		+25231		+33452
Closures	−38662		−16958		−55620
Net	−30441	90.78	+8273	72.17	−22168
Relocations:[a]					
Inmovers	+244		+3029		−
Outmovers	−3029		−244		−
Net	−2785	8.30	+2785	24.29	−
Employment Changes:[b]					
Growth	+24898		+24360		+44258
Decline	−25204		−23956		−49160
Net	−306	0.92	+404	3.56	+98
Total:					
Gains	+33363		+52620		+77710
Losses	−66895		−41158		−104780
Net	−33532	100.00	+11462	100.00	−22070

[a] Relocations between Glasgow and periphery only.
[b] Changes in employment 1958–68 by establishments in zone, including movers.

Source: Glasgow University Register of Industrial Establishments (GURIE), Department of Social and Economic Research, University of Glasgow.

In the development of policy, two issues stand out from these trends. First, the shifts of industrial location are closely linked to the possibility of influencing 'movers' to go to one location or another, be it the West Midlands or Scotland, the City of Glasgow or East Kilbride. Second, the dynamics of industrial growth and decline (in terms of the emergence of entrepreneurs, the growth of small firms into larger enterprises, and ensuring a continuity of effective management) are also clearly involved in such an overall framework of locational change. Turning to the first point, it is possible to argue that in order to obtain any given scale of locational change, it will be preferable to influence the gross intraregional changes of births, deaths, transfers and *in situ* growth (decline) of employment. It will become more difficult to generate additional employment in areas of need through interregional moves based on incentives and controls to shift firms from prosperous areas. In the past most of the firms settling in the periphery of MAS in problem areas have been assisted moves. Current regional policy has already laid greater emphasis on the growth of indigenous enterprises, but the impact of these policies has yet to be felt. In this respect there may well be greater continuity in any move towards an urban policy than might appear at first sight, for example, by the use of existing institutions. Such devices, however, will not remove the difficult choices in allocating scarce development funds among competing geographical units with varying prospects for future growth. An agency like the Scottish Development Agency will need to take closely specified geographical priorities into account, in addition to the general development prospects for an industry and the financial viability of firms.

A more selective approach to the regional problem, therefore, which recognises the need to regenerate growth from within the existing industrial structure, is also capable of recognising the need for spatial selectivity. Many parts of the assisted areas are relatively prosperous and regional-development priorities will lean towards the urban areas in need. Will concentration on urban areas in decline not push regional policy away from a concentration on the areas of proven growth potential such as New Towns and other peripheral sites as well as many existing towns and non-metropolitan sub-regions? Is it not time to recognise that the relative economic advantages of urban areas and of the large metropolitan areas are passing, if not passé? There are no definitive answers to the proposition 'let the cities wither'. All that is possible at this stage is to clarify two points that follow from the policy (dare one say slogan?) to 'revitalise the inner city'. The first involves the geographical dimension of an urban policy and the second relates to its social basis. It should be made clear that the analysis of this chapter has not been primarily concerned with the wastelands in the inner areas of many large and medium-sized metropolitan areas. Indeed, perhaps the greatest future asset of these areas will be to possess larger uncommitted tracts of land. Unfortunately, the minds of many planners and valuers are occupied with an image of these areas rebuilt to a fairly narrow range of uses. The typical reaction of local planners to the growing problem of the inner city has been to resolve to 'sell' it to incoming industrialists. All the evidence suggests that the relative decline embraces the entire city and that the main 'cause' has been the lack of new investment. It would be unrealistic to propose a delay in resolving the relationship of the evident decline of the inner areas to broader national and regional trends. It does, however, reinforce the case for tackling the urban dimension within a more spatially selective regional policy.

This approach is reinforced by the fact that the basis of an urban policy is similar to the original case for a regional policy. The major premise of the argument is that there are imperfections in the operation of land markets to secure the optimal distribution of economic activity over space. Not even in socialist economies is there an attempt to plan the most important deviations from the optimal distribution–an ideal that (to recognise the tenets of welfare economics) is set not by economic laws alone but by the addition of social value judgements. that, to recognise the tenets of the new welfare economics, is set not by economic laws alone but by the addition of social value judgements. The minor premise is that locational adjustments that are in accord with changes in the optimal distribution of industry frequently entail social costs, which should be compensated for by public policy. It may be objected that 'social' goals tend to distort the operation of regional economic policy and should be met under a different policy, the auspices of another department or a different budgetary allocation. It is, however, naive to believe that the political process could, or should, break down policies into separate compartments. An urban economic policy will almost certainly increase the likelihood of pursuing quasi-social policies with economic measures. It can be justified if it diverts public funds and resources to correcting the external diseconomies created by urban decline and thus encouraging potentially viable enterprises. Also, by removing some of the related spatial inequalities in opportunities for employment (and in levels of income), it may improve the accessibility of employers to a larger pool of labour. The danger is, of course, that instant policies will be suggested and adopted for apparently 'new' problems; the almost-daily proposal for solving the urban problem is evidence enough of that danger.

Notes

1. In Table 8.1 the Metropolitan Areas (MAS) are based upon a definition similar to the American Standard Metropolitan Statistical Area (SMSA). This concept has been applied to Great Britain and other nations (International Urban Research, 1960). Briefly, there should exist an urban core or central city of at least 50,000 population which, together with an urban periphery, should reach a total population of not less than 100,000. The periphery comprises surrounding areas that either are connected to the central city by travel-to-work patterns or have an average density of population and may be regarded as an extension of the built-up area of the central city. In Table 8.2 the SMLAS and MELAS were derived by a team engaged on a comparative study of urbanisation in Great Britain and the United States of America (Hall *et al.*, 1973). The urban cores were defined as local authorities with a minimum density of employment of five jobs per acre; metropolitan rings

had not less than 15 per cent of the population commuting to the urban core. These constituted the Standard Metropolitan Labour Area (SMLA) to which could be added an outer metropolitan ring with area components which were assigned to the SMLA to which the majority (without a specified minimum) of its commuters travelled. The total SMLA plus outer ring was termed a Metropolitan Economic Labour Area (MELA). Comparing the alternative definitions, MAS and SMLAS are similar and in total include approximately two-thirds of the population of Great Britain. The least homogeneous areas are the outer metropolitan rings, which include largely rural areas in many MELAS but in the South East and West Midlands contain many of the smaller commuter settlements closely related to the urban cores.

2. This work was undertaken by the author as part of the Metropolitan Industrial Location Project which was financed by a grant (RAP 123) to the Department of Social and Economic Research, University of Glasgow, from the Centre for Environmental Studies. His colleagues on that project were Gordon C. Cameron and John R. Firn.

References

Alonso, W. (1964) *Location and Land Use*. Cambridge, Mass.: Harvard University Press.
Brown, A. J. (1972) *The Framework of Regional Economics in the United Kingdom*. Cambridge: Cambridge University Press.
Dixon, R. J. and Thirlwall, A. P. (1975) *Regional Growth and Unemployment in the United Kingdom*. London: Macmillan.
Firn, J. R. (1976) 'Economic Microdata Analysis and Urban-Regional Change: the Experience of GURIE' in J. K. Swales *et al.*, 'Establishment-Based Research: Conference Proceedings', University of Glasgow, Urban and Regional Studies Discussion Papers, No. 22.
Great Britain (1976) Department of the Environment. *British Cities: Urban Population and Employment Trends 1951-71*. London: HMSO.
Hall, P., Gracey, H., Drewett, R. and Thomas, R. (1973) *The Containment of Urban England*. London: Allen and Unwin.
Holmans, A. E. (1964) 'Restriction of Expansion in South-East England', *Oxford Economic Papers*, Vol. 16, pp. 201-16.
House, J. W. (1976) 'The Geographer and Policy-Making in Marginal Rural Areas: the Northern Pennines Rural Development Board' in J. T. Coppock and W. R. D. Sewell (eds.), *Spatial Dimensions of Public Policy*. Oxford: Pergamon Press.
Hughes, J. T. and Firn, J. R. (1973) 'Employment Growth and Decentralization of Manufacturing Industry: Some Intriguing Paradoxes' in *Papers from the Urban Economics Conference*. Conference Paper 5. London: Centre for Environmental Studies.
Humphrys, G. (1962) 'Growth Industries and the Regional Economics of Great Britain', *District Bank Review*, No. 144, pp. 35-56.
International Urban Research (1959) *The World's Metropolitan Areas*. Berkeley and Los Angeles: University of California Press.
Keeble, D. (1965) 'Industrial Migration from North-West London 1940-64', *Urban Studies*, Vol. 2, pp. 15-32.
Keeble, D. (1968) 'Industrial Decentralisation and the Metropolis: The North West London Case', *Transactions of the Institute of British Geographers*, Vol. 44, pp. 1-54.
Lloyd, P. E. and Mason, C. M. (1976) 'Establishment-Based Data for the Study of Intraurban and Subregional Industrial Change: the Manchester Study' in J. K. Swales *et al.*, 'Establishment-Based Research: Conference Proceedings', University of Glasgow, Urban and Regional Studies Discussion Papers, No. 22.
Mattila, J. and Thompson, W. (1955) 'The Measurement of the Economic Base of the Metropolitan Area', *Land Economics*, Vol. 31, pp. 215-28.
Mayer, W. and Pleeter, S. (1975) 'A Theoretical Justification for the Use of Location Quotients', *Regional Science and Urban Economics*, Vol. 5, pp. 343-55.

Mills, E. S. (1974) 'Sensitivity Analysis of Congestion and Structure in an Efficient Urban Area' in J. G. Rothenberg and I. G. Heggie (eds.), *Transport and the Urban Environment*. London: Macmillan.

Moore, B. and Rhodes, J. (1973) 'Evaluating the Effects of British Regional Economic Policy', *Economic Journal*, Vol. 83, pp. 87–110.

Perloff, H. S., Dunn, E. S., Lampard, E. E., Muth, R. F. (1960) *Regions, Resources and Economic Growth*. Baltimore: The Johns Hopkins Press.

Richardson, H. W. (1973) *Regional Growth Theory*. London: Macmillan.

Scottish Council (Development and Industry) (1962) *Report on the Scottish Economy*. Edinburgh: Scottish Council (Development and Industry).

Stone, P. A., (1975) 'Balancing the Optima', *Built Environment*, Vol. 1, pp. 186–9.

Tooze, M. J. (1976) 'Regional Elasticities of Substitution in the United Kingdom in 1968', *Urban Studies*, Vol. 13, pp. 35–44.

Wingo, L. (1961) *Transportation and Urban Land*. Washington, D.C.: Resources for the Future.

CHAPTER 9

Spatial Structure as a Factor in Economic Adjustment and Regional Policy

*John B. Parr**

Introduction

The role of a region's spatial structure in influencing the level and character of its economic development is one that has not traditionally been stressed, either in regional economic analysis or in the framing and implementation of regional economic policy. The term 'spatial structure' is difficult to define succinctly, but it may be viewed in terms of one or more of the following perspectives: (a) the geographic distribution of the regional labour force, capital stock and infrastructure; (b) the settlement structure or urban system of the region, particularly with respect to the geographic distribution of the urban and rural population, the size distribution of urban centres, the central place structure of the region and the relative importance of specialised-function centres; (c) the spatial interaction or 'circulation' within the region, involving commuting flows, the intraregional movement of commodities, as well as flows of funds within the region. Although these three perspectives tend to be closely interrelated, it may sometimes be possible to capture the character of the spatial structure in a particular region by focussing attention on one of them. The intention of this chapter is to explore the role of spatial structure in influencing the economic performance of problem regions. The importance of the spatial structure in the formulation of regional policy will then be examined, with particular emphasis on the strategy of planned growth poles.

The Significance of Spatial Structure

As already mentioned, the development of regional economics has tended to neglect the internal structure of the regional economy, or more precisely

* Department of Social and Economic Research and Centre for Urban and Regional Research, University of Glasgow.

its spatial structure; the works of Boudeville (1966), Richardson (1973) and Vining (1955) represent notable exceptions in this regard. While there have been fairly impressive innovations in regional economic analysis (such as those relating to growth models, econometric modelling, and techniques of input–output analysis), their practical application to regional-policy problems has been weakened by the lack of a framework incorporating spatial elements of the type referred to.

The importance of spatial structure in the application of regional economic analysis to regional policy can be illustrated by way of a simple example, concerning the regional employment multiplier. A given increase in final demand within a particular regional industry, in addition to creating a direct employment expansion, will also be accompanied by an indirect (interindustry-based) employment expansion as well as an induced (consumption-based) employment expansion, the latter two elements together forming a Type II regional multiplier effect (Moore and Peterson, 1955). While the overall magnitude of the regional employment multiplier will be largely independent of the location of the direct expansion,[1] the exact intraregional dispersion of the multiplier effect will depend on where within the region the direct effect is located. For example, the dispersion pattern of regional multiplier effects accompanying a direct effect in the dominant regional metropolis would not be the same as those that would occur were the direct effect located in a small urban centre in the periphery. Both patterns of dispersion would be related to the spatial structure of the region and in particular to the hierarchical structure of the urban system and the pattern of spatial interdependencies within the region.

Considerations such as these are clearly of relevance in a policy context. Schemes to create work in regions of high unemployment frequently assume that the regional employment multiplier effects stemming from the direct expansion in employment will contribute further to the relief of unemployment. From a region-wide viewpoint, this assumption may be reasonable enough. However, only if the spatial structure of the region is explicitly introduced into the analysis is it possible to determine whether the distribution of multiplier effects bears any relation to the distribution of unemployment. Such a procedure may reveal that the part of a region with relatively high unemployment (where the direct employment creation has been sited) is experiencing few multiplier effects and is therefore benefiting mainly from the direct effects, while the part of a region with relatively low levels of unemployment is the recipient of the bulk of the multiplier effects. Under these circumstances it might be necessary to modify the policy, perhaps with greater sectoral selectivity in the initial creation of employment, as a means of localising the multiplier effects to a greater extent in those areas of the region with high unemployment.

The spatial structure of a region is usually regarded as some reflection of the nature of regional economic activity. Thus, a region with a major export base in natural-resource exploitation could be expected to possess a different spatial structure from that of a region with an export base in fabricative manufacturing. The contrasting spatial structures would reflect differences between the major activities in terms of such factors as minimum efficient plant size, predominant locational orientations and agglomeration tendencies. The relationship between economic activity and spatial structure can be approached from a slightly different perspective. Thus it might be argued that given the type and scale of economic activity, there is a particular spatial structure (or set of alternative structures) that is optimal in terms of efficient operation. This question has been examined by von Böventer (1970) in a theoretical analysis that attempted to derive optimal size distributions, as well as optimal spatial distributions, of cities.

Although the nature of economic activity within a region will exert an influence on its spatial structure, it is no less true, though perhaps less obvious, that the spatial structure can influence the nature and intensity of economic activity within the region and more generally the process of regional economic adjustment. If it is accepted that a particular set of economic activities gives rise to a distinct spatial structure, then this very spatial structure (because of its high degree of fixity) will influence the range of economic activities that can be suitably located within the region during some subsequent period. And if the region is trying to effect a sectoral transformation of its economy, the spatial structure may be retarding this process: potentially usable resources such as labour and infrastructure might be available in the 'wrong places' and in the 'wrong quantities', relative to the requirements of the potential replacement industries. It becomes evident that the spatial structure represents one of several constraints in the process of regional economic adjustment—a process that is often at the very centre of regional development. As a constraint, the spatial structure may place limits on the range of possible sectoral adjustments open to the region. Such a constraint may sometimes be weak, the spatial structure being of such a nature as to be able to sustain a wide range of alternative activities. On other occasions, however, the constraint may be severe in the sense that the spatial structure is suitable for few activities that are expanding nationally or are in the process of relocation.

The spatial structure can also be viewed as a factor that influences a region's success in the arena of interregional competition. Such a competitive process among regions may be viewed either with respect to particular economic activities or on an overall basis. Obviously a wide range of supply side forces is likely to influence the competitiveness of a given region, including the nature of regional supply functions for labour and capital, the resource endowment of the region, and the location of the region in terms of access to input supplies and markets, as determined by the structure of interregional transport costs (Stolper and Tiebout 1978).

However, from what has been argued already, it is clear that the overall competitiveness of a region (and thus its ability to adjust) may be crucially dependent on the nature of its existing spatial structure, i.e., the geographical configuration of its economy (Parr, 1978).

It should be emphasised that there are likely to be numerous instances when a regional structure is perfectly appropriate for the kinds of sectoral change that would be logical for the region by virtue of its present factor endowment and its general pattern of development to date. In such cases the spatial structure exerts no appreciable influence on the process of regional growth or adjustment, other than a purely facilitative or permissive one. This possibility, together with the fact that spontaneous or planned changes in the spatial structure are generally not accomplished within a short period of time, may have caused the significance of the spatial structure to be underestimated. More seriously, perhaps, it may have led to the spatial structure being given an inadequate (or at least inappropriate) emphasis in regional planning and regional policy.

Spatial Structure and Economic Adjustment in Problem Regions

Most developed nations contain problem regions within their boundaries, and Great Britain is no exception. The characteristics of these lagging or problem regions are familiar and typically include such features as below-average per capita income levels, above-average rates of unemployment, slow growth or decline in the overall levels of economic activity, sensitivity to fluctuations in the national economy, inefficient or outdated infrastructure systems and pressing fiscal problems, although this latter problem is less serious in Great Britain than in many nations. The problem region condition is usually associated with a declining export base, an accompanying downward multiplier effect on the export-linked and regionally oriented sectors, and a labour outmigration response that is inadequate to maintain full (or nearly full) employment.

The problem is, of course, not as straightforward as this. Within a national system of regions, virtually no region is immune from contraction of certain export sectors or sectors of specialisation (Chisholm and Oeppen, 1973). The crucial question appears to be whether the region has the ability to adjust to this exogeneously induced change (Segal, chapter 10 of this volume). The adjustment would be based on a re-utilisation of the available regional resources by alternative export sector activities (or even by local-sector activities if regional import substitution were a possibility) for which the region would be locationally competitive. It is the absence or non-appearance of an appropriate intraregional adjustment mechanism, along with the low level of interregional mobility of resources, that eventually gives rise to the problem region condition.

The Role of Spatial Structure

Such an adjustment process with respect to regional resources can be extremely complex, but usually involves such aspects as the re-employment of labour, the utilisation of the existing stock of regional infrastructure in a different manner, and (perhaps less frequently) the conversion of fixed capital, such as industrial buildings, to alternative production uses. Where there is a high degree of specificity of existing factors of production or regional resources, the extent of the adjustment process may be severely limited. Leaving this important question aside, there exists a further factor that constrains the adjustment process. This concerns the spatial distribution of these available resources. The relative inflexibility of such a spatial distribution may significantly reduce the effective extent of the adjustment process. What frequently happens is that a spatial structure that may have been eminently suitable for some earlier or existing set of economic activities may now be quite inappropriate for potential replacement activities which, if they could be successfully implanted within the region, might contribute to the maintenance of the regional economy at something approaching its former level.

The role of spatial structure is perhaps most dramatically illustrated in the case of a region with a declining export base in resource exploitation and raw-material-oriented industries. Such a decline releases resources (mainly in the form of labour and infrastructure) that might be suitable for industries new to the region. However, because of the locational characteristics of the declining industries, these resources will only become available in small quantities at a relatively large number of locations. By contrast, the locational requirements of the potentially new activities may be such as to favour relatively few, large-scale units, perhaps located in clusters (if agglomeration economies are important). If such a situation obtained, a mismatch would occur between existing supplies of regional resources and potential demands for them. This would render the region unsuitable or unattractive for the new activities (the aggregate availability of resources notwithstanding) and thus make regional economic adjustment very difficult. While this discussion of adjustment problems relating to the spatial structure within resource-based regions has been phrased in general terms, it is nevertheless possible to recognise elements of these kinds of problems within areas of Great Britain such as the Highlands and Islands of Scotland, North and Central Wales, and the western part of South West England. Certain of the declining and non-industrialised coalmining areas also tend to display problems of this type.

Urban–Industrial Regions

The problem of inappropriate spatial structures can also exist in a wholly different setting, and one that is of greater importance, as far as the regional problem in Great Britain is concerned. This involves a region's spatial structure being dominated by one or more large metropolitan areas that were at one time the location of industrial complexes with very elaborate patterns of inter-industry linkage. These metropolitan areas may have represented powerful concentrations of economic activity and decision making, having been the location for much of the region's traditional export activity. The structural contraction of these industries gives rise to problems of slow growth or decline, accompanied by unemployment and excess capacity in the infrastructure. Factors of production and infrastructure thus become available, and as with the case of the resource-based region, the question arises as to whether these resources will be an attraction for replacement industries, which may originate within the region or may be drawn from other regions. This is likely to depend in part on whether the existing spatial configuration of these resources will be conducive to the development of such activities, and if not, whether it can be adapted to meet these different requirements.

Evidence suggests that in Great Britain the potential replacement industries are eschewing metropolitan locations, despite the availability of labour and infrastructure (Hughes, chapter 8 of this volume). Of the numerous forces encouraging such a tendency, an important one is the high costs of operation within such large urban centres, particularly with regard to the cost of land and labour and the costs associated with congestion and other negative externalities. Moreover, because of the tendency toward increased firm size, many of the favourable externalities of the metropolitan areas can now be internalised, with the result that for these larger firms (as well as foreign and extraregionally owned branch plants) the metropolitan location has ceased to be as crucial as it once was.[2] Post-war changes in transport technology have also weakened the grip of metropolitan areas as locations for production. Although it is difficult to generalise about the overall impact of these various forces, the locational preference of firms in a wider range of sectors appears to be shifting increasingly in favour of medium-sized centres, particularly those located within easy reach of metropolitan areas. Within a particular region, however, the earlier patterns of centralisation and metropolitan dominance may have seriously retarded the development of economically independent medium-sized centres that could accommodate these changed locational preferences. This absence of appropriately sized centres may be a factor in the diversion of potential development away from the region, particularly since it is likely to be in competition with other regions (possibly in other countries) that do not suffer from this drawback.

The problem may not lie with the region's urban size distribution but rather with the geographic distribution of centres. Appropriately sized centres with a potential for development may exist but are located in a less developed part of the region, removed from the large metropolitan concentrations. These independent centres may have particular site advantages such as access to a newly discovered resource or to a deepwater harbour. Alternatively, the development of motorways or other regional transport facilities may have conferred an increased locational advantage on certain of these centres. Furthermore, because of the less intense pattern of development in this part of the region, such centres may enjoy a level of urban amenity superior to that existing in the metropolitan areas of the region—a factor that cannot be overlooked in contemporary locational decision making. However, the development of these centres would require a greater degree of intraregional labour mobility, as well as a willingness to make the politically difficult decision to divert infrastructure investment and social expenditures away from the declining or stationary metropolitan areas to these less developed but promising centres.

Problems of adjustment may still exist even when modifications to the spatial structure can be achieved relatively easily, and this is perhaps the more usual situation in Great Britain. A region may contain sufficient centres of an appropriate size that are strategically located so as to afford convenient access to the services of a metropolitan area and that, if developed, would contribute to overall regional economic growth. Indeed, an efficient (and in this case decentralised) spatial structure may be evolving within the region, in response to changing locational conditions, and official policies may be assisting this process, either unintentionally or by design (Stone, chapter 6 of this volume). Ultimately, however, a point may be reached when those responsible for the region's development decide that the costs of continuing with this more competitive but decentralised regional spatial structure are too high, particularly in terms of the various backwash effects encountered by the inner districts of the metropolitan areas. Because of this, there may be a deliberate attempt to retard or to reverse trends toward decentralisation.[3] By pursuing such a policy to assist the metropolitan areas, decision makers might well find themselves in the difficult position of not being able to promote a more competitive regional spatial structure, whilst at the same time trying to persevere with a spatial structure that cannot accommodate the locational preferences of potential economic activity within the region. It is probably not forcing the issue to suggest that problems of the type discussed in this sub-section may be contributing to the adjustment difficulties experienced in the urban–industrial regions of Great Britain such as Central Scotland, North West England and North East England.

Determinants of Adjustment

In practice, the required spatial restructuring of regional resources is difficult to accomplish, due largely to such factors as impediments to labour migration and the general immobility of the infrastructure. Public policy can obviously be instrumental in moulding a more favourable spatial structure for a particular region and this will be explored further in the following section.

The principal difficulty, however, is the formidable array of political pressures that militates against such a modification of the spatial structure: decision makers are under strong pressure to allocate public expenditures on the basis of where population and economic activity are presently located and not where (in the interests of long-term overall regional welfare) they 'should be' located. And in this connection the planned run-down of certain communities (or parts thereof), however rational such a policy may be, is particularly difficult to achieve.

Policy considerations apart, the extent to which restructuring can be effectively accomplished appears to depend on two general factors. The first concerns the dimension or scale of the region. For a region with a large area and a low population density, the adjustment is likely to be difficult. However, at the opposite extreme, for a small compact region with a relatively high population density, the spatial-adjustment problem tends to be potentially less serious. The relatively short distances involved facilitate adjustment by means of commuting and ease the informational and economic impediments to migration (Yapa, Polese and Wolpert, 1969). A second factor influencing the adjustment process is the period of time over which it is required to take place. If the adverse influences affecting the region are spread over a long period (e.g., thirty years), the adjustment might be accomplished relatively smoothly through the usual market mechanisms, such as outmigration of labour and/or the development of new economic activity, perhaps in a modified locational setting. If, on the other hand, comparable adverse influences occur within a short period, as is often the case, the adjustment process is rendered difficult, and the degree to which the regional spatial structure is suitable for the establishment and operation of alternative activities thus becomes a critical factor.

The arguments raised in this section need to be placed in perspective. In particular, it should be stressed that the fundamental difficulties of adjustment faced by a region frequently relate to problems that do not directly involve the spatial structure, such as poor entrepreneurial and managerial capabilities within the declining sectors (preventing a range of possible product and technical adjustments), an outmoded educational system, conservative attitudes within the labour force, rigidities in the social structure, etc. (Segal, chapter 10 of this volume). Nevertheless, the possibility that an inappropriate regional spatial structure may be contributing to the difficulties of adjustment, thereby exacerbating these more fundamental problems, should not be overlooked.

Spatial Structure and Regional Policy

Public intervention in the form of regional policy is the usual response to economic-adjustment problems of the type considered in the previous section. In Great Britain, regional policy has been concerned mainly (though not exclusively) with fostering economic conversion, i.e., the development of new sectors of economic activity within a region to replace those that have been facing slow growth or decline. This has been attempted by the improvement of labour skills, the upgrading and extending of infrastructure and the granting of financial inducements to firms, all in the expectation of stimulating employment-generating investment, not only from within the region but (more likely) from external sources. However, in striving for such an economic conversion, the extent to which adjustment is being hindered by problems related to the regional spatial structure needs to be considered. Such an approach to regional policy in a problem region is a central theme in so-called 'growth pole policy'.[4] It is recognised, of course, that regional policy that takes explicit account of existing or planned spatial structures can assume a variety of forms. However, the policy of planned growth poles is singled out for attention because it is able to illustrate a major theme of this chapter.

Growth pole policy, as a strategy for regional development, has been pursued in a number of countries, including Great Britain, although currently it tends to be neglected. Growth pole policy is viewed here as an interrelated set of sectoral and spatial policies aimed at improving the locational competitiveness of a problem region, either in terms of selected industries or on an overall basis. It represents a strategy of public investment designed to achieve a structural modification of the regional economy in both sectoral and spatial terms. Before examining the nature and limits of growth pole policy in the context of a problem region, several assumptions are made. First, the region exists within a mixed economy of the West European or North American type. Second, the economic and political justifications for intervention are taken as given, as is the decision to incur expenditure within the region. Third, it is assumed that the implementation and funding of the policy rest either with the central government or with an autonomous regional government. Finally, the focus is on the individual region. The approach is thus partial in nature, and important interregional considerations that may have a bearing on the formulation of policy are not taken into account.

Elements of Growth Pole Policy in a Problem Region
Within this general setting, growth pole policy can be seen as comprising three broad elements. The first involves the concentration of infrastructure at a selected number of locations (poles) within the region. This is based on the assumption that for certain industries the locational attractions of the region will be enhanced if infrastructure is provided in a concentrated pattern (Rosenstein-Rodan, 1961). For a resource-based region this would usually involve a centralised pattern of infrastructure availability, relative to the existing spatial structure. However, in the case of an urban–industrial region, which already has a relatively highly centralised spatial structure,

the pattern of infrastructure provision may well tend toward relative decentralisation, i.e., concentrated decentralisation. Nevertheless, it is not difficult
to conceive of situations where the pattern of planned infrastructure availability would match or even surpass the existing level of centralisation
in the regional spatial structure. In both types of region the infrastructure
would not be entirely new, inasmuch as certain elements of the existing
infrastructure would be coordinated with (or integrated into) the new
pattern. Concentration of infrastructure at a system of planned growth
poles could be attractive to certain activities by virtue of the creation
or extension of a range of urbanisation economies previously lacking or
poorly developed within the region, particularly in connection with transport
facilities (such as airports, freight terminals and motorway connections),
public-utility systems and municipal services. To the extent that such a
strategy of concentration raises the competitiveness of the region, it represents
a more 'effective' spatial allocation of infrastructure investment than a
dispersed pattern based on proportionate district shares, or one based on
districts most in need.[5] This strategy may still need to be buttressed with
financial inducements to potential incoming firms. These might be restricted
to firms willing to locate at the poles, although it is often suggested that
no such restriction should exist (Wilson, chapter 4 of this volume).

A second element in a policy of planned growth poles relates to the
sectoral structure of the regional economy, and in contrast to the first
element is more concerned with the composition of industrial investment
at the planned poles. This second element attempts to raise the competitiveness of the region by the establishment of key or propulsive industries
which would have the potential for stimulating the development of backward
and forward linkages. This would involve either existing firms within the
region or firms new to the region.[6] In the former case the prospects may
not always be encouraging (James, 1964; Lever, 1974). In the latter case,
each key industry would need to be of a sufficiently large scale that either:
(a) potential upstream suppliers (backward-linkage industries) would be
assured of a minimum demand for efficient production within the region;
or (b) potential downstream users (forward-linkage industries) would be
accessible to a source of low-cost inputs. These requirements, along with
the locational setting of the region, would limit the range of activities
that could be established as key industries.[7] In general, however, the attraction to the region of external investment in linked industries would be
more likely to succeed if the capacity of each key industry was concentrated
in large-scale plants at a limited number of planned poles, rather than
distributed within the region among small-scale, high-cost plants at a larger
number of poles. Thus for each key industry, scale considerations would
restrict the number of plants to a few or only one and, depending on
the number of key industries that were established, this would effectively
limit the total number of poles.

The location of the linked industries is less clear cut. These would tend to locate at the poles if they were sensitive to the precise location of their respective key industries, as would be the case if agglomeration economies of the industrial-complex type were important (Isard, Schooler and Vietorisz, 1959). In other cases, however, spatial juxtaposition of the linked industries and their relevant key industries might not result in agglomeration economies and the linked industries would be free to locate at other poles or at non-pole locations within the region.[8] This would permit the establishment of a larger number of planned poles, which might be of advantage in the geographic redeployment of the regional labour force as part of the growth pole policy. This second element of growth pole policy represents, in effect, an alternative to the first. Both elements are designed to achieve the objective of making the region more attractive as a location for economic activity, but the means adopted in each case are different. There is no reason, of course, why an actual policy should not involve a combination of both elements. In fact this will occur to some degree, even if emphasis is placed on the second element. The successful establishment of a key industry within a region and the subsequent attraction of linked industries to it are both likely to require investment in the infrastructure, even though this is not the primary policy instrument.

There exists a third element in the policy of planned growth poles, which in many respects is complementary to the previous two. Whereas the first two elements are concerned with increasing the regional demand for labour, the third element is concerned with the regional supply of labour and, specifically, with ensuring that adequate supplies of labour are available as economic activity locates itself at the poles. The importance of improved population mobility in this connection has been stressed by Wilson (1964, p. 21). In an initial period, this might be achieved by modifications to the 'circulation' within the spatial structure such as improved public transport, thereby facilitating commuting to the poles. Subsequently, the improvement of highways, which would probably be undertaken in any case in connection with the build-up of the poles, might permit the commuting field to be extended. Such transportation improvements, apart from easing any labour supply difficulties at the poles, would also tend to be of benefit to the labour force. Work by Sugden (1976) on a problem area in the North Region of Britain has demonstrated that the relative accessibility of centres to employment opportunities tends to be an important determinant of the level of local unemployment rates.

Over the long run, policies to improve mobility would tend to place less stress on daily commuting and encourage, by means of grants for removal, the permanent relocation of the labour force and dependents at the poles, with an increasing share of investment in social overhead capital being made at the poles rather than in other parts of the region.[9] In general, it could be expected (on the basis of gravity-model and intervening-opportunity explanations of migration) that the very establishment of poles would increase the general level of intraregional mobility, particularly with respect to 'poleward' migration. Although, as was stated above, this third element is essentially complementary to the first two, it is nevertheless possible that certain conflicts could arise. In the case of a particular region it might be found that for a given level of expenditure the number and location of poles necessary to maximise the inflow of jobs to the region would be such as to produce an inadequate commuting and migration response and thus an insufficient supply of labour at the poles. While this problem is unlikely to persist in the long run, it could pose serious difficulties of a programming nature in the short run.

Nature of the Policy

Some perspective on growth pole policy is gained by contrasting it with the more traditional regional-policy options of bringing work to the workers and bringing workers to the work. Both of these policies are concerned with factor movements: in the former case the movement involves capital and in the latter case, labour. A serious defect of policies of this kind is the lack of an adequate specification of the origin and destination of the relevant factor movements. Furthermore, there is a tendency for the two policies to be regarded as mutually exclusive alternatives. Clearly, a mixing of the two policies is feasible. Indeed, this is the very essence of a growth pole policy applied to a problem region. Both types of factor movement are involved, and the nature of these movements is specified within the context of the region: capital moves from other regions (and even possibly from within the region) to particular regional locations or poles, while labour moves to these same locations from other parts of the region. In the words of a study on a problem area in the North West Region, '. . . the problem should be viewed, not as one of moving work to the workers, or vice versa, but as one of moving the work, and the workers if necessary to the places where it will be most efficiently performed' (Economist Intelligence Unit, 1959, p. 150).

Discussions of growth pole policy frequently stress the fact that such a policy involves the steering of investment to those centres that appear to have the best prospects for growth, or centres that may even be 'natural' growth poles in their own right; see Note 4. This would be in contrast to the politically less controversial policy of proportionate expenditure shares for each centre or district, and also in contrast to the policy of channelling expenditures into the most depressed areas. However, the view that growth pole policy favours the 'best' centres (centres most able to sustain rapid growth) is too narrow a conception of the policy. While locational selectivity is quite likely to figure prominently in growth pole policy, it should be seen as part of the more fundamental objective of raising the overall competitiveness of the region and activating a spatial structure that would reflect and cater to the locational requirements of the new economic activity associated with this improved competitiveness. Nor should growth pole policy be regarded as purely a spatial policy. Its distinctive feature is that it strives for a coordination of the sectoral and spatial components. A growth pole policy will, of necessity, involve substantial long-run changes in the spatial structure, as a result of a concentrated pattern of public and private investment and the redistribution of labour force and population that derives from this. However, the policy will need to take account of the kinds of activity that can be expected to locate within the region and, if it is to be effective, it will inevitably be concerned with the level and sectoral mix of investment at the poles.

The centrepiece of growth pole policy is the poles themselves, though this should not be allowed to divert attention away from the remainder of the region. If the policy proceeds according to plan, the poles can be expected to experience employment growth. However, two types of growth need to be distinguished here. First, there is the growth that occurs in response to investments in the infrastructure and/or key industries, this growth being of an essentially short- to-medium-term nature and involving the establishment of new firms from the outside. A second kind of growth is of a more long-term type and is based on the performance of firms once they have become established. In many cases the extent of the regional problem might be such that only growth of the first type could realistically be expected. However, it is not inconceivable that the poles may emerge as highly efficient (i.e., profitable) locations. The initial implantation of firms may give rise to further agglomeration economies, conferring an advantage on recently established firms and encouraging the setting up of additional ones, which may further enhance the development of agglomeration economies and growth prospects for the initially established firms. Under these rather fortuitous circumstances the growth rates of early established (or even indigenous) firms at the poles could actually exceed those for comparable firms in other regions—the 'planned' poles would then have assumed certain of the characteristics of 'natural' growth poles. In such cases the policy would have exceeded its primary objective of raising the locational competitiveness of the region. This would have been achieved in the short run with the attraction of economic activity into the region. The fact that over a subsequent period the growth rates of firms at the poles were above the corresponding industry growth rates nationally would be an indication that the policy had induced a longer-term and more substantial improvement in the competitive position of the region, at least as far as the growing sectors are concerned.

The successful pursuit of growth pole policy is likely to depend not only on the selection of industries to be established at the poles but on the locational selection of the poles. The selection of pole industries is part of the broader problem of deciding upon the economic activity to be promoted in problem regions. This is an involved question, which has been dealt with adequately elsewhere (Klaassen, 1965; 1967), so that attention can be turned to the other major aspect of selection: the locational pattern of the poles. Even though part of the object of the policy is to effect a transformation of the spatial structure, the selection of the poles will obviously have to pay close attention to the nature of the existing regional structure. Work by Morrill (1973) has drawn attention to some of the important considerations involved with the size and spacing of poles in policies of this kind.

The problem has also been approached in terms of the size and frequency of poles. In dealing with this question, considerable emphasis has been placed on economies of scale in the provision of public services, and in particular evidence is frequently presented about the 'U'-shaped marginal cost curve for the provision of infrastructure. To quote Cameron (1970): 'The published evidence on the shape of the marginal cost for social and economic overhead capital as towns increase in size is scanty, unstandardised and conflicting'. While attention should be given to cost considerations, this has to be weighed against the likely stream of benefits, particularly with regard to the inflow of private investment and the associated employment. A cost-minimising solution is of only limited significance, and the usual criterion employed in resource allocation of this type is based on the maximising of net benefits. Only where the discounted benefits under alternative size-frequency configurations of poles are approximately similar (and this is extremely unlikely) can attention be focused on cost-minimising approaches.

Finally, the two kinds of selection process (with regard to the economic activities at the poles and with regard to the size, frequency and location of poles) cannot be undertaken separately, since important interdependencies exist. For example, the locational preferences and characteristics of the industries selected for promotion within the region are likely to influence decisions relating to the configuration of the poles in terms of their size, frequency and location. Conversely, the nature of the existing spatial structure of the region would limit the range of feasible pole configurations, and thus limit the range of industries that would be suitable for promotion at the regional poles.

Growth Pole Policy in Practice

In the early 1960s growth pole policy was still sufficiently novel (and inadequately understood) that extravagant claims were made for it, and it tended to be regarded as a panacea for regional-development problems, whatever their precise nature. However, the actual record of growth pole policy during the subsequent period has been disappointing, both in Great Britain and elsewhere (Moseley, 1974). Why has the success of the policy fallen so far short of expectations? One reason may be that the policy has been applied indiscriminately or with an inadequate appreciation of its underlying logic. Obviously, for certain problem regions a growth pole policy would not be appropriate, because of such factors as the particular character of the existing spatial structure, the locational requirements of potential incoming economic activity or the likely nature of the commuting and migration responses. The pursuit of growth pole policy under such circumstances would obviously produce unsatisfactory results.

The generally poor record of growth pole policy may also be related to the manner of its implementation. There are several factors involved here. First, a growth pole policy is fraught with uncertainty and risk, the more so because of its highly selective nature. The commitment of available investment funds to a few centres implies that if the policy fails, it is likely to involve a substantial misallocation of resources. Even though decision makers may accept the basic premises of growth pole policy, they are nevertheless likely to be hesitant about commiting substantial investment funds to a few centres. A second question involves the differential impact of the policy resulting from selective concentration of investment. If the policy is successful and the region's aggregate welfare is improved, an almost inevitable accompaniment of this success is the heightening of intraregional differences. These differences would not necessarily relate to incomes (though this would be particularly serious) but would certainly involve differences in access to employment and differences in the availability and quality of a range of consumer services. Again, decision makers may be concerned about embarking upon a policy that might have these results.

A further consideration, not unrelated to the second, concerns the public acceptability of growth pole policy. It could be safely anticipated that there would be considerable opposition from political representatives of centres that were not designated growth poles. Although it might be possible to demonstrate that a growth pole policy (among several policy options) would maximise the aggregate increase in regional welfare, the nature of the policy is such that these benefits would tend not to be distributed in conformity with the existing population, and the economies of many non-designated centres may be required to continue in stagnation or decline. Indeed, the very success of the policy is likely to be conditional upon the redistribution of population away from a number of non-designated centres. The opposition to a growth pole policy from such a non-designated centre is thus based on a fundamental 'regional-versus-local' conflict of interests—what is in the best interests of the region is not in the best interests of a given locality. In opposing the policy, a non-designated centre might feel that if the policy did not proceed, it would have a reasonable chance of receiving at least *some* public funds, since expenditures for development would then be likely to be made on a proportionate basis or on a needs basis. Since, by the very nature of growth pole policy, relatively few centres would be selected as poles, there would be a strong likelihood of an in-built majority against the policy within the region and in favour of one involving a more even distribution of investment.[10]

The various problems described above may be deemed sufficiently serious that it is decided to follow the policy in modified form. This typically involves a decision to expand the number of poles over what was originally felt to be the optimal number and to reallocate expenditures among the larger number of poles. While such a modification runs counter to the underlying logic of the policy and thus lowers the likely level of overall benefits, it may appear to reduce the degree of risk involved, it decreases the possibility that wider intraregional differences in levels of welfare might emerge and it may avoid a crucial element in the political opposition to such a policy. Sometimes the modification is slightly different, with extensive areas rather than centres being designated.[11] Whatever its particular form, this 'watering down' process, if carried beyond moderate lengths, may seriously threaten the very basis of the policy. Even though such a watering down may be resisted at the planning stage, it can still occur (for a similar set of reasons) during the implementation stage, with further poles being added or zones being expanded. It is but a short step from here to the virtual abandonment of the policy with plans for sectoral and locational selectivity becoming shelved in the scramble to acquire *any* activity at *any* location within the region.

Spatial Structure and Regional Policy: A More General Framework
The poor record of growth pole policy can thus be traced to two broad causes: first, the application of the policy in situations where it was inappropriate on technical grounds; second, modification of the policy in a manner that ran counter to the very logic of the policy. It should, of course, be recognised at the outset that growth pole policy may be inappropriate for certain kinds of regional-development problems. This in no way implies that policies designed to foster economic conversion should neglect spatial-structure considerations; it does mean, however, that alternative strategies have to be employed. Clearly, what is needed is a much broader framework for regional-development policy that takes full account of the interrelationships between regional economic performance and regional spatial structure and within which growth pole policy would be one (but only one) element. The availability of such a framework would enable decision makers to differentiate between those situations when growth pole policy could be effectively applied and those situations when some other strategy would be more appropriate.

Conclusions

It was argued earlier that if regional economic analysis is to contribute more fully to the understanding and solution of regional problems, it must be able to accommodate the influence of the spatial structure. Admittedly, there may be instances when the spatial structure exerts a negligible influence on the process of regional development, but this hardly justifies the general exclusion of spatial-structure considerations from regional economic analysis. In some respects, problems relating to the spatial structure can be regarded as a form of market failure. More generally, they represent barriers to the kinds of equilibrating adjustment mechanisms that are so central to many regional growth theories. It is perhaps worth stressing the fact that were it not for the existence of space and the frictions and imperfections that this creates, there would be no need for the subject of regional economics. If it is accepted that space exerts such effects, it is unreasonable to suppose that these operate on an interregional basis only and that their influence ceases at the boundary of a region—any more than their influence ceases at the boundary of an urban area. Few people would dispute the fact that the internal structure and workings of an urban economy are heavily influenced by the role of space. For some reason, however, we seem reluctant to recognise the possibility that space may exert corresponding (though obviously quite different) effects within a region. All too often in regional economic analysis, the region is treated either as an undifferentiated territory or as a dimensionless point, i.e., as if it is wholly lacking in spatial structure. Such a simplication is often misleading and can have serious implications for the diagnosis of problems and the formulation of policies.

From what has been said, it is clear that public intervention designed to influence the economic performance or welfare of a given region cannot afford to neglect the relationship between regional economic growth and regional spatial structure. In general, policies aimed at transforming the sectoral structure of a problem region must consider the extent to which these are consistent with the existing spatial structure or its feasible development in the future. Conversely, policies with a direct bearing on the nature of the spatial structure (such as investment in transportation facilities, New Town development and other aspects of physical planning) will have only a limited effectiveness, unless there is an explicit recognition of the needs of economic activity that at present exists within the region or might reasonably be expected to be located there. Regrettably, there is frequently a gulf between these two facets of regional policy, regardless of the level at which it is undertaken. Part of the problem is the tendency for different departments of government to be responsible for the two strands of policy.[12] Furthermore, there is a traditional difference in outlook and emphasis between those involved with economic policy and those involved with policies that seek to modify the spatial structure.

While such a dichotomy in regional policy between economic aspects and physical ones is not desirable, it is nontheless well established, and for this reason the dangers that stem from it should be recognised. Reference has already been made to the desirability of dovetailing these two elements of policy and to the need for administrative coordination—a need that is particularly strong if each element is embedded in its own bureaucratic structure. More serious perhaps is the danger of one element of policy having ascendancy over the other in the formulation and implementation of policy. It is obvious that regional economic policy cannot be formulated *in vacuo*, and physical or spatial-structure policy made to follow or 'fit in' as best it can. By the same token, economic policy should not be subordinated to physical policies that regulate or transform the spatial structure. The possible difficulties in this latter case with respect to oil-related development in Scotland have been examined by MacKay and Mackay (1975, pp. 138–49). The regional problem is seldom of such a nature that one of the two elements of regional policy can be clearly subordinated to the other, and for most problem regions the two elements must be considered in conjunction. That they are not treated in this way usually stems from the fact that there exists no framework for intervention of the type mentioned at the end of the previous section. Without such a framework it can be virtually guaranteed that regional policy will become fragmented and thus in danger of containing internal inconsistencies, with the inevitable result that its effectiveness will be impaired.

Notes

1. If the direct employment is located close to the boundary of the region, or if the input structure (particularly with regard to imports) varies systematically within the region, then it is possible that the overall multiplier effect may not be independent of the location of the direct employment.

2. For smaller firms and certain medium-sized ones, and more generally single-plant firms, the large metropolitan area is likely to be important in view of the access to external economies. It will also continue to serve as a seed-bed or nursery for many new firms, although it is frequently alleged that recent physical planning policies, particularly with regard to urban renewal and the elimination of non-conforming land uses, may have done serious damage to this role.

3. The recent reappraisal of New Towns and the decision to place less emphasis on New Towns and to direct resources towards the inner districts of metropolitan areas (Great Britain, 1977) are examples of this line of thinking.

4. The term 'growth pole' was originally employed by Perroux (1955) to describe a sector of rapid growth (within a market economy) which exerted a dominant and propulsive influence on other sectors. Perroux (1955, pp. 317–18) also used the term to describe an urban agglomeration in which this same phenomenon was present. Subsequently, the term came to be employed in a regional planning sense; see, for example, Kuklinski and Petrella (1972), and for earlier thinking on growth poles in regional planning, Scottish Council (1952; 1962). It is important, therefore, to distinguish between the 'natural' growth pole based on market forces and the 'planned' growth pole based on conscious public-policy decisions (Parr, 1973). The terms 'growth point', 'growth centre' and 'development pole' are sometimes used to describe the planned growth pole, in order to distinguish it from the natural growth pole. Nevertheless, a clear distinction between the two usages is not always made, and more seriously perhaps the underlying characteristics of 'natural' growth poles are sometimes used to justify a planning policy based on 'planned' growth poles—a procedure of dubious validity.

5. If this is, in fact, the case, it should be possible to construct a response function, indicating (in the first instance) the inflow of investment into the region under different levels of infrastructure concentration.

6. A variant of this second element would involve the outright establishment of industrial complexes (sets of linked activities) at one or more poles (Luttrell, 1972). Frequently, however, the planning authority lacks either the necessary policy instruments or the technical expertise to engage in such an approach, and it would tend to be employed only where industrial planning figured prominently in regional policy.

7. Rigid adherence to these requirements would not be justified if the key industry was a large employer and/or if the linked industries were unlikely to develop in the short term but could be realistically expected to do so in some subsequent period.

8. Even though no economies may result from the linked industries locating in the immediate proximity to the respective key industries, the linked industries might still be drawn to the region in view of the transport cost advantages of accessibility to the market or accessibility to input supply, represented in either case by the key industry.

9. Hansen (1966) draws a distinction between social overhead capital (e.g., housing, hospitals, schools) and economic overhead capital (e.g., roads, water supply, electricity).

10. This is likely to be the case whether regional policy is administered by an autonomous regional authority or by a central or federal one. It is noteworthy that growth pole policy is usually only considered when the competent authority is central or federal in character, and thus not responsible solely to the electorate of the region in question.

11. This may have been the case in the early 1960s when it was decided to designate eight 'growth areas' in Central Scotland (Great Britain, 1963a) and a rather extensive 'growth zone' in North East England (Great Britain, 1963b). In the Scottish case, Cameron and Reid (1966, p. 48) have noted that 'If we exclude Glasgow and Paisley and all land over 650 feet high, growth areas cover a large proportion of the remainder of Central Scotland'.

12. The establishment of Regional Economic Planning Boards in 1964 was designed to avoid the very problem within the context of the individual regions (McCallum, chapter 1 of this volume).

References

Boudeville, J. R. (1966) *Problems of Regional Economic Planning*. Edinburgh: Edinburgh University Press.
von Böventer, E. (1970) 'Optimal Spatial Structure and Regional Development', *Kyklos*, Vol. 23, pp. 903–26.
Cameron, G. C. (1970) 'Growth Areas, Growth Centres and Regional Conversion', *Scottish Journal of Political Economy*, Vol. 21, pp. 19–38.
Cameron, G. C. and Reid, G. L. (1966) *Scottish Economic Planning and the Attraction of Industry*. University of Glasgow Social and Economic Studies, Occasional Paper No. 6. Edinburgh and London: Oliver and Boyd.
Chisholm, M. and Oeppen, J. (1973) *The Changing Pattern of Employment: Regional Specialisation and Industrial Localisation in Great Britain*. London: Croom Helm.
Economist Intelligence Unit (1959) 'A Study of the Prospects for the Economic Development of N.E. Lancashire', Economist Intelligence Unit, London.
Great Britain (1963a) Scottish Development Department. *Central Scotland: A Programme for Development and Growth*. Cmnd. 2188. Edinburgh: HMSO.
Great Britain (1963b) Board of Trade. *The North East: A Programme for Regional Development and Growth*. Cmnd. 2206. London: HMSO.
Great Britain (1977) Department of the Environment, Scottish Office and Welsh Office. *Policy for the Inner Cities*. Cmnd. 6845. London: HMSO.
Hansen, N. J. (1966) 'Some Neglected Factors in American Regional Development Policy: the Case of Appalachia', *Land Economics*, Vol. 42, pp. 1–9.

Isard, W., Schooler, E. W. and Vietorisz, T. (1959) *Industrial Complex Analysis and Regional Development*. New York: John Wiley.

James, B. G. S. (1964) 'The Incompatibility of Industrial and Trading Cultures: a Critical Appraisal of the Growth Point Concept', *Journal of Industrial Economics*, Vol. 13, pp. 90–4.

Klaassen, L. H. (1965) *Area Economic and Social Redevelopment*. Paris: Organisation for Economic Co-operation and Development.

Klaassen, L. H. (1967) *Methods of Selecting Industries for Depressed Areas*. Paris: Organisation for Economic Co-operation and Development.

Kuklinski, A. R. and Petrella, R. (eds.) (1972) *Growth Poles and Regional Policies*. Paris and The Hague: Mouton.

Lever, W. F. (1974) 'Manufacturing Linkages and the Search for Suppliers and Markets', in F. E. I. Hamilton (ed.), *The Industrial Firm and Locational Decisions*. London: John Wiley.

Luttrell, W. F. (1972) 'Industrial Complexes and Regional Economic Development in Canada', in A. R. Kuklinski (ed.), *Growth Poles and Growth Centres in Regional Planning*. Paris and The Hague: Mouton.

MacKay, D. I. and Mackay, G. A. (1975) *The Political Economy of North Sea Oil*. London: Martin Robertson.

Moore, F. T. and Peterson, J. W. (1955) 'Regional Analysis: An Interindustry Model of Utah', *Review of Economics and Statistics*, Vol. 37, pp. 368–83.

Morrill, R. L. (1973) 'On the Size and Spacing of Growth Centers', *Growth and Change*, Vol. 4, pp. 21–4.

Moseley, M. J. (1974) *Growth Centres in Spatial Planning*. Oxford: Pergamon.

Parr, J. B. (1973) 'Growth Poles, Regional Development, and Central Place Theory', *Papers of the Regional Science Association*, Vol. 31, pp. 173–212.

Parr, J. B. (1978) 'Regional Competition, Growth Pole Policy, and Public Intervention', in W. Buhr and P. Friedrich (eds.), *Konkurrenz zwischen kleinen Regionen—Competition among Small Regions*. Schriften zur öffentlichen Verwaltung und öffentlichen Wirtschaft, Vol. 23. Baden-Baden: Nomos Verlag.

Perroux, F. (1955) 'Note sur la notion de "pôle de croissance"', *Economie Appliquée*, Vol. 8, pp. 307–20.

Richardson, H. W. (1973) *Regional Growth Theory*. London: Macmillan.

Rosenstein-Rodan, P. M. (1961) 'How to Industrialize an Underdeveloped Area', in W. Isard and J. H. Cumberland (eds.), *Regional Economic Planning: Techniques of Analysis for Less Developed Areas*. Paris: Organisation for European Economic Co-operation.

Scottish Council (Development and Industry) (1952) *Report of the Committee on Local Development in Scotland*. Edinburgh: Scottish Council (Development and Industry).

Scottish Council (Development and Industry) (1962) *Report on the Scottish Economy*. Edinburgh: Scottish Council (Development and Industry).

Stolper, W. F. and Tiebout, C. M. (1978) 'The Balance of Payments of a Small Area as an Analytical Tool', in R. Funck and J. B. Parr (eds.), *The Analysis of Regional Structure: Essays in Honour of August Lösch*, Karlsruhe Papers in Regional Science, Vol. 2. London: Pion.

Sugden, R. (1976) 'Travel Costs and Unemployment Rates: Some Implications of a Search Theory of Unemployment', Department of Economics, University of York.

Vining, R. (1955) 'A Description of Certain Spatial Aspects of an Urban System', *Economic Development and Cultural Change*, Vol. 3, pp. 147–95.

Wilson, T. (1964) *Policies for Regional Development*. University of Glasgow Social and Economic Studies, Occasional Paper, No. 3. Edinburgh and London: Oliver and Boyd.

Yapa, L., Polese, M. and Wolpert, J. (1969) 'Interdependence of Commuting and Migration', *Proceedings of the Association of American Geographers*, Vol. 1, pp. 163–8.

CHAPTER 10

The Limits and Means of 'Self-Reliant' Regional Economic Growth

N. S. Segal*

Introduction

This chapter is concerned with an interrelated set of some of the most important, even if imperfectly understood, issues in regional economics: what are the processes by which a regional economy develops? what role can the region itself play in this process? what are the public policies required to develop this role so that, in the case of an economically backward region, special assistance can in due course be withdrawn? In other words, the chapter is about the concept of regional 'self-reliance' or, put another way, the 'strength' of a regional economy within its national context. Before trying to elaborate what is meant by these terms, it will be helpful to make clear that the chapter is written with respect to the problem of old mining and industrial regions in Great Britain; the issues raised have a wider application, but the conclusions reached are done so within the stated frame of reference. Also, the views put forward happen to have been developed in the course of preparation of a development strategy for a particular Economic Planning Region of Great Britain, the North (Northern Region Strategy Team, 1977), so that there is inevitably a bias in the arguments presented. Certainly, the arguments do not apply equally to each of the main regions of Great Britain, but it would take a far longer chapter than the present one to explore fully the situation in each case.[1]

The Nature of a Strong Regional Economy

In the British context a strong regional economy may be described as one that, over the longer term, is not continually dependent on a special resource transfer from the rest of the country in order: (a) to sustain a level of prosperity no less than the national average; and (b) to generate new job opportunities for its population such that the rate of unemployment

---

* Coopers and Lybrand Associates Limited, London.

(recorded and disguised) and the net balance of migration are acceptable from a national point of view. It does not matter for present purposes whether or not such a 'definition' can be expressed in exact statistical terms, or whether or not central government has an explicitly quantified national framework for the regional distribution of population and employment. It is sufficient to note that interregional disparities in the above indicators have persisted for many decades in Great Britain and that for the past fifty years or so governments have deliberately attempted to redress them.

This concept of a strong regional economy, capable of generating its own growth without permanent special aid from elsewhere, requires a little elaboration. There are three main points to make. First, it is not an economy that is able to produce all that it needs. That is impossible and undesirable for any region in a country such as Great Britain which is so interdependent internally and so dependent on foreign trade externally. Rather, it is an economy that is itself capable of adjusting to internal and external changes (changes in markets, technology, labour and raw material supplies, and the like) without permanent outside assistance; see Parr (chapter 9 of this volume). Second, it is an economy that competes effectively for mobile industry or other resources from outside, by virtue of its own advantages of infrastructure, skills, or other factors, rather than by virtue of special subsidies from central government. Third, a strong regional economy would still receive financial transfers from central government, of two main types. For one thing, resources would be transferred through both the social-security system and the system of central-government support for local authority services. But in general, in the long term, a strong regional economy would not have above-average reliance on such welfare provision and income support, except insofar as there were special demographic features such as an above-average presence of pensioners in the population. A further type of transfer from the central government would involve situations where the scale and pace of adjustment required of a regional economy (e.g., the contraction of coalmining in the North in the 1960s) were too great for the region to be able to cope with unassisted. In such circumstances, an injection of special aid from the rest of the country is both necessary and desirable.

The key feature of a strong regional economy is its ability to adapt—to adapt its attitudes, skills, products, supporting institutions and infrastructure in response to constantly (but unpredictably) changing economic circumstances.[2] Of course, such an ability to adjust in response to change (which may conveniently be labelled an economy's 'supply response' or 'supply capability') is vital to the long-run development of any modern economy, no less for a nation than for a region. Hence, in examining a region's economic strength in its national or interregional context, it is generally the relative (not the absolute) quality of its supply response that is important.

Moreover, in such an assessment one must bear in mind that, unlike the case of a nation, a region's supply response is conditioned by the economic and other functions that it performs within the country as a whole, which are a complex function of locational and historical factors. And in planning for a region's economic development, due account must be taken not just of all these factors but also of the rather limited range of policy instruments available.

Characteristics of Peripheral Regions with a Past Specialisation in Mining and Heavy Industry

It is not a coincidence that the urban and industrial regions of the country that have experienced the most serious economic problems for the past fifty years or so have been those whose economic strength and prosperity in the nineteenth century were based mainly on coalmining, iron and steel production, shipbuilding and heavy engineering. It is conventionally argued that the reasons for these regions' persistent twentieth-century difficulties lie in a decline in demand for their basic products. But this is hardly a convincing long-run explanation, and in any case it is a reasonably valid description of external markets only in the case of coal. The real questions to be answered are: (a) why have the regions' specialist industries failed to benefit from *growing but changing* markets in their own and related industries? and (b) why have the regions failed to generate new and different activities on a sufficient scale to compensate for the decline in the traditional industries?

These questions can be combined and put more generally: why has the supply response of each of the regions concerned been so limited? There are many possible levels at which such a broad question can be answered. At the sector-specific or even company-specific level, for instance, one can identify in each of the industries concerned a number of factors in, say, national policies or in the organisation of the British market that have impeded innovative and dynamic development. The regions concerned, because of their specialisation in these industries, would thus have been especially adversely affected by such unfavourable factors. This is a valid argument, but it is not a sufficient one: 'ideal' policies or 'ideal' market conditions never exist in practice, and the markets in which all the industries operate are international not national, as well as being multi-product. In any event, an enterprising and efficient company will be successful even in a difficult environment. Apparently, therefore, there has not been a sufficient number of such companies in the problem regions.

In the final analysis one must examine the problem at a more aggregate level: are there any characteristics peculiar to these regions that have militated against their having a well-developed supply capability? Looked at in this way, the answers are not hard to find, and for convenience can be dealt with in two parts: the historical influence of the specialist industries, and certain features of the spatial distribution of economic activity within the country as a whole.

Long-Term Consequences of Specialisation in Coalmining and Heavy Industrial Activity[3]
Two crucial features of the economies under review are, first, the minor role played by small manufacturing businesses and, second, the relative lack of development of a professional capability in management, market research, corporate planning, research and development, and other special-ised white-collar skills so necessary to economic development. The principal causes of limited entrepreneurship and professional capability are to be found in the nature of the regions' particular industrial specialisation and their past pattern of development. These causes, not all of which are exactly applicable in every case, are summarised under three headings for the sake of convenience:

(a) The nature of the traditional products: heavy and large products, often of a 'one-off', non-standard design, and hence unsuited to small firms; large, indivisible capital requirements, and hence barriers to entry of small firms; cyclical demand, and hence appreciable sub-contracting limited to peak periods only, and also conservatism induced in the workforce; physical layout of factories and plant not suited to new and fast-growing light consumer goods industries; production technologies demanding strength, endurance and manual skills, rather than independent analysis and judgement and advanced formal education; emphasis on traditional craft skills and little encouragement of occupational mobility; concentration on capital and intermediate goods, and hence a tendency to emphasise production, rather than marketing and the identification of new product and market opportunities.

(b) The nature of the traditional firms in these industries: a high degree of vertical integration, and hence a small demand for external inputs; old-fashioned corporate organisation, and hence a slow adoption of modern management methods and limited demand for specialised man-agement skills, as well as low functional mobility of managers; very large size of establishments and paternal management style, and hence a limited opportunity for individual initiative and advancement, with reliance on collective action instead.

(c) The geographic settlement pattern associated with the industries: dispersed and highly self-contained labour markets, each dependent on a single industry or even a single employer, and hence extremely limited opportunities for occupational mobility or career development; small local markets with limited purchasing power and range of demand, and hence a limited scope for local consumer goods production.

These three factors, so evident in South Wales, West Central Scotland, and North East England (as well as in those areas of Europe and the

United States whose nineteenth-century booms were also based on the same industries), go back many generations. Their influence is still powerful despite radical changes in the industrial and spatial structures of the regions concerned over the past fifteen years.[4]

The Regional Distribution of Different Types of Economic Activity
In addition to the above factors, which derive directly and indirectly from the nature of the industries concerned, further constraints on the regions' supply capability result from the roles that they perform within the national economy. It was long held that these regions, with comparatively small populations and their substantial distance from the main markets of the country (and hence high transport costs), were not especially attractive as locations for consumer goods industries. The rapid development over the past two decades of the regions' communications infrastructure and of sophisticated national distribution systems has now, however, greatly reduced if not eliminated such locational disadvantages. Although the situation varies from one industry to another, the peripheral regions tend to suffer no major penalties with respect to the availability and costs of physical supplies or to the ease and cost of access to markets.[At the same time, however, a far more fundamental constraint on the peripheral regions' supply capability results from the continued dominance of London and the South East as the administrative and business centre of the country. ǀ For the peripheral regions this dominance imposes certain difficulties and high costs in performing those high-level activities (e.g., market research and intelligence, specialised financial and technical services, etc.) that depend on regular formal and informal access to knowledge and ideas. Thus a company based at any appreciable distance from London, and for which such information is important (and most companies engaged in exporting and in high value-added markets fall into this category), must almost certainly devote well above-average resources of staff and time to gaining such information in order to remain competitive (Northern Region Strategy Team (1976a)).

These latter problems have been reinforced by the secular trends nationally towards industrial concentration and towards the location of ownership and of headquarters functions in and around London (Firn, 1975; Northern Region Strategy Team, 1976b). Because of the agglomeration economies that accrue from such corporate and spatial concentration, which have been only partly offset by the advanced telecommunications systems so far available, the pressures on a new or already established company are indeed *not* to carry out these high-level activities in more distant locations. Consequently, although as a result of regional policy since the early 1960s there has been a very high rate of investment in manufacturing industry in the old industrial regions, there has also been a strong tendency for firms to engage exclusively in production operations in these regions. Within the services sector too, other than in some aspects of public administration, new employment has been in lower-level occupations (e.g., clerical and sales), rather than in higher-level decision-making jobs in business services, research and development, etc. The effect of these tendencies for routine or low-level economic activities to be undertaken in the old industrial regions has, of course, been to reinforce their relative weakness, already long present, in precisely those skills, opportunities and attitudes that play the leading role in initiating modern economic growth and change.

The Impact of Regional Policies on the Long-Term Development of the Old Industrial Regions

As elaborated in Part 1 of this volume, government policy for dealing with the problems of the old industrial regions has relied chiefly on encouraging industries undertaking new, footloose investment to establish their operations in these regions. In terms of raising the demand for labour, and particularly of compensating for the massive job losses suffered in the coal industries during the 1960s, these policies have achieved impressive results (Moore and Rhodes, 1973). On a longer-term view, they have been an essential step in diversifying the economic base of the areas out of the excessive concentration on a narrow range of industries, in expanding and modernising the physical infrastructure and in integrating the formerly separate labour markets.

Whether because of convergence in the industrial composition of employment towards the national average, or because of a high rate of investment in manufacturing industry, highways, New Towns, etc., or because of impressive numbers of new manufacturing jobs created compared with what would have happened in the absence of policy, or because of several other favourable indicators, it would be premature to conclude that the basic problems of the old industrial regions have been solved or even are near to being solved. It is evident that by and large policy has not been focused directly on increasing, in the terminology of this chapter, the regions' supply capability. Consequently, it would be wrong to expect that regional policy would necessarily have resulted directly in increases in entrepreneurship, new-company formation, product and market development, and in overcoming the other deep-seated weaknesses in the regional economies. These conclusions are not really a criticism of policy as it has been applied up to now; after all, in the past fifteen years or so the scale of job loss in the traditional industries has been such that the overriding priority has had to be the provision of new jobs by the fastest means available, and to a degree this need still persists. Rather, the conclusions lead on to the further conclusion that now so much has been achieved by way of structural change, infrastructure development and rationalisation of the settlement pattern, it is possible to start framing policies more specifically so as to take the regions through to the next stage of their development.

Before examining the nature and feasibility of the new policy measures needed to this end, it is important to consider whether, even if not its immediate aim, the standard regional-policy measures would over the long term indirectly induce an improvement in the supply capability of problem regions. In the previous section it was argued that the principal constraints on this supply capability derived from the inheritance of a particular pattern of past industrialisation. It could be argued, therefore, that the process of changing the industrial structure, in which regional policy has played a crucial role, will inevitably set in train secondary processes that will strengthen the supply capability. For example, if the regions' dominant products are no longer heavy, large and 'one-off' in nature, but light, standardised and made in long production runs, then perhaps greater opportunities exist for sub-contracting work, this being well suited to small, local firms. Similarly, new industries introduce different skills and attitudes into the labour force; there is a rising number and diversity of contacts with the outside world. These and many other influences at work, resulting from the economic and physical changes brought about by regional policies, constitute powerful forces of modernisation. Obviously there is some truth in these arguments, as is indeed evident to long-time observers of the development of the regions in question. Even so, these secondary processes of change cannot but be slow and uncertain.

Moreover, it must be remembered that it is the regions' relative, not absolute, supply capability that matters; and on this score the outlook is by no means bright. This conclusion stems from the observations in the previous section about the nature of the industrial change that has taken place, in particular, the pronounced tendency to narrow functional specialisation in all sectors of industry. Thus, for instance, the sharp increase in the proportion of manufacturing industry, consisting of subsidiary and branch operations generally carrying out only production activity, means that major purchasing and marketing decisions, as well as all the strategic planning decisions, are likely to be made outside the region and thus do not normally take account of prospective local supplies and markets. Hence only limited backward and forward linkages, both in goods and in business and related services, have tended to develop between new industry and the local economy.[5] The dominance (in these respects) of other parts of the country thus continues. Similarly, arising from the functional distribution of economic activity in the country as a whole, the upgrading of job opportunities (and hence in the long run of skills and capabilities) in the old industrial regions has tended to lag significantly behind that elsewhere.

There is a further aspect to this question of the nature of the industrial changes so far effected in the old industrial areas. This is that despite the substantial changes in industrial structure there have not been comparable changes in what might be termed the associated professional and institutional infrastructure. In their hey-day the traditional industries gave rise to, and were supported by, professional and technical associations as well as research and teaching establishments in the local area. Also, the leaders of these industries, both in the unions and in management, naturally came to play an extremely prominent role in political and civic affairs. Now, while the industries themselves have waned, their influence in the ways described is still strong. This persistence in the influence of the traditional industries is not just because institutions and attitudes tend to be conservative and slow to change. It is also because the new industries have generally not established close links with the universities and polytechnics and other professional bodies, nor have they constituted a significant new source of local leadership. The as yet limited integration of the new industries into the whole fabric of the local economy is, of course, chiefly a consequence of their production-only orientation as satellite units of multi-plant companies based elsewhere, so that their local need for a supporting professional base is limited. Three other contributory factors exist: the plants' management is often fairly junior, which limits the supply of new local talent; where management is more senior, it is likely to be highly mobile with a career path that leads away from the local economy; and because of the wide range of new industries introduced, there is generally an insufficient concentration of any one industry to stimulate the creation of specialised, new institutional structures.

In sum, therefore, the old industrial regions of the country may be said to be going through a crucial but uncertain period of transition. Many structural changes have been effected and many other changes set in motion. But all these changes have yet to be consolidated and, because of secular trends in the spatial organisation of the British economy, have taken place in such a way as not to close the relative gap in the all-important spheres of entrepreneurial opportunities and high-level job opportunities between the regions and the country as a whole.

The Next Phase of Regional Economic Development: A Greater Policy Emphasis on Supply Capability

If the above diagnosis is accepted, and clearly there is considerable room for disagreement with the various lines of argument advanced, then it is not hard to think of policy measures to combat the fundamental weaknesses still remaining in the old industrial regions' supply capabilities. This section indicates broadly the scope of such measures within the framework of national economic policies. (The final section of this chapter goes on to discuss their feasibility and desirability.) It is obviously not possible here to engage in a detailed and comprehensive discussion of policy options or the necessary balance among the different types of policy. All that is attempted is an indication of the broad directions that future regional policy would steadily need to take (over and above the continued application of conventional policies for the attraction of mobile industry) in order to encourage directly the development of an enhanced supply capability. The measures can be classified into four basic kinds.

First, a special effort is needed to encourage a faster rate of small firm formation and to ensure the survival and development of newly formed enterprises. Such an effort should probably focus principally on manufacturing and on certain business services (e.g., commercial and technical design), because of their key role in the regions' long-term development. Moreover, since a lack of entrepreneurship is one of the fundamental reasons for the long-standing economic difficulties of the old industrial regions, public policy towards the promotion of small firms should show deliberate bias in favour of these regions. A contrasting view of the role of small firms is provided by Swales (chapter 11 of this volume).

Of the various policy instruments needed, a critical one is the provision of management and technical advisory assistance to help translate ideas into sound business propositions and to help small firms through the difficult period of start-up and consolidation. There also needs to be an active effort to take advantage of the regions' changing industrial structure and to help develop increased market opportunities for small firms; one possibility would be to establish within each region a formal information system on the products, capabilities and requirements of local producers. Special encouragement for exporting would also be helpful. A further vital policy area concerns the provision of finance. There is no systematic evidence of finance being unavailable in support of sound, and hence fairly risk-free, proposals. Rather, the conventional sources of capital are very reluctant to take risks, so that for lack of funds some projects do not even get through an experimental or pilot stage, while others do go ahead but are unable to develop fully. There are many possible financial devices (on top of the efforts to help prepare better projects) to encourage a greater degree of risk-taking by the lending institutions—one possibility would be for the public sector to provide a special guarantee facility, the powers for which are already available under the 1972 Industry Act.

Second, special efforts are needed to develop the range of functions carried out in the regional economies. The thinking underlying this statement is that it will only be through the availability in the regional economies themselves of a wide range of job opportunities, including those of a high-level and strategic-planning nature as argued earlier, that the local human resources will be developed to the fullest extent possible. Of course, there is something of a chicken-and-egg problem involved in this: will the job opportunities really materialise if the local skills to fill them are not already available? Apart from the fact that interregional migration flows constitute a ready source of specialised skills so that a particular region's skill shortfalls can be (and usually are) met from outside until local capabilities develop, the real answer must be related to the fact that individuals (and hence also whole economies) develop through creating or taking advantage of opportunites that were not open to them before. Economic development experience the world over supports the validity of this contention (though the processes, usually being inter-generational, are inevitably very slow), and it would be a pessimist who felt that the prospects for comparable processes of manpower development in the old industrial regions of Great Britain were anything other than favourable.

There are many possible ways of stimulating a wider range of economic activity in the problem regions, and most of them will fortunately serve more immediate ends in addition to those of long-term human resource development. Thus, for instance, even the 'healthy' parts of the existing shipbuilding and heavy engineering industries would need to be far stronger in their corporate planning, marketing and product development activities if they want to move continuously, and far faster than they have to date, into higher value-added world markets. To achieve this end would inevitably require expansion and strengthening of these strategic activities and this would probably also result in a greater local demand for specialised business services. Together, these two developments would lead to an increase in the variety of white-collar jobs, especially at the high-level end. Similar considerations apply to other sectors of 'indigenous' manufacturing industry, where the principal need is for modernisation and improved long-run competitiveness.

With respect to the increasingly important branch plant sector, the need is to ensure that they expand their operations *in situ*, in particular that they diversify the range of functions carried out, and that they become more fully integrated in every way into the local economies. (One might say that, in a sense, the branches need to grow roots.) It would be hard to disagree with such laudable aims. But do the policy instruments exist? The answer is 'yes', notably under the selective financial assistance provisions of the 1972 Industry Act and in the powers available to the National Enterprise Board and the Scottish and Welsh Development Agencies, though they have as yet been little used at the regional level. It is also possible that regional policy might be tailored to give a strong incentive to companies to undertake activities of the type described in the regions in need of growth and diversification. The future introduction of increasingly sophisticated telecommunications systems will undoubtedly contribute to this end, by helping offset the additional costs of undertaking non-routine activities away from the main markets and decision-making centres of the country. Similarly, there are social and psychological costs, and ultimately economic losses, resulting from excessive spatial concentration of high-level activities in the South East, as well as from an exclusive emphasis on economies of scale in establishing large production-only units outside the South East; it is already possible (even if not statistically evident as it is in the United States) that these two pronounced post-war trends are already moderating, and policies could be deployed to hasten such a counter-trend.

(Third, the old industrial regions will need to pay very careful attention to the provision of what might be loosely termed 'social overhead capital', as well as to the quality of the environment in which people live and work. For good and valid reasons, the emphasis until now on housing provision, town centre redevelopment and various public services has tended to be on quantity–on getting things done without particular regard to aesthetic or other wider, qualitative considerations. Although there is a continuing need for 'more', there is also an important and growing need for 'better'. If the regions are to modernise and grow in the economic sense discussed above, they must be able to attract and retain a wide variety of personnel of different interests and life-styles. The regions must thus deliberately set out to provide an attractive physical environment as well as housing and educational, recreational, social and cultural facilities to suit a wide variety of tastes. A 'roofs over heads' approach to housing or to other public service provision is no longer sufficient (an argument that, fortuitously, is reinforced by the current and prospective constraints on public expenditure).

Fourth, institutional development must proceed in close association with economic change, both as catalyst and as consequence. One does not have to think in terms of grand new institutional edifices or be an advocate of devolution to recognise the need for modernisation and greater relevance of existing institutions and to conclude that improvements could be effected even within the existing institutional framework. The universities, polytechnics, professional societies and public and private representative bodies all have a role to play, individually and jointly, in stimulating economic change and in reflecting in their activities and their personnel the changes that have already taken place. Leadership and enterprise in these matters are no less important than in the direct production activities noted earlier, even if the policy instruments (public appointments, encouragement of collaborative research, other verbal exhortation, etc.) are markedly less tangible.

The Feasibility and Desirability of Regional 'Self-Reliance'

There can be no real doubt about the feasibility of the populous, old mining and industrial regions of the country being capable in the long term of 'self-reliance' in the sense used here. There is no fundamental obstacle of economic structure, geography, or human resources that stands in the way of such a goal. It is essentially a matter for national policy as to whether or not to apply the requisite volume and composition of resources to achieve this end, and at what pace it should be achieved. Thus the crucial issue is one of desirability: what are the net benefits (or costs) to the country as a whole of deliberately promoting regional self-reliance? This represents a classic problem of growth versus equity, as well as of the inter-temporal and spatial distribution of costs and benefits. An exact balance sheet of these costs and benefits would be hard enough to compile qualitatively, let alone to measure quantitatively on a consistent basis. In such circumstances, the policy analyst (especially if he is working at regional rather than national level) tends to eschew a formalised and empirical approach, and rather to argue from the premises of his own value judgements; this is, albeit regretfully, the approach adopted here. The argument is, in essence, very simple and consists of four main strands.

First, there is the question of the need for special remedial policies and subsidies to the old industrial regions, in respect of their persistent shortfall in the demand for labour relative to the available supply, and in respect of the associated social and environmental problems. Since these measures have been used in one form or another for some fifty years, and the problems are by no means solved, it is difficult to avoid the conclusion that some more direct means of tackling the problem, other than redistributing jobs and other resources from the rest of the country, should be used.

Second, in a country as small and densely populated as Britain, with a fairly long-established pattern of settlement, it is hardly realistic in the latter part of the twentieth century to think in terms of radical shifts in the interregional distribution of population. Therefore, while it would be futile to plan in too precise a way, and while it would be necessary to allow the population distribution to vary in accordance with relative economic and demographic circumstances, it must be assumed that the old industrial areas of South Wales, West Central Scotland and the North East will remain indefinitely as major employment and population centres.

Third, the British economy has not performed well by international standards. This extends beyond the current issues of inflation, unemployment and (until recently) the balance of payments. *The* fundamental issue, indeed one that has underlain the country's relative economic decline since before the turn of the century, is the lack of competitiveness in international trade and the sluggish growth in output. The national economy simply cannot afford open-endedly to go on propping up major regions of the country; all regions ought to be brought as rapidly as possible to the point where they do not need to rely permanently on special subsidies but are able to make a positive net contribution to the national economy. Moreover, the weaker the national economy, the weaker is its ability to undertake major redistributive programmes.

Fourth, within the framework of the national industrial strategy, the government is becoming increasingly involved at the micro-level in promoting the efficiency and long-term competitiveness of major sectors of British industry and of encouraging a steady shift into higher value-added activities (Cameron, chapter 14 of this volume). These are strikingly similar to some of the basic needs, identified earlier, of the economies of the old industrial regions. It is hardly surprising that national and regional aims should be converging, now that traditional regional policy has coped so well with large-scale job loss and has brought about such rapid (even if not yet completed) structural change. Hence, execution of the national industrial strategy might conceivably offer an opportunity to tackle the regions' fundamental weaknesses within a coherent national programme, as well as to reconcile effectively the vexing issues of national economic efficiency versus equity in the geographic distribution of economic activity.

For these four main reasons, therefore, the case for a regional policy that is quite specifically directed towards raising the regions' long-run supply capability is a strong one. This is not to say that such a policy is easily implemented or assured of steady success, especially when the continuing poor performance of the national economy so severely constrains the degrees of freedom available to government across the whole range of public policy. But the choice does increasingly become one of continuing indefinitely with a system of remedial subsidies or using specific subsidies in order deliberately to be able to withdraw all such subsidies within a limited period. This is perhaps too stark a way of stating the choice, but it does help make clear my conclusion that the latter is by far the more sensible and equitable course of action.

Notes

1. The broad applicability of the arguments presented here to the old industrial and mining areas of West Central Scotland may be seen from the development strategy prepared in the early 1970s for that area (West Central Scotland Plan, 1974).

2. Thompson (1965) has argued convincingly that the real base of an urban or regional economy lies in its human resources and their skills and attitudes, rather than in its industries and products, which are more conventionally regarded as constituting the base.

3. Readers familiar with the pioneering analytical and planning work done by Hoover, Chinitz and others on the Pittsburgh Region will recognise the general (though not necessarily the particular) line of argument in this sub-section (Pittsburgh Regional Planning Association, 1963).

4. An interesting comparison of the incidence of entrepreneurship and management skills between Pittsburgh on the one hand and New York City on the other, and the reasons for the long-term persistence of such differences, is provided by Chinitz (1961).

5. For empirical evidence on this point, see Lever (1974) for Scotland, and Northern Region Strategy Team (1976c) for the North.

References

Chinitz, B. (1961) 'Contrasts in Agglomeration: New York and Pittsburgh', *American Economic Review*, Vol. 51, pp. 279-89.

Firn, J. R. (1975) 'External Control and Regional Development: the Case of Scotland', *Environment and Planning A*, Vol. 7, pp. 393-414.

Lever, W. F. (1974) 'Regional Multipliers and Demand Leakages at Establishment Level', *Scottish Journal of Political Economy*, Vol. 11, pp. 111-22.

Moore, B. and Rhodes, J. (1973) 'Evaluating the Effects of British Regional Economic Policy', *Economic Journal*, Vol. 83, pp. 87-110.

Northern Region Strategy Team (1976a) 'Office Activity in the Northern Region', Technical Report, No. 8, Newcastle.

Northern Region Strategy Team (1976b) 'Corporate Structure and Functions', Working Paper, No. 5, Newcastle.

Northern Region Strategy Team (1976c) 'Linkages in the Northern Region', Working Paper, No. 6, Newcastle.

Northern Region Strategy Team (1977) *Strategic Plan for the Northern Region* (5 volumes). Newcastle: Northern Region Strategy Team.

Pittsburgh Regional Planning Association (1963) *Region in Transition: Report of the Economic Study of the Pittsburgh Region*. Pittsburgh: University of Pittsburgh Press.

Thompson, W. R. (1965) *A Preface to Urban Economics*. Baltimore: The Johns Hopkins Press.

West Central Scotland Plan (1974) *The Regional Economy*. Supplementary Report, No. 1. Glasgow: West Central Scotland Plan.

CHAPTER 11

Entrepreneurship and Regional Development: Implications for Regional Policy

J. K. Swales*

Introduction

Most micro-economic analysis of the regional problem assumes that regional economies are either in Marshallian long-run equilibrium or are moving towards such an equilibrium. In the first case, the particular configuration of factor prices (here including transport costs) is used to explain the low level of employment in the problem regions. In the second, the existence of 'fixed' factors is emphasised, confining the regional problem to adjustment within the Marshallian short run. Whilst these two approaches are fundamentally different, they do share at least one basic premise. This is that the regional economy responds solely to changes in relative prices, that is, to changes in factor supplies, technology and consumer demand, and that it does so in a deterministic manner, disciplined by competitive market forces.

The notion that within competitive capitalism the 'invisible hand' of market forces directs individual economic agents runs through the history of economic thought. A second idea which, whilst not as influential, has a comparable intellectual pedigree, is that the organisation of production within the framework of a competitive market requires decisions to be made which are not co-ordinated through any market. Those that take, and bear the risk for, these decisions are entrepreneurs. A number of theories state that the 'supply' of entrepreneurship plays a key role in the maintenance and development of a capitalist economy. In this chapter, the role played by entrepreneurship in current British regional development will be examined, and the work of some of the authors who have dealt with this theme will be critically evaluated.

The use of the term 'entrepreneurship' might seem ill advised. First, this term has a variety of meanings, and this has been a cause of confusion in the past. The concept will be used in a very broad sense here, which

* Department of Economics, University of Strathclyde.

225

means that a number of slightly different strands of thought can be usefully dealt with under the same heading. Second, this notion is somewhat old-fashioned and might seem inappropriate in the modern British business context. As Dobb (1931, p. 560) states,

> In earlier types of business, preceding the joint stock company, it was much easier to single out the active partner of a business as an entrepreneur. With the modern prevalence of joint stock enterprise it is difficult to localise actual control over key decisions; it is difficult to identify such control with the bearing of the results of uncertainty; and it is difficult to draw a clear line of demarcation between contractual and non-contractual income.

'Entrepreneurship' will be used in this chapter to mean the exercise of managerial discretion in the running of a firm. Such discretion occurs principally where the relevant factor and product markets function imperfectly due to the complete lack of, or the high cost of, obtaining the relevant information. An investment decision, for example, will be in this sense 'entrepreneurial', as discretion exists, due partly to the lack of adequate future markets that would enforce one particular decision. This means that a number of issues will be dealt with that might normally appear under managerial economics. However, there will be no detailed consideration of the analytical consequences of the acceptance of 'alternative' theories of the firm on traditional location theory.

A number of specific topics will be examined in some detail. In the second section the work of economists who have looked at regional development in terms of the growth of a population of firms is discussed. This work seems implicitly to concern the role of the entrepreneur in bringing together and 'time binding' the other factors of production. The third section deals with the entrepreneur's task of finding and utilising the least-cost combination of factors and looks at the work of those economists who have attempted to explain differential regional economic performance as being the outcome of differences in regional economic efficiency. The fourth section considers the idea that certain types of plant are more dynamic and/or more flexible in the face of changing economic conditions. Here the issues of external ownership and indigenous new-firm formation are scrutinised. In the final section the implications of this work for regional policy are considered.

Entrepreneurship and the Birth, Growth and Death of the Firm

Leibenstein (1968, p. 75) defines one of the characteristics of the entrepreneur to be that '. . . he creates or expands time-binding, input transforming entities (i.e., firms)'. Leibenstein goes on to argue (p. 76):

It is noteworthy that the traditional theory does not explain the existence of firms as time-binding entities. The theory presented here suggests that since the production function is incomplete, firms become valuable store houses of detailed experience and knowledge. In part, this means that successful firms are entities that house successful motivational systems that can be retained only through a scheme of renewable contractual arrangements of different time durations.

The recognition that firms are organisations whose maintenance and very existence depend on entrepreneurship seems to have motivated a number of authors to look at the regional economy from a disaggregated point of view. Their argument is that the net figures for employment change obscure information that is vital for a correct understanding of the functioning of the regional economy. They maintain that it is necessary to look specifically at the various gross employment flows: the employment loss through plant closure, plant outmigration, and *in situ* decline; and the employment gain from expanding plants, new plants, and plant relocation into the region. This approach is adopted most clearly in establishment-based research, where the figures for net employment change in certain sectors of the regional economy are broken down into their constituent gross flows. An account of most of this establishment-based research being undertaken in Great Britain is given in Swales *et al.* (1976).

There are at least two important questions raised here: what is the most appropriate level of aggregation of data for the analysis of the regional economy? and what is the most cost-effective research strategy to adopt? Whilst it is not disputed that breaking down the figures for the net change in employment into their gross components gives a more detailed description of employment change, it is uncertain whether such detail has, as yet, added to our analytical understanding of why regions' growth rates differ. Again, there are practical problems with establishment-based research. In order to disaggregate figures for net employment change, it is necessary to have information on the performance of all the individual establishments within that region. Whilst developments in computer packages have made this a fairly straightforward technical exercise, the collection and processing of the necessary data have proven to be both time consuming and costly. Also, whilst establishment-based data banks generally have a good coverage of the relevant population of plants, the economic information held for each plant is often very limited. In particular, employment is normally the only factor input covered, there being no data on capital stock, investment or land. Again, in no case has information on the level of output been used in establishment-based research in Great Britain.

It is a general tenet of conventional neoclassical economic analysis that changes in demand, factor prices or technology will generate determinate net changes in output and employment. In such a theory gross employment flows are thought to be constrained only insofar as they must sum to a given net flow. To break down the net change into its gross components would be unnecessary, and, if the theory is correct, to concentrate on individual gross flows might be very misleading. Under what circumstances would the detailed specification of gross employment flows provide a clearer understanding of regional development? It might be the case that the gross employment flows within a region are more rigidly interdependent than is suggested by conventional economic theory. There might be patterns of development, with healthy regions exhibiting a different configuration of gross flows from problem regions. Moreover, the economic problems within a region might be attributable to a deficiency in just one of the gross components of change. For instance, it might be that the poor performance of certain regions can be correctly explained as being the result of a lack of new-firm formation, a deficiency that would have an effect on all the other gross flows.

Evidence from the more prosperous regions does not support the hypothesis that there are consistent patterns of gross employment flows. Gudgin (1974) examines the components of manufacturing employment change for the East Midlands in the post-war period. When the regional figures were broken down into smaller geographical areas, Gudgin (1974, p. 493) found that:

> The variations . . . which occurred within the region were not on the whole very dramatic, although it is interesting to see that similar rates of net growth in manufacturing employment could be achieved in rather different ways. The similarity in overall growth was the result of the cancelling out of underlying differences rather than underlying uniformity.

This supports the conventional view that broad market forces generate a given net change that can be made up of various configurations of gross flows.[1]

Perhaps a more telling criticism is that it is difficult to discern the micro-economic foundations of such an approach, that is, the particular theory of the firm it implies. A 'life-cycle' theory seems the most appropriate, though Penrose (1952) has warned against the confusing nature of biological analogies in economics. This lack of a strong analytical base is all the more worrying because of the small amount of previous work in this area. This means that it is difficult to evaluate the performance of a region even against empirical results from other regions. However, even if it were the case that present work throws up a number of distinct 'types' of region, characterised by particular patterns of gross flows of employment, it still might be very difficult to discern the cause of regional decline without further research of a more detailed kind. These points are very important in relationship to the expected cost-effectiveness of establishment-based research.

An alternative reason for studying gross flows might be that, although in the long run net employment change is determined by cost and demand changes, the adaptive mechanism whereby a region adjusts to changes in market forces might crucially depend on the values taken by some or all of the gross employment flows. In particular, if a high rate of unemployment within a region is the manifestation of long-run disequilibrium, it is probable that all the gross employment flows could be increased simultaneously. However, it also seems likely that some flows will be more sensitive to changes in economic forces than others. If this is so, not only can the government affect the speed of regional adjustment to economic change, but also by concentrating on certain gross flows it should be able to increase the cost-effectiveness of its regional policy.

This thinking seems to underlie at least some British regional-policy measures. In particular, a big effort has been made to persuade firms to migrate to, or set up subsidiaries in, assisted areas. Hypotheses regarding such locational decisions have been placed in a coherent analytical structure and have been the subject of empirical testing (Townroe, 1972; Ashcroft and Taylor, chapter 2 of this volume). However, it is clear that the other gross employment flows have not been studied in such depth; the results have been mainly descriptive and non-analytical, testing intuitive hypotheses rather than coherently presented theories. A summary of such work is provided by Gudgin (1974). Establishment-based data banks could help here in generating a sampling frame and giving important employment information. But the limited amount of data that are generally held for each establishment means that more detailed information on a select number of firms is necessary to study successfully the economic and behavioural forces that underlie individual gross flows.

The issues that have been raised in this section are clearly important. Good *prima facie* arguments have been presented for supposing that an understanding of the determinants of gross economic flows is crucial for a correct explanation of net economic change. Moreover, it seems likely that British regional policy in the post-war period has reflected, at least implicitly, an acceptance of some of these arguments. However, there are a number of points relating to economic method that must be noted. First, merely because conventional economic theory has mainly concentrated on net flows, this does not mean that gross flows can be studied without recourse to economic theory at all. Moreover, the finding that gross employment flows are important would not necessarily require anything further than a more sophisticated reformulation of conventional theory. Second, although establishment-based research has a number of strengths, particularly in the detailed employment data that it provides, it has serious weaknesses too. It has been noted that such research is expensive, and that it does not provide information on a number of important economic variables. It might be added that the emphasis on the establishment could well be inappropriate for the study of decisions taken by multi-plant firms.

These observations suggest that the study of the gross components of net economic change at the regional level should be tackled in a hybrid way. Basic quantification of the gross flows and a comprehensive sampling frame could be provided by an establishment-based data bank. More detailed explanation would require more specific study of smaller samples, using some information not included on the data bank. There are clear complementarities between establishment-based and more conventional research into gross employment flows. This is fortuitous because, in order to justify its cost, an establishment-based data bank should be used intensively.

Entrepreneurship and the Efficient Use of Resources

In this section the notion that differential regional economic performance might be explained by regional differences in the efficiency of resource use is examined. Traditionally, economists have separated two aspects of efficiency in production: allocative efficiency and technical efficiency. More recent work has stressed the quantitative significance of technical, as against allocative, inefficiency, and has emphasised the role of management in the attainment of technical efficiency. For instance, Leibenstein (1966, p. 394) argues that 'Managers determine not only their own productivity but the productivity of all co-operating units in the organisation'. He maintains that empirical work suggests '. . . that firms and economies do not operate on an outer-bound production possibility surface consistent with their resources. Rather they actually work on a production surface that is well within that outer bound' (p. 413). A movement towards the outer-bound production possibility surface depends crucially on managerial motivation and the entrepreneurial ability both to complete the inputs for a production process and to determine the exact nature of incomplete labour contracts and loosely defined production functions.

A number of authors (Cameron, 1971; West Central Scotland Plan, 1974) have suggested that the poor employment record of at least one region is partly to be explained by the relative technical inefficiency of manufacturing plants within that region. There are two main problems with this claim. First, it is very difficult to substantiate. Where previous attempts have been made to identify interregional efficiency differences in Great Britain, one-factor efficiency measures have generally been used. For reasons related to data accessibility, such studies have normally been restricted to making interregional comparisons of output per employee, unit labour cost or profitability.[2] The results from these studies are limited insofar as the efficiency measures used do not properly take into account all factor inputs. Moreover, consistent and statistically significant results have not been obtained, and on the basis of these studies, it is not possible to claim with any confidence that there are interregional differences in technical efficiency.

The second major problem is that the qualitative aspects of technical inefficiency have generally been ignored. This difficulty stems from the vague way in which this subject has been treated. If there are regional differences in managerial performance, it is important to know what factors generate this inefficiency, and what specific forms it takes. Is it that the region uses outdated plants, or that it does not choose best-practice techniques, that it uses all factors inefficiently, or that it only uses some factor inputs inefficiently? Is it that managerial inefficiency is related to the culture, to the business environment in general, or to particular market conditions in specific industries? At present we do not have well worked-out analytical structures to suggest which of these we would expect to be the case, nor has enough work been undertaken to specify empirically even the most general hypotheses. If progress is to be made, more analytical rigour must be applied and further detailed empirical studies need to be undertaken.

Entrepreneurship and Dynamic Change

In this section the notion of entrepreneurship in its most conventional form is examined. This is the role played by the entrepreneur in seeking out new markets and innovating in both product design and production technique. Clearly, in a dynamic capitalist economy these functions must be carried out for a firm to survive. It has been argued that certain types of plant might be managed with more entrepreneurship than others. In particular, the management within externally owned branch plants is thought to be constrained in the type of decisions that it can make, long-term strategic policy being decided at head office. Moreover, in these plants the generally low level of local linkages and the concentration of top management outside the region is believed to have a detrimental effect on local entrepreneurship. On the other hand, indigenous new-firm formation is often thought to be synonymous with entrepreneurship.

Before these topics are looked at in more detail, it might be useful to consider a potentially misleading linguistic ambiguity. It is common to call the owner–manager of a firm, an 'entrepreneur'. It is also common for dynamic adaptability, innovation and risk taking to be known as 'entrepreneurship'. However, the fact that it is difficult to identify the classical 'entrepreneur' in many modern economic organisations does not imply that such organisations do not act 'entrepreneurially'. On the other hand, although most small firms are managed by an 'entrepreneur', this does not automatically mean that they are managed with a high degree of 'entrepreneurship'.

In evaluating the role of new firms in regional development, two particular viewpoints will be considered in detail. The first is that regional industrial adaptability depends crucially upon the rate of new-firm formation. The second is that new firms are particularly innovative.

Chinitz (1961), in contrasting New York and Pittsburgh, suggests that one of the causes of Pittsburgh's lack of diversification out of declining industries is a low level of new-firm formation. He argues that Pittsburgh's particular industrial structure generates within the local population neither the incentive nor the skills needed to set up new firms. The local economy is seen as particularly vulnerable to changes in demand and technology because of a lack of entrepreneurial adaptability. Although this might be true in the case of Pittsburgh, does the argument have general validity? Does the rate of new-firm formation play a crucial role in regional industrial adaptability? We might partially answer this question by considering whether the existence of a high level of new-firm formation is either a necessary, or a sufficient, condition for regional adaptability. There seems no good *prima facie* reason why high levels of new-firm formation should be a necessary condition for regional adaptability. Thompson (1965, p. 44) believes that '. . . entrepreneurship—inventiveness, promotional artistry, organisational genius, venturesomeness and so forth—lies at the very heart of industrial development'. However, he does not see such entrepreneurship as being restricted to new firms or even private companies. It can also exist equally well in the operation of local government, public corporations and universities.

Similarly, it seems that a high level of new-firm formation is not a sufficient condition for regional industrial adaptability. This follows from the findings of studies that have looked at inter-industry differences in new-firm formation. New-firm formation is relatively high in those industries with low economies of scale, that is, those industries characterised by small average plant size (Gudgin, 1974). Where small firms are concentrated in specific industries, agglomeration economies might be built up, given the higher level of local linkages in the sales and purchase patterns of small firms (Lever, 1974; Keeble, 1969). Specialisation at the level of the firm here produces both economies of scale and the flexibility associated with small-scale organisation. Such agglomerations are likely to generate a high level of new-firm formation. Moreover, these new firms are necessary to maintain the population of small firms intact, if it is correct that for small firms there is a negative relationship between performance and age (Boswell, 1973). Such an economic structure will give a region short-term advantages both in terms of relatively low-cost production and adaptability to small changes in demand and supply conditions. However, the long-run position is not so clear cut. First, such agglomerations might not be adaptable to fundamental changes in technology or shifts in demand. A historical example here is the demise of the Birmingham Gun Quarter (Allen, 1929; Wise, 1949). Also, if intra-industry external economies of scale have been gained through a heavy concentration of employment within a small number of industries, the regional economy might be relatively specialised and therefore vulnerable to future national shifts in demand. The role of new-firm formation in regional industrial adaptability is clearly complex. The discussion above only casts doubt on two extreme hypotheses. It might in practice be the case that a high level of new-firm formation is crucial for regional industrial adaptability. Unfortunately, at present, we lack the information to make a reasonable judgement.

We now turn to the second question concerning the innovative potential of new firms. Although Beesley (1955) states that new firms tend to develop new products, empirical studies do not support the notion that new firms are prolific innovators. Kamien and Schwartz (1975) in their recent survey of the literature found that per capita research and development activity was highest for large, but not the largest, firms. Moreover '. . . a market structure intermediate between monopoly and perfect competition would promote the highest rate of inventive activity' (Kamien and Schwartz, p. 32). Given the very small average size of new firms (Firn and Swales, 1978) and the negative relationship between the rate of new-firm formation and industrial concentration (Gudgin, 1974), it seems unlikely that new firms are important vehicles for innovation.

It is sometimes asserted that, whilst large companies undertake the bulk of innovation, the really important improvements in technology have been made by the individual inventor, working alone or as the head of the small research team (Jewkes, Sawers and Stillerman, 1969). In this view, the quantitative evidence on the relative research intensity of different types of firm might be misleading. New firms might introduce more basic and far-reaching innovations than established, large corporations. However, many of the inventions made by individuals are licensed to large companies, mainly because many inventors would make bad businessmen (Jewkes, Sawers and Stillerman, 1969, p. 82) and the costs of producing and marketing a new product are very large in comparison to the research and development costs (Maddock, 1973). Although there is no evidence on the qualitative aspects of new-firm innovation, some work has been done on small firms. Freeman (1971) finds that even when adjustments are made for the quality of innovation, small firms innovate less than larger firms.

Having looked at new-firm formation in some detail, we now consider the entrepreneurial implications for the regional economy of having plants owned outside the region. There seem to be two important issues here. The first is that decisions concerning economic activity in one region might be taken outside that region. The second is that the economic behaviour of externally owned plants might have external effects on locally owned plants.

Sant (1974) reports a conference discussion, part of which centred on regional entrepreneurship and the 'branch plant syndrome'. Here it was argued that it is '. . . necessary to guard against sweeping generalisations about branch plants. In particular it [is] not possible, at this stage, to characterise with any real understanding the nature of decision-making inside branch plants' (Sant, 1974, p. 259). The argument is that the location of ownership and of control do not always coincide, and that many branch plants might have a high degree of local autonomy. However, this seems to beg a very important question. Why is local autonomy in economic decision making deemed to be particularly desirable? Let us imagine a branch plant that is purely a production unit. It is located in an assisted area, the headquarters being in a non-assisted area. All research and development, marketing and investment decisions are taken at the headquarters. Within the firm, entrepreneurial decisions are being made, some of which might be implemented at the branch plant. It is difficult to see why such decisions will be any the worse for the region for having been taken outside the region. Indeed, if there are economies of scale or external economies there might be real advantages to having these activities centralised (Crum, 1976).

Parsons (1972, p. 100) argues:

> Business theory indicates that local factory profits are returned to the head office, where decisions are made on a corporate basis, which will not always result in a re-investment at the local level if higher rates of return exist elsewhere.

This argument implies that multi-regional firms aid the mobility of capital between regions in search of the highest rate of return. However, this can have undesirable consequences for a particular assisted area only if that region is a relatively unprofitable location. Conversely, if a region has an overall cost advantage, the existence of externally owned plants might increase the rate of investment and the generation of employment.

Holland (1976, p. 127) states that, in contrast to neoclassical perfect or pure competition, modern competitive conditions are '. . . much more in line with the combination of leap-frogging, throat cutting and devil-take-the-hindmost which characterises Marx's analysis of concentration'. However, he maintains that large ('meso-economic') corporations do not produce in the less developed regions because of '. . . the low priority given to maximisation of profit in the general growth strategy of the firm—of which location is but one factor taken into account among many others' (Holland, 1976, p. 140). Holland is arguing here that large firms do not profit maximise and for a number of reasons prefer to produce in the more developed regions. This theory has a popular appeal and is linked with the accompanying belief that branch plants are hit hardest in times of recession. It is difficult to find empirical justification for these arguments against externally owned plants. Forsyth (1972) found that for his sample of us-owned manufacturing firms in Scotland there was no clear evidence that the degree of local control affected growth or profitability. Atkins (1973, p. 349) compared the performance of a sample of British parent plants with the performance of their branches, and concluded that '. . . between 1966-1971, a period of contraction in manufacturing employment, mature branch plants maintained their employment better than their parents'. Finally, Clark (1976) studied all manufacturing and mining plants in the County of Skaraborg, Sweden, for the years 1968-73. He classified all plants that, directly or indirectly, were more than 50 per cent owned by individuals resident in the county as parent plants. All other plants were classified as branch plants. Clark (1976, p. 297) concluded that: (a) employment in small branch plants is *more* cyclically sensitive than employment in small parent plants; (b) employment in large branch plants is *less* cyclically sensitive than employment in large parent plants; and (c) in the County of Skaraborg, at least, the latter effect dominated the former so that, overall, employment in branch plants is *less* cyclically sensitive than employment in parent plants.

Another important point is that external ownership is often prevalent in growth industries. Firn (1975) studied the extent of external ownership in Scottish manufacturing industry in 1973, and found a significant positive relationship between the UK rate of growth of output in a sector for the period 1964–73 and the proportion of that sector's Scottish employment that was in externally owned plants. In the five fastest-growing SIC Orders, only 13.5 per cent of total employment in Scotland was in locally owned plants. Firn (1975, p. 405) states:

> . . . it cannot be argued that such [externally owned] enterprises that have established themselves in Scotland have had an unwelcome effect, for they have undoubtedly brought with them new products, processes, and technologies that might not have been developed indigenously.

The question of the effects of a high level of external ownership within a region on local entrepreneurship is more complex. First, as stated earlier, externally owned firms generally have a low level of local linkage (Lever, 1974). This implies that, in assessing the relative contributions made by indigenous and externally owned plants to the generation of aggregate demand within the local economy, adjustments must be made to the multiplicand in the Keynesian multiplier equation (Swales, 1975). Clearly, the closure of a plant with high local linkages has, *ceteris paribus*, a more important effect on the regional economy than the closure of a less well integrated plant. The government is aware of these considerations, which have been prominent in the debates over government support for a number of major firms, e.g., Upper Clyde Shipbuilders and British Leyland.

However, this is only part of the story. It has been argued that because multi-regional firms internalise professional services that local firms buy in the market, this reduces the quality of such services available to indigenous firms. Furthermore, the low level of linkages implies less local sub-contracting, which is thought to be an important source of income for indigenous small firms (Parsons, 1972; Jacobs, 1969). The effect is to reduce the local small-firm sector, which the Bolton Report on small firms (Great Britain, 1971) takes to be the seed-bed for potential entrepreneurs.

On a related theme, it has been suggested that the personnel structure of branch plants discourages the formation of locally based new firms. Firn (1975, p. 411) states that because of the large number of branch plants in Scotland, senior management and professional jobs are a relatively small proportion of the total labour force, so that

> ... young Scottish professionals wishing to enter companies at middle manage-
> ment levels are increasingly forced to leave Scotland. This in turn will reduce
> the potential pool of entrepreneurs, for it is from within such management
> levels that the majority of the founders of new enterprises seem to emerge.

Such an assertion must be tentative, for our knowledge of the factors affecting new-firm formation is limited.[3]

On the other hand, there are mechanisms whereby externally owned firms might stimulate indigenous enterprise. We have seen that, in Scotland at least, externally owned firms are predominant in the fast-growing sectors of the economy. There might be a potential here for the diffusion of management and production techniques to local firms. In examining the diffusion of technology by American-owned plants in Scotland, Forsyth (1972, pp. 155–6) found that '... the preconditions for diffusion of technology by US owned firms through the channels of purchasing from, selling to, competing with, and losing staff to the indigenous sector were established but were not very well developed'.

Empirical work suggests that the stereotype view that new locally owned firms are dynamically entrepreneurial, whereas externally owned plants are not, is incorrect. The rate of new-firm formation is related most consistently to economies of scale within an industry. Some studies find a positive relationship between the rate of growth of an industry and the rate of new-firm formation, but others find a negative relationship (Gudgin, 1974). Similarly, there is no reason to believe that new firms are particularly active in the introduction of new products. On the other hand, externally owned plants seem to be concentrated in growth industries, to have relatively stable levels of employment, and to use relatively advanced techniques.

Entrepreneurship and Regional Policy

In the preceding three sections differing approaches have been adopted to evaluate work on various aspects of regional entrepreneurship. Two common themes run through this review. First, entrepreneurship is important for economic development, and regional differences in entrepreneurship might be a correct partial or complete explanation of differences in regional economic performance. For example, it is almost a truism to state that in a dynamic capitalist economy a region's long-run economic viability will depend on its ability to adapt to changing demand, costs and technology. Rigidity, in the face of economic change, might well be the cause of the economic problems of at least some regions. Second, work in this area is generally inconclusive. More analytical rigour and empirical research are needed before economists are able to evaluate accurately the contribution of entrepreneurship to differential regional economic performance.

This having been said, a number of economists have argued quite vigorously that the economic problems of particular regions are based on entrepreneurial factors. The West Central Scotland Plan (1974) and the Scottish Council of the Labour Party (1977) both locate the problems of West Central Scotland in local entrepreneurial failure, resulting in the region's being dependent on external sources for future employment and technological change. They have argued that the aim of regional policy should be to attempt to stimulate growth in locally owned plants, especially through the encouragement of new-firm formation. Whilst the region would have to rely on employment generated through plant movement in the short run, they have argued that over the longer period the region should become more economically self-reliant; see also Segal (chapter 10 of this volume).

Such arguments are heavily dependent on the proposition that there are deficiencies in the management of locally owned firms. As has been shown already, this proposition is very difficult to prove. However, even were it proven beyond doubt, it is not clear that the correct policy recommendation would be to favour locally owned industry unduly, in order to strengthen local management. There seems to be a number of particularly pertinent questions. Given that we know so little about the causes of the alleged management failure, how much confidence can we have that this problem can be adequately dealt with? If emphasis is put on the new-firms sector (because of the poor 'track record' of existing locally owned firms), how cost effective will government aid be, given the very small size of new firms and the high death rate in their formative years?[4] Finally, how far will such a policy be constrained by the existing concentrated industrial structure? It might well be impossible to build up locally owned capacity in an industry with high barriers to entry.

The difficulties encountered in trying to answer these questions weaken the case for a regional policy that concentrates on stimulating indigenous growth in assisted areas. But this is not to suggest that the issues that have been raised in this chapter have no relevance for government regional policy. There are three specific areas where either the goals of regional policy or the means of achieving those goals might be fruitfully reconsidered.

First, British manufacturing is increasingly dominated by large firms. It is estimated that, in 1973, the largest 100 firms in manufacturing produced half of total output. It is predicted that by 1984 this proportion could reach two-thirds (Prais, 1974). The decision-making process in large firms almost certainly differs from that in small firms. Not only are different elements likely to be important, but different criteria might be applied in assessing the relative weights of the various elements in any entrepreneurial decision. In relating these differences to size, a very crude index is being used. Organisational status clearly is another characteristic of a plant that might well affect entrepreneurial decision making (Crum, 1976; Yannopoulos and Dunning, 1976). This has potential implications for the particular form and degree of discrimination embodied in the optimal regional policy.

Second, within manufacturing industry located in the assisted areas, it is likely that there is a high level of external ownership. Firn (1975) reports that, in 1973, only 41.2 per cent of manufacturing employment in Scotland was in Scottish-owned firms. Similarly, Fessey (1976, p. 1) states:

> . . . in recent years large enterprises using computers and integrated accounting systems to control their operations often treat factories and other units at a number of different locations as a single accounting entity . . . . In such cases, for example, purchases may be made and stocks held centrally, and it is impossible to provide statistics for such items related to particular regions. . . . Currently, establishments which make returns to the census of production covering local units in two or more standard regions between them account for getting on for one third of total employment in manufacturing.

These findings raise a number of issues relevant for regional policy. The high levels of external ownership and control that are reported here underline the fact that even the peripheral regions are strongly integrated into the British economy. This suggests that regional policy should be regarded as an integral element of national economic policy, particularly industrial policy. This runs counter to the notion that regional policy should attempt in particular to encourage indigenous development. The spatial separation of decision making from implementation might mean that such decisions are made with relatively low amounts of information (Green, 1977). Regional policy might therefore usefully seek to improve the quality of information held by firms. Alternatively, regional policy could be implemented in such a way as to take account of systematically biased information. The existence of high external ownership in assisted areas has also focused attention on the issue of local autonomy. It has been argued above that there is little evidence to suggest that a high level of external control in the regional economy adversely affects the economic performance of that region. However, local autonomy might still be a politically sensitive issue. In this case, it could be adopted as a political or social goal of regional policy.

Third, increased industrial concentration has been accompanied by a centralisation of decision-making functions (Crum, 1976). This leads to a polarised economy, with a concentration of highly paid decision makers in one location (in Great Britain, the South East). In general, there are good economic reasons why this is the case. However, it clearly raises important problems concerning the goals of regional policy. Should the government, for political and social reasons, redress the inequality that is generated by these economic forces?

Thompson (1965) argues that regional development is the process of adaptation to economic change, a process that is crucially dependent on local entrepreneurship. In contrast, British data suggest that most British regions will rely increasingly on *external* entrepreneurship for future economic development. As the individual regions become more integrated into the British economy, regional policy must be formulated as an integral part of national industrial policy. An understanding of this point should affect both the goals and instruments of British regional policy.

Notes

1. Beesley (1955), in his analysis of inter-war data from metal industries in the West Midlands conurbation, reports a similar kind of finding. There is a significantly higher rate of new-firm formation in the NW 'zone' of the conurbation, than in the SW 'zone'. However, when employment in all new plants (branch plants, subsidiaries, in-migrant plants and new firms) is examined, there is only a small difference between the relative performance in the two 'zones'. Beesley (1955, p. 59) argues that this '. . . tends to show . . . fortunate circumstances for the SW zone, that in a time of boom it happened to have attractions for firms from an exceptionally prosperous neighbour wishing to employ large amounts of unskilled labour . . .'. However, these observations might be correctly explained as being due not to good fortune, but to the working of similar economic forces in the two 'zones' which would generate similar net employment effects.

2. Dixon and Thirlwall (1975, pp. 156–69) and O'Donnell and Swales (1978) are exceptions. Dixon and Thirlwall (1975) measure a region's technical efficiency by comparing that region's actual net output per employee in manufacturing with the output per employee predicted from a national aggregate production function for all manufacturing industry. However, the parameters of the aggregate production function are estimated using a side relation of the CES production function that requires data only on net output, labour inputs and the wage rate (Arrow, *et al.*, 1961; Brown and de Cani, 1963). This procedure has been criticised by McDermott (1977) and O'Donnell and Swales (1977). O'Donnell and Swales (1978) use two-factor efficiency measures in an unsuccessful attempt to measure interregional differences in technical efficiency in the Mechanical Engineering industry.

3. Smith (1967) looked at a sample of 52 American new firms. He classified 65 per cent of the owners as being 'craftsmen', having an essentially technical, non-managerial background. Gudgin (1974) suggests that this proportion might be even higher in British new firms. However, 'opportunist' entrepreneurs, who made up the remaining 35 per cent of Smith's sample, were much more successful, on average.

4. A measure of the small size of new firms in the West Midlands and West Central Scotland conurbations is given in Firn and Swales (1978). The average employment in 1972 of new independent firms set up in the period 1963–72 was 16.9 for the West Midlands and 17.5 for West Central Scotland.

240   *Neglected Aspects in Regional Policy*

References

Allen, G. C. (1929) *The Industrial Development of Birmingham and the Black Country 1860–1927*. London: Frank Cass.

Arrow, K., Chenery, H. B., Minhas, B. and Solow, R. (1961) 'Capital–Labour Substitution and Economic Efficiency', *Review of Economics and Statistics*, Vol. 43, pp. 225–50.

Atkins, D. H. W. (1973) 'Employment Change in Branch and Parent Manufacturing Plants in the UK 1966–71', *Trade and Industry*, Vol. 12, pp. 437–9.

Beesley, M. (1955) 'The Birth and Death of Industrial Establishments, Experience in the West Midlands Conurbation', *Journal of Industrial Economics*, Vol. 4, pp. 45–61.

Boswell, J. (1973) *The Rise and Decline of Small Firms*. London: Allen and Unwin.

Brown, M. and de Cani, J. (1963) 'Technological Change and the Distribution of Income', *International Economic Review*, Vol. 4, pp. 289–309.

Cameron, G. C. (1971) 'Economic Analysis for a Declining Urban Economy', *Scottish Journal of Political Economy*, Vol. 18, pp. 315–45.

Chinitz, B. (1961) 'Contrasts in Agglomeration: New York and Pittsburgh', *American Economic Review*, Vol. 51, pp. 279–89.

Clark, U. E. G. (1976) 'The Cyclical Sensitivity of Employment in Branch and Parent Plants', *Regional Studies*, Vol. 10, pp. 293–8.

Crum, R. (1976) 'Non-Productive Employment and Large Corporations: A Survey', School of Social Science, University of East Anglia, Norwich.

Dixon, R. J. and Thirlwall, A. P. (1975) *Regional Growth and Unemployment in the United Kingdom*. London: Macmillan.

Dobb, M. (1931) 'Entrepreneur', in E. R. A. Seligman (ed.), *Encyclopaedia of the Social Sciences*. London: Macmillan.

Fessey, M. C. (1976) 'Establishment Based Research and the Business Statistics Office', in J. K. Swales et al., 'Establishment-Based Research: Conference Proceedings', University of Glasgow, Urban and Regional Studies Discussion Papers, No. 22.

Firn, J. R. (1975) 'External Control and Regional Development: the Case of Scotland', *Environment and Planning A*, Vol. 7, pp. 393–414.

Firn, J. R. and Swales, J. K. (1978) 'The Formation of New Manufacturing Establishments in the Central Clydeside and West Midlands Conurbations 1963–1972: A Comparative Analysis', *Regional Studies*, Vol. 12, pp. 199–213.

Forsyth, D. J. C. (1972) *U.S. Investment in Scotland*. New York: Praeger.

Freeman, C. (1971 *The Role of Small Firms in Innovation in the U.K. since 1945*. London: HMSO.

Great Britain (1971) Department of Trade and Industry. *Report of the Committee of Inquiry on Small Firms*. Cmnd. 4811. London: HMSO.

Green, D. H. (1977) 'Industrialists' Information Levels of Regional Incentives', *Regional Studies*, Vol. 11, pp. 7–18.

Gudgin, G. H. (1974) 'Industrial Location Process. The East Midlands in the Post War Period', unpublished PhD thesis, University of Leicester.

Holland, S. (1976) *Capital Versus the Regions*. London: Macmillan.

Jacobs, J. (1969) *The Economy of Cities*. Harmondsworth: Penguin Books.

Jewkes, J., Sawers, D. and Stillerman, R. (1969) *The Sources of Invention*. London: Macmillan.

Kamien, M. I. and Schwartz, N. L. (1975) 'Market Structure and Innovation: A Survey', *Journal of Economic Literature*, Vol. 13, pp. 1–37.

Keeble, D. (1969) 'Local Industrial Linkage and Manufacturing Growth in Outer London', *Town Planning Review*, Vol. 15, pp. 163–88.

Leibenstein, H. (1966) 'Allocative Efficiency vs x-Efficiency', *American Economic Review*, Vol. 56, pp. 392–415.

Leibenstein, H. (1968) 'Entrepreneurship and Development', *American Economic Review, Papers and Proceedings*, Vol. 58, pp. 72–83.

Lever, W. F. (1974) 'Regional Multipliers and Demand Leakages at Establishment Level', *Scottish Journal of Political Economy*, Vol. 11, pp. 111–22.

McDermott, P. J. (1977) 'Capital Subsidies and Unemployed Labour: A Comment on the Regional Production Function Approach', *Regional Studies*, Vol. 11, pp. 203–10.

Maddock, I. (1973) 'Can Science-Based Companies Survive?' *New Scientist*, 6 September 1973, pp. 566–70.

O'Donnell, A. T. and Swales, J. K. (1977) 'Production Functions, Factor Substitution and Regional Economics', paper presented to the ssrc Urban and Regional Study Group, Glasgow, May 1977.

O'Donnell, A. T. and Swales, J. K. (1978) 'Regional Efficiency in the u.k. Mechanical Engineering Industry', paper presented to the Annual Conference of the Scottish Economic Society, Edzell, September 1978.

Parsons, G. F. (1972) 'The Great Manufacturing Corporations and Balanced Regional Growth in Britain', *Area*, Vol. 4, pp. 99–103.

Penrose, E. (1952) 'Biological Analogies in the Theory of the Firm', *American Economic Review*, Vol. 42, pp. 804–19.

Prais, S. J. (1974) 'A New Look at the Growth of Industrial Concentration', *Oxford Economic Papers*, New Series, Vol. 26, pp. 273–88.

Sant, M. (ed.) (1974) *Regional Policy and Planning for Europe*. Farnborough: Saxon House.

Scottish Council of the Labour Party (1977). 'An Industrial Strategy for Scotland', Glasgow.

Smith, N. R. (1967) *The Entrepreneur and His Firm*. East Lansing: Graduate School of Business Administration, Michigan State University.

Swales, J. K. (1975) 'Regional Multipliers and Demand Leakages at Establishment Level: A Comment', *Scottish Journal of Political Economy*, Vol. 12, pp. 101–3.

Swales, J. K. et al. (1976) 'Establishment-Based Research: Conference Proceedings', University of Glasgow, Urban and Regional Studies Discussion Papers, No. 22.

Thompson, W. R. (1965) *A Preface to Urban Economics*. Baltimore: The Johns Hopkins Press.

Townroe, P. M. (1972) 'Some Behavioural Considerations in the Industrial Location Decision', *Regional Studies*, Vol. 6, pp. 261–72.

West Central Scotland Plan (1974) *The Regional Economy*. Supplementary Report, No. 1. Glasgow: West Central Scotland Plan.

Wise, M. J. (1949) 'On the Evolution of the Jewellery and Gun Quarters in Birmingham', *Institute of British Geographers. Transactions and Papers*, Vol. 15, pp. 59–72.

Yannopoulos, G. N. and Dunning, J. H. (1976) 'Multinational Enterprise and Regional Development: An Exploratory Paper', *Regional Studies*, Vol. 10, pp. 389–99.

PART IV

Regional Policy
in an Emerging
Political Framework

Within a mixed economy the nature of policies pursued is conditioned to some extent by the objectives and structures of government. The instruments of policy and expenditure commitments to particular programmes are generally influenced by political as well as economic circumstances. The political framework for regional policy in Great Britain has undergone marked changes since regional policies were first instituted. Some of these changes have been secular in nature, whilst others have appeared more dramatically in a relatively short span of time. For example, the role of the state in the British economy has evolved gradually since the 1920s, but changes in the level of government from which regional policy is implemented have largely been confined to the period since 1970. This final part of the volume seeks to examine some of the consequences for regional policy of both types of change.

In Great Britain, the central government has traditionally been the level of decision making for regional development and regional policies. However, since 1972 marked changes have occurred (and are being proposed) regarding the levels at which control over regional-development policies is exercised, although central-government control over regional policy still predominates. With entry into the European Community in 1972 certain national-level powers have been transferred 'upwards'. Even though most of the policies are still operated by the central government, these policies are now subject to general rules for assistance which are laid down by the Community. Also, with entry into the Community, problem regions are now eligible for a range of Community development incentives, which, though presently small in scale and effect, could become important in the 1980s.

By contrast, at a sub-national scale, the central government has recently responded to a complex set of regional political pressures by proposing to transfer, or devolve, certain executive powers to assemblies in Scotland and Wales. As far as regional-development policies are concerned this would represent a 'downward' transfer of power. Although the possibilities for a radical departure from former policies are not very great in the immediate future, there could ultimately be scope for carefully articulated regional-level policies that cater more efficiently to the requirements of the region. However, this would result in regional-level policies for some regions but national-level

243

policies for regions with no devolved power. This situation would be complicated by the unequal political–economic power exerted by the different levels of government, and it remains to be seen whether such a structure could emerge as stable and workable. The role of regional-level policies in the regions to which power had been devolved would be further complicated, particularly in Scotland, by the pressures for political independence. Whatever the outcome, it is clear that regional policy, as traditionally implemented, cannot remain unaffected with the move toward devolution.

The growth of regional policies in Great Britain after the depressed period of the 1930s and again since the 1960s was accompanied by the expansion of policies and expenditures in other areas of social and economic concern. During the last fifty years there has, with minor interruptions, been a sustained shift in the 'mix' of the British economy away from the private and towards the public sector. Policies to transfer resources among groups of individuals or regions have grown in importance, as have policies of subsidy and taxation to influence the choice patterns of households and firms. At the same time, state production of marketable and non-marketable goods and services has also expanded. There is now a widely held view that the mix of the British economy has shifted too far towards the provision of non-marketable public services and that the export base of the nation requires expansion and restructuring to attain growth and income objectives. A national Industrial Strategy has been proposed that intends to develop and encourage the growth of particular industrial sectors. This national Industrial Strategy, one element of which involves the National Enterprise Board, is expressed largely in sectoral rather than regional terms. In common with the majority of sector-based policies, the strategy is likely to have substantially differing regional impacts. Existing regional policy must therefore be examined, not only in relation to its ability to coordinate investment with the Industrial Strategy but also in terms of the possibilities for compensating for the differential impacts of sector policy. The extension of the role of the state into the field of industrial development and the associated change in government objectives has far-reaching implications for the future of regional policy. Indeed, with these changes, it is likely that the very definition of the term 'regional policy' will need to be reconsidered.

CHAPTER 12

Regional Policy in a European Framework

M. C. MacLennan*

Introduction

The aim of this chapter is to provide an assessment of the effect of membership of the European Communities (the Community) on British regional
policy. The chapter will be divided into three sections. The second section
will examine the provisions in the Treaty of Rome that grant the Commission
of the European Communities powers over the extent and type of financial
assistance given by member countries to promote regional development.
The third section will examine the financial assistance made available
by the Community through various agencies to supplement the national
British effort. The final section will examine the efforts of the Community
to influence the manner in which British regional policies are carried
out so that they may be compatible with the Community objective of
narrowing the divergence between the richer and poorer regions of the
Community, which is seen as a serious stumbling block to the economic
and monetary and ultimately political union of member countries—the
fundamental objective of all Community policies.

The Community and British Regional Incentives

Member countries are not free to grant whatever financial assistance they wish
in order to promote regional development. Articles 92 to 94 of the Treaty
of Rome confer upon the Commission the power to review and if necessary
to call for the modification or withdrawal of any aids granted to particular
firms. Exception is specifically made in Article 92.3(a) for 'aid to promote
the economic development of areas where the standard of living is abnor-
mally low or where there is serious under-employment' and in Article
92.3(c) for 'aid to facilitate the development of certain economic activities
or of certain economic areas where such aid does not adversely affect
the common interest' (Great Britain, 1972). This restriction and the powers

* Department of Political Economy and Centre for Urban and Regional Research, University of Glasgow.

conferred quite deliberately on the Commission, as opposed to the Council of Ministers, are intended to prevent distortions of trade and competition incompatible with the Treaty. The qualifying clauses reflect the concern stated in the Preamble to the Treaty and in Article 2 to reduce differences in living standards in the different regions of the Community.

The Regional Aid Rules

In 1971 and 1975 the Commission published two sets of rules establishing certain criteria that all regional aids must respect (European Communities, 1971; 1975a). These rules were designed to encourage member countries to agree on a number of economic principles that should govern regional aids and that would allow them to be measured, compared and assessed on a uniform basis. The results represent a considerable intellectual and political achievement on the part of the Directorate-General for Competition in the Commission, and mark a considerable advance on the juridical, case-by-case procedure of earlier years. Examination of cases does, of course, form a part of the rules but it is set in the framework of agreed criteria and can be limited to a relatively small number of significant cases.

The essential feature of the aid rules is that regional aids are subject to control in all regions of the Community. Initially, in the 1971 rules, only aids in the 'Central Areas' of the Community were subject to control. It was felt that it was in these regions, defined as those areas with the highest degree of industrialisation and the highest levels of income per head in the Community, that the risk of aids distorting competition and trade was greatest. There was concern, too, that countries would indulge in a costly, wasteful and futile overbidding for mobile investment and jobs, which would serve only to neutralise the efforts of poorer countries to develop their less developed regions. Accordingly, a maximum limit of 20 per cent net grant-equivalent was set on the aid that could be granted, leaving the other less developed regions of the Community, the 'Peripheral Regions', to be dealt with at a later date. Member countries were expected to vary the actual aid given within the limit of 20 per cent according to the needs of sub-regions within the Central Areas receiving assistance.

In the 1975 rules this binary classification was refined into four different classes of regions in which different limits and conditions were attached to aids granted by member countries. These were as follows:

(a) In Greenland, Ireland, the 'Mezzogiorno' and Northern Ireland the aid ceilings are fixed at the maximum levels attainable by measurable aids on 1 January 1975. The Commission may, however, ask for the examination *in advance* of individual cases where the investment projects have a cost greater than £10m and where aids envisaged exceed 35 per cent net grant-equivalent, in all the above regions except Greenland.

(b) In the French regions eligible for industrial development grants, in certain assisted areas in Italy other than the Mezzogiorno and in the assisted areas of Great Britain on 1 January 1975 with the exception of the Intermediate Areas, an aid ceiling of 30 per cent will be observed at the latest within a three-year period.

(c) In West Berlin and the areas bordering East Germany and in certain assisted areas in Denmark an aid ceiling of 25 per cent is fixed.

(d) In all 'Other Regions' of the Community the aid ceiling remains at 20 per cent, but this should be reduced as quickly as possible.

These rules will be re-examined at the beginning of 1978 when particular attention will be paid to the relationship between the level of aid and the number of jobs created. The extension of coverage to all regions of the Community reflected the view of the Commission that control of regional aids was not to be seen in terms of a conflict between measures aimed at the removal of barriers to free trade and competition and concern for the regional imbalances that this provoked, but as a means of combining the two principles, to form a policy promoting expansion through free trade but permitting regional subsidies to the extent that they were necessary to allow all regions of the Community to benefit equally from this model of development.

The ceilings on aid given were defined in terms of the maximum aid that could be accorded to a given investment project expressed in terms of a percentage grant-equivalent, net of tax. Agreement was reached among member countries on a key (variable from one country to another) indicating the 'typical' breakdown of investment costs between land, buildings and plant and machinery, a uniform rate of discount (8 per cent) to be employed in all calculations, and a reference interest rate that would allow 'soft' loans to be converted into grant-equivalent. It was essential that all aids be measurable in advance in terms of this given investment merely by reference to the legislative or administrative documents in which the aid details were published. This property was baptised 'transparency'; aids that could not be so measured were termed 'opaque'. The Commission attaches the utmost importance to this notion of transparency. If aids are opaque, it is unable to carry out its mandatory task of assessing whether or not the aids are compatible with the Treaty. The doctrine was, therefore, evolved that all aids that remain opaque are incompatible with the Treaty and should be rendered transparent or withdrawn. Aids given to labour costs, fuel costs, transport costs or accorded selectively project by project must be capable of quantitative translation into the form: x per cent net grant-equivalent of a given investment project measurable in advance.

On this important point the preparatory work on the 1975 rules encountered a major difficulty. In certain peripheral regions in different member countries, aids had been introduced, in some cases accounting for a large proportion of total expenditure on regional aids, that could not be measured. After much technical and political discussion involving the full cooperation of member countries, a compromise formula was reached. It was agreed that regional development was a complex problem, the resolution of which member countries understood in a fullness and depth denied Commission officials. No longer would opacity *per se* render aids incompatible with the Treaty. Measurement, however, was still crucial, and new methods of calculation would be sought to render all aids transparent. This admission represented a considerable concession by the Commission. It is, however, important not to read too much into it, for the Commission has consistently argued that the Treaty of Rome does not permit aids that serve only to shore up declining industries, subsidise operating costs or meet costs that are properly the responsibility of any competitive firm, notably commercial risks and the establishment of reserves to replace capital equipment (European Communities, 1972; Great Britain, 1973a; 1973b. Aids that are compatible with the Treaty are those that subsidise to the appropriate extent the initial costs of new operations, after which the firm must rely on its competitiveness to survive. It is, therefore, reasonable to infer that even if certain types of aid can be measured either in terms of a notional investment project or on some other basis, they are unlikely to meet the compatibility condition, other than by securing exceptional treatment.

As well as fixing aid ceilings, both the 1971 and 1975 rules contain the additional requirements that the industrial and geographical incidence of aid should be clearly established, and that in cases where the project aided is large it should be examined individually, *a posteriori*, in terms of the rules. These provisions are designed to ensure that regional aids do not go to industries where chronic excess capacity exists and that they are not scattered too widely in small localities or available over too wide an area. It is also forbidden to grant regional aid to a firm or industry and at the same time to award it regionally differentiated sectoral aid.

The Effect of the Aid Rules on British Regional Incentives

The Treaty of Accession laying down the terms of British entry to the Community requires the United Kingdom to accept the 1971 rules in their entirety. The impact of the rules on British regional policy is thus inescapable and has, in fact, been significant. In several important respects the British system of regional aids appeared to infringe the Community rules and this has given rise to lengthy discussions between the Commission, the United Kingdom and other member countries. One brief but rather acrimonious incident, which required the intervention of the Prime Minister, Mr Heath, occurred in June 1973, when the Commission wished to classify substantial areas of the United Kingdom, including some Development Areas and Special Development Areas, as 'Central'. This proposal, which would have required a reduction in the aid granted in those areas, and which constituted an interference by the Commission in the classification of areas for regional-policy purposes by the British government, was strongly resisted, and both the Development Areas and Special Development Areas were left temporarily unclassified (European Communities, 1974, p. 77). The 1975 rules quietly included both types of area under the same category of region. The Commission's willingness to adopt a flexible and 'political' approach was further demonstrated when it agreed to treat as 'exceptional' the upgrading of Edinburgh and the industrial areas on the South Wales coast (which had been classified as 'Central') from Intermediate Area to Development Area status (McCallum, chapter 1 of this volume).

Another problem that arose immediately was the existence of the Regional Employment Premium (REP). Although the REP has now been abandoned in Great Britain (though not in Northern Ireland), the problems raised by this aid are of wide general interest, and touch on essential differences of view between the Commission and the United Kingdom on the role of regional aids in regional development and regional policy. The REP was unacceptable to the Commission because it could not be measured in terms of the Community formula; it appeared to be a classic example of an opaque aid. Furthermore, it seemed to infringe almost every canon of compatibility in that it constituted a continuing subsidy to operating costs available to all firms in the assisted areas and was unconditional on any investment activity, whether new investment or replacement investment. The British approach in the discussion was to insist that the issues of measurability and compatibility be clearly distinguished. It was argued that the term 'aid' is defined in the Treaty of Rome solely in terms of its purpose and anticipated effect on regional development and on the 'common interest' of the Community. This is clearly a matter to be resolved by economic and political argument, and is in no sense merely a question of whether or not aids can be measured.

The British defence of REP rested on the argument that in order to reduce the differences in employment levels in regions of the Community, it was logical to subsidise labour costs. Such aid would directly encourage fuller employment while the effect of aid to capital costs in this respect was indeterminate. The resultant increased employment would lead to increased output by bringing unused resources into active use; the more even utilisation of capacity throughout the economy thus made possible would, in addition, permit a higher overall level of demand in the economy, bringing benefit to the more prosperous and congested regions as well as to the less developed regions. The common interest of the Community would therefore be served. There would obviously be an effect on trade, but this would also arise in the case of aid to capital costs. The weakness of this argument from the Commission's standpoint was that the REP, by reducing operating costs, might simply keep afloat firms whose resources might have been used more productively elsewhere, or, if the REP was used to finance investment, to help with the replacement of plant rather than the creation of new investment and new jobs. Trade would have been adversely affected, and the common interest damaged, with no certainty that the increased output from the REP could be sustained without indefinite continuation of the subsidy. If this was the case, then regional development was not assured, and the common interest adversely affected; consequently, the aid was incompatible. The Commission also pointed out that the REP could not be defended as the regional equivalent of a necessary currency devaluation. Devaluation is the alteration of a currency's parity by an amount that is within reasonable limits, measurable by the extent to which its unit costs exceed those of its competitors. This disparity is more easily calculable than are regional differences in competitiveness. Moreover, the devaluation imposes a penalty on the devaluing country in the form of higher import prices. Directly and through its repercussions on wage costs, this generates forces that compel firms to increase their competitiveness if the advantage of devaluation is to be maintained. No corresponding incentive to increase efficiency existed in the case of the REP.

It is clear that, despite periods of pragmatic silence and flexibility, the Commission will continue to maintain pressure against any regional aids that do not encourage long-term improvements in industrial competitiveness. The REP was not immediately attacked because the British government made it a minor but potentially troublesome element in its renegotiation discussions, and because the Commission was not uninfluenced by the fact that the time-limit of seven years set for the subsidy rendered it degressive in its effect. The basic philosophical opposition, however, remained. One important reason for the Commission's standpoint is not simply a belief (though this is genuinely felt) that regional development can be achieved only by enabling all regions in the Community to participate in a process of economic development based on free trade and competition. It has its origins also in the fact that the Community is not a unitary state. While it may be possible for the British government to accept the need to press ahead pragmatically with measures to reduce unemployment in its own less developed regions without examining too closely the long-term effectiveness and costs of any measure adopted, the Community cannot. In the Community the costs will be borne by other countries, in both their less developed and their prosperous regions, as trade is affected and capacity in certain industries maintained at an artificially high level by the British regional assistance. This point is well taken by other member countries. They note the foreign investment effort of British companies in such fields as property development, and are well aware that the British assisted areas are not the south of Italy or the west of France but regions where the conditions for an industrial regeneration are, despite all difficulties, more propitious.

The Commission's approach pays more attention to the micro-economic and long-term effects of regional policy than does the British. It is not sympathetic to arguments, such as those developed by Moore and Rhodes

(1973), that so many jobs can on certain assumptions be attributed to periods of strong regional policy of which the REP was an important element. The real question is whether these jobs might have been created more cheaply and on a more secure basis by other types of incentive. The Commission is here adopting an export-led growth model at the regional level. Regional aids must be directed towards new projects in industries and locations where there is a reasonable assurance that the firms concerned will be able to survive the forces of interregional and international competition. A further consequence of the discussions about the REP was a systematic challenge by the British to the method of aid measurement established in the 1971 rules. The British argued that, instead, all aids could be rendered measurable in terms of internal factor costs in manufacturing industry. This denominator would comprise capital costs including gross profits, as a measure of 'normal' profits, and labour costs. Since the ratio of labour costs to capital costs could be shown to be relatively stable over a number of years (at a value of 70 : 30), it would be possible to use this ratio as a key to express aids to capital and labour in terms of a total cost base. The use of such a base would give a measure of incidence that was both less partial and more relevant to a concern for free competition than the existing Community method, which related aid to only one part of total costs.

The Commission, together with other member countries, examined the British proposal in some depth, but the obligation to publish new aid rules by 1975 to incorporate the new member countries' aids interrupted this work before a solution had been found. The British proposal, however, was directly responsible for the statement in the 1975 aid rules that established the questions of measurability and compatibility as separate issues. The Commission staff was not, however, readily going to be persuaded to relinquish a notional investment project as the basis of measurement. It pointed with reason to a number of technical difficulties. The capital–labour key was not as stable in other countries as the British figures suggested; nor was the 70 : 30 value appropriate to all other countries. Furthermore, the values of the key varied widely among individual industries, thereby making it inappropriate as an element in a calculation that was to serve as a means of measuring the theoretical *maximum* aid to be given in regions. It was necessary, too, to know the total *amount* of REP payments, so that they could be expressed as a percentage of labour costs. This infringed the conditions of transparency, which required that the aid be measurable in *advance* of any payments and by reference only to the legislation governing the aid. To await an accounting statement of actual payments made would not do. The application of such an average key to individual cases would also clearly be meaningless.

Such objections have led the Commission back to the investment project as the basis for measurement. But in response to British and Italian complaints they have now admitted that measurement and control of all aids in terms of investment only may well introduce a bias in favour of capital-intensive projects. The present Commission rules, where aid is related only to capital costs, mean that a capital-intensive industry offering very few additional jobs may receive a very much larger subsidy in relation to its total costs than one that is labour-intensive, even if they are both in the same region and governed by the same limits. Transparency is being achieved here at the expense of logic and effectiveness. The Commission's response has been to agree to introduce alternative forms of aid ceiling: either *x* per cent of investment (the existing system) or *x* units of account per job created per new investment project. This meets the British criticism and permits the measurement of aids not easily or logically expressed in terms of investment only, e.g., aids to service industries or premiums per new job created (European Communities, 1977a, p. 101). The trouble is, however, that the Commission still insists that the concept of new investment be incorporated in the measurement formula. This means that aids like REP would not be measurable. More important, however, is the fact that it condemns as immeasurable the main British regional incentive, the Regional Development Grant (RDG).

The problem is that the RDG is available automatically in respect of all investment undertaken in the assisted areas and not simply new investment, which is the case in most other member countries. The Commission staff is not happy about such an arrangement. In the first place, it is argued that since the RDG is granted for simple replacement of plant and equipment it is in a sense a continuing aid. Its nominal value after tax will, therefore, understate its real value to businessmen, since they will be able to count on its renewal. Allowance must be made for this in setting aid ceilings, lest they mask the real value of British aid and consequently fail in their function of controlling overbidding. A further and perhaps even more fundamental objection is that, in any event, it is unacceptable to aid mere replacement of investment. This does not ensure the creation of new jobs and is a normal commercial obligation incumbent on firms. A possible way round the problem would be to define a typical new project in terms of the establishment of a new enterprise by creation or transfer, the extension of an enterprise or the fundamental reorganisation of rationalisation of an enterprise. By making assumptions about 'typical' or 'average' asset lives, the value of an RDG to the new project could be calculated. It would then be possible to calculate the value of any renewal element, over and above the typical project.

Whether or not any of these methods come into operation, they emphasise another continuing strand of thought in the Community on the process of regional development, namely, that new investment only should be eligible for subsidy. To subsidise mere replacement is tantamount to admitting that, even with aid to fixed costs, normal profits are not being earned in the long run by the firm concerned and resources should consequently be transferred to other industries. This is a slight modification of the standard textbook doctrine: after enjoying aid to fixed costs, earn normal profits in the long run or shut down. It could, however, be argued that this approach is a shade too austere. The refusal to subsidise mere maintenance of employment neglects the fact that any fresh equipping of a firm will permit it through embodied technical progress to operate better-practice techniques, which may in turn enable it to respond for the first time, or more effectively, to competition and, in particular, to the market opportunities offered by firms installing new investment in the region concerned. It is, after all, indigenous firms in a declining industrial area that are most likely to be mere 'replacers', while at the same time being capable of doing different things with their new equipment. Given the importance of indigenous firms in any British regional-development exercise, it may be important not to dismiss this possibility too readily (Segal, chapter 10 of this volume). If firms do shut down, resources employed in them may be transferred out of the region permanently. It should also be borne in mind that the encouragement of a shift in activities as well as of expansion by indigenous firms is an essential precondition for the successful creation of industrial complexes, which it is the aim of aid to new investment to create. What may therefore seem wasteful aid may, if considered in a slightly wider view, be an essential complement to the cumulative process of regional development. It should be noted, finally, that in the United Kingdom selective assistance under the Section 7 of the 1972 Industry Act is available for the most part only to new projects in the Commission's sense of the term, and it is only such projects that are taken into account in the granting of Community aid. There is, therefore, a fairly clear preference for 'acceptable' projects.

It is worth dwelling a moment longer on the Commission's views on selective aid. In many respects the Commission's concern that aid be given only as an initial and once-and-for-all stimulus to new investment by firms who will then operate competitively can best be met by some form of selective assistance, as long, of course, as the criteria employed are consistent with such an aim, and as long as the bureaucratic procedures are efficiently and quickly carried through. If, however, the aid is to be measurable in advance, the criteria employed must be so standardised as to reduce to some extent the possibilities of selectivity. For example, to make the assistance provided under the 1972 Industry Act compatible with the Commission's rules, it would be necessary to know in advance the percentage of investment eligible for aid, the duration of the loan, the periods of grace (if any) granted in respect of repayment and the amount of interest subsidy available in relation to an agreed 'reference' rate of interest representing the cost of borrowing on the open market. It should not be impossible to meet these conditions, but they do set limits on the selectivity exercised. The Commission has agreed on a temporary basis to permit the establishment of a special aid scheme to encourage the transfer of service industries under Section 7 of the 1972 Industry Act (European Communities, 1974, p. 78), but the general examination of the British regional aid system is still in preparation, so the matter is not yet settled.

Rather less clear is the status in the Commission's eyes of any regional aid that may be present in the financial operations of the National Enterprise Board, the Planning Agreements, the Scottish and Welsh Development Agencies, the provision of advance factories, reductions in rent on factories, and the regional-aid element that may be deemed to exist as a consequence of cross-subsidisation by the nationalised industries and of some of the social obligations that these industries are compelled to accept. In an even more doubtful category is aid conferred as a result of the preferential treatment accorded to tenders submitted for public contracts by firms in the assisted areas. The Commission's views on these various types of aid have not been definitively expressed, but a number of points may be made. As far as preferential contracts and the practice of permitting or requiring public undertakings to incur commercially unjustified costs are concerned, the Commission is feeling its way towards the establishment of procedures that will allow it to distinguish between the legitimate offsetting of such costs and the granting of advantages that are incompatible with the common market. Article 90 of the Treaty of Rome specifically requires public undertakings to respect the competition rules. It does, however, contain an escape clause, which allows that undertakings that operate 'services of general economic interest' shall obey the rules insofar as they do not obstruct the performance of the particular tasks assigned to them. A rider is then added that trade must not be affected to an extent contrary to the interests of the Community.

The Commission has been slow and cautious in its approach to the powers conferred on it by Article 90, but the growth of state interference in private industry in recent years, much of it containing a regional inflection, must compel it to clarify its position; otherwise it will be open to the understandable criticism that it is continuing to act as if the Community were a universe of competition on the classical model and not, as is the case, an increasingly corporatist economic confederation (Holland, 1976, pp. 76–95). The most probable immediate outcome is that member countries will be asked to indicate why Article 90 should not be applied in particular cases and actions, rather than pursued in respect of specific departures from it (European Communities, 1977a, pp. 143–6). The promotion of regional development may well be one such defence. It should be kept in mind here that the control over regional aids is much more strictly applied than controls over other subsidies available on a national level and other policies that affect trade, and that there have until now been no Community regional-policy guidelines in the light of which the regional aids may be systematically examined. This is not to argue for the granting of *carte blanche* to a whole range of occult regional aids. There is much merit in the control system ingeniously hammered out for regional aids when other policies were enjoying much less success. What is needed is their analysis in terms of their effectiveness as regional-policy measures and not simply their effects on trade.

The issue of opaque aids to the private sector, many of them granted through the medium of state agencies, is currently receiving much attention in the Commission. It is highly improbable that a system of control based on measurement in advance will be possible. Indeed, the Commission has already suggested that in some cases the best that can be done is to request member countries to measure the aid granted themselves and set limits to the amount available. This would have the additional merit of forcing governments, as well as the Commission, to look more closely at the costs and effectiveness of their aid systems.

The preparation by the Commission of a new set of rules to enter into force in 1978 will come at the same time as the examination by the Commission of the whole British system of regional aids. This examination is likely to highlight many of the problems and differences in approach discussed above. The problems of unemployment throughout the Community will make it difficult for the Commission to press too hard for a change in the British pattern of aids, and the British assisted areas are likely to remain broadly classified as they are in the 1975 rules. At the same time the analysis by the Commission of the economies of the assisted areas, in order to establish whether the aids for which they qualify are appropriate, is likely to be a detailed one and a reclassification or even descheduling of some assisted areas may be requested. The Commission has shown a readiness to hold its hand regarding the British aid system (*Economist*, 1974), but there may well be pressure from other member countries to reduce the extent of the assisted areas and to ensure that regional aids in a highly industrialised country with an extensive structural problem do not degenerate into a widespread social-welfare policy for a large range of ailing industries. It will be a matter of much interest to see how the Community reacts to its most extensive problem of industrial decline, as opposed to regional underdevelopment. The British government may have to argue strenuously to persuade the Commission and its partners that its regional aids are the appropriate measures to deal with this problem.

As to the form of British aids, the selective assistance available under the 1972 Industry Act will certainly raise problems, but the movement to more flexible measurement rules discussed above is likely to allow agreement to be reached, though probably with some reduction in the British government's freedom to determine *ad hoc* its selective assistance. The removal of the REP should help to take the sting out of this part of the examination.

It should, however, be noted that in June 1977 the Commission requested the Dutch government to discontinue its practice of awarding investment grants for replacement investment and to deschedule some areas added to the list of assisted areas. This suggests that the RDG will come in for similar criticism, which may or may not be forestalled by the technical device referred to above. The multi-sectoral, industrial nature of the British regional problem is also likely to force the Commission to bring forward proposals for examining the sectoral incidence of regional aids. The discussion of regional aids in general and the examination of the British system of aids will take place in the context of the renewal of the Community's own Regional Development Fund and the publication of the guidelines for a Community regional policy, to which topics it is now necessary to turn.

The Emergence of a Community Regional Policy and its Effect on British Regional Policy

The Community's role in undertaking positive measures to promote regional development has been much more limited than its purposeful and sophisticated efforts to coordinate regional aids. Indeed, it may be said that the existence of a regional policy at the level of the Community dates only from March 1975, when, fifteen months after the date set, the European Regional Development Fund and the Committee on Regional Policy were established (European Communities, 1973b; 1975b). This decision equipped the Community for the first time with a means of financing regional development and an institutional framework within which the regional policies of member countries and the Community's own policies and expenditures could be progressively coordinated and developed to reduce the regional disparities within the Community.

In order to assess correctly the impact on British policy of these developments, it is essential to indicate why the Community considers it necessary to operate a regional policy of its own in addition to member countries' policies: in other words, the *specific* justification of a regional policy at Community level. The major reason offered is that the regional imbalance in the Community constitutes an impediment to economic and monetary union, which was formally adopted at the summit meeting in The Hague in 1969, and reaffirmed at the Paris summit in 1972, as the goal to be achieved by the Community by 1980. In a series of stages outlined in the Werner Plan in 1970, the permitted margins of adjustment of member countries' exchange rates would be progressively narrowed until the Community became effectively a single-currency area with exchange rate parities irrevocably fixed. *Pari passu* with this process, countries would undertake the coordination of their economic policies. One of the concerns expressed at the 1972 summit was that the continued divergence between the economies of the richer and poorer regions of the Community would make it impossible for certain governments to surrender control over their economic policies, and if they did, would force them into protectionist measures to shelter their economies. Either way, economic and monetary union would not be achieved and the customs union itself would be threatened. The way to avoid this, it was decided, was to establish a regional policy at the Community level.

The argument here is tangled. If it is assumed that, in the context of economic and monetary union, countries become regions and balance of payments problems become regional problems, what is being advocated is a Community regional policy as an alternative to the means of adjustment employed in national economic management. But Community regional policy is defined as a means of promoting development in the problem regions *within* the national regions of the Community, which is a related problem but by no means the same thing; there is, therefore, a certain ambiguity surrounding the word 'region' (Wilson, 1975). Were Community regional policy to be envisaged as a substitute for short-term adjustment mechanisms, the amount of the transfers would be enormous and would require political and administrative institutions at Community level. It is the role of economic and monetary union to bring such federal bodies into existence eventually but not to require them as a condition of success for an early stage of its development. Even then, the term regional policy would be so stretched as to constitute a misuse of language. The really significant regional problem in the context of economic and monetary union is one of national regions (the United Kingdom, Italy and Ireland) where an amalgam of factors produces a higher propensity to inflate and lower levels and rates of growth of productivity than in the 'first division' countries of the Community.

A regional policy at the Community level does, however, have a role to play. If it is held that inflation is generated or aggravated by excess demand in the more prosperous regions, which is diffused to the less prosperous regions in the form of higher rates of wages and earnings unjustified by productivity levels there, and if, further, it is assumed that economic and monetary union may exacerbate such tendencies by stimulating migration into the more prosperous areas and destroying the money illusion, which renders wage rates in the richest areas of the Community not obviously comparable to trade unions in the least developed, some effort at the Community level to encourage development in the less developed regions is both appropriate and helpful. If a monetarist view of inflation is taken, then economic and monetary union could be harnessed to persuade member countries to desist from a fruitless adherence to national control over demand management policies, which will run against the brick wall of a given natural rate of unemployment. If one recent scheme were adopted, this would be achieved by creating a European currency (the Europa), which would be expressed in terms of a weighted basket of national currencies with its purchasing power held constant by periodic adjustment according to the weighted average of inflation rates in national economies (*Economist*, 1974; Parkin, 1976; Cairncross, 1974, chapters 2 and 3). If floated initially as a 'parallel' unit of account along with national currencies, the Europa would discourage inflationary credit policies, since these would simply encourage a movement out of the inflating economy's currency into Europas. This radical proposal, which strips national governments of an illusory sovereignty over credit policy, would discipline inflationary policies and would foster European unity. The growth of the supply of Europas would be determined by a European banking authority. A Community regional policy incorporating Community regional aid would be a useful adjunct to the new monetary system. It would help to loosen the constraint of natural unemployment and aid high-inflation economies to soften the impact of increased unemployment, which would be produced in these economies if at *the Community level* money supply growth was limited to a rate close to the growth of Community output.

Whichever view is taken (the Keynesian or the monetarist), the conclusion is clear that any Community regional policy should be seen as an addition to other policies at both the national and the Community level. Where large areas of an economy suffer from multi-sectoral uncompetitiveness, regional policy may be an important element in any corrective action, but it is only part of the answer. The other main reason for the priority given to regional policy at the Paris summit was the British insistence on financial compensation to offset the contribution they would have to make to the Community budget and in particular to the financing of the Common Agricultural Policy. The large new regional problem of industrial decline and urban decay that British entry brought to the Community was adopted as an appropriate economic argument to underpin a political claim to a share of Community revenue.

This is not to say that the Community had not given consideration to regional policy before the decision to move towards economic and monetary union (Lind and Flockton, 1970; Van Ginderachter, 1973; Cros, 1974). The difference is that prior to this commitment neither the will nor the need to have a Community-level regional policy existed. Apart from the 'Mezzogiorno', which was treated in a special protocol, and to which the European Investment Bank (EIB) was to devote particular attention, the problem of regional disparities was considered a national responsibility of member countries to be resolved primarily by national policies.

The 1977 Guidelines

In June 1977 the Commission submitted to the Council of Ministers a set of guidelines for a regional policy at Community level (European Communities, 1977b). The first significant feature of this document is that a Community regional policy is still presented as a necessary condition for 'deepening' integration, although the objective that regional policy must now serve has been rebaptised 'convergence of the economic policies of member states' rather than 'the attainment of economic and monetary union'. As the Commission puts it (European Communities, 1977b, p. 4),

... not only do the less developed regions fail to integrate fully within the Community, but the problems to which they give rise become an increasingly heavy burden on national economies and thus increase the pressure on the public authorities concerned to refuse the constraints inherent in the mechanism of Community integration.

From this position it is natural that the Commission should go on to advocate a more extensive role for regional policy, a role that would establish it as a framework within which the structural changes required in the Community economies have to be considered. All Community policies must contain a regional-impact assessment (Thomson, 1976) and there must be coordination of Community policies and financial aids and national policies to ensure their compatibility with the aims of Community regional policy. Already the Commission has set up a special task force outside the normal departmental structure to coordinate the different funds that have a bearing on regional development, to ensure that the Community's agricultural policy and the arrangements governing imports from Mediterranean countries do not adversely affect regional development in the Community. The regional impact of the increasing problems being experienced in a wide range of industries and possible solutions to them in member countries are also being examined. Within the Commission, it has been shown that the activities of the European Agricultural Guidance and Guarantee Fund (EAGGF) in the agricultural regions have not aided the regions in greatest need, and that some safeguards for the Community's Mediterranean regions will have to be written into the Community's external policy on imports from Mediterranean countries. Studies are currently underway on the textile, motor vehicle and steel industries, which pay particular attention to the regional impact of developments in these industries and policies towards them (European Communities, 1977c).

This comprehensive approach to regional policy at the Community level is in many respects laudably ambitious, but it will require not only a considerable effort of data collection but the delineation of a regional-development strategy for the Community as a whole. The elements of this strategy will be discussed in the following sections, which deal with the main instruments of Community regional policy, the European Regional Development Fund and the regional-development programmes.

The European Regional Development Fund

In March 1975 the Community established the first of its regional-policy instruments. It created the European Regional Development Fund to provide investment grants under prescribed conditions to industrial and service activities and either grants or interest rebates on EIB loans to infrastructure (European Communities, 1975b). This aid is to be additional to member countries' own expenditure on regional development, thus enabling member countries to meet more effectively the obligations of economic and monetary union. As well as a small Fund management committee, a Regional Policy Committee of senior civil servants from member countries and staffed by the Commission was set up to provide a planning framework for the operations of the Fund and to coordinate national regional policies and the Community's own policies and expenditures into a more coherent and comprehensive policy of regional development. The hope here is to encourage member countries, as far as a confederal structure like the Community can manage, to direct their regional-development efforts more effectively to reduce the regional disparities that block economic and monetary union. The shadow of ambiguity still hangs around the adjective 'regional', but it is clear that reliance on financial transfers alone is rejected.

It is time now to turn to the impact of this new approach and the new institutions on British regional policy. After almost two years of acrimonious haggling (Wallace, Wallace and Webb, 1977), the British quota of aid from the Fund was fixed at £150m in 1975 prices for the initial period of the Fund's operation, which ended in December 1977. This sum represented 28 per cent of the Fund's total resources of £650m and was available to approved projects receiving British regional subsidies in the assisted areas. The Fund can contribute up to 50 per cent of national-aid expenditure up to a total of 20 per cent of the value of the investment undertaken for industrial projects; infrastructure projects may be financed to the extent of 30 per cent. The ceilings fixed by the regional-aid rules apply to the combined aid given. The decision to set national quotas in advance was the inevitable result of countries' insistence on the principle of *juste retour*, that is, a country getting out of the Community what it puts in. The British aim was to be a net gainer from the Fund both during the transitional period up to 1976 when its contribution to the Community budget (effectively to finance the Common Agricultural Policy) was increasing by stages, and afterwards. The estimated net gain to the end of 1977 was £60m (Van Ginderachter, 1973; *Economist*, 1973).

The linking of Fund aid to national regional aids was agreed only after lengthy attempts, involving much cartography, to define 'objectively' those regions in the Community that should be designated as eligible for Community regional aid. Space prevents a full account of the ingenious and unabashedly self-interested formulae advanced in the discussions, which resulted at one point in the publication of a map on which the eligible regions covered a very extensive area of the Community territory. The extreme negotiating bids ranged from a British demand for a Fund of £1,500m to a German proposal of a mini-Fund of £300m, but limited to the United Kingdom, Ireland and Italy. It is reasonable, if politically naive, to question what much of this discussion had to do with regional development (European Communities, 1973a; Van Ginderachter, 1973).

The amount of aid granted by the Fund to the United Kingdom was very small. Between 1973 and 1976 it was £95m. This has to be set against estimates of expenditure on regional aids in Great Britain for the year 1976–77 of £593m (Great Britain, 1977, pp. 381–82). Moreover, the real impact of the aid is difficult to assess because of the method of payment. The submission of projects eligible for aid must be made through national governments; aid is then paid directly to national governments. The Community insists that the aid must be genuinely additional to what the national effort would otherwise have been. The British government has been able to give only verbal assurance that as far as possible it will respect this condition in general terms. What the British government is not prepared to do is to 'top up' national aids to any individual project. This general assurance as to additionality poses real problems, particularly in the present climate of restrictions on public expenditure. Even in the case of infrastructure, where the projects have been concentrated on local-authority schemes and the Fund aid paid to local authorities, the aid merely reduces their need to borrow and consequently their interest repayments. The restrictions on public expenditure again make it impossible for local authorities to authorise correspondingly larger investment, so that additionality is here respected only in a putative and potential sense. It might be thought that 'topping up', which has not been practised in any member country, would give greater and more tangible assurance of additionality. But as the Commission itself recognises this would result in discrimination between projects. It is also of limited usefulness in the British case since the projects submitted are all in receipt not only of the automatic RDG but of additional selective assistance. The discipline of the aid ceilings leaves limited scope for laying Fund aid on top of these national aids (European Communities, 1976a).

The initial Fund regulations laid down certain conditions as to the type of project eligible for aid. Industrial projects must have a minimum investment cost of £25,000 and either create ten new jobs or ensure the maintenance of existing jobs. If the latter condition is invoked, evidence of a conversion or restructuring plan must be submitted to ensure that the firms receiving the aid have the prospect of being competitive; even so, preference is to be given to job creation. The second version of the condition represents a hard-fought victory for the British approach against Commission doubts and French and German hostility. It is a further example of the fundamental difference of approach between the British and the Community approach to regional development. It offers further confirmation of the British suspicion that the Commission has still to come to terms with the techniques required to promote regional development in large areas dominated by declining industries. On the Commission side, and in Paris and Bonn, it serves to confirm the view that British regional policy is really a social welfare operation covering large tracts of an industrialised economy mismanaged at both the micro and macro level.

Infrastructure is another contentious subject. The Fund rules are strict on the point that infrastructure projects will be eligible only if they are directly linked with industrial projects. This restriction is understandable. The Commission and certain member countries are fearful that without it a large part of the Fund could be used to refinance public expenditure that has only a tenuous relationship to regional development. The definition of direct linkage has, however, proven a ticklish problem. It has made the selection of projects difficult and has caused some genuine irritation on the part of British local authorities unaccustomed to thinking in terms of this particular Brussels subtlety.

On 1 January 1978 the Regional Fund was endowed with a fresh allocation of resources. After an initial substantially higher request by the Commission, the Council voted the Fund £382m for its operations in 1978 within a three-year draft budget of £1220m (European Communities, 1977b). These monies will be distributed according to the existing national quotas, save for a tranche amounting to 5 per cent of the new allocation which will be distributed on a non-quota basis to finance specific actions required to deal with particular regional problems of special urgency. The Commission had to fight hard to get even this very limited discretionary power.

The United Kingdom's attitude towards the pressure to create a larger Fund and a significant non-quota section was decidedly lukewarm. The prospect of entry into the Community of Greece, Portugal and Spain, all countries with sizeable problems of regional underdevelopment, would mean that the United Kingdom could soon cease to be a net recipient of Fund assistance with little hope of compensation elsewhere; *juste retour* is not a principle that dies easily. On the other hand, the European Parliament, which now has the right of amendment over Regional Fund expenditure, has recently strongly reiterated in a lengthy and interesting report its disapproval of the quota system (European Communities, 1977d).

The Commission links its proposal for a two-part Fund to a new classification of recipient regions. Category 1 regions are those where underdevelopment is considered a permanent and long-term problem. In the cases of Italy and Ireland the countries concerned do not possess the financial capacity to deal effectively with the problem. In such regions the Fund's role is to provide general support which must be, at the least, maintained for a period of years and directed towards the creation of a sound economic base. Infrastructure investment with its high cost and long pay-off period is singled out as particularly important and it is with this in mind, and under the enthusiastic prompting of the European Parliament, that the Commission has agreed to loosen the restrictive and contentious interpretation of eligible infrastructure to include all expenditure 'which contributes to the development of the region in which it is located'. For particularly important projects the maximum aid is to be raised from 30 to 50 per cent of costs (European Communities, 1977b, pp. 30–1; 1977d, pp. 39–41 and p. 46).

These changes are significant. They represent a conscious if cautious move to establish a system of revenue sharing that will take into account the need to reduce inequalities in the relative intervention capacity of the different member countries as regards regional development. This reflects a growing interest in the Community in the notion of 'fiscal federalism' and in the methods used in established federal governments to redistribute resources among their constituent provinces. Just as unitary or federal states maintain economic and monetary union by equalising and stabilising interregional flows through the channels of central government or federal government finance, the recent MacDougall Report (European Communities, 1977e) prepared for the Commission has examined the ways in which the Community might facilitate convergence and a move towards such a union by gradually building up a system of financial transfers, channelled through Brussels between member countries.

At present the Regional Fund is a system of specific-purpose, conditional grants with quotas and a global ceiling—a standard formula, in fact, for regional-policy operations in federal states. But the language of the new arrangements for Category 1 regions suggests a loosening of the conditions, which moves this part of the Fund's aid closer towards general-purpose transfers more usually associated with government expenditure aimed at the redistribution of income among individuals. The explanation is that if Italy and Ireland, and *a fortiori* any new member countries, are to be induced to deny themselves trade and exchange rate adjustments and if excessive interregional migration is to be avoided, compensating financial transfers are required. The next logical step must be to base the Fund's operations in these regions less on individual projects and more on medium-term regional programmes, however difficult it may be. Such an arrangement is required anyway on narrower economic grounds. The use of infrastructure deliberately laid down in advance as a means of promoting economic development is incompatible with aid awarded on the basis of individual, discrete projects or the simple unconditional transfer of global sums to reduce inequalities in regional incomes.

From the British point of view it is of interest that Northern Ireland is included with Greenland and the French overseas departments as the remaining Category 1 regions requiring this more general support. It is, however, not argued that the regional intervention capacity of the United Kingdom is at the same level of inadequacy as that of Ireland or Italy. It is open to doubt whether infrastructure is now a crucial factor in promoting development in Northern Ireland. The major British concern may, however, be the pressure that is being exerted by the European Parliament, and to which the Commission itself is showing new signs of sympathy, for the adoption of an allocation formula for Fund aid to the neediest regions along the revenue-sharing lines discussed above. Need would be determined by a weighted indicator combining two measures. The first is the imbalance relative to the Community average of Gross Domestic Product (GDP) per capita together with one of three indicators: a high unemployment rate, a high net outmigration and a heavy dependence on agriculture or declining industries. The second is a measure of the intervention capacity of states in regional development, calculated as the ratio of the GDP of regions with no substantial imbalances to the GDP of regions where substantial imbalances exist (European Communities, 1977d, pp. 38 and pp. 40–1). The employment of such an indicator would almost certainly lower the British share of the Fund and indeed require an alteration or abolition of the quota system. The entry of new member states would enhance this effect and require a larger Fund.

Category II regions, which include the assisted areas of Great Britain, are those in which manufacturing industry and agriculture have experienced low growth of incomes, migration drain and unemployment, associated with structural change on a scale such as to affect the common market. Category III regions comprise regions, not necessarily scheduled as national assisted areas, in which Fund aid will be granted to supplement national aid made available to counteract unforeseen developments and compensate any regionally deleterious effects of other Community policies. Category IV regions are frontier regions. In Category III and Category IV regions, only non-quota aid will be available, the decision to assist depending on the regional-impact analyses discussed above.

For Category II regions a certain level of aid will be assured but its continuance will be subject to a review every two years by the Commission. If the region's problems, and particularly its unemployment, are not such as to threaten the functioning of the Community, Fund aid will no longer be guaranteed, though it may qualify for non-quota aid applicable to category III regions. It is aid to productive investment rather than infrastructure that is deemed most important here. What is required is to induce the transfer of investment funds from the richer regions to employ underutilised labour, rather than the creation *ab ovo* of an economic base. The Commission's proposals foresee an increasing emphasis on specific actions in Category III regions and consequently a run-down of aid to Category II regions and, by implication, an increase in non-quota aid.

The hand of the Brussels free-competition school, which produced the national aid rules, can be discerned here. Even large areas of industrial backwardness do not constitute a reason for indefinitely continuing aid, and the emphasis on aid to new investment rather than to total costs remains firmly embedded. Obviously, there will be no dramatic cutting-off of Fund aid, but it is clear that the problems of the British assisted areas are deemed capable of solution in a foreseeable future and the British economy generally capable not only of paying its share of this effort but of contributing to the more intractable difficulties of the Category 1 regions. On the other hand, another Commission proposal could, if implemented, be of considerable benefit to British regional policy. The Commission proposes to use the Regional Fund to finance interest rebates on loans granted by the EIB to private firms, loans made under Article 56 of the European Coal and Steel Community (ECSC) Treaty, and possibly on other loans granted by the Community (European Communities, 1977b, pp. 52–60). The amount of the rebates will vary up to 5 percentage points for the first five years of the loan, but shall not exceed 40 per cent of the cost of long-term borrowing on the capital market of the member country concerned or reduce the effective interest rate below 4 per cent. A ceiling of £32,500 per job created or maintained will be operated. For small firms employing less than 500 persons, with net assets of less than £20m, and in which larger enterprises hold no more than a one-third share, a system of global loans is to be introduced. The loans will be granted to appropriate intermediary agencies. This extension of the interest rebates hitherto available only on loans granted under Article 56 of the ECSC Treaty is intended to relieve the interest cost and indirectly, the exchange rate risks associated with loans denominated in the European unit of account, a basket of European currencies. These risks have much reduced the attractiveness of EIB loans to private companies. The loans are aimed mainly at firms in Category II and Category III regions where loan finance is more appropriate in the Commission's view, since it taps a wider source of investment funds than a fixed-budget Fund subject to tight constraints, and directs aid of a non-continuing kind to firms whose operations will have met the commercial vetting of the EIB.

The Commission has considered using some of the non-quota part of the Fund to guarantee directly EIB loans against exchange risks, but this ran into opposition in the Council, not surprisingly from strong-currency member countries. The EIB is also jealous of its autonomy and extremely cautious about allowing the Commission to intervene and to introduce an element of 'softness' into its lending policy. The exchange rate risks have severely limited the use of the EIB loan facility by British firms. Only those firms with sufficient foreign-exchange earnings have been able to use it. EIB loans to British regions have consequently gone mainly to public-sector undertakings where a Treasury guarantee is available. Many of these projects are highly capital intensive and would probably have been financed anyway. The regional-development potential of the EIB facilities has, therefore, not been used as fully or effectively as it might. The situation has been somewhat eased by the decision of the Treasury at the beginning of 1978 to guarantee a limited measure of protection against adverse movements in the exchange rate to private firms in receipt of EIB loans.

Community Regional Programming and its Impact on British Policy

While the bulk of the Community's attention has so far been devoted to the establishment of the Regional Fund, it has always been recognised that it could form only a minor part of a regional policy at the Community level. The Fund was and is needed as a political earnest of Community concern, but the work of the Regional Policy Committee is likely to assume growing importance. Its task is to coordinate the regional policies of member countries and the Community's own expenditures more effectively to reduce regional disparities in the Community. It was entrusted with the task of preparing the model outline for regional-development programmes to be prepared by member countries by the end of 1977. These programmes will serve as the framework for the project aid given by the Fund. The Committee has also to give an opinion on all infrastructure projects costing more than £5m for which Fund aid is claimed. It has the further task of keeping under study and review the effectiveness of both national and Community aids and policies, and is specifically charged to examine disincentive measures in the prosperous regions of the Community (European Communities, 1975b). It is important to note that the Committee is a Committee of the Council staffed by the Commission. This is the result of pressure from certain member countries, particularly France, who refuse categorically to hand over control of regional policies to the Commission. It is, therefore, essentially a coordinating body and in no sense a supranational regional planning agency of the Community; its membership will ensure that!

The regional-development programmes have not yet all been completed, but a common outline has been prepared by the Commission and a preliminary programme submitted by the British Government (European Communities, 1976b; Great Britain, 1977). According to the common outline, the programmes are to present an analysis and not simply a description of the regional problem. They are as far as possible to present quantified targets for a medium-term period covering regions the size of which is to be determined by member countries. In particular, the Committee is seeking reliable estimates of the number of jobs that have to be created or maintained and the target rates of growth of regional income, together with the changes in industrial structure and manpower mix required to achieve these targets. The targets must be realistic, that is to say, compatible with national economic policy, and not simply 'an inventory of regional needs or aspirations'.

Having established the targets, the programmes must give full details and provide estimates of the cost of regional-policy measures. Separate estimates are to be made of infrastructure cost, the cost of aids to investment, the cost of other aids and subsidies to particular industries as they effect the regions concerned and, finally, social expenditure that may be deemed relevant to regional development, including the cost of tax reductions and exemptions. The different sources of this finance must be specified and this expenditure related to national public-expenditure plans or forecasts; it is recognised that it is difficult to attribute some expenditure to specifically regional objectives. In addition, information is required on the volume of investment (affecting regional development) by state-controlled companies or major private companies with whom agreements exist. Finally, the responsibilities of the different agencies involved in implementing the programmes and the arrangements for their coordination are to be specified. Annual information statements on the progress achieved by the programmes are required.

How may British regional policy be affected by the obligation to prepare programmes of the kind sketched out above? Neither the Community outline nor the admittedly preliminary British regional programme (Great Britain, 1977) deal in terms of the resource cost of regional development; nor is the financial 'clawback' by the national exchequer from an increase in regional output requested or provided. Nor is any information provided on the gross costs of regional-development incentives. Even in a preliminary exercise this cannot be said to be encouraging. As far as expenditure on infrastructure is concerned, a fair amount of detail is provided of projects eligible for Regional Fund aid, but it is specifically stated that it is not possible to estimate the part of total infrastructure expenditure attributable to regional-development requirements.

While the section of the programme (Great Britain, 1977) dealing with Scotland gives some forward estimates of employment trends, it is pointed out that specific objectives for regional policy in terms of jobs or of unemployment rates are not established in advance, since the regional problem is a continuing and changing phenomenon much influenced by national and international economic circumstances. It is emphasised that no attempt is made to select or identify particular industries as suitable for particular regions. Brief analyses of the economies of the assisted areas are also provided, which, together with the details of infrastructure works, serve as background information to Regional Fund project applications. But they in no sense constitute even the outlines of regional plans or strategies.

In its examination of the British submissions, the Commission is likely to press with due tact for more quantification and to contrast the British approach to regional programming with the practices of other countries. While the imposition of such a discipline is useful, there is a danger that, through discretion if nothing else, the Commission may limit itself to rather academic costing and forecasting exercises that do not touch some of the problems of regional development, which lie in the economic, institutional and social structure of the regions. A positive feature of the programme outline is its concentration on future needs and possibilities in the less developed regions rather than, as was the case in the haggling over the

Fund, past problems and present symptoms. Since the Commission is concerned to reduce disparities between regions in the Community and not simply within one country, it is likely to single out areas in countries where both problems and future growth possibilities exist on a scale large enough to have an impact at Community level. It would not be difficult to define two or three such areas in the British problem regions. By this means an indirect reconsideration of the growth area concept pioneered in the 1964 Central Scotland Plan may at least be initiated (Parr, chapter 9 of this volume). Such an approach may be dovetailed with the request in the programme outline for information on large state and private investment projects in the regions. Here specific mention is made of possible agreements that may exist between governments and private firms. Such information could be used to identify industrial complexes that are emerging or that are envisaged in certain regions.

The idea of agreements involving special packages of aid including special infrastructure provision, with firms large enough to constitute the core of a group of related industries, is now in varying forms accepted in several countries in the Community. Were these to be set in the context of growth areas delineated from the information supplied by the programmes, a small number of Community growth areas might be capable of identification. In such areas it might be possible through a working party of the Regional Policy Committee to consider their development as a whole, bringing together the questions of aid, infrastructure provision, government contracts, training facilities, service industry growth and urban and physical planning. This would be one way of introducing more effectiveness and flexibility into the aid rules and the operations of the Fund, which clearly cannot continue to operate indefinitely on the basis of aid given to individual projects on an annual basis. It should commend itself to the 'payer' countries as a means of exercising constructive control over the expenditure of the Fund. If such work were carried out by the Regional Policy Committee, fears of any supranational influence should be suitably allayed. Such a procedure would also be a more effective way of concentrating aid than the energetic demands of the European Parliament for a more 'objective' selection of regions eligible for aid. The previous efforts at 'objective' definitions are scarcely encouraging, resulting as they did in each member country seeking to maximise the area within its own territory eligible for assistance.

The proposed coordination of the Regional Fund, the guidance section of the EAGGF and the Social Fund is inevitably going to lead to a greater emphasis on programmes rather than projects. The Social Fund is already organised on this basis, while the EAGGF is moving away from project-based aid. It is, however, no simple matter to disburse aid on this wider basis until the regional programmes have been prepared and examined and constitute a sound enough frame to serve as the basis for 'envelopes' of aid. It is possible, however, to make a start by concentrating Fund aid on larger projects, multi-stage operations or closely linked projects, whether large or small; preference is already indicated in the Fund regulations for such projects. Such a shift of emphasis would compel the Fund to commit money to projects several years ahead. Large projects or programmes cannot be effectively financed on an uncertain annual basis; this merely spawns marginal activities. If the programmes are developed successfully, the Fund should, of course, be organised on a medium-term basis coterminous with the programmes. Excessive bunching of payments in particular years would have to be avoided, but within limits countries could vary the timing of their claims on the Fund within the planning period. But the European Parliament will still demand its annual check on allocations.

The major lacuna in the Community's regional strategy is coordinated action on development controls in the congested areas, which are rendered even more attractive by the Community's own centripetal effects. The British Industrial Development Certificate (IDC) system is the most extensive example of such controls, but there are similar controls on development in the Paris and Lyons areas and in limited areas around Turin and Milan. It is fully recognised by the Commission that while such controls are an essential element in any successful regional policy, they touch on the trade-off between growth and a redistribution of economic activity, which no member country is prepared to yield to a Community authority. It is also plain that Germany, having so far eschewed such controls, is scarcely likely in the present economic climate to have them imposed for the benefit of other less competitive economies. The British problem here, though there is admittedly no hard evidence, is not to lose investment and jobs through continuing to impose its own relatively severe controls.

The new coordinating task force accords this problem high priority, but the difficulties are great. One ingenious suggestion is to supplement the Community's financial resources by a tax on land values or the increase in land values and use the proceeds for regional development (Balassa, 1973; Cairncross, 1974). Since the increase in land values is partly caused by Community pressures, this would be appropriate. Action through the price mechanism, apart from other advantages, would also avoid the very difficult task of coordinating different national administrative procedures. Another more directly interventionist possibility is to use an agreed Community IDC system, operated by the Regional Policy Committee, to persuade all large multi-national firms seeking a location to site at least x per cent of jobs in approved areas (Holland, 1976, p. 93). It is, however, much more likely that the Community will begin with an inventory of present disincentive measures and, initially at least, seek some low-level agreement on minimum disincentives. It may not be impossible in a time of political pressure for regional decentralisation to get member countries to agree to a common code of practice that embodies the principle that only activities able to prove that location in congested areas is essential are permitted to locate or expand there. This could be reinforced by an agreement to remove progressively over a period of, say, five years, all regional aids in the old Central Areas, or Other Regions as they were designated in the 1975 rules. The coordination of Community funds should involve a close check on the proportion of aid flowing from the Social Fund or the EAGGF guidance fund to firms located in prosperous or congested areas.

There is a good case for a British initiative on the subject of disincentives. A possible approach would be to propose a study by a working party of the Regional Policy Committee on the costs of concentration and congestion, including the provision for foreign immigrants in the large urban centres of the Community. It can scarcely be argued that this is well tilled territory in any member country, and it would allow the Community to be more precise about the real-resource cost of regional development. The British assisted areas might stand to benefit if a careful analysis were available that compared the costs of location in rundown but redeemable areas with a history of industrial aptitude (as well as problems) with the costs in areas where expansion can be achieved only by the continued import of foreign labour, pollution and increasing congestion.

References

Balassa, B. (1973) 'Regional Policies and the Environment in the European Common Market', *Weltwirtschaftliches Archiv*, Vol. 109, pp. 402–17.
Cairncross, A. (ed.) (1974) *Economic Policy for the European Community*. New York: Holmes and Meier.
Cros, J. (1974) 'Les déséquilibres géographiques dans la CEE face aux objectifs de l'union économique et monétaire', *Revue d'Economie Politique*, Vol. 84, pp. 145–72.
The Economist (1973) 'Regional Fund. Ready for the Last Round', Vol. 249, 24 November, pp. 63–4.
The Economist (1974) 'Will Labour be Trapped or Saved by the State Aid Web?', Vol. 251, 4 May, pp. 76–82.
European Communities (1971) Commission. 'Régimes généraux d'aides à finalité régionale', *Journal Officiel des Communautés Européennes* (Communications et Informations), Vol. 14, 4.11.71, pp. 1–13. An English translation of this document is to be found in Great Britain (1973a, pp. 138–57).
European Communities (1972) Commission. 'First Report on Competition Policy', annexed to *Fifth General Report on the Activities of the Communities*. Brussels: Office for Official Publications of the European Communities.
European Communities (1973a) Commission. 'Report on the Regional Problems in the Enlarged Community (Thomson Report)', COM (73) 550 Final, Brussels. The text of this report is published in *Bulletin of the European Communities*, Supplement, No. 8, 1973.
European Communities (1973b) Commission. 'Proposal for a Regulation on the List of Regions Eligible for Assistance from the European Regional Development Fund', *Official Journal of the European Communities* (Information and Notices), Vol. 16, 6.12.73, pp. 26–30.
European Communities (1974) Commission. 'Third Report on Competition Policy', annexed to *Seventh General Report on the Activities of the Communities*. Brussels: Office for Official Publications of the European Communities.

European Communities (1975a) Commission. 'General Regional Aid Systems' COM (75) 77 Final, Brussels. A summary of this document appears in 'Third Report on Competition', annexed to *Seventh General Report on the Activities of the Communities*. Brussels: Office for Official Publications of the European Communities.

European Communities (1975b) Council of Ministers. 'Regulation Establishing a European Regional Development Fund; Council Decision of 18th March, 1975 setting up a Regional Policy Committee', *Official Journal of the European Communities* (Legislation), Vol. 18, 21.3.1975, pp. 1–8 and 47–8.

European Communities (1976a) Commission. 'European Regional Development Fund. First Annual Report (1975)', *Bulletin of the European Communities*, Supplement, No. 7, 1976.

European Communities (1976b) Commission. 'Outline for Regional Development Programmes', *Official Journal of the European Communities* (Information and Notices), Vol. 19, 24.3.76, pp. 2–5.

European Communities (1977a) Commission. 'Sixth Report on Competition Policy', annexed to *Tenth General Report on the Activities of the Communities*. Brussels: Office for Official Publications of the European Communities.

European Communities (1977b) Commission. 'Community Regional Policy. New Guidelines', *Bulletin of the European Communities*, Supplement, No. 2, 1977.

European Communities (1977c) Parliament. 'European Regional Development Fund. Second Annual Report (1976)', Working Document, 224/77, *Official Journal of the European Communities*, 1977–78.

European Communities (1977d) Parliament. 'Report of the Committee on Regional Policy on Aspects of the Community's Regional Policy to be developed in the Future' (Delmotte Report), Working Document, 35/77, *Official Journal of the European Communities*, 1977–78.

European Communities (1977e) Commission. 'Report of the Study Group on the Role of Public Finance in European Integration', Brussels.

Great Britain (1972) *Treaty Establishing the European Economic Community.* Cmnd. 4864. London: HMSO.

Great Britain (1973a) House of Commons. Expenditure Committee (Trade and Industry Sub-Committee). Session 1972–73. *Regional Development Incentives: Minutes of Evidence.* House of Commons Paper 327, pp. 254–79. London: HMSO.

Great Britain (1973b) House of Commons. Expenditure Committee (Trade and Industry Sub-Committee) Session 1973–74. *Regional Development Incentives: Report.* House of Commons Paper 85, Chapter 11, 'Britain in Europe'. London: HMSO.

Great Britain (1977) Department of Industry. 'Regional Development Programme for the United Kingdom', *Trade and Industry*, Vol. 26, pp. 358–62, 381–82, 419–23 and 488–93.

Holland, S. (1976) *The Regional Problem.* London: Macmillan.

Lind, H. and Flockton, C. (1970) *Regional Policy in Britain and the Six.* Chatham House European Series, No. 15. London: Political and Economic Planning.

Moore, B. and Rhodes, J. (1973) 'Evaluating the Effects of British Regional Economic Policy', *Economic Journal*, Vol. 83, pp. 87–110.

Parkin, M. (1976) 'Monetary Union and Stabilisation policy in the European Community', *Banca Nazionale del Lavoro*, No. 29, pp. 222–40.

Thomson, G. (1976) Address to the Regional Authorities Conference, Paris, Tuesday, 7 December 1976.

Van Ginderachter, J. (1973) 'La politique régionale de la Communauté, justifications, modalités et propositions', *Revue de Marché Commun*, No. 170, pp. 468–86.

Wallace, H., Wallace, W. and Webb, C. (eds.) (1977) *Policy-making in the European Communities.* London: John Wiley and Sons.

Wilson, T. (1975) 'Economic Sovereignty' in J. Vaizey (ed.), *Economic Sovereignty and Regional Policy.* Dublin: Gill and Macmillan.

CHAPTER 13

Devolution: The Changing Political Economy of Regional Policy

*John R. Firn and Duncan Maclennan**

Introduction

During the past decade there have been two major constitutional debates in the United Kingdom regarding the level of government at which sovereignty over different economic, political and legislative powers should be exercised. The first of these concerned the United Kingdom entry into the European Community. The second, and as yet unresolved, debate is about the devolution of certain economic and political powers from the central parliament at Westminster to new elected legislative assemblies in some of the constituent regions of the country, initially to Scotland and Wales.[1] This chapter is concerned with the second of these constitutional developments. It will attempt to examine the main economic components of the type of devolution proposed for the United Kingdom and it will focus on the uncertain relationship between devolution and regional economic policy. It is clear that the two debates on constitutional change that have taken place have much in common. Both have encompassed an extraordinarily complex and interrelated set of economic, legal, political and social issues; in each case the final decision will, with hindsight, be seen to have been based on and to have evolved out of broad and rather imprecise political attitudes and criteria; and both have clearly demonstrated the apparent limitations of economic analysis and prescription in policy areas of fundamental importance.

Therefore, we make no effort to develop a model of the whole of the devolution process, but instead we confine our attention to trying to identify the main issues of the debate in which economic analysis has an important part to play. In the next section the concept of devolution is explored, and the pressures behind the demand for greater regional self-government are discussed. This is followed by a brief history of both

* Department of Social and Economic Research and Centre for Urban and Regional Research, University of Glasgow.

the demand for devolution in Scotland and the government responses to such demands. Attention will then be focused on some of the main public-finance aspects of political devolution. Finally, the complex relationship between devolution and regional economic development policies will be examined, with particular attention being paid to the possibilities of introducing effective economic policies at sub-national levels.

The Concept of Devolution

The Definition of Devolution

For the purposes of this chapter it is convenient to assume that the organisational structure of government in nation states can be divided into unitary, federal and devolved systems, although in the real world it is possible to find systems that contain features from all three types. Pure unitary and federal systems are relatively easily defined. In a unitary state, central government makes all decisions, and these are deemed to be equally binding and effective in all the constituent regions. Further, the power over, and accountability for, all economic, legislative and political functions is retained by the central government, although it is possible to achieve a degree of decentralised decision making in the regions via either administrative devolution or decentralisation. However, pure unitary states are relatively uncommon in practice, especially in large countries with mixed economies, where central governments usually co-exist with a variety of semi-devolved administrative and political entities, the most important of which are probably municipal governments.

In a federation, the central government may retain control over certain economic powers and functions, especially those relating to policies for general macro-economic control and redistribution, whilst allowing sub-national states to have sovereignty over a variety of well-defined economic and legislative functions. The vertical relations between central and local administrations and legislatures are generally precisely defined, often in considerable constitutional detail, and an important characteristic of federal systems is that all comparable sub-national units have similar and equivalent economic and legislative controls and powers allocated to them for policy purposes. It is also usual to find the central authorities controlling local behaviour by economic incentives as well as by political controls, as through, for instance, the use of specific grants to influence the level and content of local-expenditure patterns. It is also worth noting that the major federal systems, such as Australia, Canada, India, West Germany and the USA, are all relatively large states comprising distinct and diverse regional economic, political and cultural structures, which often reflect the existence of earlier independent political states that have come together to form the present political unit.

In contrast to unitary and federal systems, the devolved system is much harder to define satisfactorily. Basically, devolution is now seen to refer to a constitutional arrangement where one or more of the regions or sub-regions of a nation gain, or have granted to them, a degree of economic, political and legislative sovereignty that falls short of the status achieved by a member state in a federal system, but that is substantially greater than the status of subordinate units in a unitary system. Unfortunately, it is not possible to be definitionally more precise, because experience has revealed that devolution, as a political structure, can lie virtually anywhere on the continuum between pure unitary and pure federal systems.

Where the existence of devolution reflects regionally based political pressures, then important operational characteristics serve to distinguish devolution from federalism. With devolution, economic, legislative and administrative powers may be unevenly distributed across a set of otherwise similar regions. Further, the political origins of devolution are likely to result in an unclear constitutional relationship between central and regional governments. Compromises, contradictions and specific regulations, most of which are produced to meet the demands of an individual region, are likely to condition the rules relating central to regional governments. Operationally, federalism and devolution are likely to be quite distinct.

The term 'devolution' may also be restricted to certain functions of government. It is common to distinguish legislative and administrative devolution. First, there is legislative devolution, which means that the regions involved have been given elected parliamentary assemblies that have the powers to legislate in certain well-defined areas, including economic and administrative affairs. Second, there is administrative devolution, which is taken to imply that a region has a degree of independence in the administration of its affairs. This generally takes the form of regional ministries and civil servants that are separate from the main central ministries and administration, and although it is possible to have a high degree of administrative devolution without legislative devolution (as in Scotland), the existence of regional legislatures or parliaments normally implies an accompanying separate regional administrative system. Administrative decentralisation falls below the level of subordinate powers that we would define as devolution. It normally is taken to mean the existence in the regions of major offices of central ministries and agencies whose civil servants have an above-average degree of discretion in the decisions they can make at the regional level. In practice, such decentralisation can be almost as powerful as full legislative and administrative devolution. It is important, however, not to confuse devolution and decentralisation, for whereas the former can be seen essentially as the granting of new economic and political sovereignty to institutions at a regional level, decentralisation is really a limited increase in the regional levels of administrative discretion within the existing administrative structure of central government.

Both for reasons of convenience and for analytical purposes, we shall use the term devolution to mean a political system in which one or more regions in a nation state are enjoying both legislative and administrative devolution, with an accompanying degree of sovereignty over economic and political affairs that stops short of those implied by federalism.

The Pressures for Devolution

Discussion of the devolution issue has grown steadily during the last decade, but it is often forgotten that similar demands for increased regional autonomy have become relatively commonplace in other developed economies, particularly in Western Europe, since the mid-1960s. In some regions devolution arguments are merely the continuing expression of a distinct regional consciousness or awareness, as in Bavaria, the Jura and perhaps North East England, and usually they are not accompanied by an active local political movement. Indeed, evidence presented to the Kilbrandon committee (Great Britain, 1973; Craven, 1975) suggested that all the major British regions had a distinct regional identity and an expressed desire for greater regional control of their affairs. Thus if equal devolution of powers was to be granted by central government to all such regions, devolution would represent a genuine shift of beliefs regarding the desired level of economic control over regionally oriented functions. The present piecemeal approach is open to less flattering interpretations.

Where strong regional political parties become an active vehicle for the expression of demands for autonomy, asymmetrical devolution, partly reflecting regional bargaining power, is likely to emerge as a constitutional form, at least in the short run. Before looking in detail at the arguments for devolution and its economic implications, it is important to have some understanding of why powerful regional demands for autonomy may arise. The reasons for the development of distinct and powerful political forces in sub-national regions are complex, and although each case tends to display a number of unique features, nearly all share certain common factors that have helped regional politicians shape a general feeling of discontent into movements that can present effective challenges to the existing central governments.

There are almost invariably strong historical grounds for particular regions regarding themselves as something more than mere regions. Within any geographical area there are always centripetal and centrifugal economic and political forces in operation and as the balance of these forces alters, a new political equilibrium may emerge. Historically, many of the areas now pressing for some degree of local autonomy or self-government had their present territorial structures determined in periods of conflict when dominant regions and states expanded their boundaries to include peripheral areas that were previously independent or parts of other states. Cooperative reasons for uniting individual smaller states into larger entities have also occurred, as for instance with the British experience where the national boundary has been in part cooperatively determined.

The existence of well-defined economic and cultural regions is a necessary condition for regional political movements to emerge, and the impetus for autonomy tends to accelerate in an area where the population perceives the existence of significant differences in history, language and culture between itself and the inhabitants of other regions within the nation state. The tendency for such distinct regions to persist in a nation state over long periods of time may also reflect an incomplete integration of the region into the economy and society as a whole. The cultural and historical bases of demands for regional autonomy may be strengthened if the region is spatially peripheral to the dominant economic and political centres of the nation state, and if the citizens in such regions feel that they are far removed from the locus of real economic and political power. This may result in citizens of the periphery perceiving that they constitute an isolated minority which is unable to participate effectively in the political and administrative systems under which it is governed. In turn, this effect may be compounded by a more understandable belief that the periphery is excluded, by location, from the relatively well-rewarded job opportunities of the dominant regions, and also from a variety of public and private consumption activities that are solely centrally located.

The condition of the regional economy may also shape pressures for change. A sense of personal disadvantage may be heightened if the regions of the periphery have had expanded export bases that are now undergoing a long process of decline. The existing dependence of such peripheral regions on declining primary or industrial sectors means that their real rate of economic growth may be below that of the nation as a whole, and this produces all the usual symptoms of relative economic stagnation. Heavy unemployment, low activity rates, lower incomes (frequently rein- forced by higher real regional prices) and poorer economic and social overhead capital combine to produce persistently high levels of outmigration (which, if biased towards the young, the enterprising and the skilled, pro- duces a resentment at the long-term impact of a regional 'brain-drain', although it may also improve the region's receipts of private transfers in its invisibles account) and a continued reliance upon direct subsidisation by the rest of the nation. Such subsidisation may in turn engender a resentment at dependence by the receiving region and a simultaneous resentment at diverting resources by the prosperous regions, which consider themselves entitled to the profits of their success (Wilson, chapter 4 of this volume).

The problems of peripheral regions have long been recognised by economists (Robinson, 1969; Hansen, 1974) as producing political effects, but more recently it has been realised that what is important is not so much the actual levels of economic disadvantage as the perception of them by the regions concerned. Indeed, in most European countries the deployment of active regional policies and the growing ubiquity of national economic policies have meant that the interregional differences within nations of a wide range of economic and social indicators have been appreciably reduced. However, part of this reduction in spatial disparity has recently been due to a comparatively greater deterioration in the indicators in the more prosperous areas, especially in the wake of the 1973–74 world recession (Randall, chapter 5 of this volume). The determinants of interregional differences in the perception of relative economic and political disadvantages is an extremely interesting research area that has so far remained virgin territory for the regional analyst, despite its obvious importance for policy makers.

A further intriguing research issue concerns the factors that cause such disillusion to be translated into direct political action, and more especially, into forms of political activity that threaten to remove a region from a national political system. One interesting possibility concerns the use of an 'exit–voice' framework (Hirschman, 1970) to analyse the demand for devolution, whereby the inhabitants of regions begin to demand (voice) an improvement in their conditions when it becomes more difficult for individuals to leave (exit) the declining areas to seek better economic opportunities elsewhere (Firn, 1977b). However, much more work is required to understand the forces that cause regions, such as Scotland, to switch from an 'exiting' to a 'voicing' form of behaviour, although the substantial narrowing of interregional differentials in Great Britain may be one of the more important factors.

One final point that is worth making here is that it is possible for both the degree and the intensity of the pressures for devolution to differ quite markedly among regions in the same country, because of the existence of different cultural, economic and political traditions. This can perhaps be most clearly seen within the British Isles, where such factors have resulted in unique systems of regional government existing in or being proposed for Scotland, Wales, Northern Ireland, the Channel Isles, the Isle of Man, and the Shetland Islands (which have achieved a degree of autonomous taxation powers relating to the oil facilities located there). Thus, the tasks of administering the nation state can be seriously complicated by virtue of the central government having continuously to take account of the demands and needs of a heterogenous collection of sub-national administrative, political, and legislative, structures and systems.[2]

Devolutionary Pressures and Responses: the Scottish Example

The pressures for devolution, as well as the responses by central government, are well illustrated by the case of Scotland. In Scotland, Union with England has always been subject to waves of criticism, although such attacks have been historically based on romantic patriotism rather than detailed economic arguments. Bills to introduce 'Home Rule' for Scotland were a feature of successive Parliaments after the First World War until 1928 when national economic and political concerns came to dominate government discussion.[3] The devolution issue lay dormant until 1968 when regional political interests, now focusing on the economic disadvantages of London-based government, were sufficiently powerful to persuade the Government to set up the Royal Commission on the Constitution in April 1969 under Lord Kilbrandon.

The Royal Commission took four years to examine the constitutional options that it considered were open to the United Kingdom. Volumes of evidence were collected and a wide range of economic and political expertise was utilised. However, when it finally reported in 1973, it was far from unanimous in the recommendations of its members and thus it did little to clarify the situation with regard to the best form of government for Scotland and Wales, although it did reach an overall broad conclusion that some form of devolution was desirable (Great Britain, 1973). But the context of the political economic environment in which the Royal Commission operated changed substantially between its establishment in 1969 and its reporting in 1973. Particularly important in this respect was the discovery, in 1970, of oil and gas in the North Sea around the Scottish coast. The poor absolute and relative performance of the Scottish economy, along with prospective North Sea oil revenues, became central in the devolution debate. Central government became crucially involved in the discussions surrounding the use of oil revenues and many Scottish politicians, aware that the direct benefits of oil exploitation were limited in relation to the massive indirect effects that principally benefited the rest of the United Kingdom, saw independence or devolution as a vehicle for obtaining or retaining a vastly increased proportion of North Sea benefits. It is probably this factor rather than any altruism towards the Scots that has resulted in the pragmatic, asymmetrical devolution arrangements of the 1978 Scotland Act (Great Britain, 1978a). The return of the Labour Government in 1974 saw the long process of translating the Royal Commission's recommendations into legislative proposals. A new urgency was given to the debate with the substantially larger representation of Scottish Nationalist MPs in Parliament following the two elections of 1974. Moreover, in the 1970s the increasing probability of minority governments made major parties peculiarly sensitive to the geographic bases of their political power.

A series of White Papers on devolution followed (Great Britain 1974; 1975), and eventually the Scotland and Wales Bill was introduced into the House of Commons in November 1976. Bitterly opposed by the majority of Conservative MPs and by a substantial proportion of the Labour Party (especially the MPs from assisted areas outside Scotland and Wales who feared that their industries would be put at a substantial disadvantage if Wales and especially Scotland were granted the powers contained in the Bill), the Bill failed to get through the House of Commons, and with the Labour Party struggling to hold on to power with a minority of seats, the proposals for devolution were finally deferred to the following parliamentary session. A further White Paper followed (Great Britain, 1977a) and in late 1977 separate devolution bills for Scotland and Wales were introduced into Parliament (Great Britain, 1977b; 1977c). A hard parliamentary battle began during which the Government suffered some notable defeats before eventual victory. At the time of writing the eventual outcome of the Acts (Great Britain, 1978a; 1978b) remains unpredictable as their implementation is dependent upon a favourable referendum vote. However, the events of the last decade, plus the prospect of oil, have ensured that the demand for devolution, at least in the case of Scotland, will not disappear.

Although the granting of legislative devolution is still to be implemented, it is important to recognise that past government responses to regional political pressures have now resulted in an advanced state of administrative devolution in Scotland. The retention, after the Union, of distinctive legal, educational and religious systems, has always meant that Scotland had a regionally unique administrative structure. These differences were emphasised and expanded in 1885 when the post of Secretary for Scotland was revived. The 'Home Rule' pressures of the 1920s resulted in further administrative change with the Scottish Secretary becoming a Minister of State and the Scottish Office being established to serve his needs.[4] After the transfer of the Scottish Office from London to Edinburgh in 1939, there were few changes in Scotland's administration until the 1960s, when the Scottish Office began to develop an interest and expertise in a number of hitherto centralised areas such as physical planning. The changes of the early 1960s were partly achieved by outside political pressure, but largely stemmed from a growing professional competence within the Scottish Office. The Scottish Development Department was created in 1962, and from it stemmed a number of highly regarded planning studies, including the 'growth areas' programme (Great Britain, 1963) and the plan for the Scottish economy (Great Britain, 1966). One could argue that, rather than being passively neutral, Scottish civil servants have played a major role in developing regional policies and plans. A unitary system need not have uniform effects.

The 1960s also saw a growth of interest in the Scottish economy, and the Scottish Office developed a steadily growing technical expertise, which included the formation of the Economics and Statistics Unit in 1970 and the Scottish Economic Planning Department in 1973. However, the most important parts of the central administration dealing directly with economic matters remained centralised through all these changes, and no one could conceive of a Scottish Treasury, or Scottish Departments of Industry or Employment. In 1975, however, under the pressure of the renewed demand for devolution outlined above, the administration of Regional Development Grants, selective financial assistance and the industrial sector schemes of Section 8 of the 1972 Industry Act were transferred to the Scottish Office from the Department of Industry, whose Scottish office than became the Industrial Development Division of the Scottish Economic Planning Department. Subsequently, the devolution White Paper (Great Britain, 1975) promised the transfer of most of the remodelled employment and training functions of the Manpower Services Commission, and this was implemented by 1977. The formation of the Scottish Development Agency in December 1975 marked the most dramatic step forward of all, for it effectively enabled the Scottish Office to invest directly in and support manufacturing enterprises, as well as undertake land and urban renewal schemes, build factories, and help small businesses and craftsmen. The exercise of these various powers means that Scotland is almost as powerful as a state in a federal nation, and there can be little doubt that the developments outlined above have favoured Scotland (and to a lesser extent Wales), relative to the English regions.

The increased integration of such administrative powers may be almost as effective as legislative devolution or even federal status in terms of ability to implement policy, especially since by far the largest number of daily operational decisions taken by the regional civil servants (e.g., who should receive loans, which public expenditure projects should be given priority, etc.) are not political matters in the traditional sense, but rather the natural outcome of working to set criteria that allow a degree of initiative. Further, the interests of Scotland, Wales and Northern Ireland in national policy areas are safeguarded by virtue of the fact that they alone of the regions of the country have direct representation (Secretaries of State) in the Cabinet of the central government. These Secretaries of State are uniquely able to present coherent regional views on national policy issues, being briefed about the possible impacts of decisions on these three regions by the civil servants in the three respective regional administrations.

This growth of decision making in Scotland, Wales and Northern Ireland has resulted in virtually complete administrative devolution being introduced. Thus there are now civil servants in regional ministries with considerable powers over expenditure and planning in three regions of the United Kingdom, for which they are not accountable to the regional populations concerned, except indirectly via the national Parliament. Not only is it possible for such civil servants to remain uninformative about the purpose, quality and value of the goods and services provided to these regional populations, it is also certain that they have considerable influence on the mix of goods and services provided in the regions, the speed with which they are provided, and the priority of areas that receive them. It may be claimed, therefore, that in each of these three regions of the

United Kingdom, and perhaps above all in Scotland, there is a regional government without a regional parliament, and because of this the case for legislative devolution can be made with some force.

The failure to grant legislative devolution to Scotland, when compared to the continued growth there of administrative devolution, appears to be based on a fear that the union of political control and a sophisticated regional administration might result in forces that threaten the essential unity of the country (Tait, 1975). This view has been encouraged by a failure to consider the economic-policy implications and possibilities of a devolved political system, which, in turn, reflects the absence of a comprehensive understanding of the nature of the economics of devolution.

There have been no economic arguments advanced, either for reversing the above trends in administrative and legislative devolution for Scotland or for the economic benefits that might be obtained from a more centralised system of administration in which all regions and all individuals were treated absolutely identically. Instead, those who have been against devolution have tended to rely on destructive criticism of their opponents' proposals without advancing a reasoned case to the contrary. Because of this, it can be argued that the main focus of the serious debate about regional political systems has been pulled towards the independence end of the continuum.

We have argued above that the essentially asymmetrical and unique nature of devolution makes it a difficult issue for economic analysis, and comprehensive examinations of the economics of devolution are still relatively rare. Perhaps the first, and still one of the most sophisticated contributions, is that of McCrone (1969), although a careful reading of the Kilbrandon Report and the recent series of White Papers on devolution does show a steady expansion in the range of issues that are considered relevant. In the rest of this chapter we shall concentrate on outlining the two areas that are central to the political economy of devolution, namely, the public finance of devolution and the regional economic development aspects of devolution.

The Public Finance of Devolution

In assessing both the level and the effectiveness of expenditure and revenue-raising powers that can be devolved to regions like Scotland and Wales, it is necessary to take into account the general economic and political objectives of central government. Most importantly, the central government is concerned to preserve, both initially and in the long term, the unity of the United Kingdom. To do this, government must ensure that it retains sufficient economic powers to achieve its own macro-economic and redistributive policies in the face of any contrary challenges from the regions. At the same time, government is concerned both with increasing local choice and democracy within the regions, and with raising the operational levels of efficiency in regional administrations. As will be seen, the simultaneous achievement of such a wide range of central and regional objectives will not be easy, especially in the area of devolved public finance (Dawson, 1972).

The Improvement in System Efficiency

A major argument, as yet unproven, in favour of devolution is that regional governments use resources more efficiently and effectively in undertaking expenditure at a regional level than central governments. The improvements in such resource utilisation would appear to result from gains in both technical and x-efficiency. The distinction between technical efficiency and x-efficiency by Leibenstein (1977) has some important implications for our understanding of the economic aspects of devolved government.

In terms of the technical efficiency of regional-resource use, it is assumed that a regional government and its administration will have a more informed understanding of local needs, problems, potentials and priorities, as well as the ability to interpret national and regional trends in greater detail. Decentralised statistical and economic-information systems can also help improve the efficiency of regional-resource use, and this will be reinforced by the shorter vertical chain of command between the main components of the regional political system. Such administrative improvements are typical of technical efficiency arguments for devolution (Wilson, 1976, p. 28), as are the gains to be made via implementing policy packages that more accurately represent the preferences of the regional population. However, the possibility cannot be ignored that devolution may be followed by increased system inefficiencies or costs, especially if the regional administrations are asked by an inexperienced regional government to implement non-feasible or non-reconcilable policy programmes that would have been avoided by central government.

Although improvement in technical efficiency is an important element of the pro-devolution case, the gains from higher levels of x-efficiency may be even more important in the long term. The oft-quoted example of such gains is the cathartic response of re-motivated regional populations who, having been granted autonomy, will work harder and more responsibly at their chosen occupations, and who will simultaneously display increased entrepreneurship and initiative. Empirical evidence to support this remains totally absent, but improved motivation is always claimed as one of the virtues of independence in the third world. Such improved motivation and innovation may apply to both governments and electorates, and although we may thus view efficiency stemming from such sources as an important separate input to the overall regional production function, '. . . we must keep in mind that it is unlike other inputs in that it cannot be purchased in the market place, nor is it readily measurable' (Leibenstein,

1977, p. 314). It is not clear, in the case of Scotland, why such effects will occur, particularly if workers and employers are still part of the national system of taxation, trade unions, etc.

Devolution and Public Expenditure

Two major arguments are commonly advanced in favour of the central government of a nation such as the United Kingdom devolving expenditure functions to lower levels of government. First, as shown in the previous section, a substantial proportion of this expenditure is already controlled by regionally decentralised administrations that are not politically directly accountable to the respective regional populations. Although this argument has special force in Scotland and Wales, it is also of some significance in the English regions. The second, and more complex, contention is that many of the expenditure functions undertaken centrally are not pure (national) public goods, and as such a more satisfactory provision of these could be undertaken at the regional level. This second argument is a principal economic rationale for devolving public expenditure, and although generally valid it is not, as we shall try to demonstrate, convincing in all circumstances.

The central theoretical principle of the regional public goods argument is quite simple: in a centralised system of provision the nation is deemed to be the operational level of the public consumer's 'club'. Thus individuals may be 'coerced' into experiencing a pattern of public expenditures that is at variance with their own preferences and consequently with the principles of efficient economic allocation. However, some public goods can be efficiently produced at sub-national levels and in such cases it is possible for regions to provide a level and mix of public provision that accords with local preferences. In turn, the conventional model (Tiebout, 1956) suggests that individuals and corporations may relocate in order to maximise their satisfaction in relation to the tax/expenditure characteristics of a local area.

However, the simple Tiebout model may be rather oversimplified in relation to the characteristics of regional economies. First, there may be instances of goods and services that do not fall naturally into an existing level of government and thus regions with devolved powers may have to coordinate expenditure policies with lower-level regions or regions without such powers. Central government can forestall this difficulty by retaining functions with marked and complex spillover patterns. For instance, it may be relatively simple to identify the interregional spillovers of a river pollution control scheme but it is unlikely that the benefits from locally financed university education could be traced through an integrated set of regions. Thus central governments should aim to devolve functions in which there are no scale economies operative above the regional level and where there are small or easily identifiable spillover effects among regions.

A second objection to the simple model is that it assumes individuals can select, or move to, their preferred fiscal area. In the British context the alternative choices are limited and the regions with devolved powers are sufficiently large that the costs of moving outside them are probably non-marginal. Hence, minority groups and areas within the regions scheduled for devolution may prefer to remain within the existing unitary framework. For instance, within Scotland the remoter northern and oil-related assisted areas may not wish to have their pattern of regional services dominated by the preferences and objectives of the urban and industrial areas of the Central Belt (Gaskin, 1975). With the advent of devolution it may also be the case that certain functions (for instance, public-sector housing policy) should be shifted upwards from a local to a regional (sub-national) level.

The Tiebout model also assumes that services are financed on a 'benefit-taxation' basis, but for some goods it may be either technically or politically impossible to introduce benefit taxes or user charges. If such a system is impossible, then regional-level fiscal policies may generate substantial interregional changes in real-income distribution: two identical consumers living in different regions may receive quite different real-income benefits from the consumption of the same volume of a given good. If corrective cross-subsidies are not transferable across fiscal boundaries then the economy may be segmented into a series of regions among which labour and factor mobility is seriously diminished or distorted. The present regional pattern of council house subsidies determined by local authorities is a good example of effective public-sector price distortions having important distributional and regional-development effects. One final reservation regarding the simple public-choice model is that it is relatively static and fails to consider the developmental consequences of public expenditures. The current pattern of central-government expenditure in the regions affects such areas as education, housing and transportation, all of which influence the long-run wealth-creating capacity of the region. Should central government permit a regional authority to reallocate expenditure from such functions to the public provision of non-wealth creating activities such as parks and sporting facilities? It is an important question, for such a reorientation might exacerbate the economic problems of a region, create greater demands for needs-related expenditure and grants from the central government, and distort national sectoral policies.[5]

The above discussion suggests that central government should devolve functions for which there are different regional preferences, in which national economies of scale are unimportant, in which spillovers are negligible or easily identifiable, and which are not likely to generate substantial non-transferable subsidy differences. The present list of functions proposed for devolution (regional taxation and industrial-development powers excepted) appears generally to satisfy these criteria (Great Britain, 1978).

The benefits from enhanced local fiscal choice and expenditure may be rather limited in practice. The degree of freedom available to alter in any significant manner either the level or the mix of public-sector (or indeed of induced private-sector) expenditure in a region with devolved powers, is reduced by a number of factors. Most patterns of expenditure at a regional level have a certain degree of inertia caused by the need to maintain currently supplied services, and thus expenditure on wages, replacement capital goods, and other inputs frequently leaves little scope for major shifts in resource use in the short term. In a relatively highly integrated nation such as the United Kingdom there are also difficulties in changing standards of provision for many public goods, and regional consumers are still continuing to move towards a national uniformity of tastes. The bureaucracy at a regional level may also tend to work in the direction of continuity of past standards and goals, as civil servants will still be heavily influenced by the legacy of existing internal analysis and advice, as well as the impacts of continued liaison with their equivalent colleagues in the central-government bureaucracy. All the above factors imply that the sovereignty of devolved regional legislatures may initially be quite limited and although improved fiscal choice remains an important theoretical argument for devolution, it has received scant political attention.

Regional Revenue and Taxation

Just as central government must select expenditure functions for devolution in relation to its overall objectives, so it must select a financing arrangement for the regional polity. A variety of financing systems are available for regional authorities: at one extreme, central government may fix a block grant that will fund the region's activities, and at the other, financing can arise from purely local taxation. The system chosen reflects central-government beliefs on a range of factors, and, at least in theory if not in practice, the system is evaluated on a Paretian basis.[6]

The centre must decide on the extent to which regional self-determination is a good thing and how far it is prepared to sacrifice macro-economic controls and objectives to that end. In this respect, under the present devolution proposals, which affect some 15 per cent of the United Kingdom Gross Domestic Product (GDP), the granting of full fiscal powers to regions may not seriously affect macro-economic targets determined at the centre. But the central authorities have to consider their commitment to interregional equalisation schemes. If an increasing proportion of taxation were to be retained and used within the revenue-generating region, then existing equalisation schemes would be less effective and require redesign.

The issue of regional and local taxation schemes in spatially compact and integrated economies such as the United Kingdom has received recent attention from two Royal Commissions (Great Britain, 1973; 1976).[7] This chapter has little new to add on this topic and our remarks on regional-taxation schemes are general rather than specific, though we note in passing that regional-taxation schemes are implemented in a large number of developed, integrated economies where central and local public expenditures are important. The objectives rather than the bases for regional taxation are probably the most important regional economic issues. Benefit-oriented taxation for the provision of local public goods is not likely to have harmful allocation, distribution or stabilisation effects. Regional taxation for stabilisation purposes is unlikely to occur given the importance of centrally controlled monetary flows, the extreme openness and the high import propensities of regions. Of greater significance at the regional level is the possibility that regions, if they could find a suitable non-mobile tax base, would raise revenues to stimulate industrial development or subsidise new enterprises. In a pure federal system such strategies, unless they shifted the overall investment demand schedule, could lead to a locational subsidy 'war' with zero-sum regional location gains.

Additional problems arise in the selection of a tax base for the regional polity, especially that of the openness of the regional economy compared to the national system. No matter what potential source of regional-level revenue one examines, the high degree of interregional integration makes the location of tax incidence uncertain unless all regions have similar systems and levels of taxation, and it must be remembered that devolution centres on an asymmetrical sub-national political system. It is an unfortunate paradox that the drive for devolution occurs in an era when national factor and product markets are becoming increasingly integrated. Thus corporate taxation becomes very difficult in a region where a majority of the operating enterprises are organisationally subordinate units that do not form profit centres for the companies involved (Firn, 1975). Personal taxation presents problems of equity and of evasion via individuals choosing to reside in the 'softest' tax region. Even more difficult to overcome is the fact that those regions that are the most likely candidates for devolution are the poorer ones, having simultaneously high public-sector subsidy and expenditure requirements and a relatively small personal tax base. Indirect taxation is also difficult to envisage in poor regions, and natural-resource taxation, especially of such potentially high-yielding sources as oil and gas, does not normally escape the control of central government.

Regional-taxation possibilities are further complicated by the desire of the central government to avoid a multiplicity of tax levels and systems operating within a single nation, as this can both substantially increase the administrative costs involved and also encourage evasion, thus reducing the net tax yield.[8] Because of this, most devolved tax systems aim to operate by shifting certain centrally administered taxes downwards to the regions (sales and turnover taxes being favourites for decentralisation), rather than by introducing yet more taxes, which may well be politically unacceptable in a heavily taxed nation.

The present devolution arrangements for Scotland and Wales have, after a thorough government examination of the possibilities for regional-taxation schemes (Great Britain, 1977a), initially ruled out the granting of direct revenue-raising powers to these two regions, and have instead proposed a block grant system, under which a lump sum will be allocated to the assemblies each year to cover the expenditure functions that will be devolved. This system will tend to minimise problems of vertical control in the macro-economic spheres, and, further, the assemblies are specifically required to take account of national economic policies in areas such as incomes and consumer affairs. But at the same time, it politicises the negotiations on the level of the block grant, does not guarantee any limit to the grant, and does not promise to be an easy way of maintaining interregional equity. There is a danger that Scottish and Welsh aspirations for revenue may run ahead of the resources allocated to them via the block grant, especially in the presence of annual North Sea revenues equivalent to 60 per cent of Scottish GDP.

Reference has already been made to regional transfers via public expenditure and taxation policies and to the increased regional scrutiny and rivalry over public allocations that may follow devolution (Wilson, chapter 4 of this volume). The previously favoured public expenditure position of regions such as Scotland, which may have reflected a genuine long-term desire to attain regional parity, may now have to be forsaken if Scotland demands a calculated basis for local expenditures. Devolutionists, keen to argue the efficiency benefits of local expenditures, must beware that similar rational arguments will not reduce the size of the Scottish expenditure budget if devolution is to be a long-term political success. The budgetary losses could easily outweigh the benefits of local choice.

Devolution and Regional Policy

This final section is not concerned with traditional regional policy, since it has been covered in Part 1 of this volume. Instead, we intend to examine three key issues where devolution comes into direct contact with the existing framework of regional economic development theories and policies.

The Possibility of Devolved Economic Policies
Little thought has so far been given to the types of economic policy that might be employed by devolved regional governments, although it is possible that in the near future the United Kingdom will see such regional administrations, complete with the full panoply of economic ministers, civil servants and advisers. What will be the objectives that such a regional government will attempt to pursue? What will be the policy measures and tools that

it will employ? What will be the chances of the regional government being successful in its efforts? These are all questions of fundamental importance, yet it is clear that so far very little attention has been paid to them, either by central government or by those actively involved in the debate.

In examining this critical area, it must first of all be borne in mind that a region operates in a different context from a nation. First, the local economy is very much more open than a national one, even if the latter is a member of a customs union such as the European Community. Thus, the freedom of action of a regional government is greatly reduced and will tend to be more responsive than initiatory, which in turn may influence the policy objectives pursued. Second, in the sectors of the regional economy producing marketed outputs, the regional government will almost certainly be faced with a continued trend towards integration of regional enterprises into national and international corporate structures, as well as a growing (national) public-sector presence. Third, the development of a distinct regional administration could, unless care is exercised to avoid the possibility, result in the civil servant in the region being *more* isolated from national economic policy formulation, which again would reinforce the move to a responsive style of economic policy. None of these possibilities in themselves is an argument against devolution, but they do represent some of the difficulties that new regional administrations will face.

Because of the above, it is certain that the economic-policy objectives followed by a regional government will be largely a reflection of national goals, although it is possible to conceive of a situation where regional–national goal conflicts could occur, as is discussed below. At a more general level, it can be assumed that the longer-term economic objectives of a regional government will include increasing the region's relative rate of economic growth, lowering the region's level of economic dependence (and thus reducing its reliance on fiscal and other types of interregional transfers), and improving the region's ability to respond flexibly and effectively to the changing pressures upon it from internal and external sources. It is assumed that within these broad goals there will be detailed spatial and sectoral objectives, as well as the more usual desire to maximise the efficiency of resource utilisation. But even broad economic-policy objectives such as these assume a fairly sophisticated theoretical and practical understanding of how a regional economy operates, and it also presupposes that thought has been given to the formulation of coordinated regional-development policies. In these areas of regional economics it cannot be denied that much remains to be done, although the work of Tinbergen (1967), and more recently Lindbeck (1976), would seem to provide regional-policy theorists and practitioners with a basis from which to start.

The question of the tools of regional economic policy is even more complex, for few of the national mechanisms for controlling an economy are capable of effective devolution. The chief means of implementing policy decisions will obviously be through the use of a region's expenditure in those areas where it has coordinating and planning competence, but it may well rely on more specific mechanisms and institutions to tackle detailed policy objectives, an example being the use of regional-development corporations in regional industrial policies. But the political backing and potential threat of secession that will lie behind the regional government could well result in its most effective policy tool being its ability to bargain with national ministers and central-government departments.

It is obviously impossible to predict the success that a devolved government would have in achieving its policy objectives, but if its major regional-growth goals were attained, it could produce an interesting conflict between regional economic growth and interregional equity that has been little discussed so far in the devolution debate.

Interregional Growth and Equity
Outside the world of static equilibrium theory the concept of interregional balance is one that has never been fully investigated by regional economists, and yet it is something that lies at the very centre of the devolution debate. If regions, dissatisfied with their relative economic status within the nation, demand and are granted a large measure of autonomy, and then use their newly gained economic sovereignty to improve their relative economic performance, it is obvious that the existing, perhaps traditional, interregional differences in levels of development will be changed.

At both national and international levels, development economics has shown that growth proceeds in an unbalanced fashion (see, for example, Hirschman, 1958), and the evidence from economic historians would seem to show that this has also been the normal mode for regional development, with different industries, enterprises and entrepreneurs stimulating and leading growth at different periods. Consequently, as the distributions of industries and enterprises are not interregionally even, different regions have alternately led and lagged in the process of overall national economic growth, and this would suggest that interregional growth disparities are a normal feature of development.

In the post-war period there has emerged the view, obviously deep-seated in government and the civil service, that regional policy must concern itself with striving for an essential equality between regions and that, because of this, regional policy must continue to be administered from the centre.[9] The desire to maintain interregional parity (a concept that has conveniently never been defined) obviously stems from fears that effective interregional competition might develop in the area of industrial development, for example, and thus produce wasteful expenditure on industrial-promotion schemes. There is also the concern that competition could result in interregional trade barriers (Great Britain, 1975, para. 20), although with the degree of integration existing in the United Kingdom, fears regarding the latter would seem to be completely groundless. It is, however, interesting to note that in the United States, growing rivalry between states, or more accurately between groups of states, is beginning to give cause for concern (Jusenius and Ledebur, 1977).

Yet, and here the basic conflict within the concept of devolution emerges starkly, unless the regions that demand and are granted devolution are also allowed to use their new autonomy to try to improve their economic position, the advantages of devolution will be diminished, with increased benefits from devolution only arising in relation to fiscal choice. If this happens, the drive for political independence will be reinforced. If less attention is paid in future to the interregional-parity goal, it might be argued that a removal of checks to interregional competition will also produce an improvement in national economic growth, accepting the Hirschman thesis. Of course, in the real world, the alternatives are never so stark, and it would be surprising if any region with devolved government could make a substantial change in its comparative growth rate, purely on the basis of its own policies, at least in the short term. Nevertheless, the fears that devolution would put Scotland and Wales at a real long-term economic advantage over the other regions played a large part in the defeat of the Scotland and Wales Bill in the House of Commons in early 1977. Again, in late 1978, MPs from the English assisted areas voiced similar concerns in their opposition to devolution.

Regional Industrial Policy
The emphasis on increased economic autonomy, which forms one of the essential policy objectives likely to be encountered in a region with devolved government represents a sharp break with the past tradition of centralist intervention in regional economic development. A regional orientation towards greater economic self-determination is an important component in the economics of devolution, as it effectively concentrates analytical attention on the constraints and weaknesses that are present *within* a regional economy, and this in turn results in policy measures designed to improve the supply capability and efficiency of the local industrial and commercial sectors. This emphasis on what has come to be termed indigenous growth, as distinct from the externally based development that is typical of traditional regional policies, is an important advance, but it is one that is hard to translate into effective action (Segal, chapter 10 of this volume).

Post-war regional policies have certainly achieved much in terms of providing new employment opportunities for regions such as Scotland (Moore and Rhodes, 1974), and have helped these regions diversify away from their old industrial bases towards the newer high-technology sectors. Indeed, this has been so marked in Scotland that it has developed a greater degree of similarity in its industrial structure to the national average than any other region (Gardner and Dougharty, 1977, p. 80). But behind such relative improvements there is the knowledge that many of the regional industries, especially in the critical export-oriented manufacturing sectors, remain heavily subsidised and non-competitive due to such factors as weaknesses related to the age and vintage of their capital stock, the low productivity of much of their workforces, the absence of modern effective management, and a reliance on externally generated technology. It is now being increasingly realised that such weaknesses may be best tackled by the introduction of detailed sector-based regional industrial strategies (Firn, 1977a), involving the use of regional-development agencies, such as the Scottish Development Agency, that have the ability to understand the detailed workings of major industrial sectors, as well as the financial resources necessary to engage in schemes to improve regional industries and enterprises. This emphasis on improving regional industrial competitiveness becomes more important in the context of an international decline in the role of manufacturing sectors, increased third-world competition, and the growth in protectionism in international trade. Legislative devolution is not a necessary concomitant of such a strategy. However, a successful Scottish Development Agency may be imperative for effective devolution in Scotland.

The central government and its advisers have unfortunately shown little evidence of detailed thinking about the industrial-development aspects of devolution,[10] and yet the industrial expectations raised by the prospects of devolution have run substantially ahead of the possibilities of implementation. It must be remembered that most of the major industrial developments that will take place in regions such as Scotland, either with or without devolution, will have non-regional origins. But despite this, regional industrial policies have a role to play in such areas as the encouragement of local entrepreneurship, the provision of adequate industrial premises, and more importantly the development of a more micro-oriented view of the region's problems and potential. This latter requirement is essential if the direct investment and assistance powers of such bodies as the Scottish Development Agency are to be employed in the catalytic fashion that is envisaged. There is also a need to ensure, in the case of the United Kingdom, that regional industrial strategies are coordinated with the national strategies and, indeed, with those of the European Community, but this in turn requires a much improved understanding of regional industrial economies at a sectoral and sub-sectoral level. It is in this area that the Scottish Development Agency, for instance, intends to be active, in the belief that profitable investments in Scottish companies can only be made on the basis of comprehensive and continuing appraisals of the prospects for their respective industries. This new and important orientation in regional policies has so far received little detailed consideration from regional analysts,[11] but it is one which will form the core of the economic-development policies that might be expected under devolution.

Notes

1. The special, and in some ways atypical, case of Northern Ireland will not be discussed in detail here, even though it has experienced varying degrees of administrative and legislative devolution (Wilson, 1976).

2. Britain is not without experience of such complexity. The British Empire at its height (say between 1900 and 1914) contained a bewildering range of constitutional systems, ranging from Dominion Status to mere protectorates, all of which had to be more or less administered by the Colonial Office in London.

3. For detailed histories of the long history of devolution and the government response, see Kellas (1976) and Harvie (1977).

4. A brief history of the early days of the Scottish Office can be found in Hanham (1969), whilst recent developments are covered in Kellas (1976).

5. This particular issue may become more important in Britain because of increasing public ownership of manufacturing industry. If a regional government wishes to build infrastructure, and if essential capital components can only be supplied at a loss via a nationalised industry, the classic dilemma emerges.

6. One comment on the Paretian approach to devolution is noteworthy: 'once real-world assumptions are allowed full play, the Paretian case for political decentralisation evaporates in its entirety. For the world in which local governments are provided only with partial taxation powers, supplemented by substantial grants-in-aid from central government, and in which the process of fiscal decentralisation is one in which decisions about the scale of provision are made at central government level, and only decisions about the design of activity are delegated to lower layers, is not the world of Tiebout' (Rowley and Peacock, 1975, pp. 130–1).

7. Official and unofficial taxation proposals suggested for devolution are referred to in Great Britain (1975, paras. 106–10 and paras. 227–9), Heald (1975), Wilson (1976) and Great Britain (1977a, paras. 5–65).

8. In the United Kingdom, taxation appears to be increasing system costs. The late 1960s and early 1970s have seen a number of suggestions for new forms of taxation: new local income taxes were proposed by the Layfield Report (Great Britain, 1976) and the first devolution proposals of the 1974 Labour Government suggested new regional surcharges on the local authority rates (Great Britain, 1974). Attempts at radically revising the whole tax system, via the introduction of tax-credits, were suggested, but never got further than the outlining of possibilities in a government Green Paper.

9. A statement of this view that the maintenance of interregional parity is paramount was provided by the Royal Commission on the Constitution (Great Britain, 1976, Vol. 1, paras. 605–7), although the key sentence seems to reflect a basic contradiction: 'In general, although under a system of devolution the central government would still need to control expenditure *for the purpose of equalising regional growth and levels of employment*, this control would be exercised in relation to expenditure still in central hands, and not to any great extent over regional expenditure' [emphasis added]. This would seem to show that a degree of confusion exists in the minds of those responsible for drafting devolution legislation about the relationship between interregional economic parity and the possibility of devolved economic powers. The implied contradictions appear to be largely irreconcilable.

10. For an example of the views of devolved industrial-development policies typically held by government advisers and civil servants the reader is referred to Smallwood (1976).

11. The impact of devolution and decentralisation upon regional policy is briefly discussed in Firn (1977a), Kellas (1977) and Moore and Rhodes (1977).

References

Craven, E. (ed) (1975) *Regional Devolution and Social Policy*. London: Macmillan.

Dawson, D. (1972) *Revenue and Equalisation in Australia, Canada, West Germany and the U.S.A.* Research Paper, No. 9, Royal Commission on the Constitution. London: HMSO.

Firn, J. R. (1975) 'External Control and Regional Development: the Case of Scotland', *Environment and Planning*, Vol. 7, pp. 393–414.

Firn, J. R. (1977a) 'Industrial Policy' in D. I. Mackay (ed.), *Scotland 1980: The Economics of Self-Government*. Edinburgh: Q Press.

Firn, J. R. (1977b) 'Devolution: an Exit-voice Model of Regional Policy', paper presented to the British Association meeting, University of Aston, September 1977.

Gardner, J. W. and Dougharty, J. E. (1977) 'Regional Accounts: Further Estimates for 1975, including regional fixed investment', *Economic Trends* No. 289, pp. 79–98.

Gaskin, M. (1975) 'Centre and Region in Regional Policy' in M. Sant (ed.), *Regional Policy and Planning for Europe*. London: Saxon House.

Great Britain (1963) Scottish Office, Development Department. *Central Scotland: A Programme for Development and Growth*. Cmnd. 2188. Edinburgh: HMSO.

Great Britain (1966) Scottish Office. *The Scottish Economy 1965 to 1970: A Plan for Expansion*. Cmnd. 2864. Edinburgh: HMSO.

Great Britain (1973) Royal Commission on the Constitution. *Report*. Vol. 1, Cmnd. 5460; Vol. II, Cmnd. 5460–I. London: HMSO.

Great Britain (1974) Privy Council Office. *Devolution within the United Kingdom. Some Alternatives for Discussion*. London: HMSO.

Great Britain (1975) Lord President of the Council. *Our Changing Democracy Devolution to Scotland and Wales*. Cmnd. 6348. London: HMSO.

Great Britain (1976) Royal Commission on Local Government Finance. *Report*. Cmnd. 6543. London: HMSO.

Great Britain (1977a) Lord President of the Council. *Devolution: Financing the Devolved Services*. Cmnd. 6890. London: HMSO.

Great Britain (1977b) House of Commons. *Scotland Bill*. London: HMSO.

Great Britain (1977c) House of Commons. *Wales Bill*. London: HMSO.

Great Britain (1978a) Public Acts. *The Scotland Act, 1978*. London: HMSO.

Great Britain (1978b) Public Acts. *The Wales Act, 1978*. London: HMSO.

Hanham, H. W. (1969) 'The Development of the Scottish Office' in J. N. Wolfe (ed.), *Government and Nationalism in Scotland*. Edinburgh: Edinburgh University Press.

Hansen, N. (ed.) (1974) *Public Policy and Regional Economic Development*. Cambridge, Mass.: Ballinger.

Harvie, C. (1977) *Scotland and Nationalism: Scottish Society and Politics, 1707–1977*. London: Allen and Unwin.

Heald, D. A. (1975) 'Financing Devolution', *National Westminster Bank Quarterly Review*, November, pp. 6–16.

Hirschman, A. O. (1958) *The Strategy of Economic Development*. New Haven, Conn.: Yale University Press.

Hirschman, A. O. (1970) *Exit, Voice and Loyalty: Responses to Decline in Firms, Organisations and States*. Cambridge, Mass.: Harvard University Press.

Jusenius, C. L. and Ledebur, L. C. (1977) 'The Northern Tier and the Sunbelt: Conflict or Cooperation?' *Challenge*, Vol. 20, pp. 44–9.

Kellas, J. G. (1976) *The Scottish Political System* (2nd ed.), London: Cambridge University Press.

Kellas, J. G. (1977) 'Decentralisation and Devolution: Policy making in education and regional development in Scotland', paper presented to the European Conference for Political Research, West Berlin, March-April, 1977.

Leibenstein, H. (1977) 'x-Efficiency, Technical Efficiency, and Incomplete Information Use: A Comment', *Economic Development and Cultural Change*, Vol. 25, pp. 311–16.

Lindbeck, A. (1976) 'Stabilisation Policies in Open Economies with Endogenous Politicians', *American Economic Review*, Vol. 66, pp. 9–19.

McCrone, G. (1969) *Scotland's Future: The Economics of Nationalism*. Oxford: Basil Blackwell.

Moore, B. and Rhodes, J. (1974) Regional Policy and the Scottish Economy', *Scottish Journal of Political Economy*, Vol. 21, pp. 215–36.

Moore, B. and Rhodes, J. (1977) 'The Economic and Financial Implications of Devolution', paper presented to the British Association meeting, University of Aston, September 1977.

Robinson, E. A. G. (ed.) (1969) *Backward Areas in Advanced Countries*. New York: St Martin's Press.

Rowley, C. K. and Peacock, A. T. (1975) *Welfare Economics: A Liberal Restatement.* London: Martin Robertson.

Smallwood, C. (1976) 'Financing the Assembly', *New Edinburgh Review*, No. 31, pp. 22–8.

Tait, A. (1975) 'The Economics of Devolution—A Knife Edge Problem', Fraser of Allander Institute, Glasgow, Speculative Paper, No. 2.

Tiebout, C. M. (1956) 'A Pure Theory of Local Expenditure', *Journal of Political Economy*, Vol. 64, pp. 416–24.

Tinbergen, J. (1967) *Economic Policy: Principles and Design.* Amsterdam: North-Holland.

Wilson, T. (1976) 'Devolution and Public Finance', *Three Banks Review*, No. 112, pp. 3–29.

CHAPTER 14

The National Industrial Strategy and Regional Policy

Gordon C. Cameron*

Introduction

At present the national economy is facing a now familiar set of problems. A low growth rate, high unemployment and under-utilised capacity, difficulties with the non-oil balance of payments and an internationally high rate of inflation are all causes of concern. Policies to control wages and prices and a general restraint on public expenditure represent government attempts to manage the domestic economy in the short run. For the longer run there is a growing consensus that the current ills of the economy are partly due to an excessive growth in the public sector, which, on the whole, produces non-tradeable and non-exportable goods and services and provides limited opportunities for productivity growth, but also to a persistent decline in the international competitiveness of manufacturing activity. For the first problem, the Wilson and Callaghan Governments have shown a willingness to control the rate of public expenditure growth, thereby freeing resources for more directly productive activities. For the second they have developed an 'Industrial Strategy', the objectives of which have been outlined by the Secretary of State for Industry, Mr Varley, and involve the '. . . patient building up of viable industrial capacity at sectoral and plant level . . .' (Varley, 1976).

This strategy, which covers the whole of the United Kingdom, has four component parts: planning agreements between the government and major companies; financial aid to achieve industrial change in the private sector; state intervention into and involvement with private economic activity through special state agencies; and diagnostic exercises and cooperative planning covering roughly forty key manufacturing sectors. Ostensibly, each one of these components has been selected so as to improve productivity growth over the medium-to-long run. Institutionally, they are to be the

* Department of Town and Regional Planning and Centre for Urban and Regional Research, University of Glasgow. Several of the tables in this chapter were prepared by Derrick Johnstone who has provided the author with excellent research support and ideas. Naturally, he bears no responsibility for any remaining errors of fact or judgement.

building blocks of a new and flexible relationship between government, the trade unions and private industrial enterprise, based on the recognition of the interdependence of decision making in a mixed economy. Thus the planning agreements are seen as mechanisms for linking government financial aid to *major companies* in the private sector within a clear programme of investment, product development, finance and marketing. The broad theme running through *financial assistance*, both general and selective, is that of improved competitiveness through productivity growth. *State intervention* through the National Enterprise Board and associated agencies is also geared to aiding companies and sectors to restructure, to the identification of growth opportunities and to the solution of specific problems retarding the growth of particular companies and sectors. Finally, and at a broader industrial sectoral level, the *planning exercises* are attempts to draw management, unions and the government together in a search for methods of eradicating constraints on the growth of industries in which the nation should have a comparative advantage.

Taken together, these initiatives represent a commitment to a much more vigorous and much more subtle industrial strategy than has ever been attempted in the nation before. But they raise an intriguing question. For over forty years, albeit with periods of lesser concern, British governments, Conservative and Labour alike, have used a battery of measures to encourage private activity to accelerate the development of certain regions of the nation (the assisted areas) allegedly suffering from weaknesses in their economic structure. And yet, if national industrial policy is increasingly concerned with national manufacturing efficiency and competitiveness, is regional policy, with its emphasis on aiding the less prosperous regions, an unnecessary restraint upon future manufacturing competitiveness? Conversely, is it appropriate to argue, as was done in the National Plan (Great Britain, 1965), that regional policy '. . . has a key role to play in the achievement of faster growth. One of its major aims is to make use of the reserves of unused labour in some regions of the country and to speed up industrial growth where it is lagging'.

Even if these questions are unanswerable in precise technical terms or unlikely to be posed in this form because of politicians' unwillingness to specify explicit trade-offs between policy goals, there remains the essential need to provide coherence between the mechanisms chosen for a national industrial strategy and for regional development. A recent report (Organisation for Economic Co-operation and Development, 1975) captures this well when it argues: 'As . . . regional policies assume a more active and autonomous role it becomes increasingly important to understand the interaction between them and national industrial policies so as to avoid possible inconsistencies and conflicts'. Equally, as the national industrial policy becomes more explicit and clearly more concerned with the performance of particular sectors, there is a corresponding need to re-evaluate the objectives and methods of regional industrial policy. And if the reader remains unconvinced, one statistic may carry some conviction. In the years between 1968 and 1974, approximately 60 per cent of manufacturing investment in the United Kingdom was made by establishments in the assisted areas.[1]

This chapter is concerned with identifying the interactions between national industrial policy and regional policy, and the mechanisms necessary to achieve some coherence between the policy goals of industrial growth and regional development. It has a simple structure. In the next section we attempt to explore some major elements in the emergence of the Industrial Strategy. In the subsequent sections, we investigate the possibilities for conflict between the two levels of policy and in the last section we attempt to establish some simple guidelines for the harmonious integration of national industrial policy and regional policy.

The Industrial Strategy

The Industrial Strategy (Great Britain, 1975b) was initiated in November 1975. Broadly speaking, it falls into the category of industrial policy, which is concerned with solving specific restraints on the performance of key sectors. In this it is neither the broad macro-type 'planning' that seeks to create the general framework in which private economic activity can flourish, nor a formal indicatively planned system with precise and inter-related targets for all of the major productive sectors, government, investment, trade and so on. Instead the stress is upon a 'framework of analysis and discussion of practical means of improving performance in particular industries—a framework which will be reviewed and adjusted in the light of experience and changing circumstances' (Great Britain, 1975c, p. 1). From the very beginning the focus has been upon particular types of industry, notably those that, on past performance, are likely to be successful in the future, those with a disappointing recent history but with good prospects for competitive performance and those whose performance is critical to the success of other industries.

Initially, thirty-seven sectors were chosen for particular scrutiny both with regard to short-term barriers to their growth in the hoped-for upturn in the economy of 1976–77, but also with respect to their medium-term growth problems and especially their contribution to the balance of payments. The thirty-seven Sector Working Parties, made up of industry, trade union and government representatives, and operating within and through the National Economic Development Council (NEDC), reported in August and December of 1976. Of the problems specified, the government decided to pay most attention to: (a) facilitating exports, particularly the possible deficiences in export credit finance, and the problems of breaking into new markets; (b) industrial restructuring and particularly the rationalising of production in individual firms; and (c) product development. In addition, the government, whilst encouraging the sector working parties to move on from the generalities of how exports are to be increased and imports reduced to the specifics of investment, employment, finance, technology and methods of improved operation, has introduced a number of schemes to encourage investment in particular sectors and schemes to accelerate investment more generally and also has chosen five sectors for detailed attention. These five sectors (industrial engines, construction equipment, office machinery, electronic components, domestic electrical appliances) were selected because they are amongst the world leaders, or can be expected to make significant improvement in their performance. The objective is to use industrial policy to encourage these sectors to achieve specified medium-term objectives and particularly to improve their rate of return on capital invested, their capacity to export and their ability to satisfy domestic markets hitherto dependent upon imports. As yet no evaluation has been made of the benefits of the Industrial Strategy, though it is abundantly clear that its success will depend upon the willingness of individual companies to accept the recommendations of the tripartite committees and to adopt them into actual company practice. In the next section we address ourselves not to these micro considerations but to some general aspects of assistance to industry.

Assistance to Industry: Some General Criteria

We have seen that the Industrial Strategy is an attempt by government, in collaboration with the private sector and with trade unions, to improve the performance of a large part of manufacturing activity and more specifically to encourage competitiveness in a limited range of sectors. But here the precise context and objective of assistance is at stake. If, as seems appropriate given the whole thrust of the strategy, the emphasis is upon the rate of return, viability and sound commercial practice, then how does this relate to social goals such as the relief of heavy localised unemployment or a better interregional balance of economic activity? This question has been recognised as having validity. Thus, according to the Department of Industry (Great Britain, 1976c, p. 37), where the private costs and benefits are less than the ultimate social costs and benefits flowing from any set of private decisions, there may be a case for government involvement to redress the divergence through information provision, taxation, planning controls or subsidies, viz:

> The most clear cut illustration of this is provided by the programmes, whether general or selective for promoting employment in the Development Areas, which in one form or another have been the longest established and most continuous of all Government schemes for industry.

Here, the oft-stated purpose is to avoid the social costs of unemployment and migration that flow from private decisions not to invest in certain areas on a scale sufficient to absorb the available supply of local labour. But if the Industrial Strategy is to succeed, how should claims for assistance from industry *outside* areas of high unemployment be judged? The note cited above also argues (Great Britain, 1976c, p. 36):

> ... apart from the employment criterion the balance of payments has provided the most clearly identifiable [criterion] ... Rationalisation schemes represent a particular type of situation in which the benefits ... accrue to an industry as a whole and in consequence to the balance of payments rather than to particular companies and therefore ... justify help from the Government. Sectors of industry indentified as of special significance to the economy or designated as of high priority in any strategic policy of government should be given *due priority* in assessing the merits of applications for assistance.

In terms of efficiency the Department of Industry seeks to aid companies that can become viable and maintain profitability with specified and controlled aid and thereafter do not require continuing subsidies apart from those such as Regional Development Grants available to all eligible enterprises. However, and here the dilemma is portrayed by two possibly opposed objectives (Great Britain, 1976c, p. 38),

> In considering an assessment of viability along with an assessment of the social costs and benefits involved, the Government have always been more prepared to give proposals for assistance the benefit of the doubt as to the prospects of viability where the social cost of withholding assistance would be particularly high—in particular in areas of persistent high unemployment where the creation of new employment is specially difficult.

Contrast this statement with another in the same document (Great Britain, 1976c, p. 38):

> The Government are conscious of the desire for job security and of the natural resentment of redundancy which require that all reasonable measures should be taken to provide the former and avoid or cushion the impact of the latter. *At the same time* if we are to break through the balance of payments constraint and thus achieve more room for manoeuvre in the management of the economy *more and not less emphasis will be required on competitiveness* in home and export markets. Failure to achieve this would in the end be the enemy of job security. [Emphasis added]

The objective of the next section is to scrutinise how the government has pursued these different objectives of policy—the provision or retention of employment in areas of high localised unemployment and the increased competitiveness of particular sectors of manufacturing activity. This section will focus upon the post-1972 Industry Act period and will discuss the issues in the context of aggregate expenditure decisions.

Trends in Regional Expenditure

For our purposes it is imperative to answer one seemingly simple question: has regional policy already been submerged beneath the national Industrial Strategy? The short answer is 'no'. However, there is an important qualification. As assistance to particular sectors and companies, *regardless* of their location, has been a rapidly growing feature of central-government activity in the last eighteen months (and this at a time of public expenditure restraints), then regional policy, with its emphasis upon shaping the distribution of economic activity so as to favour the assisted areas, has become relatively less important. This is not to argue the case in terms of absolute expenditure on regional objectives. Indeed, if we compare real regional preferential expenditures in 1971–72 (the year of the enactment of the Industry Act) with those in 1975–76, then there has been a growth overall of nearly one-third in real terms, from £507m to £669m (Great Britain, 1977a, p. 370). Information on employment likely to be generated by regional preferential assistance also confirms this picture of a strong commitment to regional employment goals. Thus the level of job creation after 1972 compares very favourably with a period generally recognised to be one of 'strong' regional policy—the mid-to-late 1960s.[2] And finally, anticipated regional expenditure, as outlined in the White Paper on Public Expenditure (Great Britain, 1977c) shows a further strong commitment in the period 1977–79.[3]

Specifics of the Industrial Strategy

Despite this apparently clear-cut picture, we have to dig deeper and look at some specific actions of the government, partly under the 1972 Industry Act, and partly under the 1975 Industry Act. Four areas are of particular concern: those measures under Section 7 of the 1972 Act to aid companies in acute financial difficulties; Section 8 measures to encourage investment in particular sectors; contra-cyclical schemes to accelerate investment and assistance under Section 8; and the 1975 Industry Act, which sets a framework for the buying of state equity in particular companies.

Section 7 Assistance under the 1972 Industry Act (Assistance 'Outside the Normal Guidelines')

One part of the 1972 Act gives the Secretary of State powers to aid companies facing severe financial difficulties on a 'once-and-for-all' basis. This assistance can be used to aid companies anywhere in the United Kingdom, regardless of the local employment situation. In practice, it has been used almost entirely within the context of Special Development Areas, Development Areas or Intermediate Areas and as such has been a regional-aid measure.[4]

Section 8 Assistance under the 1972 Industry Act (Sectoral Schemes)

A very different picture emerges with schemes to encourage investment in thirteen industrial sectors regardless of the location of the establishments putting forward the projects for subsidy.[5] So far over £260m has been allocated for assistance in individual manufacturing sectors and just under one quarter (£56m) has actually been committed after approval of a submitted request for project assistance (Great Britain, 1977b, Appendix U). The objective of these schemes is to encourage investment, whether to modernise and perhaps extend facilities or alternatively to rationalise production facilities. The assistance given varies from scheme to scheme, but normally consists of grants for plant and equipment and for buildings, interest relief grants and sometimes loans to encourage rationalisation and mergers, and grants to cover consultancy fees for small firms involved in project investments. Some of these schemes appear to have been very successful. For example, over 500 of the country's 825 ferrous foundries applied for project assistance (under the Ferrous Foundries Scheme) in the eighteen months between August 1975 and December 1976. By the termination date of the scheme, 193 projects already had been approved and assistance amounting to £32.6m offered. These schemes are expected to generate a total investment of £150.4m with a total expansion of capacity of 23 per cent for iron foundries and 17 per cent for steel foundries. In addition, employment generated by these projects will result in a manning increase of about 2,500 (Great Britain, 1977a, p. 227).

The apparent success of this and other sectoral schemes has led the Government to extend their coverage so that they now embrace thirteen separate industries. But from our point of view the question is, how do they affect or relate to regional policy? One obvious fact is that companies in specified sectors within the assisted areas may claim the 'normal' regional incentives *and* the sectoral assistance. Let us take, for example, an electric component manufacturer in a Development Area in Scotland engaged on a £1m development. Half of the project costs are accounted for by a new building and half are involved in plant and machinery installations. This company can claim 20 per cent as a Regional Development Grant on both the building and plant and machinery components. This would amount to a total grant of £200,000. Of the residue of £800,000 project costs, additional sectoral assistance could be claimed provided only that the total subsidy to total project costs did not exceed 50 per cent. In particular industries, especially those already concentrated within the assisted areas, many companies have taken advantage of this 'double form' of subsidy. For example, in the Wool Textile Scheme, of the £4.5m offered to companies to modernise or eliminate marginal capacity, almost 90 per cent has been obtained by assisted-area plants. Certainly, this form of sectoral assistance is less absolutely than that given to the industry in the form of Regional Development Grants.[6] Nonetheless, to an industry locationally concentrated within the assisted areas, the effect of sectoral assistance is that of an additional regional aid. The experience of the Wool Textile Scheme seems to have been paralleled by that of the Clothing Scheme where over £11m of the total project costs of £13.6m in submitted and considered applications for assistance have emanated from assisted-area plants. By contrast, less than half of the schemes considered under the Foundry Scheme came from assisted-area plants and only approximately 40 per cent of the machine-tool companies seeking aid came from assisted areas (Great Britain, 1976c).

Though many of these schemes are at an early stage of development, it is possible to trace out some of their broad implications for regional development. First, in all of the schemes, existing assisted-area producers are eligible for these sectoral subsidies and many seem to have taken advantage of them. However, since they are nationwide in their coverage, these sectoral schemes are liable both to encourage and to provide justifications for expansions and rationalisations *in situ* and thereby reduce the propensity of plants within these sectors to establish production units within the assisted areas. This reduced mobility is made even more likely by the marked easing of the Industrial Development Certificate (IDC) control, which, in recent years, has almost ceased to be a mechanism for refusing permission to expand in non-assisted areas. Instead, it appears to be being used as a 'registration' device whereby government can scrutinise proposed developments and either press the financial advantages of developing in an assisted area or encourage *in situ* investment.

Accelerated Investment

The objective of this scheme (in operation from April 1975 to September 1976) was to bring forward planned investment projects that had been shelved or postponed. This was established partly as a contra-cyclical device to create employment but also to stimulate investment in advance of the hoped-for upturn in the economy. Each project had to satisfy four criteria: (a) the project should be for new investment or modernisation (or both) and the capital cost, including working capital, should normally exceed £500,000 (initially, the lower limit was £2.5m); (b) the project should be a net addition to the firm's capital investment programme in this country, which would not take place or would be deferred but for government assistance; (c) the project should be commercially sound and lead to an improvement in the balance of payments; (d) construction work on the installation of plant should be planned to commence before September 1976.

There is very little doubt that this scheme has been successful. The £78m in interest relief grants and £6m in loans are ultimately expected to generate £640m of net investment. The bulk of this investment is expected to be undertaken before the end of 1979, which suggests a net annual

TABLE 14.1

Regional distribution of accelerated projects, April 1975–September 1976.

Area	Projects	Assistance in millions of pounds	Project cost in millions of pounds
West Midlands	24	8.5	75.2
North Western	14	7.9	59.0
Eastern	13	15.7	112.9
East Midlands	11	1.6	18.0
South Western	11	3.0	33.2
Yorks. & Humberside	11	21.8	138.5
London & South East	10	2.2	23.0
Scotland	6	2.1	33.3
North	5	3.1	31.3
Wales	2	2.2	15.7
Other[a]	13	16.2	100.8
Total	120	£84.3 m	£640.9 m

[a] Project spread over more than one region

Source: Great Britain (1977a, p. 154).

addition to aggregate manufacturing investment in the period 1976–79 of approximately £200m or 4–6 per cent. Once again the assisted areas appear to have benefited, as Table 14.1 makes clear, although the new-employment impact falls much more heavily outside these areas, with 8,300 jobs being created in non-assisted areas, 1,800 jobs in assisted areas, and 2,700 spread over assisted and non-assisted areas. As with the sector schemes, the development of competitive capacity prior to the upturn in demand is liable to reduce the propensity of some plants to seek an assisted-area location for development. In previous cycles, the flow of new plants into the assisted areas was most vigorous at the point when capacity restraints and labour shortages prevented increased *in situ* output (Ashcroft and Taylor, chapter 2 of this volume). Then, the combination of IDC controls, exhortation, inducements, a more elastic supply of labour at given wage rates and the availability of advance factories in the assisted areas encouraged a favourable response. The modernisation and extension of plant and buildings prior to a demand upturn is liable to provide some companies with scope for accommodating a relatively vigorous growth in output, and *time* to plan and construct further *in situ* expansions or modernisations.

The Government has decided to extend this type of scheme but on even more liberal terms. The *Selective Investment Scheme* will be available to any company in manufacturing anywhere in the country that has a development project of more than £500,000. £100m have been allocated initially for projects that enhance 'national prosperity . . . but which would not go forward in the proposed form without help from the Government'.

For example, help would be justified if a project was carried out earlier, on a larger scale, more efficiently or with a larger range of product developments. But all projects must be commercially viable and result in a significant improvement in performance. Indeed, assistance (normally interest relief grants) will be linked to performance on a case-by-case basis.

The introduction of these schemes (sectoral, accelerated and selective) represents a fundamental shift in governmental policy towards industry. Not only does it reflect a move away from standard 'blanket' subsidies towards a philosophy of case-by-case appraisal, specific-project support and more effective inducement, but it also indicates an increased willingness to aid companies where they are presently located rather than an attempt to shift the geography of their investment decisions. It is, of course, the case that companies covered by these schemes and operating within the assisted areas can obtain higher inducement benefits than companies in non-assisted areas. In this narrow technical sense there has been no diminution in the relative financial advantage of investing in an assisted area. But in a context where (a) many non-assisted-area companies will prefer the simplicity and certainty of an *in situ* expansion with guaranteed financial assistance as compared to the greater uncertainty of an assisted-area location even with ostensibly higher financial assistance (and this for how long?) and (b) IDC policy increasingly reflects the cogency of private-company arguments that operating performance, exports and import-substitution production are all liable to be affected adversely in the short-to-medium run if *in situ* expansions are refused, the outcome is liable to be a reduced flow of new investment projects from non-assisted to assisted-area locales.

The Role of the National Enterprise Board (*NEB*)

The prime objective of the NEB is the extension of public ownership into areas of profitable manufacturing industry so that the NEB shall make acquisitions on its own account only when it sees the prospect of an adequate rate of return within a reasonable period. However, another of NEB's purposes is to aid the creation or safeguarding of employment opportunities in areas of high unemployment. Accordingly, the Secretary of State will make 'directions . . . to provide assistance from time to time to companies in financial or managerial difficulties' (Great Britain, 1976a, p. 634), and he will have to be satisfied (Great Britain, 1976a, p. 634) that

    1. the NEB can effectively discharge its employment responsibilities in areas of high unemployment particularly through regional offices in the North East and North West of England; and

    2. in considering the expansion of an existing operation or the development of a new undertaking, the NEB examines the case for location in an area of high unemployment with a particular intent to site the development *if possible* in such an area. [Emphasis added]

The language used here is significant. Areas of high unemployment are not defined, and whilst there is some degree of commitment to the North and the North West Regions (and Scotland and Wales have their own agencies), it is entirely conceivable that any area of relatively high localised unemployment could qualify for the NEB's special attention, particularly in view of the convergence of regional unemployment rates (Randall, chapter 5 of this volume). And even the special attention given to the assisted areas need not result in action, if there is a strong case, on grounds of commercial viability, against siting developments in such areas.

Drawing all these strands together we can see that more rapid assisted-area development remains a goal of government; but the importance of competitiveness, a healthy balance of payments and the equalisation of unemployment rates among regions has resulted in the generation of a range of schemes and individual exercises of aid that benefit companies and sectors outside the assisted areas. Furthermore, although assisted-area plants have benefited from the sectoral schemes and the accelerated investment scheme, their overall net effect is liable to be a reduced propensity for non-assisted-area plants to locate new projects in assisted areas. This is especially so given the sharply reduced use of the IDC control as a weapon for refusing *in situ* or non-assisted-area growth, and no *net improvement* in assisted-area inducements to offset this greatly enhanced capacity to expand *in situ*.

Some Possible Conflicts

If the arguments of the preceding section are correct, then the success of regional policy over the next few years will be much more dependent than hitherto upon the performance of establishments already operating within the assisted areas. But equally, the success of the Industrial Strategy is dependent upon increasing the number of sectors of industry that are able to withstand import competition and to export a high proportion of their output. And this, in turn, requires concentration upon the techniques, the products and the establishments at the most efficient end of the competitiveness spectrum. An NEDC document (Great Britain, 1974, p. 13) captures this well when it argues:

> . . . the average level of industrial productivity is low in most sectors of manufacturing compared with other industrial economies like Germany and the U.S. Around this low average there is a fairly wide spread of productivity in different establishments within particular industries. As time passes there appears to be little tendency for the average to move closer in the U.K. to the moving horizon of the most efficient techniques and organisation. The observed growth of productivity reflects an industrial structure which changes only slowly. It measures the trend of technical progress rather than industry's potential—under different circumstances—for getting closer to this moving horizon . . . If the growth of average industrial productivity is to be faster than the old trend rate in the U.K. there will need to be progressive changes in the balance of output resulting from an increasing concentration of investment upon the techniques, the products and the establishments at the most efficient end of the spectrum.

But how are assisted-area plants likely to fare if there is a growing concentration upon the establishments at the upper end of the competitiveness spectrum? Is the spectrum of assisted-area establishment performance, sector-by-sector, generally at the lower end of each sector's spectrum seen from a United Kingdom level? Or do the assisted-area establishments tend to have approximately similar levels and ranges of competitive performance as their non-assisted-area counterparts? The answer to these questions is central to the development of regional policy. If public subsidies are used to improve the competitiveness of assisted-area plants that are currently operating well below the national average (an average that itself is internationally uncompetitive), then even a successful use of subsidies may simply move the assisted-area plants up to the national average.) Accordingly, the creation or retention of employment in assisted areas through the use of subsidies may ameliorate social problems but do little to move the average productivity of given national sectors towards the internationally moving horizon of best techniques and practice. Put in a different way, if the nation is to change its manufacturing competitiveness trend upwards, it will need to put more emphasis upon the accelerated growth of plants that are competitive already, rather than upon those that use up scarce national capital in achieving a level of performance that is already below an internationally competitive average.

In contrast to all of this, if assisted-area plants mirror national-average performances, then there is no inherent conflict between a regional policy that generates a preferred locational pattern of job opportunities and a policy favouring faster industrial growth nationally. To test whether assisted-area plants and sectors are nationally competitive or not would be a mammoth task, calling for measurements of operating efficiency, changes in market shares, export competitiveness, the internal use of subsidies, and so on. We cannot attempt such a diagnosis but instead we focus upon a simple indicator of assisted-area performance. Essentially we are concerned to establish whether *net output per employee* is above, much the same as or below that of sectors within the non-assisted areas. We have taken the year of most recent statistics (1971) as a reasonable date for this cross-sectional analysis (which comes eight years after the introduction of vigorous regional-policy measures), though obviously a later year would have been preferable.

There are several conceptual and operational difficulties associated with the use of net output per employee as a measure of efficiency (Swales, chapter 11 of this volume). Conceptually, there are inherent biases in using a single-factor measure of productivity. Operationally, industrial categories may cover a wide range of output mix within a given class; regions may specialise in different stages of the production process; firms may be multilocational but only report statistics in their headquarters region. Even where appropriate statistics are collected (Fessey and Browning, 1971), they may not be publicly available. Accordingly, there are large gaps in the data, especially in highly concentrated industries. Bearing all of these points in mind, we shall now examine the productivity record, region-by-region, of all manufacturing industry, of the five 'super' sectors chosen for rapid development under the Industrial Strategy and finally of the engineering industries that form a very large proportion of the approximately forty industries chosen for special scrutiny under the Industrial Strategy. Initially, thirty-seven industries were chosen for special consideration, but this was increased.

Patterns of Productivity

In terms of general productivity the assisted areas do not appear to operate at a disadvantage. Indeed, they tend to have a higher net output per employee than two of the major non-assisted areas (the East Midlands and West Midlands), though the South East and also East Anglia had higher productivity than all of the assisted areas in 1971. Furthermore, the relatively strong showing of the assisted areas is not accounted for by a level of wage and salary payments that inflates the regional net output figure. Thus, if we subtract from regional net output the aggregate of wages and salaries paid and divide the residue by the number of employees, we have a rough measure of employees' contributions to net output. Once again both the South East and East Anglia have a productivity lead but the assisted areas taken as a whole have exactly the same level of productivity as the non-assisted areas as a whole. This pattern is repeated when we disaggregate the overall productivity figures by Order Headings (Table 14.2). Once again the South East stands out clearly with an above-average productivity in no less than fifteen of the sixteen order headings. In contrast, one allegedly 'strong' region (the West Midlands) has only four headings with above-average productivity and is bettered by no less than four of the assisted areas. Indeed, if we portray by means of a frequency distribution (weighted by employment) the difference in produc-tivity between the assisted areas and the non-assisted areas, then there is very little to choose between the distribution of the two sets and all of the difference is explained by the productivity performance of the South East (Table 14.3).

This generally favourable finding on the assisted areas' productivity seems, however, to be subject to an important qualification. Capital expendi-ture in manufacturing industry has been heavily concentrated in the assisted areas and to a degree far in excess of these areas' net output and employment shares. Table 14.4 shows the assisted areas' share of net capital expenditure for 1963, 1968, 1970 and every year between 1971 and 1974. It also shows, for selected years, shares of net output and of employment. What is surprising about Table 14.4 is that the assisted areas persistently had

310

Regional Policy in an Emerging Political Framework

TABLE 14.2

Net output per employee as a percentage of the United Kingdom average (manufacturing industry, Orders 3–19), 1971

	All Manufac-turing	3	4	5	6	7	8	9	10/11	12	13	14	15	16	17	18	19	Number of orders with above-average productivity
Assisted areas:																		
North	96.9	88.4	30.9	98.0	71.2	110.5	92.6	75.5	81.2	110.1	108.2	93.9	102.1	97.5	95.4	101.9	104.5	6
Yorks. & Humberside	90.9	81.6	79.6	92.8	96.1	95.7	98.1	93.4	91.3	97.8	100.0	105.6	88.7	107.1	92.5	84.5	91.8	2
South West	100.8	103.4	49.4	83.5	102.6	91.0	108.3	93.4	109.2	107.5	116.8	121.8	135.9	106.4	99.6	90.6	102.0	10
North West	98.8	92.0	143.1	102.5	106.8	91.0	89.3	98.7	95.0	99.6	92.3	98.0	92.9	105.0	97.1	90.7	93.9	4
Wales	101.6	88.7	106.6	87.8	109.4	97.3	90.3	100.0	98.6	94.7	130.1	88.8	83.1	110.0	97.5	115.2	90.2	5
Scotland	102.8	119.0	67.3	91.4	89.0	99.6	91.7	106.7	109.6	100.4	86.2	109.6	104.9	103.9	91.6	91.5	113.0	8
Northern Ireland	90.2	107.6	59.0	111.9	206.0	83.6	88.9	84.2	72.0	90.7	125.5	87.3	70.4	97.1	82.8	81.5	93.1	4
Non-assisted areas:																		
East Midlands	89.4	115.9	54.5	90.3	92.3	98.4	96.3	92.1	70.2	87.5	91.8	120.8	104.9	104.6	101.7	87.0	87.3	5
East Anglia	103.1	95.1	—	110.6	101.3	98.0	118.0	94.2	107.3	116.3	98.5	85.8	107.7	109.3	115.5	89.6	84.1	8
South East	110.2	103.7	128.5	108.3	103.0	110.5	104.2	112.4	106.4	104.8	116.8	100.5	107.0	115.3	104.6	111.5	97.9	15
West Midlands	93.3	90.8	35.7	90.1	110.3	93.4	90.3	85.5	105.0	96.5	114.8	73.1	90.8	76.1	95.0	86.7	116.7	4
Percentage by industry of all manufacturing's net output in the United Kingdom	100.0	13.1	1.3	9.2	6.4	13.0	1.9	9.2	10.6	6.2	6.0	0.4	3.3	4.0	3.1	8.1	4.1	—

Source: Great Britain (1975a).

TABLE 14.3

Net output per employee in manufacturing industry, 1971

	Net output per employee in thousands of pounds	Orders with net output per employee					
		at or above national average		more than 10 per cent below national average		more than 10 per cent above national average	
		Number	Percentage of manufacturing employment	Number	Percentage of manufacturing employment	Number	Percentage of manufacturing employment
Assisted areas:							
North	2.46	6	37.0	5	34.5	2	20.4
Yorks. & Humberside	2.31	3	20.7	4	21.5	—	—
South West	2.56	10	62.3	2	4.6	3	8.0
North West	2.58	4	26.1	1	1.4	1	2.5
Wales	2.58	6	54.8	4	17.2	3	13.8
Scotland	2.61	8	52.9	3	12.7	2	25.8
Northern Ireland	2.29	4	55.6	9	34.2	3	29.8
Non-assisted areas:							
East Midlands	2.27	5	29.7	5	19.3	2	15.0
East Anglia	2.62	8	44.2	4	25.4	4	12.1
South East	2.80	15	95.4	—	—	6	45.9
West Midlands	2.37	4	40.1	5	9.1	3	21.4
UNITED KINGDOM:	2.54						

Source: Great Britain (1976d, Table 10.2).

TABLE 14.4

Percentages of United Kingdom net output, employment and capital for manufacturing industry (assisted areas and non-assisted areas), selected years

Year		Percentage share	
		Assisted areas	Non-assisted areas
1963	Capital	53.2	46.7
	Employment	49.3	50.7
	Net output	47.8	52.2
1968	Capital	57.0	43.0
1970	Capital	61.0	39.0
1971	Capital	62.3	37.7
	Employment	49.6	50.4
	Net output	48.6	51.5
1972	Capital	61.6	38.4
	Net output	48.9	51.0
1973	Capital	57.7	42.3
1974	Capital	57.9	42.1

Source: figures on capital are taken from Great Britain (1976b, pp. 414–15) and figures on employment are taken from Great Britain (1975a).

a share of new-capital investment higher than their share of employment and (probably) their share of net output. In the earliest year, 1963, the disparity amongst these aggregates was not marked, though even here the assisted areas made heavier calls upon capital investment relative to output and employment than did the non-assisted areas. However, by the later years a marked disparity had developed between the assisted areas' call upon national investment and their share of national net output. The latter remained almost unchanged over the 1963–73 period whilst the investment share increased markedly reaching a peak of 62.3 per cent in 1971 but never falling below 57.0 per cent. With a relatively static share of employment over the period, this evidence suggests that the marginal net capital invested per worker in the assisted areas was substantially in excess of that for the non-assisted-area worker. Equally, the marginal-capital/marginal-output ratio was higher in the assisted areas.[7]

These figures generate an intriguing set of questions. On the face of it, it appears that assisted-area manufacturing is becoming more capital intensive than non-assisted-area manufacturing, and that the productivity of the new capital employed is lower. However, the heavier outlays upon new capital could reflect a number of different factors, amongst which the following four possibilities are worth considering: (a) a 'catching-up effect' after years of low investment when the average age of capital had increased and/or the technological appropriateness of capital had declined;

(b) a difference in the structure of industry between assisted and non-assisted areas, either in the type of product produced or the stage of production of a given product; (c) a heavier allocation of capital to areas of declining product demand leading to poor utilisation of capital; (d) a less effective utilisation of capital because of over-manning and other restrictive practices.

It was the conventional wisdom in the 1960s that explanation (a), the catching-up effect, was the reason for a high marginal-capital/marginal-output ratio in the assisted areas. With so much old and worn-out capital around, so the argument went, we could expect that heavy marginal additions to the capital stock would be required *for many years* before the average age and appropriateness of capital improved and the average-capital/average-output ratio fell. There is no simple way of testing this hypothesis, since we have no regional data on capital depreciation. However, it is not an argument that can be used indefinitely and it might be reasonable to have expected a more marked increase in the assisted areas' productivity relative to that of the non-assisted areas over a period as long as eleven years. The second explanation, namely that the structure of economic activity in the assisted areas is weighted by capital-intensive industries and/or that in given activities such areas concentrate upon the capital-intensive stages of production, carries much more conviction. It is certainly the case, as many studies have made clear (Chisholm and Oeppen, 1973), that the industrial structure of the assisted areas has become much more like that of the nation. But a closer scrutiny of which industries have invested most heavily in the assisted areas reveals a very interesting picture. If we break the seventeen Order Headings into five groups, then the unusually heavy concentration in the assisted areas has been in the group embracing coal, petroleum, chemical products and metal manufacture (Orders 4–6). In 1971 no less than 81 per cent of this group's capital expenditure was focused upon the assisted areas, and unlike all the other four groups, this was a proportion markedly out of line with the assisted areas' share of group net output.

The principal explanation for this discrepancy is quite straightforward. In 1971 metal manufacturing industries accounted for approximately 23 per cent of the net output of the coal, petroleum, chemicals, metals, group. However, they invested no less than 42 per cent (£357m) of the group's capital expenditure (£857m), which represents an 'excess' investment of £16om. And since most of the metal manufacturing industries are highly concentrated within the assisted areas, much of this 'excess investment' was in such areas and particularly in Yorkshire and Humberside where the British Steel Corporation was engaged in a major programme of capital modernisation. Thus, although the assisted areas have tended to place a heavy call upon capital resources and one that was in excess of their contribution to national net output, a major explanation for this 'extra' capital expenditure is found in the modernisation programme of the British Steel Corporation.

Productivity and the Industrial Strategy Sectors

The 'Super' Sectors

Up to this point we have looked at productivity for very broad industry groupings and all the evidence suggests that the assisted areas lag behind the South East but have, on average, a productivity level similar to that of the other non-assisted areas. When we scrutinise particular industries (and initially we look at the five 'super' sectors chosen for rapid development under the Industrial Strategy), the picture does not look so favourable for the assisted areas. The reader will recall that these 'super' sectors are industrial engines, construction equipment and mobile cranes, office machinery, electronic components and domestic electrical appliances. Of these sectors, one, electrical components, has already been chosen for sectoral assistance and all the others are thought to be particularly suitable for rapid development. The question that must be asked is as follows: is this rapid development likely to be focused heavily or even relatively heavily within the assisted areas or are the assisted areas likely to be 'also-rans' in the wake of the output growth of the non-assisted areas?

Using data on net output productivity for 1971 in these super sectors is not particularly revealing. The number of omissions from industrial engines is so great that no area conclusions can be drawn. In construction equipment, the non-assisted areas tend to have a strong productivity record whereas the assisted areas are much weaker. For office machinery, no general conclusions are possible but one fact is clear. The South East has a strong productivity position and dominates national employment with almost half of all employees being employed there. The position in electronic components is that three regions (the South East, the North West and the South West) have a strong productivity record, whereas everywhere else is weak. Once again the South East dominates employment with almost one out of every two employees located there. With the last sector (domestic electrical appliances), the data are too deficient to draw any general conclusions, though once again the South East has a marked productivity advantage and a fairly strong employment share.

Given these data differences in individual industries, we have looked at productivity for all super sectors together over the four years 1970 to 1973 (Table 14.5). This is more revealing and shows that the South East has a marked lead and also that there is very little difference between the performance of the assisted areas as compared to the non-assisted areas excluding the South East. We cannot speculate on the reasons for the disparity in productivity performances. However, we can conclude that in four of the five sectors the productivity advantage of the South East is quite marked and in two of the sectors the South East dominates employment. This suggests that South East companies are liable to be in an especially favourable position to take advantage of any organised

TABLE 14.5

Net output per employee in the super sectors in relation to the national average, 1970–73

	Observations	Number of sectors with net output per employee		
		at or above national average	more than 10 per cent below national average	more than 10 per cent above national average
Assisted areas:				
North	7	—	6	—
Yorks. & Humberside	7	—	7	—
North West	13	3	8	2
South West	15	1	12	1
Wales	5	—	5	—
Scotland	8	3	3	3
Northern Ireland	6	3	3	3
TOTAL	58	10	44	9
Non-assisted areas:				
East Midlands	9	2	4	—
East Anglia	11	—	9	—
South East	16	11	3	4
West Midlands	12	4	4	4
TOTAL	48	17	20	8

Note: Super Sectors consist of: Industrial Engines (MLH 334); Construction Equipment and Mobile Cranes (part of MLH 336 and part of MLH 337); Office Machinery (MLH 338); Electronic Components (MLH 364); Domestic Electrical Appliances (MLH 368).

Source: figures derived from various issues of the PA series of the *Business Monitor*.

efforts to improve sectoral performance. Thus an establishment that has already attained a relatively high productivity level is liable to generate a larger marginal growth in output from a given injection of investment funds than one that starts from a lower level of productivity. In the case of the first type of establishment, marginal improvements to basically sound technology and to appropriate production methods may yield high returns, whereas a lower level of productivity may reflect the need for a fundamental (and costly) change in technology and in working practices. We return to this point after the next sub-section, where we consider productivity in the seventeen engineering industries chosen for special attention under the Industrial Strategy.

Engineering Industries

A similar analysis to that carried out on the Super Sectors was completed for an additional seventeen Minimum List Heading (MLH) industries within engineering. In twelve cases the MLH corresponded to a Sector Working Party (SWP) operating under the Industrial Strategy. In the other cases, the MLH heading did not exactly coincide with an SWP but the data were generated as a reasonable indication of levels of productivity (Table 14.6). We have already suggested that the productivity performance of the assisted-

TABLE 14.6
Engineering industries selected for Sector Working Parties and for productivity analyses

Name	Minimum List Heading	Comments
Machine tools	332 and 339.9	Analysed separately
Fluid power equipment	333 part ⎫	No way of separating out
Pumps and valves	333 part ⎭	from Census of Production figures
Textile machinery	335	
Industrial trucks	337.1	
Mining machinery	339.1	
Printing machinery	339.2	
Space heating, etc.	339.4	
Food and drink packaging machinery	339.7 ⎫ 339.8 ⎭	Not analysed separately
Process plant fabrications	341 (part) ⎫	No way of separating out
Constructional steel	341.4 ⎭	from Census figures
Gear transmission equipment	349.3	Data only for 349.1
Scientific instruments	354	
Heavy industrial equipment	361 ⎫	No way of separating
Industrial equipment	361 ⎭	
Telecommunications	363	
Electronic consumer goods	365.2	
Electronic computers	366	
Radar, radar and electronic capital goods	367	

areas plants in the super sectors was generally poorer than the performance of the South East. With the engineering industries the picture was even less favourable to the assisted areas. Table 14.7 shows that in 1971 over three-quarters of all the industries within the assisted areas operated at productivity levels below that of the nation as a whole. The one exception to this general pattern was Yorkshire and Humberside where almost as many industries operated above the national level as below it. In every other assisted area the picture was unfavourable. A similar conclusion applies to two of the non-assisted areas (West Midlands and East Midlands) where only one-third of all recorded industries operated at or above national productivity levels in 1971. With the two remaining regions, the South East showed a very marked lead position with fourteen out of sixteen industries operating at or above the national average. East Anglia was the only other region where there were more above-average than below-average industries.

The picture then is very clear. The South East had an exceptionally strong position when measured against other domestic regions and only two other regions (East Anglia and Yorkshire and Humberside) showed some signs of productivity strength. When we disaggregate this picture for 1971 by means of a frequency distribution, almost one-fifth of all the industries within the assisted areas operated at very low levels of productivity, here defined as less than 80 per cent of the national level. By contrast, within the non-assisted areas a roughly similar percentage operated at levels much in excess of the average (120 per cent and above). The other interesting feature is the high proportion of assisted-area industries operating just below the national average (90.0–99.9 per cent), with a similar high proportion operating at just above the average (100.0–109.9 per cent) in the non-assisted areas (Table 14.7). There is no evidence that the picture for 1971 was markedly different in 1970 or 1972.

In terms of individual industries there are three industries in which the South East dominated employment (more than 40 per cent of the national employment) and had a marked productivity lead (more than 15 per cent above average productivity). These three industries were: (a) Printing and book-binding machinery (MLH 339.2); (b) Broadcast receiving and sound reproduction equipment (MLH 365); (c) Electronic computers (MLH 366). In a further four industries the South East had between 25 per cent and 39 per cent of national employment and a high level of productivity (more than 15 per cent above the national average). These were: (a) Pumps, valves and compressors (MLH 333); (b) Mechanical handling equipment (MLH 337); (c) Ball and other roller bearings (MLH 339); (d) Telephone and telegraph apparatus (MLH 363). In all of these cases there is a *prima facie* case for asking whether the productivity advantage of the South East should be encouraged by an explicit government policy.

TABLE 14·7

Net output per employee in the Industrial Strategy engineering sectors in relation to the national average, 1970–72

| | Observations | | | Number of sectors with net output per employee | | | | | | | | |
| | | | | at or above national average | | | more than 10 per cent below national average | | | more than 10 per cent above national average | | |
	1970	1971	1972	1970	1971	1972	1970	1971	1972	1970	1971	1972
Assisted areas:												
North	9	11	10	5	2	3	1	5	6	3	1	2
Yorks. & Humberside	15	14	14	2	6	4	8	5	6	—	2	2
North West	14	15	13	2	2	3	8	7	8	2	1	—
South West	12	10	12	2	1	4	7	5	6	1	—	3
Wales	8	8	6	2	3	3	4	1	2	1	1	—
Scotland	12	10	9	3	3	3	7	5	5	2	2	2
Northern Ireland	6	7	8	2	2	1	4	5	3	2	2	1
TOTAL	76	75	69	18	19	21	39	33	35	11	9	10
Non-assisted areas:												
East Midlands	11	11	10	5	3	4	3	1	2	2	1	1
East Anglia	7	7	7	3	4	6	2	1	1	1	2	5
South East	16	16	14	15	14	11	—	1	—	11	9	4
West Midlands	13	11	13	3	4	8	7	5	4	1	1	3
TOTAL	47	45	44	26	25	29	12	8	7	15	13	13
Total of MLHs covered	17	17	16									
Percentage of cells where net output per head was unobtainable	28	32	31									

Source: figures derived from various issues of the PA series of the Business Monitor.

We return to this question in the concluding section. Finally, there is one industry (MLH 341, Industrial plant and steelwork) which is well represented within the assisted areas and which has very low productivity in at least four assisted areas. This industry presents a case for consideration as to its suitability for further growth within several of the assisted areas.

Conclusions

The last few years have seen the emergence of an industrial policy that emphasised problem-solving within industrial sectors selected because of their favourable growth prospects. This has not replaced regional policy with its emphasis upon bringing greater employment opportunities to regions that have experienced persistently high unemployment. But since unemployment has been high relative to the national average in a large number of regions (some of which do not fall within the category of assisted areas) and since the Government has shown a desire to aid major companies in their restructuring activities regardless of their location, the overall effect has been a spreading of subsidies over a much larger area of the nation. This has been accompanied by a marked easing of IDC controls and the operation of a number of schemes to encourage contra-cyclical investment, industrial restructuring and more rapid growth. The net effect of all of these activities has been to encourage growth *in situ* and to reduce the propensity of companies to establish plants within the assisted areas.

In the longer term a critical and unresolved question is whether there is a conflict between a policy that encourages growth within a limited number of given sectors and regional policy. We have argued that if there is very little difference between the productivity of industries in different regions of the country, then it is perfectly consistent for government to permit companies either to expand within the non-assisted areas or to set up within the assisted areas and thereby claim a higher level of subsidies. If a company chooses the extra subsidies, the real-resource cost of its development in the assisted area is likely to be no greater than if it had developed outside the assisted area. The social benefit achieved is the creation of local employment with only a transfer payment (the subsidy) as an offset, and even this may replace or partially replace existing transfer payments to the local unemployed. However, if the productivity of given industries is markedly lower in the assisted areas, then subsidies to encourage expansion in such areas are liable to reduce the overall national growth potential of such activities. We have carried out simple investigations of the available data to see whether there is a potential problem. Though our data are deficient in a number of respects, there is sufficient evidence to suggest that the South East possesses a clear productivity lead in a number of 'super sectors' and in most of the engineering industries chosen for rapid development under the Industrial Strategy. Only East Anglia approaches the South East in terms of productivity 'strength in depth'. All of the remaining assisted and non-assisted areas have a much more patchy productivity record.

A number of conclusions can be drawn from these findings. If the Industrial Strategy, with its special emphasis upon rapid growth in key sectors, succeeds, the major regional beneficiary will be the South East, precisely because this region has a heavy concentration of national employment in a high proportion of the selected industries. It may even be the case that incremental productivity gains may be more likely in the South East than elsewhere. Thus a company that starts from a relatively high productivity base may find it easier to convince its workforce of the necessity of further improving company productivity. By contrast, a company starting from a lower productivity base may require much greater perseverance to achieve national-average productivity, especially if the route forward necessitates making workers redundant in areas already suffering the socially and personally corrosive forces of unemployment. There is a second point. If certain *industries* have generated externalities in particular areas that permit high productivity performance, IDC policy should continually recognise this fact and only seek diversions to other regions if there is unequivocal evidence of unacceptable local social costs flowing from new developments in the South East and/or clear evidence that operating costs in the assisted areas are likely to be no higher, without subsidy, within a relatively short project-installation period. In this context we have provided some illustrations where the productivity advantage of the South East is so marked that it would make nonsense of an Industrial Strategy, which seeks competitiveness and rapid growth, to encourage companies to engage in the time-consuming process of establishing new assisted-area plants.

With regard to assisted-area subsidies, there appears to be no good economic reason why the level of subsidy in such areas should be higher for those *sectors* that have been selected under Sectoral Assistance Schemes and where the level of assisted-area productivity is low relative to non-assisted areas. Whilst there is a social justification for such a practice, it only makes economic sense if the level of assisted-area productivity is already relatively high. Subsidies in sectoral schemes should be used to make relatively strong companies commercially stronger and not to help weak companies nearer to the margin of competitiveness. Finally, assisted-area development will have to be based increasingly upon the development of new sectors of activity rather than 'stealing' growth from regions that have pioneered their development. For this reason the role of agencies like the Scottish and Welsh Development Agencies and the activities of the NEB will be pivotal.

Notes

1. This is a rough approximation since many of the assisted areas exist within given Economic Planning Regions and investment data only relate to Economic Planning Regions as a whole; see Table 14.9.

2. The estimated annual additional employment expected to arise from projects under the Local Employment Acts and Section 7 of the 1972 Industry Act in Special Development Areas, Development Areas and Intermediate Areas averaged 76,000 in 1966–1967 to 1968–1969; 80,000 in 1969–1970 to 1971–1972; and 88,000 in the period 1972–1973 to 1975–1976, the last period including some employment 'safeguarded' (Great Britain, 1976a, p. 385; 1976b, Appendix G, Table 6 and Appendix F, Table 1).

3. As a percentage of Trade, Industry and Employment expenditures, regional support and regeneration accounted for 24.2 per cent in 1976–77 and is expected to be 21.5 per cent in 1978–79.

4. In 1974–75 all the assistance went to companies in Special Development Areas. In 1975–76 the bulk of the assistance went to Ferranti, with its employment concentrated in Manchester and Edinburgh.

5. The industries are as follows: wool textiles; clothing; ferrous foundries; machine tools; paper and board; non-ferrous products; electronic components; printing machinery; textile machinery; poultry-meat processing; red-meat slaughtering; instrumentation and automation; drop forgings.

6. In 1975–76 the wool textile industry received £1.2m in aid under Section 7 of the 1972 Industry Act, £7.8m from Regional Development Grants and £3.9m from the sectoral scheme for the industry.

7. The 1971 marginal (net) capital expenditure per employee was £353 in the assisted areas and £210 in the non-assisted areas. Over the period 1963–71 net output in the assisted areas grew in money terms by just over £4,400m and this was associated with an annual increase in capital investment of £800m. Net output increased in the non-assisted areas by almost £4,600m but with a much lower annual growth in capital expenditure of £350m.

References

Chisholm, M. and Oeppen, J. (1973) *The Changing Pattern of Employment: Regional Specialisation and Industrial Localisation in Great Britain.* London: Croom Helm.

Fessey, M. C. and Browning, H. E. (1971) 'The Statistical Unit in Business Enquiries', *Statistical News*, No. 13, pp. 13.1–13.5.

Great Britain (1965) Department of Economic Affairs. *The National Plan.* Cmnd. 2764. London: HMSO.

Great Britain (1974) National Economic Development Council. 'Industrial Performance in the Longer Run: An Approach Through Investment', NEDC (74)31, London.

Great Britain (1975a) Central Statistical Office. *Census of Production for 1971.* London: HMSO.

Great Britain (1975b) Department of Industry. *An Approach to Industrial Strategy.* Cmnd. 6315. London: HMSO.

Great Britain (1975c) The Treasury. *Economic Progress Report.* No. 69, p. 1.

Great Britain (1976a) Department of Industry. *Trade and Industry*, Vol. 22, pp. 384–5 and 631–5.

Great Britain (1976b) Department of Industry. *Trade and Industry*, Vol. 24, pp. 414–5.

Great Britain (1976c) Department of Industry. *Annual Report of the 1972 Industry Act.* London: HMSO.

Great Britain (1976d) Central Statistical Office. *Regional Statistics*, No. 12, pp. 138–41 and 197–200.

Great Britain (1977a) Department of Industry. *Trade and Industry*, Vol. 26, pp. 153–5, 226–8, 243–4 and 370.
Great Britain (1977b) Department of Industry. *Annual Report of the 1972 Industry Act*. London: HMSO.
Great Britain (1977c) The Treasury. *Public Expenditure to 1979–80*. Cmnd. 6396. London: HMSO.
Organisation for Economic Co-operation and Development (1975) *Aims and Instruments of Industrial Policy*. Paris: Organisation for Economic Co-operation and Development.
Varley, E. (1976) Speech to the American Chamber of Commerce by Secretary of State for Industry, 13 January 1976 (reported in *Trade and Industry*, Vol. 22, p. 130).

Postscript

Duncan Maclennan and John B. Parr

The chapters of this volume have each provided an analysis of one aspect of regional policy. Some of these chapters viewed the general notion of a regional policy favourably, but others were strongly critical. Throughout the volume, however, a general tone of unease was expressed with respect to present regional policies. Rather than provide the reader with a summary of the individual chapters, some of the general themes and unresolved questions of the volume are discussed. More particularly, comment is made on the likelihood of the continuance of regional policy, the probable changes in the detail and scale of policy and the possibility of efficient regional policies being pursued in the 1980s.

The Challenge to Existing Policy

Criticisms of existing regional policies stem from a variety of economic viewpoints, and such challenges vary in strength from calls for the termination of policy to suggestions for relatively minor alterations to the existing approach. Three major challenges to regional policy can be identified. The most forceful attack on policy undoubtedly comes from those who believe that intervention at the regional level should not take place. This view is shared by two quite different groups. First, there are the proponents of the efficacy of the free-market system and, second, there are those who, though not enamoured with competitive-market solutions, maintain that the problems of income and unemployment differences are more meaningfully attacked on a non-spatial basis. In general, regional economic analysis can readily respond to the views of both groups. Economic development, encompassing the growth of income and employment opportunities, does not benefit all regions equally. The differential mobility of labour and capital, primarily reflecting spatial frictions not incorporated into the economic models underlying the free-market arguments, always tends to generate income and employment disparities across regions. If these differences are allowed to persist over time, then a distinctive, possibly insoluble, regional problem may emerge that can substantially condition future national economic development. The non-intervention arguments against regional policy thus appear to be faultily based in economic theory, in addition to being contrary to the norms of economic and social policy in Great Britain.

A second serious challenge to current policy is the contention that existing measures are ineffectual and that the impotence of regional policy stems from its inadequate scale. It is maintained that regional-policy expenditure has never reached the critical minimum level required to remove the regional economic problem permanently, and that existing policy has had only limited short-term benefits. To support this view, it is frequently argued that in the post-war period the regional problem in Great Britain has not decreased in magnitude and geographic extent. The tendency for regional unemployment differentials to narrow between the traditionally depressed and traditionally prosperous regions during the 1970s should not be allowed to conceal the fact that the absolute position of the problem regions has seriously deteriorated in the last decade. Nevertheless, this argument about the ineffectiveness of policy must be modified in view of the evidence that policy has diverted a considerable number of jobs to the assisted areas and that employment prospects in such areas, though still relatively poor, have been considerably enhanced by policy. Undoubtedly, a greater expenditure commitment to regional policy in the past could have further offset continued decline in the problem regions, though the possible adverse impact on the non-assisted regions and on national economic performance is not clear.

A third challenge to existing policy is concerned with the efficiency of policy instruments. Again there is a widely held view, which is reflected in this volume, that the instruments and strategies of existing policy are economically inefficient and that the benefits of limited expenditure are seriously circumscribed by policy inadequacies. There is a general feeling that policy is not sufficiently selective in the projects and areas which it supports and is often believed to sustain plants that do not require incentives to locate in the assisted areas. For instance, regional-policy support has only recently been discontinued for activities directly related to oil exploitation activities in Scotland that would not, in most circumstances, have considered alternative locations. Furthermore, it is increasingly felt that although current policy expenditures may raise aggregate demand in problem regions, the strategy of policy does not lead to a long-run reconstructive development of the regional economic base. These two final challenges to regional policy (the scale of policy and the instruments of policy) are sufficiently serious, or at least sufficiently worthy of closer consideration, that account is likely to be taken of them as policy is modified in the future.

The Evolving Economic Context

This volume has consistently stressed the need to revise and review regional policies as the condition of the national economy changes, and the differing economic experience of Great Britain between the 1960s and the 1970s has been widely referred to. The arguments stressed above against the present form of regional policy were for the most part deductively based and independent of the performance of the economy. However, before discussing major changes in the scale and scope of regional policy, it is worth considering whether the experience of the period 1972–77 represented an aberration in the performance of the British economy, or whether such conditions will be typical of the future. Undoubtedly, the post-war economic record has been relatively disappointing, but there are some grounds for believing that the economy may revive in the 1980s, particularly as a result of the benefits of North Sea oil. A number of commentators have suggested that in the next five years the inflation rate will fall to single figures, the balance of payments will be in surplus, interest rates will fall and real income growth (at around a relatively high post-war rate of 2–3 per cent) will occur. Already there are signs that constraints on public-policy expenditure will be relaxed, if only slightly, and there is a strong case for using available government revenue to stimulate employment, since unemployment is expected to remain at the historically high rate of around 6 per cent.

There is currently no evidence to suggest that as output growth occurs it will be equally distributed over all regions. Indeed, there must always remain the possibility that the underlying geographies of market accessibility, factor productivity and factor mobility, which contribute to the formation of the regional problem, have not improved in favour of assisted areas in the last five years. It may be that modest national economic expansion can be sustained solely by utilising labour and plant in the previously prosperous areas. The historic pattern of regional inequalities in Great Britain may thus reappear as the national economic performance improves. There is already growing concern that the unemployment relatives for Scotland and the North are once again deteriorating. It may be the case that the relatively improved economic performance of northern Britain in the period 1972–76 owes substantially more to oil-related development, and its complex multiplier effects, than has been estimated in the past.

It is possible in the reasonably near future that the pattern of economic performance among regions may return to a situation more in keeping with the period prior to the 1970s, and thus perpetuate the need for regional policy. It is unlikely, however, that the detail of policy would continue as at present or revert to past patterns. The experience of the recent period has tended to increase public surveillance of policy expenditure, and this may permit past proposals for the improvement of policy to be incorporated into new policy strategies. Further, the movements toward industrial, urban and devolution policies have now gained enough strength that they must ultimately have a bearing on regional policy. Regional policy in the 1980s cannot be modelled on the experiences of the 1960s, but it is likely to survive, nonetheless. Regional policy, independent of its economic merits or demerits, also has an operating momentum of its own. It is in the nature of economic-policy formulation in Great Britain that policy programmes, especially those that are politically sensitive and electorally significant, are not rapidly abandoned even if they are economically wasteful. As is indicated within the volume, there may be more positive reasons for a substantive regional policy, but momentum alone can be expected to ensure the existence of regional policy in the 1980s.

The New Regional Policy

Although it is reasonably certain that regional policy will continue well into the 1980s, it is no less certain that its present form and scale will undergo considerable modification. Currently, there is some dissatisfaction with the present size of the regional-policy budget, but relatively little speculation has occurred regarding the future levels of expenditure. It is unlikely that real expenditure on regional policy by the European Community will increase substantially in the medium term, so that any expansion of regional policy will therefore have to be domestically financed. The situation would change dramatically, however, if full economic and monetary union were to become a reality, since this would give a new significance and urgency to regional policy within the Community.

The improvement in economic performance, a relaxation of public-expenditure restrictions and the availability of North Sea oil revenues may all contribute to an expansion in the regional-policy budget. There is a widely expressed viewpoint at present, presumably based on political pressures rather than economic analysis, that revenues from North Sea oil should be used to expand regional policy. However, new industrial, urban and devolution policies are also competing through the political system for public funds. It is not clear how the development of these related policy areas will affect the size of the regional-policy budget nor is it obvious how they will influence the detailed form of regional policy.

The emergence of a strong policy for industrial development is advocated at several places within the volume. If such a policy is adhered to, then, assuming that efficiency objectives are defined in terms of prices and costs and vigorously pursued, it is evident that industrial development will not occur equally in all regions and that the existing problem regions may benefit to a lesser extent than other regions. An industrial strategy pursuing efficiency objectives is not easy to reconcile with current regional policy.

The very existence of such a strategy may run counter to the objectives of regional policy, at least in the short term. With the growth of industrial policy, the continuation of an active regional policy may only be rational if the various sector policies contain explicit spatial-distribution objectives as well as efficiency goals.

The opinion is sometimes expressed that if economic-development policies favouring particular locations are to continue, they should be focused on the urban, rather than the regional level. This proposed new policy direction reflects the fact that the spatial perception of the unemployment problem in Britain has tended, in the last five years, to shift from an interregional to an intraregional level. Undoubtedly, the pressures of the present, whether they are of a social, economic or political nature, do draw attention to the plight of inner-city areas. It is also arguable that existing regional policies have not only acted directly against the interests of the inner cores of the southern conurbations but have failed to help the declining metropolitan cores in the assisted areas. This criticism of existing policy obviously does not constitute a case for abandoning the region (often dominated by a metropolitan area) as a spatial unit for policy.

The functional relationships within a region (for instance, the linkages between the metropolitan node and the non-metropolitan periphery) have a crucial impact on the effectiveness of policies. Whilst at any one time a particular part of a region may become the focus for policy, the overall regional structure must be borne in mind. At a more prosaic level, it is possible by a combination of social, transport and housing policies to shift the income and unemployment problems within a metropolitan area (for example, from the inner-city slum to a suburban housing estate), but the performance of the metropolitan or regional economy as a whole is a crucial factor in determining whether or not such problems may be removed. Inner-city problems may well have 'regional' economic causes. Urban-based policies should not therefore be seen as substitutes for regional policy but rather as vital complements to it.

Regardless of the spatial framework chosen for policy, the pursuit of objectives relating to the geographic distribution of economic activity will still conflict with an industrial policy, which is concerned solely with efficiency targets. However, the probability that industrial policy will be modified to allow the pursuit of specifically regional objectives may be increased by the eventual advent of devolution. The existence of regional assemblies, particularly with powers and institutions to aid economic development, not only ensures the continuance of regional policy but inevitably complicates its operation. The presence of a regional government is likely to involve the constant scrutiny of regional economic performance, and differences in performance may become politicised as the regional block grant is renegotiated. Further, the region rather than the urban area *per se* will be the effective locus of political debate and interarea political conflict, thus implying that the region will persist as a unit for policy. The complexity of policy will also increase as individual regions pursue their own policies for regional industrial development. At the same time, central government will probably need to maintain a 'national' regional policy as regions may have different degrees of success, or even failure, in pursuing locally designed industrial-development policies.

The existence of devolution and a sustained high unemployment rate (particularly if accompanied by high rates of unemployment in the southern conurbations) is likely to restrain the capacity, and indeed the propensity, of central government to maintain a regional policy of a diversionary nature. It is therefore likely that the instruments of policy will be designed either to attract foreign investment to problem regions or to stimulate indigenous economic development. Regional policy pursued by central government in the 1980s must take account of, and where necessary allow for, the policies of regional assemblies. At the same time, this national regional policy must be coordinated with urban and industrial policies. Such a complex structure of policy will be further complicated if regions do not have the same political status. Unless a uniform regional political structure emerges in Great Britain, a rational and consistent set of regional policies will be difficult to devise and operate.

Is a Complex Regional Policy Possible?

If British regional policy in the future is to be economically efficient and acceptable, then two general conditions of policy formulation must hold. First, there must be an explicit statement of regional economic objectives, and policy expenditure must be geared to some long-term strategy of regional development. It is not sufficient that policy expenditure should satisfy an electoral cycle or merely respond to the political pressures stemming from the collapse of major enterprises in assisted areas. It may well be the case that the political will for a real commitment to regional-development policy, as opposed to cosmetic tinkering in relation to aggregate demand policy, is unlikely to emerge, due to the short-lived nature of individual governments. It is probably unlikely in the British context that a long-term regional policy with clearly stated development objectives will appear.

The second condition for a satisfactory regional policy is that policy expenditure and instruments have to be closely and rationally related to any newly emerging urban, industrial and devolution policies. The level of commitment to an efficient regional policy in Great Britain is reflected in the relatively small expenditures on policy research. Moreover, the statistical and monitoring capability of the government is sufficiently low that it is unlikely to be able to design efficient regional policies of a complex nature. Undoubtedly, the British political system is responsive to regional pressures, and there is always a desire to be seen to be assisting lagging regions. However, this outward concern is not matched by either the real desire or the ability to translate policy expenditures into efficient policy outputs. Political pressures may change the scale and form of regional policy in the directions suggested above, but without more serious attention to the details of its operation, the efficiency and effectiveness of regional policy will continue to be impaired.

Index

Abercrombie, P.   8
adaptability, regional   194-8, 199, 206,
    212-13, 229, 231, 232, 233, 237
agglomeration economies   183, 203, 215,
    232
Allen, G. C.   232
Allen, K. and MacLennan, M. C.   106
Alonso, W.   183, 184
Archibald, G. C.   72
Arrow, K. *et al.*   239n.
Ashcroft, B. and Taylor, J.   47, 52, 60
assisted areas: criteria for designating
    101-2; productivity in   308-9, 309-13,
    319; reclassification of   30, 248-9, 255,
    262, 264; *see also* Development Areas;
    Intermediate Areas; problem regions;
    Special Development Areas
assisted labour mobility policy   65-79
Atkins, D. H. W.   234
Atkinson, A. B. and Flemming, J. S.   95

Barlow Report   *ix*, 5-6, 135
Beacham, A. and Osborn, W. T.   48
Beaumont, P. B.   73, 76, 77
Beckerman, W. and Associates   112
Beesley, M.   233, 239n.
Begg, H. M. *et al.*   52
birth rates   124, 133
block grants   288
Board of Trade   11-12
Board of Trade Advisory Committee (BOTAC)
    12
Bolton Report   236
Boswell, J.   232
Böventer, von, E.   193
Boudeville, J. R.   192
branch plants   *x*, 125, 220, 233-6
Brown, A. J.   4, 19, 91, 123, 175
Brown, A. J., Lind, H. and Bowers, J.
    17, 91
Brown, G.   5, 19
Brown, M. and de Cani, J.   239
building grants   14, 16, 18, 20

Cairncross, A.   258
Cameron, G. C.   123, 204, 230
Cameron, G. C. and Reid, G. L.   209n.
capacity, constraints on   47, 48, 53
Champernowne, D.   *xiii*
Chinitz, B.   223n., 232
Chisholm, M.   39n., 63, 98, 111, 115
Chisholm, M. and Oeppen, J.   194, 313
Clark, U. E. G.   235

Committee of Inquiry into the Intermediate
    Areas   17; *see also* Hunt Committee
Common Agricultural Policy   258, 260
Common Market *see* European Communities
competitive efficiency   83, 116, 124-5,
    212, 223, 230
competitiveness: international   222, 307;
    regional   193-4, 199, 200, 202-3, 205,
    222, 292
Control of Office and Industrial
    Development Act (1965)   15
Corkindale, J.   116, 152
Craven, E.   276
Crommelin, M., Pearse, P. H. and Scott, A.
    168
Cros, J.   258
Crum, R.   238
Cullingworth, J. B.   6, 9

Daniel, W. W.   68
Danielsson, A.   48
decentralisation   23, 25, 149-55, 176-7,
    196-7, 200; *see also* urban regions
decision-making   234, 238-9, 243-4, 273;
    see also entrepreneurship
declining industries   *x*, 3-4, 10, 17-18,
    114, 140-2, 150-3, 185, 195, 196, 213,
    214-15, 216, 218, 264
Dennis, R. D.   140
Department of Economic Affairs (DEA)
    15, 19
Department of the Environment   20-1
Department of Industry   25, 53
Department of Trade and Industry (DTI)
    20, 24
depreciation allowances   14, 20, 21, 103;
    see also investment incentives
'depressed areas'   4, 11; *see also* assisted
    areas; old industrial regions; problem
    regions; urban regions
Development Areas   7, 8, 12, 17, 25, 30,
    43, 63, 248-9
Development Areas Treasury Advisory
    Committee (DATAC)   7
Development Districts   12, 13, 15
devolution   *xx*, 84, 116-17, 127, 273-93,
    327-8
disincentive measures   266, 269-70
Distribution of Industry Act (1945)   7, 8
Distribution of Industry Act (1950)   10
Distribution of Industry (Industrial Finance)
    Act (1958)   10-11
Ditwiler, C. D.   168

Dixon, R. J. and Thirlwall, A. P. 183, 239n.
Dobb, M. 226

earnings and incomes 147–9, 158n.
Easterlin, R. A. 65
economic and monetary union 256, 257, 260
Economic Planning Regions 15, 19, 171, 174
economies of scale 183, 232, 236
efficiency: allocative 230; technical 230, 239n., 283; *see also* competitive efficiency
employment: distribution of 119, 134, 136–8, 142, 149–55, 203; generation of 186; gross employment flow 227–30; regional, goals of 302; by sector 119, 137, 138–40, 143–44, 147, 150–5; *see also* gross employment flows; job creation
Employment and Training Act (1948) 68
Employment Transfer Scheme (ETS) 69–71, 72–7 *passim*, 77–9
entrepreneurship 214, 216, 218, 219, 223n.; constraints on 231; definition of 225–6; local *v.* external 234, 238–9; in new firms 231–6; regional differences in 231, 236–9; and technical efficiency 230–1
Equal Opportunity Program (US) 182
establishment-based research 227, 228, 229
European Communities 98, 100, 101, 104, 256–65, 266–70; Commission 100, 116, 245–56, 259, 260–5; Committee on Regional Policy 256; Council of Ministers 258, 262; European Agricultural Guidance and Guarantee Fund (EAGGF) 259, 268; European Coal and Steel Community (ECSC) 265; European Investment Bank (EIB) 258, 265; European Regional Development Fund 256, 259–65; Parliament 262, 264, 269; Social Fund 268
expenditure, government *see* public expenditure
external economies *see* externalities
external ownership *see* branch plants
externalities 65, 89, 183, 196, 232, 285

Fessey, M. C. 238
Fessey, M. C. and Browning, H. E. 308
Finance and Local Employment Acts (1963) 14
Finer, S. E. 85
firm behaviour 172, 227, 228
Firn, J. R. 185, 235, 238, 278, 292, 293n.
Firn, J. R. and Swales, J. K. 233, 239n.
forecasting 105–6
Forsyth, D. J. C. 234, 236
Freeman, C. 233

Gardner, J. W. and Dougharty, J. E. 292

gas discoveries 160, 161; *see also* North Sea oil and gas
Gaskin, M. 285
GDP per capita 90, 91, 117–18, 119, 157; *see also* earnings and incomes
generation–distribution model of industrial movement 43, 47–50, 54–8
Goddard, J. and Spence, N. 134
grants *see* loans and grants
Green, D. H. 238
Greenwood, M. J. 65
growth area approach 13, 14, 87, 268; *see also* growth pole policy
growth pole policy 199–206, 208n., 209n.
growth services 138, 139, 142, 143, 150–1, 179
Gudgin, G. H. 228, 229, 232, 233, 236, 239n.
Gunderson, M. 79n.

Hailsham, Lord 12
Hall, P. *et al.* 134, 187n.
Hanham, H. W. 293n.
Hansen, N. J. 209n., 277
Hardman Report 25
Harris, D. F. 9, 114
Harvie, C. 293n.
Heald, D. A. 293n.
Highlands and Islands Development Board 16, 183
Hirschman, A. O. 278, 290
Holland, S. 31, 36, 234, 254
Holmans, A. E. 175
House of Commons Expenditure Committee 24
House, J. W. 183
Hughes, J. T. and Firn, J. R. 177
Humphrys, G. 175
Hunt Committee 17, 18, 19, 123, 125, 126

incentives *see* investment incentives; regional aid; tax incentives
indigenous firms 22, 23, 99–100, 186, 220, 231, 235–6, 237, 238, 253
industrial development: assistance for 28, 31, 86–7, 97, 99–103; changing patterns of 173, 325–9; regulation of 6, 7, 8, 9–10, 97; *see also* Industrial Strategy; investment incentives; new-firm formation; public expenditure
Industrial Development Act (1966) 16, 63, 111
Industrial Development Certificate (IDC) *xi*, 7, 15, 23, 25–7, 96–7, 135, 173–4, 269, 304
Industrial Development Executive 25
industrial movement: away from urban areas 134–42, 177, 184–5, 196–7; distribution of 45–7, 51, 53, 94, 173, 177, 200–1, 215–16, 229; effect of regional policy on 43–4, 47, 48, 52–8, 59–61, 97; generation of 45–7, 48–9, 57, 58; incentives for *xi*, 48, 50, 51, 52, 57, 114; *see also* investment

incentives; tax incentives; measures of
44, 50–8, 58–60, 61–3, 227, 228, 229;
postwar trends of 8, 44–5; and
productive capacity 45, 49, 53; *see also*
decentralisation; location controls;
locational change; locational choice
Industrial Strategy, national: financial
assistance 298, 302–4; major elements
of 299–300; productivity patterns
309–19; sectoral *v.* regional policy
300–2, 303–9, 319–20, 326–7
industrial structure 124–5, 126; *see also*
declining industries; industrial
development
Industrial Transference Board (ITB) 3, 4,
67, 68
Industry Act (1972) 22, 24, 27–8, 101,
102, 220, 253, 254, 255, 302, 303
infant-industry argument 86, 99, 100
infrastructure 13, 115; aid for 84,
87–8, 260, 261, 262–3, 266, 268;
investment in 20, 197, 201;
obsolescence of 126; professional and
institutional 218; regional patterns of
199–200, 209n.; *see also* social capital
innovation *see* entrepreneurship; research
and development
Intermediate Areas 17, 18, 19, 21, 23,
25, 30
intervention capacity 264
investment 8, 16, 36, 48, 57, 58, 116,
200, 202; incentives for 16, 23, 51, 52,
57, 251–3, 259–60, 300, 303, 304–6
Investment Grants 20
Isard, W., Schooler, E. W. and Vietorisz, T.
201

Jacobs, J. 236
James, B. G. S. 200
Jewkes, J., Sawers, D. and Stillerman, R.
233
job creation 22, 29, 30, 60, 162, 163–4,
192, 216, 302, 305, 321n.
Johnson, J. H. *et al.* 79n.
Jusenius, C. L. and Ledebur, L. C. 291
juste retour 260, 262

Kaldor, N. 17, 123
Kamien, M. I. and Schwartz, N. L. 233
Keeble, D. E. 48, 51, 184, 232
Kellas, J. G. 293n.
key industries 200, 201, 209n.
Kilbrandon Committee 276, 279
Kilbrandon Report 282
Klaasen, L. H. 204
Kuklinski, A. R. and Petrella, R. 208n.

labour: demand and supply factors of 8,
50, 51, 94–6, 97–8, 113, 199–202;
mobility of 3, 71, 72, 73–4, 92–3, 95,
197, 201–2; *see also* assisted labour
mobility policy; Employment Transfer
Scheme; Resettlement Transfer Scheme;
subsidies for 52, 97–8
land clearance 18, 19, 28

Law, D. 124
Layfield Report 293n.
Leibenstein, H. 226, 230, 283
Lever, W. F. 200, 223n., 232, 235
Lind, H. and Flockton, C. 258
Lindbeck, A. 289
Lloyd, P. E. and Mason, C. M. 185
loans and grants 4, 5, 7, 11, 12, 16, 18,
22, 23, 30, 57, 104, 265; *see also* block
grants; building grants; standard grants
Loasby, B. 53
Local Employment Act (1960) 11
Local Employment Act (1970) 19, 20
Local Employment Act (1972) 22
Local Employment Development Unit
(Northern Ireland) 103
location controls 48, 57–60; *see also*
industrial movement; locational change;
locational choice
Location of Offices Bureau (LOB) 14, 30
locational change 106, 184, 185, 186
locational choice *xii*, 45–7, 51, 53,
196–7, 199–202, 229
Luttrell, W. F. 209n.

MacDougall Report 85, 88, 89, 106, 263
MacKay, D. I. 103
MacKay, D. I. and Hart, R. 50
MacKay, D. I. and MacKay, G. A. 160,
208
MacKay, R. R. 52, 82
McCrone, G. 6, 17, 38n., 82, 123, 282
McDermott, P. J. 239n.
Maddock, I. 233
managerial performance *see* decision-making;
entrepreneurship
Mann, M. 72
Manners, G. 111, 115
Manpower Services Commission 78, 79,
281
market forces 84, 85, 87, 98, 225, 323
market research 214, 215, 219
Mattila, J. and Thompson, W. 175
Mayer, W. and Pleeter, S. 175
Mellis, C. L. and Richardson, P. W. 62
Metcalf, D. 124
Metropolitan Areas (MAS) 187n.; *see also*
urban regions
Metropolitan Economic Labour Area (MELA)
188n.
migration *xii*, *xiii*, 75–7, 92–4, 134; *see
also* assisted labour mobility policy; labour
mobility; outmigration
Mills, E. S. 184
mobility *see* assisted labour mobility policy;
Employment Transfer Scheme; labour
mobility; outmigration
Moore, B. and Rhodes, J. 39n., 48, 52,
53, 60, 63, 82, 119, 162, 173, 175, 216,
250–1, 293n.
Moore, B., Rhodes, J. and Tyler, P. 29
Moore, F. T. and Peterson, J. W. 192
Morrill, R. L. 204
Moseley, M. J. 210

National Economic Development Council (NEDC) 13, 81, 299
national economic growth and regional policy 112–22, 129; *see also* Industrial Strategy; National Plan
National Enterprise Board (NEB) 28, 30, 220, 254, 306–7
National Plan (1965) 15–16, 81, 111, 112–13, 115, 123, 298
Nelson, J. and Tweeten, L. 67
New Earnings Surveys (1971, 1974) 144
new-firm formation 185, 231–6, 237, 243; *see also* small-firm formation
New Towns 8, 13, 38n., 57, 115, 135, 156, 186, 207, 208n.
non-assisted areas 309–13, 317
North Sea oil and gas: costs of, to Scotland 165–7, 168; discovery of 159–60, 168–9, 279; economic benefits of 34, 35, 83, 110, 160–9, 208; employment in 119, 163–4, 166; production rates of 166, 168; taxes on revenue 167–8

Oates, W. E. 89
Odber, A. J. 38n.
O'Donnell, A. T. and Swales, J. K. 239n.
Office Development Permits (ODP) 15, 23, 25, 30, 135
office work 138, 143
Offshore Supplies Office 25
old industrial regions 213–23; *see also* declining industries
'opaque' aids 247, 248, 249, 255
'operational grants' 18, 20, 21
operative work 138, 143–4
outmigration 70, 71–2, 74–7, 79n., 162; *see also* assisted labour mobility policy; labour mobility; migration
overspill policies 8; *see also* New Towns

parity 88–90, 290, 291
Parkin, M. 258
Parr, J. B. 194, 208n.
Parsons, G. F. 234, 236
Penrose, E. 228
peripheral regions *see* assisted areas; old industrial regions; problem regions
Perloff, H. S. *et al.* 175, 179
Perroux, F. 208n.
Petroleum Revenue Tax 167
Pitfield, D. E. 4, 5, 36, 68
pole industries 203–4; *see also* growth pole policy
population trends 115, 116, 120–2, 133–4, 136–8, 149, 150, 162, 173, 177, 201, 222
Prais, S. J. 238
problem regions 19, 194–8, 199, 206; *see also* assisted areas; old industrial regions; urban regions
productivity 95, 96, 102, 230, 292, 303, 309–13, 314–19, 325
public expenditure 9, 12, 15, 18, 31; constraints on 82–3, 115, 325;

interregional transfers of 84, 88–92, 106, 107; per capita 89–90; planning of 105–6; regional disparities in 89–91, 127; in Scotland 117, 162, 284–6

Randall, J. N. 36, 124
Reesman, C. J. and Zimmerman, D. R. 75
regional aid: additionality 261; criticisms of 323–4; measurement of 247–8, 249, 251, 252, 253, 255; opportunity costs of 175; regulations on 116, 245–56, 259, 260–5, 268; selectivity of 253, 255–6; urban-oriented 179–83
regional aid rules 246–56, 268
Regional Development Grant (RDG) 22, 28, 99, 156, 252, 256, 281
regional disparities x–xi, 85–92, 112–13, 114, 123, 126–7
Regional Economic Planning Boards 15, 209n.
Regional Economic Planning Councils 15
regional multiplier 72, 91, 123, 164, 192, 208n., 235, 325
Regional Employment Premium (REP) xi, 17, 20, 23, 24, 29, 81, 97, 249–50, 251, 255
regional planning 3–6, 18, 84, 91–2, 104–6, 122–8, 174–5, 194–8, 199, 231–6; *see also* industrial development; Industrial Strategy
regional taxation schemes 104, 286–8
Rent Act (1974) 93
replacement industries 196
replacement ratios 96
research and development 126, 214, 215, 233; *see also* entrepreneurship
Resettlement Transfer Scheme 68
resource utilisation 195, 196–8, 230–1, 283
Rhodes, J. and Kan, A. 15
Richardson, H. W. 67, 183, 184, 192
Riew, J. 65
Robinson, E. A. G. 277
Rosenstein-Rodan, P. M. 199
Rowley, C. K. and Peacock, A. T. 293n.
Royal Commission on the Constitution 89, 92, 279, 286, 293n.; *see also* Kilbrandon Report
Royal Commission on the Distribution of the Industrial Population 5; *see also* Barlow Report
Royal Commission on Local Government Finance 286; *see also* Layfield Report

Sant, M. 44, 233
Schnitzer, M. 68
Scholefield, H. H. and Franks, J. R. 21
Scotland Act (1978) 279
Scotland and Wales Bill 279
Scottish Assembly 104, 117, 273, 288
Scottish Council (Development and Industry) 102, 208n

Scottish Development Agency 28, 37, 116, 117, 125, 169, 186, 220, 281, 292
Scottish Development Department . 280
Scottish Economic Planning Department 280, 281
Scottish National Party 25, 169, 279
Scottish Office 116, 280, 281
sector working parties 299
sectoral assistance 28, 31; *see also* Industrial Strategy
sectoral policy *v.* regional policy 300–2, 303–9, 319–20.
Selective Investment Scheme 305–6
'self-reliance', regional 212–13, 221–3, 237
service industries 21, 138, 139, 142, 143, 147, 152, 179, 254; *see also* growth services
Singer, H. W. 68
skill drain, regional 71–2
small-firm formation 219, 231–6, 237; *see also* new-firm formation
Smallwood, C. 293n.
Smith, B. M. D. 63
Smith, N. R. 239n.
social capital 66, 70, 201, 209n., 221; *see also* infrastructure
spatial selectivity 186, 187
spatial structure *xiv*, 174, 191–4, 195, 198, 203, 207
Special Areas 4
Special Areas (Amendments) Act (1937) 5
Special Areas Commissioners 4, 5
Special Areas (Development and Improvement) Act (1934) 4
Special Areas Reconstruction Association 4–5
Special Development Areas 17–18, 21, 25, 30, 248–9, 292
Special Temporary Employment Programme 29
standard grants 14, 22
Standard Metropolitan Statistical Area (SMSA) (US) 187–8n.
Standard Regions 171, 174
Stewart, Sir Malcolm 6
Stolper, W. F. and Tiebout, C. M. 193–4
Stone, P. A. 179
subsidies: capital 51, 52, 59, 97, 98–103; sectoral 28, 303–4, 319–20, 321n.; *see also* investment incentives; loans and grants; tax incentives
Sugden, R. 201
Sundquist, J. L. 5
'super' sectors 314–19
supply capability 216, 217–21, 223; *see also* adaptability
Swales, J. K. 235
system efficiency 283–4

Tait, A. 282
tax incentives 21, 103–4; *see also* investment incentives

Thirlwall, A. P. 65
Thomson, G. 259
Thompson, W. R. 223n., 232, 239
Tiebout, C. M. 284
Tiebout model 284–5
Tinbergen, J. 289
Tooze, M. J. 183
Town and Country Planning Act (1947) 7, 173
Town Development Act 135
Townroe, P. M. 48, 53, 229
Townsend, A. R. 140
'transparency' 247, 251, 252
Treaty of Accession 248
Treaty of Rome 245, 246, 248, 249, 254

unemployment: age distribution of 146–7; industrial structure of 114; intraregional 327; patterns of 31–5; skill distribution of 94–6, 124; urban 116, 134, 136–40, 143–4, 149–55, 177–9, 180–1
unemployment benefits 93, 94–5
unemployment, rate of: interregional disparities in 3, 34–5, 51, 118–19, 120–3, 324; in the mid-sixties 113–15; prewar 3, 4; urban 116, 124, 144–7, 155, 158n.
urban regions: decline of 134–5, 149–58, 177, 184, 196–7; employment trends in 116, 134, 136–40, 143–4, 149–55, 177–9, 190–1; industrial composition of 194–5; policies for 7–8, 35, 135, 155–8, 183–7, 192, 208n., 327; population trends in 116, 134, 136–8, 149, 150, 176, 177; skill distribution in 143–4, 146; spatial imbalance in 173, 184, 196–7; *see also* decentralisation; New Towns; overspill policies

Van Ginderachter, J. 258, 260, 261
Varley, E. 297
vertical integration 214
Vining, R. 192

wage inflation 50
Wallace, H., Wallace, W. and Webb, C. 260
Welsh Assembly 273, 288
Welsh Development Agency 28, 37, 116, 125, 169, 220
Welsh Office 116
Werner Plan 256
Wilson, T. 91, 100, 104, 201, 257, 283, 293n.
Wingo, L. 183, 184
Wise, M. S. 232

Yannopoulos, G. N. and Dunning, J. H. 238
Yapa, L., Polese, M. and Wolpert, J. 198